ORGANISATION
and
IDENTITIES

Text and readings in organisational behaviour

Edited by

HEATHER CLARK
*Senior Lecturer based at
Queen Mary and Westfield College
University of London
UK
on behalf of the East London
Business School, University of
East London*

JOHN CHANDLER
Principal Lecturer

and

JIM BARRY
*Senior Lecturer
both at
East London Business School
University of East London
UK*

INTERNATIONAL THOMSON BUSINESS PRESS
I T P® An International Thomson Publishing Company

London • Bonn • Johannesburg • Madrid • Melbourne • Mexico City • New York • Paris
Singapore • Tokyo • Toronto • Albany, NY • Belmont, CA • Cincinnati, OH • Detroit, MI

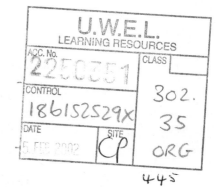

Organisations and Identities

I(T)P   A division of International Thomson Publishing
The ITP logo is a trademark under licence

British Library Cataloguing-in-Publication Data
A catalogue record for this book is available from the British Library

First edition published 1994 by Chapman & Hall
Reprinted 1995 by Chapman & Hall and 1999 by International Thomson Business Press

Typeset by Best-set Typesetter Ltd, Hong Kong
Printed in the UK by the Alden Press, Oxford

ISBN 1-86152-529-X

International Thomson Business Press
Berkshire House
168–173 High Holborn
London WC1V 7AA
UK

http://www.itbp.com

Contents

Note to the reader

Much of the language used in classic readings would now be regarded as sexist. Virtually all authors today recognize that words like 'he' and 'him', when used to mean human beings as a whole, are an expression of implicit gender power and that such usage should therefore be avoided.

Foreword

In *Organisation and Identities*, Heather Clark, John Chandler and Jim Barry have produced a text of readings in organisational behaviour which is full of good things. In particular, this is a rich quarry of material for teachers and students in the areas of organisation and management studies, economics, industrial relations, sociology and social psychology. To have it within the convenient covers of one book is to have fortunate access to a fine learning resource.

It is all too easy for textbooks in the area of organisational behaviour to refer to authors in ways which, if only for reasons of compression, do not do them justice. Here, the authors speak for themselves at sufficient length for the reader to form his or her own opinion. Indeed, I hope and believe that the appetite will be whetted and readers will be stimulated to explore further the work of authors who they may not have previously encountered. This, I think, will be one of the tests of the success of the book. When texts become a substitute for wider reading they are a pedagogic failure and should carry an educational health warning.

The editors have thrown their net widely when collecting these readings. This has a number of welcome consequences. First, the text is genuinely cross-disciplinary and a number of perspectives from within disciplines are given an airing. Secondly, there is a generous historical span in the coverage, from early on in the industrial revolution up to the present day. Thirdly, not all the work included is readily available, bearing in mind the way in which most bookshops operate and the current economic pressures on libraries. Fourth, a number of issues relating to the gender structuring of organisations are carefully raised.

All of this, it seems to me, makes for the possibility of serendipity in our own thinking, as the familiar and the unfamiliar jostle side by side in the text. This, by its nature, will not be readily amenable to measurement, but as readers we should be grateful for this creative possibility.

Teachers in this field can amuse themselves by imagining what they would have put into such a collection. With such historical, cultural and disciplinary diversity, there are many options. But this well-presented book will, in its thoughtful catholicity, surely commend itself to a wide readership and promote a critical approach to the study of organisations and society.

John Eldridge
Department of Sociology
University of Glasgow, UK

Introduction

This book is about the human aspects of organisation, and the social and individual identities that shape organisations and are shaped by them. A broad spectrum of work is presented.

Some authors are avowedly 'managerial', attempting to provide managers with solutions to the problems they face; some are anti-capitalist and anti-managerialist, at least in so far as managers are seen as serving, from this perspective, to secure continued domination and exploitation; others are simply trying to understand what is going on in organisations without, as it were, taking sides. A variety of academic disciplines is represented here, too, including psychology, sociology, and economic and social history. There is, finally, a mixture of theoretical and empirical contributions with a number of research methods employed in the latter, including observation, documentary research and experimental methods.

Taken together, the readings presented here provide a broad and complex picture of organisational life. It will be apparent that the narrow managerial and psychological bias of some approaches to 'organisational behaviour' is rejected decisively. We do not think it helps anyone – even those simply setting out to control organisational behaviour – to ignore the insights to be found in work by sociologists, social historians and others.

In any selection of readings, however, difficult decisions have to be made about what to exclude and we are acutely conscious that some things have been left unsaid. Even in the readings chosen there are limitations, including, for example, the gender-blind masculine bias of many of the authors who failed to address the experiences of women in organisations. This collection of readings attempts to go some way towards redressing this bias.

A book of readings is rarely read from cover to cover and in the precise order in which readings are presented. Indeed, one of the advantages for a reader is the ease with which it can be 'dipped into' for a particular piece or read in many different orders. Nevertheless, we have tried to organise the selected readings in a coherent way. The first part introduces the major concepts and theories which underpin current debates in organisational behaviour. The second part is concerned with critical issues which are the subject of much contemporary writing on organisations – the issues of flexibility; culture and quality; and alienation and stress.

The first chapter can be seen as setting the stage for what follows. It raises fundamental questions concerning the nature of contemporary society – industrial, capitalist or 'post-modern'? – and of the continuities and discontinuities between past and present. It also introduces the work of two writers who offer alternative ways of critically evaluating organisational life – Marx and Foucault. Much contemporary critical literature on organisations is from either a Marxist or Foucauldian perspective and anybody wishing to engage in a serious evaluation of the texts which follow would do well to begin with these readings.

The second chapter of the book explores a variety of conceptualisations of the nature of human identities and how they are formed. Contributions from psychologists and sociologists are used to show the complex nature of identities – both individual (who I am) and social (me as a student, mother, manager or whatever).

In the third chapter are to be found some of the writings on organisations that are most frequently referred to. The focus here is on the patterning of organisational relationships through different well-established forms of discipline, a term used in a broad sense to cover both structured or ordered forms of behaviour, as well as outright control. Resistance to discipline is also dealt with. Two main disciplinary forms can be discerned here – they are labelled 'classical' and 'human relations' approaches respectively. The first is formal, impersonal, rule-governed, autocratic, while the second relies more on 'positive' social relationships and building job satisfaction. Both these different approaches can be found, in approximate form at least, in contemporary organisations.

In Part Two a number of issues are dealt with around which much contemporary writing on organisations revolves: the issues of flexibility; culture and quality; and stress and alienation. The readings here bring together much of the material dealt with in earlier chapters.They raise the question of the changing nature of identities in the face of revised forms of disciplinary relations, and explore the effects on social and individual identity of disciplinary relations and structures.

We hope that together these readings will help the student of organisations to build up a complex picture of organisational life and the identities associated with it. Furthermore, we hope they encourage critical reflection and debate on the nature of these organisational realities and on the literature which seeks to understand it.

PART ONE

HISTORIES, IDENTITIES and DISCIPLINARY RELATIONS

This first part of the book outlines the major concepts and theories which underpin the current debates around organisations and identities which can be found in Part Two.

The first chapter introduces theories and debates on the context, development and changing nature of industrial capitalist society. The second outlines different approaches to the construction of individual identity and social differences. The third considers the many approaches that have been taken to the complex patterning of organisational relationships and the interaction of organisation members.

1

Histories, ideas and contexts

The readings in this opening chapter provide an introduction to the histories, ideas and contexts which underpin the study of modern organisations and identities. The starting point is the advent of Western industrial capitalism.

Societies underwent radical transformation during the period of industrialisation, moving from the traditional hierarchies of agriculturally-based feudal communities, which had dominated Europe for centuries, to urban, factory-based wage labour and the disciplines of industrial capitalism. These vast upheavals followed on from the equally dramatic religious convulsions of the Reformation, and the social and politial dislocations of the American and French Revolutions, and drew inspiration from the intellectual energy released in the Enlightenment.

The readings document how intellectuals, in awe and despair in equal measure at the magnitude of the changes, sought to explain the consequences for modern forms of organisation and identity.

In the first reading Kumar deals with an important aspect of the changes: the division of labour or differentiation. At its extreme the division of labour entailed the fragmentation or breaking down of specialised craft skills, increasing worker proficiency along a narrow range of tasks, enabling increased productive efficiences to be achieved. Although this process was not new, its marked development during industrialisation brought about changes to the organisation of work so significant that it put social stability under considerable strain. As the certainties of feudal society began to wane, intellectuals like Durkheim looked hopefully to new forms of social cohesion and integration through occupational communities.

Along with the rise of industrialisation came secularisation, and a questioning of traditionally institutionalised forms of religion and belief. Industrialisation with its new adherents tended, as Kumar puts it, to 'dethrone and disqualify all other competing religions'. The driving compulsions of rationalisation which underlay these processes and so preoccupied Weber is considered in the next section from Kumar. For Weber the forces of rationalisation denied stability to traditional social relationships, as religion, myth, magic and superstition were engulfed in the calculative pursuit of technical efficiency. As Weber saw so clearly and so pessimistically, this led to bureaucratic forms of organisation containing tightly constrained grey bureaucrats going about their grim daily tasks trapped in an iron cage of compulsively rule-governed behaviour.

The sense of suffocating social relationships is elaborated in the work of Marx, where the blame is laid at the door of the capitalist system. Friedman, in the next reading, shows how Marx saw the development of industrial capitalism as the essential framework for exploitation through accumulation of wealth and commodification. The production and sale of commodities or goods – for profit rather than for use as previously – underlies the whole capitalist system for Marx and it is the way they are produced, the social relations of production, that renders the system exploitative.

Although capitalist societies are comprised of many social groupings, Marx argued that there would, ultimately at least, come to be two fundamental classes characteristic of capitalism: the bourgeoisie and the proletariat. The former owned the means of production while the latter did not – they had to sell their power or capacity to labour in order to earn wages to survive.

The ruthless pursuit of profit led capitalist entrepreneurs to introduce ever-more productive machinery and drive down costs wherever possible, whether those costs were material or labour. The use of human beings as objects, whose labour was to be used up in the process of production, made the relationship between the bourgeois capitalist and the proletarian worker essentially exploitative with no place for expression of human creativity and individual identity.

This use of labour enabled the incorporation and modification of previously established methods of organisational control, and provided opportunities for the introduction of new ones. These are dealt with in the readings which follow. We start with Foucault, a French philosopher whose work has recently had 'an enormous influence on British and American intellectuals' (Sarup, 1983: 87). Foucault's ideas raise some very interesting questions about social control, as well as the construction of identity, issues which are dealt with further in later chapters of the book.

There are two readings from Foucault. The first reading draws on elements of Weberian and Marxist thought in order to demonstrate how forms of rationalised social control were embodied in what he calls regimes of surveillance. The use of such subtle mechanisms places emphasis on structural systems of control, involving for instance the lay-out of machinery in workshops to facilitate the overseeing of workers. Here, the gaze of the overseer is experienced by the subjects even if their immediate presence is not, inducing self-discipline and self-control throughout the workforce. This self-control is maintained just in case they are being observed, since they are never sure when they are being watched and when they are not. Furthermore, the routines of control – taking the form of timetabling in schools for example or workshop procedures – facilitate domination across a wide range of circumscribed activities. In this sense those who are subjected to such systems of regulation or discipline are shaped, in part by themselves, into identifiable organisation members such as workers or pupils.

Foucault's work has been criticised for this emphasis on social structure as effectively making, creating or moulding human subjects, and for playing down the role of human action, though his analysis which sees power as something which is exercised through social relationships does at least open up the possibility of resistance. This is demonstrated in his second reading. Nevertheless, his focus on the regulation and discipline of organisation members' understanding and behaviour is helpful in highlighting mechanisms of dominance, control, surveillance and resistance.

This theme is taken up in the reading from Bell which contrasts the nature of time experienced as something that passes under feudalism with the control of time under industrial capitalism to organise production. Here time is counted, spent usefully or wasted; time is money. Bell's reading recounts the use of the three logics of time, size and hierarchy, reaching their 'high' point in assembly-line production, the outcome of engineering rationality and the stimulus-response dictates of measured, calculated time. This, it could be argued, diminishes human spirit and calls into doubt any realisation of human potential and dignity in creative work.

Questions of human fulfilment, dignity and freedom, and concerns about denial, alienation and control engaged many academics in the wake of fascism and Stalinism from at least the 1930s onwards. Ideas have their time. Fears of social conformity exercised many thinkers whose readings appear later in the book, both before and after the atrocities of the concentration camps, which attempted to stamp out identity altogether. Organisations not only seemed like camps, prisons or asylums, they sometimes were.

It is an open question as to quite how far societies and social relationships in organisations have changed since the introduction of the large-scale assembly-line (first associated with Ford), and the recognition of its potential for the denial of freedom and creativity. The idea that capitalism has changed is certainly not new – social scientists have been all too aware of the historical movement of a 'system' of production which has taken monopoly forms and spread its tentacles ever further into the developing world. The belief that the changes are so fundamental that society itself has been transformed is not new either. Notions of industrialism (Kerr *et al.*, 1960) and post-industrialism (Bell, 1973) were attempts to signal changes in the features of capitalism so basic as to herald a new era, as nation states converged towards a model of the pure industrial society with similar social, economic and political structures where class conflict became a thing of the past and memos would flow instead of blood.

More recent arguments which centre around vague notions of post-modernism, post-Fordism and New Times, echo these earlier preoccupations, suggesting that far-reaching and fundamental social, political and economic changes are perhaps under way. The reading that seems to capture this mood is 'The Manifesto for New Times' which, while focusing on Britain, outlines recent changes in the fabric and features of Western capitalist societies, sensing the potential outlines of a new order. The post-war 'settlement', which the Manifesto sees as under strain, had been built on the twin foundations of Keynes and Beveridge, the one an economist whose ideas had been influential in bolstering economic growth, the other a Liberal who had laid the groundwork for the construction of Britain's post-war welfare state. His attack on the five giant evils of Want, Idleness, Squalor, Disease and Ignorance was contained in the now-famous Beveridge Report of 1942.

The changes mentioned in the Manifesto do, on first reading, appear to lend strong empirical weight to the New Times argument. Economic growth, for example, does not seem to have provided an ever-expanding pot of gold at the end of the rainbow of affluence; and the Beveridge Report has been criticised roundly from both left and right of the political spectrum, and from advocates of the women's movement who condemn its assumptions of female dependence. It is also the case that the women's movement has raised consciousness about women's disadvantaged historical and contemporary position in the labour force, and that attempts to highlight women's invisibility in mainstream (or 'malestream') research is a recent phenomenon. Certainly recent debates have drawn attention to multiple identities such as gender, ethnicity and class in a way not recognised before.

But the real question here is whether the developments in contemporary society herald a new era different in kind to the capitalist economic, political and social order. The differences between what has been called 'Modern Times' and 'New Times' are summarised in the reading 'Fundamental List'.

This issue is addressed directly in the final reading in this chapter. Coyle offers a rejoinder to advocates of post-modernism and, perhaps more importantly as the very concept 'post-modernism' is the subject of academic debate, to the proponents of New Times. The sense of frustration with intellectual opponents of a different persuasion to Coyle himself is most acute in this reading.

The protagonists around the New Times and post-modernism debate have chosen history, past and present, as the terrain on which to wage their battles, opening up the debate for some time to come. This focus on history, on continuities and discontinuities, is one of the more enlightened aspects of this debate as social scientists deal with their subject matter historically grounded and politically contested, in sharp contrast to so many recent managerialist attempts to abstract 'useful' strategies from the academic literature with which to gain competitive advantage over others.

The literature is beginning to reflect these important developments. Attempts to introduce visions and mission statements into contemporary organisations by management gurus can thus be seen as quests to re-enchant Weber's barren rational landscape. Concerns about job enrichment and flexibility can be viewed in historical relief, as a cry for a return to artisanal craft-work and the craft ethic in a world, it is assumed, existed once and has now been lost. These critical issues are taken up in Part Two of the book.

This chapter has offered an overview of the histories, ideas and contexts within which the individuals in the next chapter come ultimately to be who they are. We will see once again that the construction of our various identities such as male worker and female manager are not independent of context, and that in many respects human subjects are as much created by the societies and organisations in which they live and work, as they are themselves creators of their own destinies.

Bibliography

Bell, D. (1973) *The Coming of Post-Industrial Society: a Venture in Social Forecasting*, Penguin, Harmondsworth, 1976.

Kerr, C., Dunlop, J.T., Harbison, F., and Myers, C. (1960) *Industrialism and Industrial Man*, Penguin, Harmondsworth, 1973.

Sarup, M. (1983) *Marxism/Structuralism/Education*, The Falmer Press, Sussex.

Specialization and the division of labour

KRISHAN KUMAR

All known societies practise some form of the division of labour, if only between the sexes or the generations. It clearly is not a peculiar feature of industrial society. We have only to think of the occupational specialization inherent in the Indian caste system, or the craft specializations of the medieval European towns, to realize now highly developed the division of labour can be in societies that are in no way industrialized. Contemporaries in the industrializing Europe of the nineteenth century were however inclined to think that something new had arrived with industrialism. They may have been prepared to concede that a rudimentary division of labour existed in other kinds of society. But so struck were they by the enormous complexity and interdependence of parts of the new industrial economy, so impressed by the number of new specializations and the speed with which they evolved, that they conceived the change to have been of a qualitative nature, and not merely one of degree. Nevertheless the division of labour that they observed and discussed was fundamentally of the old, non-industrial type. In concentrating so much on this they often failed to notice the distinctively new form of the division of labour that was the creation of industrialism, and were responsible for a confusion of analysis that has persisted to this day.

The division of labour that they commented on was the division of labour **in society** a social or 'societal' division of labour. It was a division that arose on the basis of new or different needs and functions, necessitating the introduction of new or different structures, roles, and occupations. As before, but with a new intensity, cities and ports became specialized around coal, iron, textiles, or railway construction; new occupations, especially of the professional and technical sort, were added to the old in great profusion. The process was analogous to the growth of individual organisms. Just as, in the development from infancy to adulthood, the individual plant or animal created new specialized organs and structures to meet the changing needs of its own growth, so it was argued the growth of the 'social organism' was a constant process of division, differentiation, and specialization, in adaptive response to the changing needs of its internal and external environment. It was in fact just this biological metaphor – for some it was much more than that – that was seized upon by many nineteenth-century theorists seeking to understand the growing division of labour. In particular it was the organizing principle of two of the most influential accounts, those given by Herbert Spencer and Emile Durkheim.

Both Spencer and Durkheim made it plain that the increasing division of labour was a process of great antiquity and long duration. Indeed for both it had been an inherent, progressive, feature of the growth of society from its very origins. But both also thought that there came a point – and that point had been reached in the industrial society of their day – when the phenomenon achieved such dimension in scope and volume that it introduced a new principle of order into the society. The high degree of the division of labour, and the strict and close interdependence that it entailed, became the very basis of a new social solidarity. Both individuality and mutuality were satisfied, the first by the great variety of occupations now offered, the second by the insufficiency of any one of them to sustain individual or collective life. It was a social order appropriately seen by Durkheim as resting on 'organic solidarity', and contrasted with the 'mechanical solidarity' of less developed societies with a low division of labour where order was maintained by powerful collective sentiments and harsh punishments. In the order based on organic solidarity there was no need, and no place, for repressive or authoritarian rule. Sentiments of solidarity were created by the natural and necessary dependence of the parts on each other and on the whole.

That industrialization made for much greater differentiation and specialization is obvious and undeniable. But what has to be noticed is that such a process does not necessarily involve the dividing up of the operations of any particular **task**, or act of production. What impressed Spencer and Durkheim was the spectacular growth of new roles and tasks – rather than the splitting and fragmentation of both old and new tasks. It was the latter that was the novel accomplishment of industrialism. It was this, the **detailed** division of labour, rather than simply the division of labour in society at large, that Adam Smith in a famous passage in *The Wealth of Nations* had described and advocated. In his example of the manufacture of pins, he made it clear that the advantages to be gained from the division of labour derived essentially from dividing up the task into simple, easily learned and easily repeated operations, thereby both saving time and opening the way to further mechanization. Pins could be made by one man; the skills were by no means too diverse to be mastered by the individual artisan. But by separating out each specific operation involved and assigning each to a separate, detail, worker, 'the important business of making a pin is, in this manner, divided into about eighteen distinct operations, which, in some manufactories, are all performed by distinct hands.' As a result, each worker could be reckoned as producing upwards of 4,800 pins a day where he would have produced only one on his own (Smith, vol. 1, 1910, p. 5).

It was this aspect of the division of labour that Marx took as central to the process of capitalist industrialization. The division of labour in society he acknowledged to be an old and well-established principle; the division of labour in the workshop was the really novel and distinctive feature of industrialism. A crucial distinction between the two systems lay in the nature of authority exercised over the worker. The social division of labour implied no more than that independent producers bought and exchanged commodities among themselves, subject to no other authority than the market forces of free competition. The division of labour in the workshop, on the contrary, implied the absolute and despotic authority of the capitalist over the workers, for the commodity is produced only through the combined labour power of the detail workers, whom he alone brings together and co-ordinates in the factory. 'Manufacturing division of labour implies the concentration of the means of production in the hands of the capitalist; the social division of labour implies the dispersion of the means of production among many mutually independent producers of commodities.' Marx pointed to the paradox that

> the very same bourgeois mentality which extols the manufacturing division of labour, the life-long annexation of the worker to a partial operation, and the unconditional subordination of the detail worker to capital . . . denounces just as loudly every kind of deliberate social control and regulation of the social process of production, denounces it as an invasion of the inviolable property rights, liberty and self-determining genius of the individual capitalist. It is characteristic that the inspired apologists of the factory system can find nothing worse to say of any proposal for the general organization of social labour, than that it would transform the whole of society into a factory.

Contrasting this situation with the low manufacturing division of labour in traditional authoritarian societies, which often had an extensive social division of labour, he even thought he had found a general law:

> We may say . . . as a general rule that the less we find authority dominant in the division of labour in the interior of society, the more do we find that the division of labour develops in the workshop, and the more it is subjected to the authority of a single individual. Thus, authority in the workshop and authority in society, as far as the division of labour is concerned, are in inverse ratio to one another.
> (*Marx, 1910, vol. 1, pp. 374–77, and Marx, 1847, pp. 135–36*)

Ruskin followed the Marxian rather than the Durkheimian analysis when he commented that 'we have much studied and much perfected, of late, the great civilized invention of the division of labour; only we have given it a false name. It is not, truly speaking, the labour that is divided, but the men . . .' (Ruskin quoted in Williams, 1963, p. 147). The logical extension of this industrial form of the division of labour came at the end of the nineteenth century with Frederick Winslow Taylor and the principles of 'scientific management'. Here, in the decisive separation of a knowledgeable management from a knowledge-less workforce, of conception from execution, of mental from manual labour, was the culmination of a process that had started in the artisan's initial loss of the instruments of independent production, and his enforced enrolment as a detail worker in the factories of the early nineteenth century.

Durkheim was not unalive to this side of the division of labour. He accepted the charge that, in the industrial society of his day, the individual was often 'no longer anything but an inert piece of machinery, only an external force set going which always moves in the same direction and in the same way' (Durkheim, 1893, p. 371). But whereas for Marx this was a normal, indeed inevitable, consequence of the capitalist division of labour, to be remedied only through the abolition of the division of labour itself, Durkheim continued to believe (or hope) that such a condition of individual alienation was simply an abnormal, transitional, form of the division of labour. It was owing to the contemporary condition of the 'forced' division of labour in which, because of sharp inequalities of circumstances, individuals were not playing the parts in the division of labour for which their natural capacities fitted them. True solidarity would only come about when the division of labour was 'spontaneous', that is, when society 'is constituted in such a way that social inequalities exactly express natural inequalities', and that in turn depended on 'absolute equality in the external conditions of the conflict' (Durkheim, 1893, p. 377).

Some might have thought this almost as utopian a hope and a solution as Marx's expectation of a resolution through a future socialist revolution. But Durkheim, like Marx, believed that the temper of the times was with him, and that the tendencies were all in the direction of greater social justice, and hence a more 'spontaneous' division of labour. Meanwhile he was particularly stern with those who refused to acknowledge that the division of labour was the cardinal principle of modern industrial society, and who opposed to it old-fashioned notions of the universal man:

> We can say that, in higher societies, our duty is not to spread our activity over a large surface, but to concentrate and specialize it. We must contract our horizon, choose a definite task, and immerse ourselves in it completely, instead of trying to make ourselves a sort of creative masterpiece, quite complete, which contains its worth in itself and not in the services that it renders.
>
> (*Durkheim, 1893, p. 377*)

It was a judgement with which many of the most thoughtful observers of the nineteenth century agreed. Others may have shared Marx's feeling that the rise of the division of labour in human society was akin to the Fall in Christian theology. But, unlike him, they had lost their faith, and with the onset of industrialization, could see no hope of redemption in a society that seemed bound to push the division of labour to extremes inconceivable in earlier societies.

References

Durkheim, E. (1933) *The Division of Labour in Society*, trans. G. Simpson, The Free Press, New York (First published, in French, 1893.)

Marx, K. (1963) *The Poverty of Philosophy*, International Publishers, New York (First published in 1847.)

— (1910) *Capital*, trans. Eden and Cedar Paul, 2 vols., Dent & Sons. (Everyman edition 1930.)

Moore, W.E. (1962) 'The Attributes of an Industrial Order', in S. Nosow and W.H. Form (eds), *Man, Work, and Society*, Atherton, New York.

Smith, A. (1910) *The Wealth of Nations*, 2 vols., Dent & Sons. (First published 1776.)

Spencer, H. (1891) 'Progress: Its Laws and Causes' (1857), in *Essays, Scientific, Political, and Speculative*, 3 vols., Williams & Norgate.

Williams, R. (1963) *Culture and Society 1780–1950*, Penguin Books.

Secularization, rationalization, bureaucratization

KRISHAN KUMAR

'Alas! Alas! Religion is vanishing... We no longer have either hope or expectation, not even two little pieces of black wood in a cross before which to wring our hands... Everything that was is no more. All that will be is not yet.' (Alfred de Musset, quoted in Coser, 1965, p. 101.) Alfred de Musset's rather mawkish utterance can be found repeated a hundred times and more during the course of the nineteenth century. Of one thing most people felt certain: the industrial society was a secular society. By this they meant that, on the one hand, there was a progressive decline of institutionalized religion, and of the formal beliefs associated with religious institutions; and, on the other, these beliefs were being increasingly replaced by ones deriving their authority from science and reason, rather than from systems of revealed religion.

For the negative aspect of this view the evidence appeared incontrovertible. Industrial man was not a worshipping man – not, at any rate, of the familiar gods. 'Among the masses there prevails almost universally a total indifference to religion,' commented Engels in *The Condition of the Working Class in England in 1844*. 'In cities and large towns,' wrote Horace Mann, the author of the 1851 Religious Census of Britain, 'it is observable how absolutely insignificant a portion of the congregations is composed of artisans.' Dutiful attenders of Sunday schools in their youth, he noted, on growing up 'soon become as utter strangers to religious ordinances as the people of a heathen country'. (Quoted in Harrison, 1973, p. 151.) The census revealed, to the horror of the Victorian Establishment, that less than twenty-five per cent of the total populations of most of the large cities and industrial towns attended divine service on Sundays. The rural districts did not fare much

Abridged excerpt reproduced with permission from Kumar, K. *Prophecy and Progress: The Sociology of Industrial and Post-Industrial Society*, pp. 85–107; published by Penguin Books Ltd, Harmondsworth, 1978. Copyright © Krishan Kumar, 1978, 1986.

better, averaging out at a rate of attendance of just over twenty-eight per cent of the rural populations. Methodism was indeed the last organized religion to seize the popular mind; and after 1850 it went into a steep decline.

No one of course maintained that simple non-attendance at church equalled secularization. There were even some societies, such as the United States, where for exceptional and largely non-religious reasons church attendance remained high. But non-attendance was nevertheless very important. It was the most visible outward manifestation of the broader trend whereby religious practices, institutions, and thinking came to lose their hold over society as a whole. Typically in industrial society religion becomes a marginal and a minority preoccupation, like a hobby. There remains a decent respect for churchly supervision of the most important *rites de passage*, birth, marriage, death. Church baptisms, weddings, and burials continue to be popular. But Bryan Wilson rightly says of this that 'the church still plays its part in the lives of the many more as a service facility than as an evangelistic agency, more as the provider of occasional and re-assuring ritual than as the disseminator of vital knowledge or the exemplar of moral wisdom.' In matters as important as these the desire is still felt for some touch of the sacred, if only as a form of hopeful insurance:

> The church appears increasingly as some department of a welfare state, which might be corporately supported without personal commitment . . . to be used as and when the individual requires the performance of its services . . . It functions as a service agency providing appropriate ceremonial for prestige and status-enhancement at crucial stages of the life-cycle.
>
> *(Wilson, 1969, p. 34–5, 38)*

Both at the time and since two main objections were made to the view that industrialization and secularization went hand in hand. The first was historical: the fact that, at the very moment when England was entering on its swiftest phase of industrialization, there should occur what one historian has called 'the greatest revival of religious faith since the middle ages' (Perkin, 1969, p. 203). The Church of England was temporarily uplifted by the piety and intellectual rigour of the Oxford Movement; sects and denominations proliferated outside; Evangelicalism was part of the reigning ideology of the day.

But the paradox is easily resolved. The parallel can almost be drawn with the behaviour of species in natural evolution, when poised on the edge of extinction; in their decadent phase they give off a glorious explosion of energy, throwing up the most gorgeous and eccentric forms. So with organized religion. The Victorian revival was the prelude to virtual extinction. The emancipation, made possible by industrialism, from the old society and the old religion, led both to an intensification and a purification of religious life, and – not necessarily in the same people – away from it altogether. Harold Perkin aptly remarks that 'the existence of numerous competing sects, which was more characteristic of Britain than any other European country, provided a sequence of stepping stones by which the emancipated individual could make his way from the Church to any position of Christian belief, or at last out into the great desert of unbelief on the other side of the Jordan' (Perkin, 1969, p. 203). A contemporary neatly made the connection between free-thinking and free trade: 'The same spirit which has produced "free trade" in articles of commerce advocates likewise a free trade in religion.' The eighteenth-century Unitarianism of Priestley and his friends easily led in the nineteenth century to sceptical Utilitarianism and later, to agnostic Positivism. Methodism in its various guises and manifestations provided for the working class the stepping-stones from the Church to Chartism, and later to secular socialism. It was Carlyle who shrewdly remarked in 1838 that theirs was an age 'destitute of faith and yet terrified at scepticism'. Hence the frantic religiosity. But it could be no more than a temporary haven from the slow erosion of the traditional faith. In the end the age found new faiths. But in their secular, rational, cast of thought they marked a deep divide between the industrial society and the religious faiths of every other kind of society.

This last point leads directly on to the second, more serious objection. To the historical argument was added a psychological and sociological one. Responding to the threat of the annihilation of religion the nineteenth century discovered the universality of religion, in the individual mind and in society at large. 'There is,' wrote Durkheim in his *Elementary Forms of the Religious Life*,

> something eternal in religion which is destined to survive all the particular symbols in which religious thought has successively enveloped itself. There can be no society which does not feel the need of upholding and re-affirming at regular intervals the collective sentiments and the collective ideas which make its unity and its personality . . . What essential difference is there between an assembly of Christians celebrating the principal dates of the life of Christ, or of Jews remembering the exodus from Egypt or the promulgation of the decalogue, and a reunion of citizens commemorating the promulgation of a new moral or legal system or some great event in the national life?
>
> (*Durkheim, 1912, p. 427*)

On this view there could be no such thing as 'the decline of religion', merely a change in its forms. Religion was functionally necessary to society, the central mechanism of integration of its members and the most important source of its unifying symbols and rituals. While in the earlier part of the century some used this insight to proclaim the eternal necessity of Christianity, later, more radical, exponents of the view were too conscious of the loss of Christianity's hold on the populations of the industrial societies to rest on so untenable a position. Instead they devoted themselves to exploring the new 'secular' religions that were emerging in the age.

This proved a task of no great difficulty. From Burke onwards it became a commonplace to point to the French Revolution's substitution of the Goddess of Reason for the God of Christianity. Then there was Saint-Simon's 'New Christianity', a secular, scientific faith for the new world of industrialism, to replace the obsolete old Christianity of the obsolete old world. This shortly reappeared as Comte's 'religion of humanity', Positivism, aptly characterised by T.H. Huxley as 'Catholicism minus Christianity'. But then, too, Huxley's own scientific humanism had all the hallmarks of traditional evangelical religion, especially when urged on by his own passionate, missionary, advocacy. Once this step had been taken it was easy to discern the essentially religious character of the vast majority of the new ideologies of the century – nationalism, republicanism, socialism, even the ideology of science itself (see Kumar, 1971, pp. 111–15). Later on, and going back to the roots of the whole thing, Carl Becker elegantly mapped out the 'heavenly city' of the eighteenth-century *philosophes*, as they erected the Temple of Reason on the ruins of the temples of traditional Christianity, and transferred the golden age from an unearthly past to a terrestrial future (Becker, 1932).

Wherever industrialization took hold, its ultimate tendency was to secularise life, to de-throne and disqualify all other competing religions. In so far as a society accepted industrialism, it had to accept a mode of cognition, science, which had its own exclusive interpretation of the world, its own prescriptions for action within it, and its own, internally self-validating, procedures for testing and confirming the truth of its beliefs. To say that this description fits any and every religion is true but again misses the point: which is that industrialism has undermined and vanquished every social order which it has encountered, and that therefore secularism has triumphed over other religions to an extent and in a manner never accomplished by any previous religion.

Tocqueville caught the birth of this process in his account of the French Revolution, where he saw the revolutionaries' rationalism become 'a kind of new religion in itself – a religion, imperfect it is true, without a God, without a worship, without a future life, but which nevertheless, like Islam, poured forth its soldiers, its apostles, and its martyrs over the face of the earth' (Tocqueville in Kumar, 1971, p. 115). The secularism that was carried by the revolutionary armies was carried even further and more powerfully by the iron ships and cheap manufactured goods of the new industrial society. It is this unprecedented phenomenon of total victory which makes the rise of secularism different in kind from the rise of other religions, and which makes it perverse to deny the real break in continuity of beliefs entailed by industrialization. Whatever the actual quality of the majority's belief in science, or the extent of their knowledge of it, the fact remains that they have available explanations of the world in terms of a system of thought which for all practical purposes has ruled out the explanations of all other systems of thought.

Secularization was, in its turn, a manifestation of an even deeper-lying tendency in industrial society: the drive towards the **rationalization** of all spheres of life. Max Weber, who made the analysis of this process central to his sociology of modern society, made it clear that, as with democratization, it was a tendency that long predated the rise of industrial society. As an attitude and a practice, Weber in fact saw it as a secular distillation of certain features of Protestant Christianity, and therefore dated its origins in sixteenth-century Europe. Moreover, given the fact that perhaps the most significant aspect of rationalization was its transformation of attitudes towards economic life, it had as much claim to be the cause of industrialism as its effect. Nevertheless, by the end of the nineteenth century the origins of rationalization were less important than its contemporary expression. Having helped to give birth to industrialism, it became fused with it and was later carried by it. To become industrialized was to become rationalized, a process affecting every area of society, the most public and the most private, the state and the economy as well as the relations of marriage, family, and personal friendship.

Weber's rationalization is a complex concept, embodying a complex and not altogether coherent historical process. He himself was fond of emphasising the negative aspects of it, as in his frequent quotation of Schiller's phrase, 'the disenchantment of the world': 'The fate of our times is characterized by rationalization and intellectualization and, above all, by "the disenchantment of the world"' (Weber, 1948, p. 155). Here rationalization referred to the process whereby the world was rid of magic and mysticism, and of the populations of gods, demons, and spirits that had governed its activities in so many systems of belief. This development had matured only in the societies of the Christian religion. Indeed Church, priest and prophet had hurried it on, in their relentless drive towards the bureaucratization of church affairs, their scholastic systematizations of theology, their creations of increasingly monistic cosmologies. In this sense Weber along with several others was led to see Christianity as an **inherently** secularizing and rationalizing religion, producing almost inevitably out of itself its own demise. To this 'disenchantment' early science of course contributed; but then it must be remembered that for many centuries some of the most brilliant natural scientists were clerics, intent, in all sincerity, to demonstrate by their scientific labours the greater grandeur and power of God.

The positive qualities of rationalization can loosely be summed up by saying that it is the embodiment of the method and substance of science in the institutions, practices, and beliefs of the society. Weber was concerned to emphasize the practical bent of such a development and, above all, its reliance on the method of observation and calculation in all activities, even in those of the arts. The prime exemplar of the rational calculating mode was to be found in the economic realm, in the system of modern European capitalism, with its rationally organized labour market of formally free workers, and rational entrepreneurial activities based on exact calculations of profit and loss. The economic substance of the concept is given weight, perhaps too much so, in Julien Freund's definition of rationalization as 'the organization of life through a division and co-ordination of activities on the basis of an exact study of men's relations with each other, with their tools and their environment, for the purpose of achieving greater efficiency and productivity' (Freund 1968, p. 18).

More generally Weber applied the concept to a studied and increasing mastery over the environment, both natural and social, in which the essential tools were those of observation, experiment, measurement, and calculation. The tendency could be observed in all areas of modern culture: in the elaboration of a rational system of laws and formal procedures for handling them; in the rise of a rational system of administration with modern bureaucracy; in painting's achievement of a rational utilization of lines and spatial perspective; in the establishment of a rational system of musical notation, and of rational principles of musical structure in modern counterpoint and harmony. (See Weber's *Introdruction*, 1904–5.)

Weber was careful to point out that rationalization did not by any means necessarily imply that the populations of those societies undergoing it were any more 'reasonable' or knowledgeable individually, as compared with the populations of less rationalized societies. In terms of a better understanding of their environment they might even know less. The primitive man in the bush knows infinitely more about the conditions under which he lives, the tools he uses and the food he consumes. The modern man who takes a street-car or an elevator, suggested Weber, was not likely to know the principles on which those machines worked, nor were the driver or the elevator operator likely to be any more enlightened.

> The increasing intellectualization and rationalization does not, therefore, indicate an increased and general knowledge of the conditions under which one lives. It means something else, namely, the knowledge or belief that if one but wished one **could** learn it at any time. Hence, it means that there are no mysterious incalculable forces that come into play, but rather that one can, in principle, master all things by calculation. This means that the world is disenchanted. One need no longer have recourse to magical means in order to master or implore the spirits, as did the savage, for whom such mysterious powers existed. Technical means and calculations perform the service. This above all is what intellectualization means.
>
> *(Weber, 1948, p. 139)*

Rationalization, then, here yielded one of its ambivalences. A deeper and more serious ambivalence was revealed in Weber's distinction between 'formal' and 'substantive' rationality. The former refers to the degree to which action is governed by rationally calculable principles, the fitting of the most appropriate and efficient means to a desired end. The latter refers to the degree to which goals and values have been definitely formulated and sorted out according to a rational procedure of ranking, ascription of priorities, realization of contradictory aims and strategies for getting round this, and so forth ('from the standpoint of determinate ethical postulates', was how Weber expressed it, although he believed that the ultimate grounds of ethical choice remained irreducibly arbitrary and 'irrational'). At the abstract level the distinction was just about possible to hold. In historical reality, as Weber knew only too well, the agencies of formal rationality – strictly, the means – had a tendency to invade and undermine the quest for the attainment of substantive rationality.

The dilemma, and the common dénouement, can be illustrated from the fate of classical liberal industrial society. In theory, liberal industrial society was concerned only with the rationalization of means. Ends were seen as diverse and infinite, a matter of individual, private, desires. Hence all the characteristic concepts of liberal economic theory – 'maximization', 'optimization', 'least cost', and so on – related to a concept of rationality that was entirely concentrated on the most efficient means to a given end. In practice, however, things worked out differently. The organization of society, of work, of family life, for the realization of the most efficient means, the most rational way of maximizing output and reducing input all this inevitably affected and influenced the individual's choices, preferences, and desires. The mobilization of society for the greater and cheaper production of goods had as one of its consequences the production also of a 'consumer mentality', constraining its inhabitants to a passive and unproductive consumption of goods. It had, too, its effect on the whole way in which 'fun' and 'leisure' were perceived, and how the hard-won rewards of economic activity were spent. That is, it affected the ends satisfied by such instrumental activity. The irony was that the rationalized means, which, more than ever before, were supposed to free the individual for the pursuit of more, and more diverse, ends, ended up by enslaving him to their supposedly neutral techniques and technology. (See Marcuse, 1965, pp. 3–17.)

Weber's own nightmare about the 'irrationality' of rationalization was born of the contemplation of the most fateful and formidable agency of formal rationality: **bureaucracy**. In much of his writing, indeed, bureaucratization and rationalization are almost synonymous, so struck was he by the growth of the phenomenon, and so distinctively a western development did it seem:

> No country and no age has ever experienced, in the same sense as the modern Occident, the absolute and complete dependence of its whole existence, of the political, technical, and economic conditions of its life, on a specially trained **organization** of officials. The most important functions of the everyday life of society have come to be in the hands of technically, commercially, and above all legally trained government officials.
>
> *(Weber, 1904–5, p. 16)*

And just as the general process of rationalization, while not initially created by industrialism, was given its greatest impetus by it and later carried by it, so the more specialized deposit of that process, bureaucracy, accompanied the development of industrialism and became functionally indispensable to it. The trained official, said Weber, 'is the pillar of both the modern State and of the economic life of the West' (Weber, 1904–5, p. 26). Bureaucracy had a principled hostility to all 'irrational' considerations of person or place, religion or kinship. It adhered strictly to rationally constituted rules and formal procedures of execution. It submitted to the rationality of scientific expertise. It was consequently the highest expression of the rationalizing tendency in industrial society. Industrial society, in whatever form, capitalist or socialist, needs bureaucracy as much as it needs workers and machines. 'The dependence of the material fate of the masses on the permanently correct functioning of ever more bureaucratically co-ordinated private-capitalist organizations steadily grows, and the very thought of the possibility of eliminating them becomes ever more utopian.' So, too, 'any rational socialism will have to take over and augment' bureaucratic administration (Weber, 1948, p. 229).

But Weber's conception of the indispensability of bureaucracy to modern industrial society is accompanied by the perception of its threat to certain key values of the society. This most developed exponent of 'formal rationality' at a certain point complicates the attainment of some of the values of 'substantive rationality'. The technical, means-to-ends, rationality of bureaucracy comes to substitute itself for the goals for which it was instituted. Weber singled out here particularly the threats to individual creativity, personal autonomy, and democracy – all deeply-held values of modern western society. The rationalization of economic life, through the development of modern capitalism, and the unique prominence of economic ends in modern society, had already posed acute problems for the general health of the society and the possibilities of all-round individual development. The further, intensive, bureaucratization of society also tended to undermine the pursuit of democracy. Weber saw, along with Tocqueville, that democratization had been one of the most favourable bases of bureaucratization, through its attacks on aristocratic and monarchical privilege. But 'democracy inevitably comes into conflict with the bureaucratic tendencies which, by its fight against notable rule, democracy has produced . . . The most decisive thing here – indeed it is rather exclusively so – is the **levelling of the governed** in opposition to the ruling and bureaucratically articulated group, which in its turn may occupy a quite autocratic position, both in fact and in form' (Weber, 1948, p. 299). And reflecting, in the long term, on the bureaucratization of ever-larger sectors of social life, Weber was driven to offer a grim vision:

> Together with the machine, the bureaucratic organization is engaged in building the houses of bondage of the future, in which perhaps men will one day be like peasants in the ancient Egyptian State, acquiescent and powerless, while a purely technically good, that is rational, official administration and provision becomes the sole, final value, which sovereignly decides the direction of their affairs.

This passion for bureaucracy is enough to drive one to despair. It is as if in polities, we were deliberately to become men who need 'order' and nothing but order, become nervous and cowardly if for one moment this order wavers, and helpless if they are torn away from their total incorporation in it. That the world should know no men but these: it is in such an evolution that we are already caught up, and the great question is, therefore, not how we can promote and hasten it, but what can we oppose to this machinery in order to keep a portion of mankind free from this parcelling-out of the soul, from this supreme mastery of the bureaucratic way of life.

(*Weber, quoted in Marcuse, 1965, p. 15; and Nisbet, 1967, p. 299*)

References

Becker, C. (1932) *The Heavenly City of the Eighteenth Century Philosophers*, Yale University Press, New Haven.

Durkheim, E. (1915) *The Elementary Forms of the Religious Life*, trans. J. Swain, Allen & Unwin. (First published, in French, 1912.)

Freund, J. (1968) *The Sociology of Max Weber*, Allen Lane The Penguin Press.

Harrison, J.F.C. (1973) *The Early Victorians 1832–51*, Panther Books.

Kumar, K. (ed.) (1971) *Revolution: The Theory and Practice of a European Idea*, Weidenfeld & Nicolson.

Marcuse, H. (1965) 'Industrialisation and Capitalism in the Work of Max Weber', *New Left Review*, no. 30, March–April, pp. 3–17.

Nisbet, R. (1967) *The Sociological Tradition*, Heinemann.

Perkin, H. (1969) *The Making of English Society 1780–1880*, Routledge & Kegan Paul.

Weber, M. (1948) 'Science as Vocation' and 'Bureaucracy', in Gerth, H. and Mills, C.W. (eds), *From Max Weber: Essays in Sociology*, Routledge & Kegan Paul.

— (1930) *The Protestant Ethic and the Spirit of Capitalism*, trans. T. Parsons, Unwin Books. (First published, in German, 1904–5.)

Wilson, B. (1969) *Religion in Secular Society*, Penguin Books.

Marx's framework

ANDREW L. FRIEDMAN

1   Capitalist mode of production

It will be useful to begin with Marx's basic description or definition of the capitalist mode of production. The capitalist mode of production is peculiar to a limited period of history. It is distinguished from earlier modes of

Abridged excerpt reproduced with permission from Friedman, A.L. *Industry and Labour: Class Struggle at Work and Monopoly Capitalism*, pp. 10–19; published by The Macmillan Press Ltd, London, 1977.

production by the category of free labour. Labour is free under capitalism in two ways.

First, individual workers are free to sell and thus to **alienate** their capacity for labour or 'labour power' for a limited period of time in exchange with capitalists for money. Marx defines labour power as 'the aggregate of those bodily and mental capabilities existing in human beings, which he exercises whenever he produces a use-value of any description' (*Capital*, vol. 1, p. 164). In feudalism serfs or vassals owe their lords so much of their labour power and the serfs are born into this relationship. There is no market where labourers may exercise proprietary rights over their own labour power. But under the capitalist mode of production people do have proprietary rights over their labour power and they are free to sell their labour power for **limited** periods of time.

The second way that labour is free in the capitalist mode of production is that the workers have nothing to sell but their labour power in order to gain the means by which they might subsist. They have no independent access to means of subsistence, such as through the produce of land-holdings, and they have no other commodities which they might exchange for means of subsistence.

In the pure capitalist mode of production there are two clearly distinguishable classes. One, of people who own nothing but their labour power and who must sell that labour power to subsist – the workers. The second, of people who buy labour power and who use that commodity, combined with other commodities such as raw materials and tools or machines (what Marx calls the 'instruments of labour'), to produce commodities which they sell for money – the capitalists. With this money the capitalists acquire means of subsistence while retaining ownership of the means of production. 'He, who before was the money-owner, now strides in front as capitalist; the possessor of labour-power follows as his labourer. The one with an air of importance, smirking, intent on business; the other, timid and holding back, like one who is bringing his own hide to market and has nothing to expect but – a hiding' (*Capital*, vol. 1, p. 172).

Capital, the title of Marx's most developed treatise, is that process by which capitalists first exchange money for commodities by purchasing labour power and other means of production, then transform those commodities into new commodities (means of production and means of subsistence) in what Marx calls the 'labour process', and finally exchange those new commodities for money which enables them to start the process again. Capital, the process, is manifest in different entities at different stages – sometimes money, sometimes means of production and means of subsistence. But the process is based on the purchase and sale of labour power.

There is one other feature of the capitalist mode of production which Marx considers to be essential. Capital is not simply a process of endless alternation from money to commodities and then back to money. Capital is a **developing** process whose essential nature is that it expands; that capitalists **accumulate** more and more money representing more and more capital.

Why should this be so?

First, contained in the main features of the capitalist mode of production mentioned above are the potential ingredients for capital to expand. As a class the workers bring only their own hides to the market and as such they can only expect a hiding. But if the value of any commodity is taken to be the amount of labour time which is socially required to produce that thing, and if in return for their labour power the workers receive what is socially necessary to maintain them as proprietors of labour power (capable of making that labour power available to capitalists), then, in value terms, equivalents are exchanged. There is no exploitation. It is not in the exchange of labour power that the worker gets his hiding, but in the labour process which follows. Having sold his labour power to the capitalist for a period of time, the worker is now alienated from that labour power, and the capitalist may dispose of it as he wishes (within some bounds set by law and custom). Labour power is a peculiar commodity in that it is possible for labour power to produce commodities, the value of which is greater than the value of the means of subsistence socially necessary to reproduce that labour power. Not only has the worker become alienated from his labour power, but in so doing he has lost claim to the fruits of his labour. Surplus value created by labour power legally belongs to the capitalist and it is the form taken by exploitation in the capitalist mode of production.

What will the capitalist do with this surplus value?

The capitalist will consume part of it, but he will also plough part of it back into the process of capital in order to expand the value of his capital. Why should the capitalist abstain from immediate consumption?

First, the capitalist is driven by a desire for wealth as wealth, but second, the individual capitalist is driven to reinvest by the forces of competition. New investment embodies newer and more productive techniques for production. If an individual capitalist does not keep up with the most productive techniques his competitors will be able to sell their commodities more cheaply than him. Not only will the laggard capitalist fall behind in technique, but he will also be priced out of his commodity markets and destroyed as a capitalist. While the individual capitalist may have become a capitalist through avarice, continual abstinence is required of him due to the competitive nature of the mode of production. For Marx the character of the mode of production primarily shapes the psychology of the individuals rather than the other way around. I shall return to this theme in Section 2 below.

In the purchase and sale of labour power Marx demonstrates the **potential** for capital to expand. The purchase of labour power allows the capitalist to appropriate surplus value. In the forces of competition Marx provides a reason for that potential to be realised **continually**. This Marx calls the Law of Value, that capitalists are forced to extract surplus value from workers due to competition.

The development of capitalist production makes it constantly necessary to keep increasing the amount of the capital laid out in a given industrial undertaking, and competition makes the **immanent** laws of capitalist production to be felt by each individual capitalist, as external coercive laws. It compels him to keep constantly extending his capital, in order to preserve it.

(Capital, vol. 1, p. 555)

The capitalist mode of production may therefore be defined by two features. First, labour is free in the double sense. The worker is free to sell his labour power, but because he is also free from the possession of other commodities which he might sell, he **must** sell his labour power to some capitalist.

Second, capitalists, while having a monopoly over the means of production as a class (and therefore not being required to sell their labour power), are not monopolists over sections of the means of production as individuals. They are subjected as individuals to forces of competition which **force** them to accumulate capital – though they **may** wish to accumulate anyway.

Marx's definition of the capitalist mode of production describes the exchange relations which surround production, rather than the capitalist method of production itself. The definition merely sets out the conditions which allow exploitation to occur; the conditions which allow one group of people to appropriate surplus product produced by another group. As such, it is capable of providing a theory to explain the distribution or allocation of wealth produced by the capitalist mode of production. Most Marxists, until very recently, have concentrated on Marx's theory as a theory of value, something similar to, though not quite the same as, the value theory of classical economists like Ricardo and the price theory of neo-classical economists today – a theory of resource allocation under certain initial assumptions. But for Marx the capitalist mode of production is an historically limited phenomenon. Not only is capital a process which grows, but the capitalist mode of production is a social system which develops, changes and ultimately will be destroyed because of changes which it has itself fostered as part of its development process.

To understand how the capitalist mode of production develops and changes Marx considers a theory of productive activity itself to be necessary along with a theory of the exchanges which initiate and sustain productive activity and which distribute its fruits.

2   The capitalist labour process and the valorisation process

Productive activity for Marx is the unity of the labour process and the valorisation process.

The labour process is not in itself peculiar to capitalism. It is a fundamental condition of human existence. The labour process in its most abstract aspect is 'human action with a view to the production of use-values, appropriation of natural substances to human requirements; it is the necessary condition for effecting exchange of matter between Man and Nature; it is the everlasting Nature-imposed condition of human existence, and therefore is independent of every social phase of that existence, or rather, is common to every such phase' (*Capital*, vol. 1, p. 179).

In this abstract definition the labour process is a relation between man and nature. But in any concrete stage of history the labour process is also a social process in which **people interact**. The particular form of the social aspect of the labour process will depend on the mode of production within which that labour process is situated.

For Marx what distinguishes the human labour process from that of other animals is that human labour is conscious and purposive rather than instinctive.

> What distinguishes the worst architect from the best of bees is this, that the architect raises his structure in imagination before he erects it in reality. At the end of every labour-process, we get a result that already existed in the imagination of the labourer at its commencement. He not only effects a change of form in the material on which he works, but he also realises a purpose of his own that gives the law to his *modus operandi*, and to which he must subordinate his will. And this subordination is no mere momentary act. Besides the exertion of the bodily organs, the process demands that, during the whole operation, the workman's will be steadily in consonance with his purpose.
>
> *(Capital, vol. 1, p. 174)*.

In the abstract the labour process involves human imagination, human purpose and human will, but in a particular situation the people whose imagination, purpose and will direct the physical activity may be different from those who carry out that physical activity. This separation is increasingly incorporated into the labour process as the capitalist mode of production develops.

There are three elements to the abstract aspect of the labour process.

First, there is the work or labour itself – the personal activity of human beings.

Second, the subject of labour – nature's materials in their virgin state or worked up through previous labour into raw materials.

Third, the instruments of labour – the things which people use to mediate between themselves and the subject of their labour.

Under the capitalist mode of production the elements of the labour process are combined to produce surplus value as well as use-values. In the valorisation process commodities are used to produce other commodities, the value of which is greater than the constituent commodities. Marx calls the instruments of labour used up in the labour process (wear and tear or depreciation) and the materials used up in a given period of time **constant capital** (commonly labelled c). He calls the labour power used during that time **variable capital** (commonly labelled v). The capitalist buys the constant and variable capital at their values, at the amount of socially necessary labour time required to produce them, but labour power, v, creates commodities the value of which is greater than the value of the wages which are paid for labour power. The value which workers give to the commodities produced is therefore $v + s$, the value of variable capital plus **surplus value**. Constant capital, on the other hand, merely transfers its value to the commodities produced. Plant and equipment embody past live labour time so they have value, but it is only living labour which produces surplus value.

Therefore the value of commodities produced as part of the valorisation process equals $c + v + s$. The rate of exploitation is defined as s/v, while the rate of profit (assuming all constant capital which the capitalist purchases in one period is used up during that production period) is $s/c + v$ or surplus value as a proportion of total capital laid out.

Capitalist productive activity is a developing process which is both affected by the social relations which surround it and in turn also influences them. The effect of productive activity on the mode of production derives from Marx's view of human nature. For Marx, people's needs and abilities are not fixed. They change in the course of human activity and particularly in the course of work.

Productive activity is initiated by man 'in order to appropriate Nature's productions in a form adapted to his own wants', according to Marx. But he then goes on to say that man, 'by thus acting on the external world and changing it, . . . at the same time changes his own nature. He develops his slumbering powers and compels them to act in obedience to his sway' (*Capital*, vol. 1, p. 173).

Three characteristics or stages of capitalist productive activity are worth considering. First is what Marx calls **co-operation** – 'when numerous labourers work together side by side, whether in one and the same process, or in different connected processes' (*Capital*, vol. 1, p. 308). Co-operation is not peculiar to the capitalist mode of production, but it does distinguish capitalism in its earliest stages from the individual handicraft trades of the guilds.

While the category of free labour determines the legal possibility or potential for the extraction of surplus value, and while competition among capitalists provides the primary motivation for capitalists to try to realise that potential continuously, co-operation provides one of the main **technical** reasons which allows that **legal** opportunity for exploitation to be captured by the capitalist. To enable the capitalist to appropriate surplus value, commodities must be produced in the labour process whose value is greater than the commodities which went into it. What the capitalist pays the labourer is the cost of maintaining him for a fixed period of time, while what the capitalist receives is the labourer's capacity for working during that period of time. With co-operation a given expenditure of work by each individual labourer (a given degree of effort for a given amount of time) will produce more commodities than if those labourers were each working separately. There are many reasons for this. For example, co-operation allows common use of means of production such as buildings; it allows a great deal of work to be carried out in a short space of time at critical moments such as during harvest time; and it allows a certain uniformity and continuity in commodities produced.

A second major characteristic of the labour process under the capitalist mode of production is the development of the **manufacturing division of labour** – the separation of tasks within a workshop or where a single final commodity is being produced. This increases the productivity of labour beyond what is achieved under simple co-operation when everyone is doing the same things. The workers' dexterity at a simple operation increases with constant exercise and experience. Much of the time lost when workmen changed from one operation within the labour process to another is eliminated. Thus the amount of labour time required for the production of a fixed quantity of commodities falls. This means that commodities have fallen in value. Now if the amounts of commodities which the workers require as means of subsistence remain the same in physical terms, then the value of labour power falls. The labour time embodied in the means of subsistence required to maintain workers falls. If the amount of time the workers work stays the same, the proportion of that time representing surplus value and appropriated by the capitalist rises. This method of valorisation, increasing the rate of exploitation by cheapening commodities which enter into workers' consumption, Marx calls the 'production of relative surplus value'.

Marx considers the period when the capitalist mode of production was mainly characterised by the manufacturing division of labour as roughly from the middle of the sixteenth century to the last third of the eighteenth century (*Capital*, vol. 1, p. 318). Marx actually calls this period of capitalist development Manufacture.

During Manufacture, workers who had been trained as all-round craftsmen, often with a seven-year apprenticeship, came to be what Marx calls 'detail workers' and lost their all round craft skills.

This is one example of how the development of productive activity under capitalism can affect capitalist social relations, or the capitalist mode of production itself. The original condition which distinguished worker from capitalist, the lack of independent means of production (the lack of commodities other than his own labour power available for sale), is augmented by the degradation of workers' labour power. As the manufacturing division of labour proceeds within the labour process, the workers' general craft skills wither while their detail dexterity for a very specific operation is developed. Thus productive activity moulds a set of workers such that even if they could get access to some means of production they would no longer be able to produce entire commodities.

The manufacturing division of labour weakens the workers' position in another way. By splitting productive activity requiring general skills into component parts and filling those parts with different workers, manufacture 'develops a hierarchy of labour powers, to which there corresponds a scale of wages' (*Capital*, vol. 1, p. 330). As the individual components are simpler to master than the whole, the value of labour power is diminished. The training time required to reproduce labour power falls. There also arises a set of detail operations which require no skill at all. Manufacture 'also begins to make a speciality of the absence of all development' (*Capital*, vol. 1, p. 331). Workers are increasingly separated into skilled and unskilled. The cost of apprenticeship for unskilled workers employed is removed altogether.

As the position of the worker weakened in the market for labour power during this period, the position of the typical capitalist slowly improved. The manufacturing division of labour meant an increase in the minimum number of workers under the control of a single capitalist required for that capitalist's operation to be technically efficient. The rise in the minimum number of workmen also meant a rise in the quantity of tools and raw materials needed. So the amount of money which the capitalist must lay out to buy the labour power he needs (variable capital), and to buy the instruments of labour and raw materials (constant capital), rises. Each individual labourer's labour power represents a smaller and smaller proportion of the capital of the capitalist who purchases it.

A third major feature or stage of productive activity during capitalism is the use of **machinery** to replace labour power and to increase the productivity of the workers who remain. Machinery acts like the manufacturing division of labour to reduce the labour time necessary to produce commodities and to increase the rate of exploitation by the production of relative surplus value. The widespread introduction of machinery into capitalist production began in the last third of the eighteenth century and Marx calls the stage of the capitalist mode of production from then up to his time Modern Industry.

During this stage an equalisation or homogenisation of work activities by different workers occurs because now most workers are merely appendages to the machine rather than facets of a handicraft skill. Instead of a hierarchy of workers based on skills or tasks, most workers do unskilled work and the more important divisions within the labour force are based on age and sex.

Machines lessened both the brute strength and the level of skill required in productive activity. This allowed capitalists to employ more women and children. The employment of women and children meant that in order to produce labour power men did not have to be paid a family wage. Wages were actually reduced during this period, partly because of the pressure of women and children being added to the market as suppliers of labour power, and partly because the numbers of men looking for work was swollen due to men being thrown out of work when machines were introduced.

All productive activity is not mechanised immediately. The introduction of machinery into one labour process, by cheapening the value of labour power (production of relative surplus value), actually discourages the introduction of machinery into other labour processes. Machines have to be that much cheaper or they have to increase the productivity of the remaining workers by that much more if they are to replace cheapened workers.

During the Modern Industry phase productive activity conducted on the basis of domestic industry and manufacture survives. But this productive activity is altered in that it comes to be affected crucially by the dominant Modern Industry sector made up of highly mechanised factories. Marx renames these less technically advanced sectors 'Modern Manufacture' and 'Modern Domestic Industry' during the Modern Industry stage.

First, conditions of work in these less technically advanced sectors deteriorate markedly. The widespread use of women and children is not confined to the Modern Industry sector during this period. While the lightened character of work in the mechanised Modern Industry sector first encouraged capitalists to employ women and children there, the consequent fall in wages also forced women and children into the less technically advanced sectors to make up the family wage. There the work was harder, often more dangerous because of poor sanitary conditions, hours were longer, and pay was often lower than in the more technically advanced sectors. This is because workers come to Modern Manufacture and Modern Domestic Industry after being thrown out of Modern Industry (and agriculture) in a desperate state, because these less technically advanced sectors could only compete with Modern Industry on the basis of cheap labour and hard conditions, and because workers' power to resist such conditions in the Modern Domestic Industry sector is weaker because the workers are so spread out.

Second, in many cases domestic industry or small workshops based on manufacturing division of labour become the outside branches of the mechanised factories. The same capitalist might control productive activity in all three sectors producing the same commodity. When demand for the commodity is high workers in the less technically advanced sectors will be put to work at an exhausting pace, but when demand falls off these workers will be the first to be laid off. This occurs because the capitalist will want to keep his modern factory running at a smooth continuous pace to gain the most from his machinery. He loses out when machines are idle because the machines deteriorate physically and because of obsolescence since continual improvements occur in new generations of machinery. Idle workers, laid off because of insufficient demand for the capitalist's commodities, cost the individual capitalist nothing.

Two further characteristics of labour processes under Modern Industry are worth noting.

The first is that while Modern Manufacture and Modern Domestic Industry survive for some time into this period, according to Marx these technically backward sectors eventually become mechanised. The cheapening of labour power and the miserably hard conditions of work in these sectors eventually meet with the natural barrier of human endurance.

'So soon as this point is at last reached – and it takes many years – the hour has struck for the introduction of machinery, and for the thenceforth rapid conversion of the scattered domestic industries and also of manufactures into factory industries' (*Capital*, vol. 1, p. 442). Another reason for the eventual disappearance of the non-mechanised sectors was the Factory Acts, which began to take effect during the 1830s. By limiting hours of work and regulating some of the most unhealthy conditions of work they weakened the competitive position of non-mechanised sectors relative to the mechanised ones.

The second characteristic of the Modern Industry stage is the continual change in methods of production which occurs even in labour processes where machines have already been introduced. Machines themselves are continually being improved, replacing more and more labour power. The production of relative surplus value – the cheapening of commodities by introducing technical improvements – grows in importance.

'Modern Industry never looks upon and treats the existing form of a process as final. The technical basis of that industry is therefore revolutionary, while all earlier modes of production were essentially conservative' (*Capital*, vol. 1, p. 457). Corresponding to these changes, the functions of the labourer and the social division of labour is continually changing; that is, changes in the particular tasks performed by workers within a single labour process and shifts in capital and labour from one branch of production to another are always occurring. But because the worker has sold his labour power to a capitalist these changes in technical conditions of production mean that workers often have to be thrown out of one labour process, have to return to the labour power market, in order to be regrouped around new manufacturing and social divisions of labour. This 'dispels all fixity and security in the situation of the labourer; . . . it constantly threatens, by taking away the instruments of labour, to snatch from his hands his means of subsistence, and by suppressing his detail function, to make him superfluous' (*Capital*, vol. 1, p. 457).

This continual technical change, which is primarily labour-saving according to Marx, perpetually creates and re-creates what Marx calls an 'industrial reserve army' of labour – a body of workers out of work, 'kept in misery in order to be always at the disposal of capital' (*Capital*, vol. 1, p. 457). Through the industrial reserve army, wages are kept down to near subsistence.

The other important effect of technical change during the Modern Industry phase is that its labour power saving bias implies that the ratio of constant capital to variable capital (called by Marx the 'organic composition of capital') will rise. Because surplus value can only be extracted from labour power (constant capital merely gives up a part of its value as a commodity to the new commodities created by using up constant capital) the proportion of capital which yields surplus value will fall. If the rate of exploitation remains constant (the amount of surplus value appropriated from a given amount of labour time), then the ratio of surplus value to capital will fall. If we take this ratio as an indicator of the rate of profit generated within the system, we have Marx's law of the tendency of the rate of profit to fall.

Co-operation, the manufacturing division of labour within a single labour process and the mechanisation of the labour process each dominate the labour process under the capitalist mode of production at different stages of its development, but during succeeding stages the main characteristic of earlier stages continues to characterise the labour process, though in a somewhat altered form. In the Modern Industry stage workers still perform detail tasks but they are now details of a machine process rather than of a handicraft.

References

Marx, K. (1859) *A Contribution to the Critique of Political Economy* (London: Lawrence and Wishart, 1971).
— (1867), *Capital*, vol. 1 (London: Lawrence and Wishart, 1970).
— (1885), *Capital*, vol. 2 (London: Lawrence and Wishart, 1970).
— (1895), *Capital*, vol. 3 (London: Lawrence and Wishart, 1972).
— and F. Engels (1848) *Manifesto of the Communist Party* (Moscow: Progress).

Docile bodies and panopticism

MICHEL FOUCAULT

The classical age discovered the body as object and target of power. It is easy enough to find signs of the attention then paid to the body – to the body that is manipulated, shaped, trained, which obeys, responds, becomes skilful and increases its forces. The great book of Man-the-Machine was written simultaneously on two registers: the anatomico-metaphysical register, of which Descartes wrote the first pages and which the physicians and philosophers continued, and the technico-political register, which was constituted by a whole set of regulations and by empirical and calculated methods relating to the army, the school and the hospital, for controlling or correcting the operations of the body. These two registers are quite distinct, since it was a question, on the one hand, of submission and use and, on the other, of functioning and explanation: there was a useful body and an intelligible body. And yet there are points of overlap from one to the other. La Mettrie's *L'Homme-machine* is both a marterialist reduction of the soul and a general theory of *dressage*, at the centre of which reigns the notion of 'docility', which joins the analysable body to the manipulable body. A body is docile that may be subjected, used, transformed and improved. The celebrated automata, on the other hand, were not only a way of illustrating an organism, they were also political puppets, small-scale models of power: Frederick II, the meticulous king of small machines, well-trained regiments and long exercises, was obsessed with them.

What was so new in these projects of docility that interested the eighteenth century so much? It was certainly not the first time that the body had become the object of such imperious and pressing investments; in every society, the body was in the grip of very strict powers, which imposed on it constraints, prohibitions or obligations. However, there were several new things in these techniques. To begin with, there was the scale of the control: it was a question not of treating the body, *en masse*, 'wholesale', as if it were an indissociable unity, but of working it 'retail', individually; of exercising upon it a subtle coercion, of obtaining holds upon it at the level of the mechanism itself – movements, gestures, attitudes, rapidity: an infinitesimal power over the active body. Then there was the object of the control: it was not or was no longer the signifying elements of behaviour or the language of the body, but the economy, the efficiency of movements, their internal organization; constraint bears upon the forces rather than upon the signs; the only truly important ceremony is that of exercise. Lastly, there is the modality: it implies an uninterrupted, constant coercion, supervising the processes of the activity rather than its result and it is exercised according to a codification that partitions as closely as possible time, space, movement. These methods, which made possible the meticulous control of the operations of the body, which assured the constant subjection of its forces and imposed upon them a relation or docility-utility, might be called 'disciplines'. Many disciplinary methods had long been in existence – in monasteries, armies, workshops. But in the course of the seventeenth and eighteenth centuries the disciplines became general formulas of domination. They were different from slavery because they were not based on a relation of appropriation of bodies; indeed, the elegance of the discipline lay in the fact that it could dispense with this costly and violent relation by obtaining effects of utility at least as great. They were different, too, from 'service', which was a constant, total, massive, non-analytical, unlimited relation of domination, established in the form of the individual will of the master, his 'caprice'. They were different from vassalage, which was a highly coded, but distant relation of submission, which bore less on the operations of the body than on the products of labour and the ritual marks of allegiance. Again, they were different from asceticism and from 'disciplines' of a monastic type, whose function was to obtain renunciations rather than increases of utility and which, although they involved obedience to others, had as their principal aim an increase of the mastery of each individual over his own body. The historical moment of the disciplines was the moment when an art of the human body was born, which was directed not only at the growth of its skills, nor at the intensification of its subjection, but at the formation of a relation that in the mechanism itself makes it more obedient as it becomes more useful, and conversely. What was then being formed was a policy of coercions that act upon the body, a calculated manipulation of its elements, its gestures, its behaviour. The human body was entering a machinery of power that explores it, breaks it down and rearranges it. A 'political anatomy', which was also a 'mechanics of power', was being born; it defined how one may have a hold over others' bodies, not only so that they may do what one wishes, but so that they may operate as one wishes, with the techniques, the speed and the efficiency that one determines. Thus discipline produces subjected and practised bodies, 'docile' bodies. Discipline increases the forces of the body (in economic terms of utility) and diminishes these same forces (in political terms of obedience). In short, it dissociates power from the body; on the one hand, it turns it into an 'aptitude', a 'capacity', which it seeks to increase; on the other hand, it reverses the course of the energy, the power that might result from it, and turns it into a relation of strict subjection. If economic exploitation separates the force and the product of labour, let us say that disciplinary coercion establishes in the body the constricting link between an increased aptitude and an increased domination.

The 'invention' of this new political anatomy must not be seen as a sudden discovery. It is rather a multiplicity of often minor processes, of different origin and scattered location, which overlap, repeat, or imitate one another, support one another, distinguish themselves from one another according to their domain of application, converge and gradually produce the blueprint of a general method. They were at work in secondary education at a very early date, later in primary schools; they slowly invested the space of the hospital; and, in a few decades, they restructured the military organization. They sometimes circulated very rapidly from one point to another (between the army and the technical schools or secondary schools), sometimes slowly and discreetly (the insidious militarization of the large workshops). On almost every occasion, they were adopted in response to particular needs: an industrial innovation, a renewed outbreak of certain epidemic diseases, the invention of the rifle or the victories of Prussia. This did not prevent them being totally inscribed in general and essential transformations, which we must now try to delineate.

Napoleon did not discover this world; but we know that he set out to organise it; and he wished to arrange around him a mechanism of power that would enable him to see the smallest event that occurred in the state he governed; he intended, by means of the rigorous discipline that he imposed, 'to embrace the whole of this vast machine without the slightest detail escaping his attention' (Treilhard, 14).

A meticulous observation of detail, and at the same time a political awareness of these small things, for the control and use of men, emerge through the classical age bearing with them a whole set of techniques, a whole corpus of methods and knowledge, descriptions, plans and data. And from such trifles, no doubt, the man of modern humanism was born.[1]

---

[1] I shall choose examples from military, medical, educational and industrial institutions. Other examples might have been taken from colonization, slavery and child rearing.

The art of distributions

In the first instance, discipline proceeds from the distribution of individuals in space. To achieve this end, it employs several techniques.

Discipline sometimes requires **enclosure**, the specification of a place heterogeneous to all others and closed in upon itself. It is the protected place of disciplinary monotony. There was the great 'confinement' of vagabonds and paupers; there were other more discreet, but insidious and effective ones. There were the *collèges*, or secondary schools: the monastic model was gradually imposed; boarding appeared as the most perfect, if not the most frequent, eductational régime; it became obligatory at Louis-le-Grand when, after the departure of the Jesuits, it was turned into a model school (cf. Ariès, 308–13 and Snyders, 35–41). There were the military barracks: the army, that vagabond mass, has to be held in place; looting and violence must be prevented; the fears of local inhabitants, who do not care for troops passing through their towns, must be calmed; conflicts with the civil authorities must be avoided; desertion must be stopped, expenditure controlled. The ordinance of 1719 envisaged the construction of several hundred barracks, on the model of those already set up in the south of the country; there would be strict confinements: 'The whole will be enclosed by an outer wall ten feet high, which will surround the said houses, at a distance of thirty feet from all the sides'; this will have the effect of maintaining the troops in 'order and discipline, so that an officer will be in a position to answer for them' (*L'Ordonnance militaire*, IXL, 25 September 1719). In 1745, there were barracks in about 320 towns; and it was estimated that the total capacity of the barracks in 1775 was approximately 200 000 men (Daisy, 201–9; an anonymous memoir of 1775, in Dépôt de la guerre, 3689, f. 156; Navereau, 132–5). Side by side with the spread of workshops, there also developed great manufacturing spaces, both homogeneous and well defined: first, the combined manufactories, then, in the second half of the eighteenth century, the works or factories proper (the Chaussade iron-works occupied almost the whole of the Médine peninsula, between Nièvre and Loire; in order to set up the Indret factory in 1777, Wilkinson, by means of embankments and dikes, constructed an island on the Loire; Toufait built Le Creusot in the valley of the Charbonnière, which he transformed, and he had workers' accommodation built in the factory itself); it was a change of scale, but it was also a new type of control. The factory was explicitly compared with the monastery, the fortress, a walled town; the guardian 'will open the gates only on the return of the workers, and after the bell that announces the resumption of work has been rung'; a quarter of an hour later no one will be admitted; at the end of the day, the workshops' heads will hand back the keys to the Swiss guard of the factory, who will then open the gates (*Amboise*, f. 12, 1301). The aim is to derive the maximum advantages and to neutralise the inconveniences (thefts, interruptions of work, disturbances and 'cabals'), as the forces of production become more concentrated; to protect materials and tools and to master the labour force: 'The order and inspection that must be maintained require that all workers be assembled under the same roof, so that the partner who is entrusted with the management of the manufactory may prevent and remedy abuses that may arise among the workers and arrest their progress at the outset' (Dauphin, 199).

In the factories that appeared at the end of the eighteenth century, the principle of individualizing partitioning became more complicated. It was a question of distributing individuals in a space in which one might isolate them and map them; but also of articulating this distribution on a production machinery that had its own requirements. The distribution of bodies, the spatial arrangement of production machinery and the different forms of activity in the distribution of 'posts' had to be linked together. The Oberkampf manufactory at Jouy obeyed this principle. It was made up of a series of workshops specified according to each broad type of operation: for the printers, the handlers, the colourists, the women who touched up the design, the engravers, the dyers. The largest of the buildings, built in 1791, by Toussaint Barré, was 110 metres long and had three storeys. The ground floor was devoted mainly to block printing; it contained 132 tables arranged in two rows, the length of the workshop, which had eighty-eight windows; each printer worked at a table with his 'puller', who prepared and spread the colours. There were 264 persons in all. At the end of each table was a sort of rack on which the material that had just been printed was left to dry (Saint-Maur). By walking up and down the central aisle of the workshop, it was possible to carry out a supervision that was both general and individual: to observe the worker's presence and application, and the quality of his work; to compare workers with one another, to classify them according to skill and speed; to follow the successive stages of the production process. All these serializations formed a permanent grid: confusion was eliminated[2] that is to say, production was divided up and the labour process was articulated, on the one hand, according to its stages or elementary operations, and, on the other hand, according to the individuals, the particular bodies, that carried it out: each variable of this force – strength, promptness, skill, constancy – would be observed, and therefore characterized, assessed, computed and related to the individual who was its particular agent. Thus, spread out in a perfectly legible way over the whole series of individual bodies, the work force may be analysed in individual units. At the emergence of large-scale industry, one finds, beneath the division of the production process, the individualizing fragmentation of labour power; the distributions of the disciplinary space often assured both.

---

[2] Cf. what La Métherie wrote after a visit to Le Creusot: 'The buildings for so fine an establishment and so large a quantity of different work should cover a sufficient area, so that there will be no confusion among the workers during working time' (La Métherie, 66).

The control of activity

The **time-table** is an old inheritance. The strict model was no doubt suggested by the monastic communities. It soon spread. Its three great methods – establish rhythms, impose particular occupations, regulate the cycles of repetition – were soon to be found in schools, workshops and hospitals. The new disciplines had no difficulty in taking up their place in the old forms; the schools and poor-houses extended the life and the regularity of the monastic communities to which they were often attached. The rigours of the industrial period long retained a religious air; in the seventeenth century, the regulations of the great manufactories laid down the exercises that would divide up the working day: 'On arrival in the morning, before beginning their work, all persons shall wash their hands, offer up their work to God and make the sign of the cross' (Saint-Maur, article 1); but even in the nineteenth century, when the rural populations were needed in industry, they were sometimes formed into 'congregations', in an attempt to inure them to work in the workshops; the framework of the 'factory–monastery' was imposed upon the workers. In the Protestant armies of Maurice of Orange and Gustavus Adolphus, military discipline was achieved through a rhythmics of time punctuated by pious exercises; army life, Boussanelle was later to say, should have some of the 'perfections of the cloister itself' (Boussanelle, 2; on the religious character of discipline in the Swedish army, cf. *The Swedish Discipline*, London, 1632). For centuries, the religious orders had been masters of discipline: they were the specialists of time, the great technicians of rhythm and regular activities. But the disciplines altered these methods of temporal regulation from which they derived. They altered them first by refining them. One began to count in quarter hours, in minutes, in seconds. This happened in the army, of course: Guibert systematically implemented the chronometric measurement of shooting that had been suggested earlier by Vauban. In the elementary schools, the division of time became increasingly minute; activities were governed in detail by orders that had to be obeyed immediately: 'At the last stroke of the hour, a pupil will ring the bell, and at the first sound of the bell all the pupils will kneel, with their arms crossed and their eyes lowered. When the prayer has been said, the teacher will strike the signal once to indicate that the pupils should get up, a second time as a sign that they should salute Christ, and a third that they should sit down' (La Salle, *Conduite . . .* , 27–8). In the early nineteenth century, the following timetable was suggested for the *Écoles mutuelles*, or 'mutual improvement schools': 8.45 entrance of the monitor, 8.52 the monitor's summons, 8.56 entrance of the children and prayer, 9.00 the children go to their benches, 9.04 first slate, 9.08 end of dictation, 9.12 second slate, etc. (Tronchot, 221). The gradual extension of the wage-earning class brought with it a more detailed partitioning of time: 'If workers arrive later than a quarter of an hour after the ringing of the bell . . .' (*Amboise*, article 2); 'if any one of the companions is asked for during work and loses more than five minutes . . .', 'anyone who is not at his work at the correct time . . .' (Oppenheim, article 7–8). But an attempt is also made to assure the quality of the time used: constant supervision, the pressure of supervisors, the elimination of anything that might disturb or distract; it is a question of constituting a totally useful time: 'It is expressly forbidden during work to amuse one's companions by gestures or in any other way, to play at any game whatsoever, to eat, to sleep, to tell stories and comedies' (Oppenheim, article 16); and even during the meal-break, 'there will be no telling of stories, adventures or other such talk that distracts the workers from their work'; 'it is expressly forbidden for any worker, under any pretext, to bring wine into the manufactory and to drink in the workshops' (*Amboise*, article 4). Time measured and paid must also be a time without impurities or defects; a time of good quality, throughout which the body is constantly applied to its exercise. Precision and application are, with regularity, the fundamental virtues of disciplinary time. But this is not the newest thing about it. Other methods are more characteristic of the disciplines.

Bentham's *Panopticon*

We know the principle on which it was based: at the periphery, an annular building; at the centre, a tower; this tower is pierced with wide windows that open onto the inner side of the ring; the peripheric building is divided into cells, each of which extends the whole width of the building; they have two windows, one on the inside, corresponding to the windows of the tower; the other, on the outside, allows the light to cross the cell from one end to the other. All that is needed, then, is to place a supervisor in a central tower and to shut up in each cell a madman, a patient, a condemned man, a worker or a schoolboy. By the effect of backlighting, one can observe from the tower, standing out precisely against the light, the small captive shadows in the cells of the periphery. They are like so many cages, so many small theatres, in which each actor is alone, perfectly individualised and constantly visible. The panoptic mechanism arranges spatial unities that make it possible to see constantly and to recognise immediately. In short, it reverses the principle of the dungeon; or rather of its three functions – to enclose, to deprive of light and to hide – it preserves only the first and eliminates the other two. Full lighting and the eye of a supervisor capture better than darkness, which ultimately protected. Visibility is a trap. If the inmates are convicts, there is no danger of a plot, an attempt at collective escape, the planning of new crimes for the future, bad reciprocal influences; if they are patients, there is no danger of contagion; if they are madmen there is no risk of their committing violence upon one another; if they are schoolchildren, there is no copying, no noise, no chatter, no waste of time; if they are workers, there are no disorders, no theft, no coalitions, none of those distractions that slow down the rate of work, make it less perfect or cause accidents.

Hence the major effect of the Panopticon: to induce in the inmate a state of conscious and permanent visibility that assures the automatic functioning of power. So to arrange things that the surveillance is permanent in its effects, even if it is discontinuous in its action; that the perfection of power should tend to render its actual exercise unnecessary; that this architectural apparatus should be a machine for creating and sustaining a power relation independent of the person who exercises it; in short, that the inmates should be caught up in a power situation of which they are themselves the bearers. To achieve this, it is at once too much and too little that the prisoner should be constantly observed by an inspector: too little, for what matters is that he knows himself to be observed; too much, because he has no need in fact of being so. In view of this, Bentham laid down the principle that power should be visible and unverifiable. Visible: the inmate will constantly have before his eyes the tall outline of the central tower from which he is spied upon. Unverifiable: the inmate must never know whether he is being looked at any one moment; but he must be sure that he may always be so.

A real subjection is born mechanically from a fictitious relation. So it is not necessary to use force to constrain the convict to good behaviour, the madman to calm, the worker to work, the schoolboy to application, the patient to the observation of the regulations. He who is subjected to a field of visibility, and who knows it, assumes responsibility for the constraints of power; he makes them play spontaneously upon himself; he inscribes in himself the power relation in which he simultaneously plays both roles; he becomes the principle of his own subjection. By this very fact, the external power may throw off its physical weight; it tends to the non-corporal; and, the more it approaches this limit, the more constant, profound and permanent are its effects: it is a perpetual victory that avoids any physical confrontation and which is always decided in advance.

References

Amboise, Projet de règlement pour l'aciérie d', Archives nationales, f. 12, 1301.
Ariès, P. (1960) *L'Enfant et la famille*.
Boussanelle, L. de (1770) *Le Bon Militaire*.
Daisy (1745) *Le royaume de France*.
Dauphin, V. (1913) *Recherches sur l'industrie textile en Anjou*.
La Métherie, C. de (1787) *Journal de physique*, XXX.
La Salle, J.-B. de (1783) *Conduite des écoles chrétiennes*, B.N. MS. 11759. *Traité sur les obligations des frères des écoles chrétiennes*.
Navereau, A. (1924) *Le Logement et les ustensiles des gens de guerre de 1439 à 1789*.
Oppenheim (1911) *Règlement provisoire pour la fabrique de M.S.*, 1809, in Hayem, J., *Mémoires et documents pour revenir à l'histoire du commerce*.
'*Saint-Maur, Règlement de la fabrique de*', B.N. MS. Coll. Delamare, Manufactures III.
Snyders, G. (1965) *La Pédagogie en France aux XVIIe et XVII$_e$ siècles*.
Treilhard, J.B. (1808) *Motifs du code d'instruction criminelle*.
Tronchot, R.R., *L'Enseignement mutuel en France*, I (unpublished thesis).

The subject and power

MICHEL FOUCAULT

I would like to suggest a new economy of power relations, between theory and practice. It consists of taking the forms of resistance against different forms of power as a starting point. To use another metaphor, it consists of using this resistance as a chemical catalyst so as to bring to light power relations, locate their position, find out their point of application and the methods used. Rather than analyzing power from the point of view of its internal rationality, it consists of analyzing power relations through the antagonism of strategies.

For example, to find out what our society means by sanity, perhaps we should investigate what is happening in the field of insanity.

And what we mean by legality in the field of illegality.

And, in order to understand what power relations are about, perhaps we should investigate the forms of resistance and attempts made to dissociate these relations.

Generally, it can be said that there are three types of struggles: either against forms of domination (ethnic, social, and religious); against forms of exploitation which separate individuals from what they produce; or against that which ties the individual to himself and submits him to others in this way (struggles against subjection, against forms of subjectivity and submission).

I think that in history, you can find a lot of examples of these three kinds of social struggles, either isolated from each other, or mixed together. But even when they are mixed, one of them, most of the time, prevails. For instance, in the feudal societies, the struggles against the forms of ethnic or social domination were prevalent, even though economic exploitation could have been very important among the revolt's causes.

In the nineteenth century, the struggle against exploitation came into the foreground.

And nowadays, the struggle against the forms of subjection – against the submission of subjectivity – is becoming more and more important, even though the struggles against forms of domination and exploitation have not disappeared. Quite the contrary.

When one defines the exercise of power as a mode of action upon the actions of others, when one characterizes these actions by the government of men by other men – in the broadest sense of the term – one includes an important element: freedom. Power is exercised only over free subjects, and

Abridged excerpts reproduced from Foucault, M. 'Afterword: The Subject and 'Power', in Dreyfus, H.L. and Rabinow, P. (1982) *Michel Foucault: Beyond Structuralism and Hermeneutics; With an Afterword by Michel Foucault*, pp. 210–13 and 221–2; The Harvester Press, Sussex, 1982.

only insofar as they are free. By this we mean individual or collective subjects who are faced with a field of possibilities in which several ways of behaving, several reactions and diverse comportments may be realized. Where the determining factors saturate the whole there is no relationship of power; slavery is not a power relationship when man is in chains. (In this case it is a question of a physical relationship of constraint.) Consequently there is no face to face confrontation of power and freedom which is mutually exclusive (freedom disappears everywhere power is exercised), but a much more complicated interplay. In this game freedom may well appear as the condition for the exercise of power (at the same time its precondition, since freedom must exist for power to be exerted, and also its permanent support, since without the possibility of recalcitrance, power would be equivalent to a physical determination).

The relationship between power and freedom's refusal to submit cannot therefore be separated. The crucial problem of power is not [. . .] voluntary servitude (how could we seek to be slaves?). At the very heart of the power relationship, and constantly provoking it, are the recalcitrance of the will and the intransigence of freedom. Rather than speaking of an essential freedom, it would be better to speak of an "agonism"[1] – of a relationship which is at the same time reciprocal incitation and struggle; less of a face-to-face confrontation which paralyzes both sides than a permanent provocation.

[1] Foucault's neologism is based on the Greek ἀγώνιστμα meaning "a combat." The term would hence imply a physical contest in which the opponents develop a strategy of reaction and of mutual taunting, as in a wrestling match. (Translator's note)

Work and its discontents

DANIEL BELL

The Cult of Efficiency in America
Before Jove's day no tillers subdued the land. Even to mark the field or divide it with bounds was unlawful. Men made gain for the common store, and Earth yielded all of herself more freely when none begged for her gifts. 'Twas he that . . . hid fire from view, and stopped the wine that ran everywhere in streams. . . . Then came iron's stiffness and the shrill sawblade – for early man cleft the splitting wood with wedges; then came divers arts. Toil conquered the world, unrelenting toil, and want that pinches when life is hard.

(*Virgil*, The Georgics)

Abridged excerpts reproduced with permission from Bell, D. *The End of Ideology: On The Exhaustion of Political Ideas in The Fifties,* pp. 227–31, 271–2 and 421; published, with an afterword, by Harvard University Press, New York, 1988. Originally published by Free Press, 1960.

We assume that in efficiency, as in geometry, the shortest distance between two points is a straight line. But what if something is in the way? Within the same week, once, the problem was posed in two different places. In New York, the new Thruway pushing down from New England came smack up against the old Huguenot cemetery at New Rochelle, the burial place of the French founders of the town; should the Thruway be diverted, or the cemetery moved? In England, a new fleet of square-topped, double-decker buses found themselves unable to proceed through the ancient Gothic arch of a historic town wall; should the vault be rebuilt, the double-deckers scrapped, or the buses rerouted some distance in miles? Which was the rational course in each case? In New York the cemetery was removed; in England the buses rerouted. Each choice reflected the contrasting values of the society.

The contrasting definitions of rationality, the costs of efficiency – as applied to work – are the themes of this essay.

The new calculus of time

For about twenty years of his busy life, Jeremy Bentham, the patriarch of modern reform, devoted much of his energies to the elaboration, in minutest detail, of plans for a perfectly efficient prison. This was the famous **panopticon**, a starshaped building so intricately constructed 'that every convict would pass his life in perpetual solitude, while remaining perpetually under the surveillance of a warder posted at the center.'

Bentham, the leader of the philosophical radicals, had gotten the idea of the **panopticon** from his ingenious brother, Sir Samuel-Bentham, a famous naval architect who, while employed by Catherine the Great to build ships for Russia, had designed a factory along just those lines. For many years, in fact, Jeremy Bentham sought money from Parliament to build a 'five-storied' **panopticon**, one-half of which would be a prison, the other half a factory. The **panopticon**, he said, would be a cure for laziness, a 'mill for grinding rogues honest and idle men industrious.' (In 1813 he finally received £23,000 as compensation for money he had expended in his efforts to construct a model.)

This identification of factory and prison was, perhaps, quite natural for Bentham. Prison and factory were united in his philosophical mind by the utilitarian conceptions of tidiness and efficiency. The root of utilitarianism – this new mode of conduct which Bentham elaborated – is a passion for order, and the elaboration of a calculus of incentives which, if administered in exact measures, would stimulate the individual to the correct degree of rectitude and work. Utilitarianism provided a new definition of rationality: not the rule of reason, but the rule of measurement. With it, man himself could now be regulated. When the rule was applied by the engineer – the utilitarian par excellence – not only was work broken down in detail, but it was measured by detail, and paid for in time units defined in metric quantities.

With this new rationality came a unique and abrupt break from the rhythm of work in the past. With it came a new role of time. In the various ways it has been expressed, two modes of time have been dominant: time as a function of space, and time as *durée*. Time as a function of space follows the rhythm of the movement of the earth: a year is the curving ellipse around the sun; a day, the spin of the earth on its axis. The clock itself is round; and the hour, the sweep of a line in 360 degrees of space.[1] But time, as the philosophers and novelists – and ordinary people – know it, is also artless. There are the psychological modes which encompass the differing perceptions: the dull moments and the swift moments, the bleak moments and the moments of bliss, the agony of time prolonged and of time eclipsed, of time recalled and time anticipated – in short, time not as a chronological function of space, but time felt as a function of experience.

Utilitarian rationality knows little of time as *durée*. For it, and for modern industrial life, time and effort are hitched only to the clock-like, regular, 'metric' beat. The modern factory is fundamentally a place of order in which stimulus and response, the rhythms of work, derive from a mechanically imposed sense of time and pace.[2] No wonder, then, that Aldous Huxley can assert: 'Today every efficient office, every up-to-date factory is a panoptical prison in which the workers suffer . . . from the consciousness of being inside a machine.'

The indictment, damning if true, lays its gravest charge against the United States. Contemporary America is, above all, the machine civilization. The image of tens of thousands of workers streaming from the sprawling factories indelibly marks the picture of industrial America, as much as the fringed buckskin and rifle marked the nineteenth-century frontier, or the peruke and lace that of Colonial Virginia. The majority of Americans may not work in factories, just as the majority of Americans never were on the frontier and never lived in Georgian houses; yet the distinctive ethos of each time lies in these archetypes.

What then is the nature of work in the life of present-day America?

The watching hand of God

The contemporary enterprise was set up to obey three peculiar technologics: the logic of size, the logic of 'metric' time, and the logic of hierarchy. Each

---

[1] For a discussion of time as a function of space, see C.F. von Weizacker, *The History of Nature* (Chicago, 1949), pp. 12–13, 48–50.

[2] 'Order,' said Freud, 'is a kind of repetition compulsion by which it is ordained once for all when, where and how a thing shall be done so that on every similar occasion doubt and hesitation shall be avoided. The benefits of order are incontestable: it enables us to use space and time to the best advantage, while waiving expenditures of mental energy. One would be justified in expecting that it would have ingrained itself from the start and without opposition into all human activities; and one may well wonder that this has not happened, and that, on the contrary, human beings manifest an inborn tendency to negligence, irregularity and untrustworthiness in their work, and have to be laboriously trained to imitate the example of their celestial models." *Civilization and Its Discontents* (Hogarth Press, London, 1946), pp. 55–56.

of the three, the product of engineering rationality, has imposed on the worker a set of constraints with which he is forced to wrestle every day. These condition the daily facts of his existence.

For the man whose working day is from eight in the morning to five in the afternoon, the morning begins long before the time he is to arrive at his place of work. After a hasty wash and a quick breakfast, he is off in his car or on the streetcar, bus, or subway; often he may have to spend an hour or more in getting to the plant. (There seems to be a law, as Bertrand Russell has noted, that improvements in transportation do not cut down traveling time but merely increase the area over which people have to travel.)

Although this is the most obvious fact about modern work, few writers have concerned themselves with it or with the underlying assumption: that large masses of human labor should be brought to a common place of work. The engineer believes that concentration is technologically efficient: under one roof there can be brought together the source of power, the raw materials, the parts, and the assembly lines. So we find such huge megaliths as Willow Run, now used by General Motors, a sprawling shed spanning an area two-thirds of a mile long and a quarter of a mile wide; or such roofed-over, mile-long pavements as the Boeing plant in Wichita, Kansas.

This belief in the efficacy of size was conditioned by the type of energy first used – the limited amount of power available through the use of steam. Since steam dissipates quickly, the engineer tended to crowd as many productive units as possible along the same shaft, or within the range of steam pressure that could be carried by pipes without losses due to excessive condensation. These considerations also led to the bunching of workers in the layout of work, since the machines had to be located along a straight-line shafting.

The introduction of electric power and electric motors opened the way to greater flexibility; and within the plant these opportunities were taken. Newer work-flow designs have avoided the antiquated straight-line shafts and aisles of the older factory. Yet the outward size of the factory remained unchallenged. Why? In part because the engineer conceives of efficiency in technological terms alone; and he is able to do so because a major cost – the travel time of the worker – can be discounted. But the question can be posed: should large masses of persons be brought to a common place of work? Which is cheaper to transport: working men twice daily or materials and mechanical parts, let us say, twice a week? As Percival and Paul Goodman so pertinently note in their book, *Communitias*: 'The time of life of a piece of metal is not consumed while it waits for its truck; a piece of metal does not mind being compressed like a sardine.' What the Goodmans propose is production in 'bits and pieces' rather than integrated assembly. If the plants were located near workers' communities, the men would not have to travel; the processed materials would be brought to several places for manufacture, and the parts would then be collected for assembly. Yet the question is rarely considered, for few industries pay directly for their workers' travel time. Calculations in terms of market costs alone do not force the enterprise to take into account such factors as the time used in going to and from work, or the costs of roads and other transport to the factory site, which are paid for by the employee or by the community as a whole out of taxes.

In his travel to and from work the worker is chained by time. Time rules the work economy, its very rhythms and motions. (After consulting Gulliver on the functions of his watch, the Lilliputians came to the belief that it was his God.)

Ananke and Thanatos

In Western civilization, work, whether seen as curse or as blessing, has always stood at the center of moral consciousness. 'In the sweat of thy brow,' says Genesis, 'shalt thou eat bread.' The early Church fathers were intrigued about what Adam did before the Fall; in the variety of speculations, none assumed he was idle. He devoted himself to gardening, 'the agreeable occupation of agriculture,' said St. Augustine.

In the Protestant conception, all work was endowed with virtue. 'A housemaid who does her work is no farther away from God than the priest in the pulpit,' said Luther. Every man is 'called,' not just a few, and every place, not just a church, is invested with godliness. With Zwingli, even with dour Calvin, work was connected with the joy of creating and with exploring even the wonders of creation.

In the nineteenth century, beginning with Carlyle, man was conceived as *homo faber*, and human intelligence was defined as the capacity for inventing and using tools. If man in the Marxist sense was 'alienated' from himself, the self was understood as a man's potential for 'making' things, rather than alienation as man being broken into a thing itself. (Man will be free when 'nature is his work and his reality' and he 'recognises himself in a world he has himself made,' said Marx in his early philosophical-economic manuscripts, adopting an image that A.E. Housman later turned into a lament.) In the same vein, John Dewey argued that a man 'learned by doing,' but the phrase, now a progressive-school charade, meant simply that men would grow not by accepting prefigured experiences but by seeking problems that called for new solutions. ('Unlike the handling of a tool,' said Dewey, 'the regulation of a machine does not challenge man or teach him anything; therefore he cannot grow through it.')

All these are normative conceptions. In Western history, however, work has had a deeper 'moral unconscious.' It was a way, along with religion, of confronting the absurdity of existence and the beyond. Religion, the most pervasive of human institutions, played a singular symbolic role in society because it faced for the individual the problem of death. Where death was but a prelude to eternal life, hell and heaven could be themes of serious discourse, and domination on earth had a reduced importance. But with the decline in religious belief went a decline in the power of belief in eternal life. In its place arose the stark prospect that death meant the total annihilation of the self. (Hamlet, as Max Horkheimer points out, 'is the embodiment of the idea of individuality for the very reason that he fears the finality of death, the terror of the abyss.')

Many of these fears were staved off by work. Although religion declined, the significance of work was that it could still mobilize emotional energies into creative challenges. (For Tolstoy, as later for the Zionists in the Israeli *kibbutzim*, work was a religion; A.D. Gordon, the theoretician of the co-operative communities, preached redemption through physical labor.) One could eliminate death from consciousness by minimizing it through work. As *homo faber*, man could seek to master nature and to discipline himself. Work, said Freud, was the chief means of binding an individual to reality. What will happen, then, when not only the worker but work itself is displaced by the machine?

The manifesto for new times

B. CAMPBELL *et al.*

The new times

As we enter the 1990s Britain will be a capitalist society, riven with enormous inequalities in income, wealth and power, with key decisions taken by a minority of international financiers and industrialists. But it will be a different kind of capitalist society from Britain in the 1930s or 1950s. International capitalism is entering a distinctive phase of development. The signs are all around us.

The ownership of capital is more diverse than ever. Corporate bodies rather than powerful individuals or families play the dominant decision-making role. A greater share of our wealth is owned, indirectly, by working people, through pension funds and other institutions representing the collective product of working people, whose control is increasingly remote.

Robots and computers are familiar parts of our workplaces, just as satellite television will become familiar in our living rooms. Semi-skilled work in mighty manufacturing plants is in decline, while professional, new technology skilled jobs are growing, alongside part-time unskilled work in services. The rise of women's paid employment to more than 50 per cent of the workforce will create strong pressures for new relationships between paid employment and domestic work. So also will new political priorities which challenge the traditional settlement between patriarchal capital and patriarchal labour.

Abridged excerpts reproduced with permission from Campbell, B. *et al.* The Manifesto for New Times in Hall, S. and Jacques, M. (eds) *New Times: The Changing Face of Politics in the 1990s*, pp. 23–5 and 29–37; published by Lawrence and Wishart Ltd in association with *Marxism Today*, London, 1989.

The products, skills and communities of old industrial areas – shipbuilding in Sunderland, newspaper production in Fleet Street – are being overtaken by new centres of economic growth – Telford, Crawley, Basingstoke – based on new technology, manufacturing and services. The City of London has become a hub in a 24-hour-a-day, computer-integrated, global financial system. Multinational manufacturers and business service companies are becoming more powerful as capitalism becomes more transnational in every dimension, and more intensive in advanced countries.

A profound ecological crisis will demand a search for international regulation of economic development and the environment. The recurrence of famine increasingly demands new solutions to the consequences of the destruction of the traditional economies in the southern hemisphere by the actions of governments and big business in the northern hemisphere.

The spreading impact of *perestroika* in the Soviet Union and the opening of European nations to one another offer an opportunity to create an era of more open, co-operative international relations.

Woven into the new times of the 1990s are changes which are inevitable, changes which are desirable, and changes which are neither. If Britain is to develop in a more democratic and sustainable way in the 1990s, we have to work with the grain of the new times, to enable society to develop in a more progressive way. Progressive forces in Britain need to realign, modernise, and contest the changes underway by offering an alternative vision of progress.

Socialists are yet to develop a radical, popular appeal for the 1990s because we do not yet confidently speak the language of the future. For much of the labour and democratic movement still rests upon a world which is fast disintegrating beneath its feet. It lives in the last house of a terrace which is slowly being demolished and redeveloped.

A departing world

Two key developments laid the foundations for postwar British society. firstly, the depression of the 1930s led industry to shift from the production methods inherited from the 19th century, based on coal and steam, to the new technologies based on electricity, oil and petrol. At Ford's Dagenham plant, opened in 1931, the company introduced the mass production methods which were to have a sweeping impact on much of the rest of industry. They became known as 'Fordism'. They left an indelible mark on the economy, workers, consumers and social life. These new methods were propelled by a concentration of ownership with a wave of mergers and acquistitions, which created what are now familiar household names like ICI and GEC.

The second factor was the economic, social and political upheaval of the struggles against unemployment and fascism in the 1930s, which culminated during the second world war. Social aspirations, together with working class and democratic pressure bred by the war, propelled the Labour Party into power with a wide-ranging programme of social and economic reform –

nationalisation, the creation of the National Health Service, the expansion of public education, an enormous council-house building programme, the introduction of a system of welfare benefits, and perhaps above all, a commitment to maintain full employment through Keynesian economic policies. These were the twin pillars of the postwar settlement: a modernising capitalism and a labour and democratic movement intent on social and economic reform.

The postwar settlement created a framework to meet both companies' demands for profitable markets and popular desires for rising living standards. The institutions of the postware settlement were designed to contain struggles within manageable limits. It was not a single settlement. It was made up of several components, which became the focal point for conflict and arenas of struggle. For these settlements did not mark the end of conflict or struggle. Rather, they set the basic parameters for those conflicts, until these settlements themselves were beseiged.

The slow disintegration

The industrial and economic settlements broke apart because the modernising investment of British capital at home did not match developments abroad. Slowly rising unemployment and inflation, falling productivity and profitability threw into doubt the ability of Keynesian economic policies to keep the economy at full employment.

Faltering growth intensified industrial conflict. Constraints on public expenditure, and the ill-fated mixture of monetarism and incomes policy concocted by the Callaghan government produced strikes in both the private and public sectors. And the reaction in the labour movement, a regression to sectionalist and syndicalist forms of resistance, mirrored the government's retreat from renovation.

The legitimacy of the conservative gender settlement was increasingly challenged by an insurgent women's movement, the continued rise in women's employment, greater access to education, the introduction of the pill and more liberal legislation on divorce which gave women more control over childbirth and marriage. The abortion and divorce laws and the availability of relatively reliable forms of contraception – a historic moment in women's quest for control over their own bodies – implicitly acknowledged and contributed to the increasing instability of the patriachal family.

The women's liberation movement challenged the sexual division of labour, politicised sexual and domestic violence as expressions of a culture of sexual domination and thus challenged the ideologies of state agencies, from the police to housing authorities, for their patriarchal practices.

The conflict over the racial settlement became more open and intense, with an open embracing of racist politics by sections of the Conservative Party alongside the rise of the National Front. Successive immigration bills and racist policing, rather than protection for black communities, were challenged by anti-fascist and anti-racist movements. The poor quality and management of mass council housing, and generally the remoteness of Labour in local government from its electorate, led to mounting criticism. Community politics was born from the demands of people struggling to humanise ghastly urban social environments and gain a greater say in decision-making over their own lives.

The destruction of swathes of British cities by motorways and speculative developments which privatised – and brutalised – vast tracts of the public realm, exacerbated the housing crisis in the new and the old slums. Elsewhere in Europe mounting concern at the effects of industrialism, militarism and modernism on the social and ecological environment gave rise to green movements. The postwar settlements had survived by creating a framework to contain social conflict. But by the 1970s they began bursting at the seams.

The path from the crisis

The crisis of the 1970s provoked two fundamental developments which are shaping our times.

Firstly, there was a political struggle to coalesce discontent with the decaying postwar settlement and the impotence of the Keynesian, social democratic state. It was a struggle the labour and democratic movement lost.

The Right in the labour movement pushed an increasingly autocratic, visionless agenda which paved the way for conservative developments in education, the erosion of trade union rights and monetarist economic policies. But the Left of the movement was trapped by a complacency that the movement's future was guaranteed by history.

But there was a second, equally important factor at work, which made it much more likely that Thatcherism would succeed: capitalism's search for a successor to the regime of accumulation developed in the 1930s. As Mrs. Thatcher was struggling against opposition in the early 1980s, to pave the way for a radical shift to the right, so multinational companies were in search of new production methods, to raise productivity and profitability in the face of intensifying international competition.

It is these large companies in search of a secure position within increasingly global markets which are the key forces reorganising the UK economy. It is their response to international competitive pressures which is driving crucial changes in the technology people work with, the structure of industry, the ownership of companies, the location of investment and consumption patterns.

A second dual revolution

The postwar settlement was created by the confluence of the economic restructuring of the 1930s, and the popular impetus for social democratic reforms, which cemented the institutions of the full-employment welfare state.

The 1980s have been shaped by a different dual revolution: the confluence of Thatcherism's radical right-wing politics with an international wave of capitalist restructuring. Thatcherism has both facilitated that restructuring and been propelled by it. Thatcherism's regressive modernisation is only one path to the future. Its terms for creating the new times will be challenged by other social forces with a different vision of the future.

The new times

Britain will still be an advanced capitalist society, with key decisions taken in the boardrooms of powerful multinational companies in Detroit, Tokyo or Seoul. But it will be markedly different from the capitalism of the postwar settlement. For its component settlements are being dismantled and remade. What emerges will be the outcome of industrial, social and political struggle.

At the industrial heart of the new times will be production based on a shift to information technology and microelectronics. New technology allows more intensive automation and its extension from large to smaller companies, pulling together the shopfloor and the office, the design loft and the showroom. It allows production to be both more flexible, automated and integrated.

These changes are not confined to manufacturing. Banks and building societies propelled by fiercer competition in more international markets are also using information technology to innovate new services and products. It is seeping into the public sector and local authorities.

Work is being re-organised around new technology. Traditional demarcation lines between blue and white collar, skilled and unskilled, are being torn down in the wake of massive redundancies in manufacturing. In future, work in manufacturing will be about flexible team-working within much smaller, more skilled workforces. Services will continue to provide the main source of new jobs, fuelling the continued rise of women's part-time employment which will be at the core of the 1990s economy.

Combined with persistent mass unemployment, these changes are creating deeper divisions within the workforce. There will be more professional, highly-skilled technicians' jobs, but also more low-skill, low-wage, low-technology jobs. The economy will be marked by a division between core full-time workers in large companies and the growing number of part-timers in small subcontractors, between those in employment and the long-term unemployed.

Traditional bases for union organisation are declining. The rise in unemployment, extensive corporate restructuring and the government's anti-trade union laws, allowed more assertive managers to marginalise unions. Collective bargaining is no longer about regulating an industrial machine. It is about setting the terms for widespread restructuring of work.

These developments amount to a structural change in the economy. The economic and industrial settlements, which were at the centre of industrial conflict in the postwar settlement, are being superseded. This upheaval in the industrial and economic core of modern capitalism is one of the forces which is replacing the postwar social settlement with greater social fragmentation, diversity and polarisation.

The television industry is the sharpest example of how new technology, multinational restructuring and government legislation combine to produce more fragmented conditions of work and consumption. In the 1990s, multinational media groups will use the new satellite technologies to create European television stations. Their rise has been facilitated by the government's ideological and legislative attack on the institutions and ethos of the public-service broadcasting system established after the war.

National union agreements are being broken up. Programme production will be largely devolved to a sea of small sub-contractors, employing technicians on short-term contracts lasting anything from three weeks to six months.

The family crowded around a black and white television was one of the images of the 1950s. Their counterparts in the 1990s will be switching between a swarm of European commercial stations. One of the most important acts of mass consumption, which is vital to the quality of information in a modern democracy, will have been completely transformed.

But restructuring is promoting far more savage forms of social polarisation. A very small and very rich minority has done extremely well. But in general Britain is becoming a two-thirds, one-third society, with a growing gulf between the majority itself, highly differentiated, leading relatively comfortable lives; and the one-third trapped in poverty. The rise in home ownership in the 1980s means many working-class families will become property inheritors for the first time in the 1990s. But homelessness has grown to record levels.

The welfare state is increasingly ill-equipped to cope with high unemployment and the growth in the number of single-parent families, who are faced with the continuing privatisation of childcare and are unsupported by collective responsibility for the cost and care of children. At the same time the growth of women's employment could fundamentally undermine the legitimacy of conservative assumptions about work and welfare: that workers are men, earning for families in which women would be available to care for children, the elderly and the sick.

These social developments are creating enormous pressure for established institutions, from the family to the welfare state, to be refashioned in the new times.

A new political map is taking shape. The regions and cities of postwar industry, which bred so much of the labour movement's culture, are in decline. The concentration of newspaper production in Fleet Street in London has been dispersed to new technology printing sites, with smaller, more tightly controlled workforces. Up and down the country docks are being redeveloped into yuppie housing and retail space.

The poles of the political map of the 1990s will be the politics of race and the underclass in the inner city, and the growth of new industrial regions such as the M4 corridor, and within them growth towns like Swindon and Basingstoke. The labour movement is present in these towns. But it is not central to the spirit emerging within them, in the way that it was in Sheffield in the early part of the century or Coventry during the heyday of engineering.

The local politics of the new town has become a key site for conflict between international capital and the community. All cities, from Bridgend to Dundee and Skelmersdale, are in search of foreign investment to attract an international growth sector to their industrial estates. The competition has been intensified by government regional policy and the constraints on local authorities' abilities to plan economic development.

A vital part of this new political geography is the resurgence of nationalism in Scotland and Wales in response to Thatcherism's authoritarianism, and the disproportionate costs of restructuring they have borne.

The next decade will also be shaped by the environmental crisis bequeathed by Fordism: from the social environmental crisis of congested, polluted conurbations, and the classic product of the postwar period – the car – to the global crisis of the greenhouse effect.

The international settlement which enveloped British postwar capitalism will be dismantled in the 1990s. The two-dimensional world of superpower conflict is giving way to a more complex set of international relations. The Japanese, South Korean and Far Eastern companies will continue to disorganise the western economies, which will also be reshaped by the European integration programme. Eastern and Western Europe are likely to become more open to one another as India and China take on much more significant world economic and political roles. Resolving Britain's position within this new international order will be a key task of the 1990s.

Politics and new times

Much of postwar capitalism mirrored the mass production methods which were at its industrial heart. They became known as Fordism. In the new times, the industrial core of the economy is being transformed into what we call 'post-Fordism'. This does not mean that mass production will disappear. It does mean that in both manufacturing and services, production and work is taking on more flexible, diverse, fragmentary forms. Bargaining between workers and employers will also take on new forms to match the new conditions. Post-Fordism does not describe the whole economy but the leading edge of the most competitive modernising companies.

These changes in the industrial and economic organisation of capitalism are not determining all the changes which are shaping the new times. International, social and cultural forces are at work independently of changes in production. Post-Fordism is at the economic and industrial core of the new times, but it does not encompass and define all aspects of the new times.

The 1990s will see myriad political and social struggles. But in essence they will come down to a single question: on whose terms will this new era be moulded? Thatcherism's attempt to facilitate a 'conservative modernisation' will create privatisation, polarisation, fragmentation, public squalor and authoritarianism in the new times. Its grip will only be broken by a progressive movement gathered around the aspirations bred by the new times.

There are powerful social currents which offer an alternative path to modernisation which is more just, democratic, humane and sustainable. For on each of the central issues facing society in the new times, powerful progressive forces are developing. These movements do not necessarily share the same interests, nor do they possess properties which unite them spontaneously. But they do move to a similar rhythm:

– The green movement's response to the environmental crisis with a challenge to current economic priorities;
– The optimism that the internationalisation of the economy may be matched by a new era of more co-operative international relations, symbolised by changes in Soviet foreign policy;
– The mounting moral and political opposition to the savage inequalities Thatcherism is creating;
– Women's challenge to the traditional demarcation lines between domestic work, welfare and waged work, which will be consolidated by women's expanding presence in the labour market and the political domain;
– The widespread concern over Thatcherism's authoritarian transformation of the state;
– Nationalism's challenge to authoritarian centralism;
– Increasing doubt that the government's economic policies are capable of fully modernising the economy, through investment in research and development, training and skills.

These are not formal policies or parties. They are moods, currents and forces in society. They can trace their lineage to discontent with the postwar settlement as clearly as Thatcherism. They could offer an alternative vision of modernisation which is as credible and potentially more popular than Thatcherism's.

For these forces are in the grain of the new times. They stem from popular social aspirations. They offer the prospect of a new wave of progressive social and economic development in the 1990s.

Fundamental list: modern times and new times

Fundamental list

Modern times	New times
Fordism	Post-Fordism
Modern	Post-modern
Steinbeck	Pynchon
Le Corbusier	Venturi
Sartre	Foucault
Futurism	Nostalgia
Marlon Brando	William Hurt
Production	Consumption
Mass-market	Market segmentation
Ford	Toyota
Self-control	Remote control
Depth	Surface
Belief	Credit
Elvis	Michael Jackson
Interpretation	Deconstruction
Butlins	Theme parks
Relationships	White weddings
The Beatles	Bros
Determinism	The arbitrary
Maxwell House	Acid House
Concrete	Holographic glass
Liberalism	Libertarianism
Mass hysteria	Fatal Attraction
Humanism	Post-structuralism
Raspberry Ripple	Hedgehog Crisps
Lady Chatterley	Blue Velvet
World wars	Terrorism
Angst	Boredom
Roosevelt	Reagan
In/Out lists	New Times guides
Newspapers	Colour supplements
Z Cars	Miami Vice
Conservatism	Thatcherism
Emotion	Affectation
Dow Jones	Nikkei Index
Stalinism	Glasnost
Free love	The free market
The Titanic	Challenger
The Cabinet	The Prime Minister
Bingo	The Big Bang

Reproduced from *Marxism Today*, October 1988, p. 5.

Post-modernism

KENNY COYLE

One of the leading lights of the Post-modernist movement Ihab Hassan has said that the term Post-modernism has moved from awkward neologism to derelict cliche without having attained the dignity of a concept.

If that is what the friends of Post-modernism have to say it puts critics of the trend in a difficult position.

The series of events which have been unfolding in Eastern Europe since 1989 and which look very much like reversing the achievements of the Russian Revolution, are certain to strengthen what one French critic described as 'a groundless ideology of refusal and despair.'

Post-modernists have long argued that we are entering a period of New Times, a new epoch. If 1917 opened one historical epoch the defeat of Socialism in Eastern Europe may close it. The right-wing US historian Francis Fukuyama said in 1989 that 'What we may be witnessing is not just the end of the Cold War, or the passing of a particular period of post-war history, but the end of history as such: that is the end of mankind's ideological evolution and the universalisation of Western liberal democracy as the final form of human government.'

This is the message which is transmitted to us every single day in the media. The West and its supposedly associated ideas of freedom, the market, democracy have triumphed.

Part of the appeal of Post-modernism is its critical approach to society. It is by no means a current which necessarily encourages us to believe in the values of Western capitalism.

Yet Post-modernism offers us no hope of a way out. The world of Post-modernism is like a fairground hall of mirrors where we can never be sure which reflection, or which image is real, or to put it another way, where all images and appearances are as real as any other.

Post-modernism to paraphrase a favourite slogan of Gramsci offers us a 'Cynicism of the intellect and pessimism of the will.'

A key element of Post-modernism is its assault on the Enlightenment begun in the late 18th century. The Enlightenment stressed the rational abilities of humanity to understand and gain control of their own society. It challenged previous religious and mystical beliefs. One of its central thinkers Condorcet said the progress of humanity was inevitably linked to the progress of the human mind.

Abridged excerpts reproduced from Coyle, K. *Postmodernism. Bulletin of The Marx Memorial Library*, **117**, Winter–Spring 1992, pp. 9–11 and 14–19; published by The Marx Memorial Library.

Jean-Francis Lyotard however, argues that the:

'idea of progress as possible, probable or necessary was rooted in the certainty that the development of the arts, technology, knowledge and liberty would be profitable to mankind as a whole.'

After two centuries, we are more sensitive to signs that signify the contrary.

Lyotard therefore defines the post-modern as 'incredulity toward meta-narratives' (general or universalising theories of how societies function).

The term Post-modernism has gained currency in three areas (1) As a reaction against the International Style of architecture (2) a cultural aesthetic in literature and art (3) A shift in the economic and social organization of capitalist societies.

New times

Do we despite all the change live in an identifiably capitalist society where we continue to have class divisions and class conflict, where the economic basis of our societies is still governed by exploitation, or have we moved to a new stage in human society where previous explanations of social development no longer apply.

This aspect of Post-modernism draws upon the theories of post-structuralist philosophy on the one hand and those of post-industrialism or as it has now become known – post-Fordism on the other.

Post-modernism's emphasis on discontinuity, fragmentation and chaotic change is one that it inherited from Post-structuralism. Post-structuralism, and its post-modernist offspring emphasises change but denies stability. They emphasise inner contradiction but without accepting the possibility of identity, no matter how fleeting or temporary.

Lyotard again says: 'Let us wage war on totality; let us be witnesses to the unpresentable let us activate the difference and save the honour of the name.'

For Marxists there is not only change but also stability, but a relative stability which is a prelude to new changes. To deny this is to emphasise only one side of the equation.

So while Marxists have concentrated on questions of class power and the state, post-modernists have preferred to see power and oppression as more amorphous more all-pervasive permeated throughout society and relationships in a variety of unconnected ways rather than having some central source.

Just as importantly they emphasise the differences rather than any common interests held by groups of people, and so raise doubts about the effectiveness or the desirability of common action.

It is certainly true that the working class is not homogenous and a central part of any socialist strategy has to be how to overcome divisions based on race or gender but such an approach is certainly well within the boundaries of Marxist politics.

Many will recognise these questions about the relative importance of special oppression as having been central to the debates within British Marxism for some time.

But it is not just class which has to be junked as an overambitious generalization. A dangerous attempt to capture some universal truth. Because if class has become redundant as a category because of other conflicting identities, how does that leave analyses based on gender or racial oppression. 'Women' after all are no more free of difference than the 'working class'. What sense is there in a feminist analysis which seeks to offer a universal explanation of women's oppression.

Michelle Barret the author of *Women's Oppression Today* first published in 1980 has written in her introduction to the 1988 edition:

'Here lies, perhaps, the greatest challenge to the assumption within which *Women's Oppression Today* was written: the discourse of Post-modernism is premised on an explicit and argued denial of the kind of grand political projects that both 'socialism' and 'feminism' by definition are. But post-modernism is not something that you can be for or against; the reiteration of old knowledges will not make it vanish. For it is a cultural climate as well as an intellectual position, a political reality as well as an academic fashion.

But why stop at metanarratives based on class or gender? Stuart Hall hasn't.

'We can no longer conceive of the 'individual' in terms of a whole and completed Ego or autonomous 'self'. The 'self' is experienced as fragmented and incomplete, composed of multiple 'selves' or identities in relation to the different social worlds we inhabit.'

The plurality of New Times is such that we can exist only in a schizophrenic sense where we can't rely on our own identities. This is ultimately absurd. The fact is that we live one life not several, our ability to choose which other 'worlds' we wish to inhabit is very much dependent on our position in this world. What gender we are, what race we belong to and of course what class we come from. These are interconnected questions.

Our development as individuals is conditioned by and affected by other individuals in society. And it is through collective action that we can achieve the fulfillment of our individual needs.

Post-Fordism

I want now to turn to post-Fordism because it is argued that it is the development of new technology and its effect on production and class politics that have determined all the other aspects of Post-modernism. In arguing this the post-Fordists have constructed one of the most mechanical and technologically deterministic arguments that has been put forward on the left for many years. What does the term mean?

Post-Fordism is consumption-led, it uses computer-based just in-time production and distribution which allows retailers to avoid over-stocking. Niche marketing targets specific groups of consumers, design becomes a major selling point as commodities are no longer bought just for use value but also for the lifestyle denoted by their design, a colour supplement consumer capitalism.

Industrial production is superseded by services. Hi-tech flexible specialisation means an almost infinite variety of goods not the limited, standardised products of Fordism. The workforce is divided into two: a multi-skilled work force with high wages and job security pitted against an underclass subject to poverty, and long term unemployment. This creates a one-third two-thirds society with the underclass the one-third of the population.

There is a disintegration of state-regulated national economies. Multinational expansion undermines sovereignty. Together all these factors weaken the traditional coherence of the labour movement and result in the decline of class-based politics.

'Between 1926 and 1988, the proportion of people in the UK employed in service industries rose from 33 per cent to 69 per cent, a mirror image of the relative decline in those employed in manufacturing and production: from 68% to 31%.' (*Manifesto for New Times*).

Our first quibble is a statistical one. According to figures quoted by the *Financial Times* the high point of the British industrial workforce was reached in 1955 when industry accounted for 48 per cent of employment, and never therefore accounted for a simple majority. The counter-position of services and industry is also misleading: railway workers long accorded a semi-elite status in the working-class movement as part of the Triple Alliance are regarded as service workers.

It is also interesting to note that in the highly advanced capitalist economy of Japan between 1964–82 there was a fall in the services share of GDP and a rise in manufacturing from 24.1–39.9%.

The post-Fordist analysis ignores the replacement of manufactured goods for services such as washing machines for laundrettes; television, VCRs, hi-fi systems to replace cinema and theatre.

There is little evidence of the breaking up of mass markets as a new range of mass produced durables, walkmen, CD players, microwaves, dishwashers are joining the longer-standing items such as cars, fridges, washing machines etc. The introduction of high technology for flexible manufacturing is highly expensive requiring high-volume production to cover expenses.

Employment in manufacturing has grown 2,500% in South Korea since 1956. Between 1971 (when Fordism went into decline and 1982 year of worst industrial layoffs) rose 14.1% in the 36 leading industrial countries and between 1977–82, a period of recession it increased from 173 to 183 million.

Marxists had already identified the working class as the decisive agent for change 65 years before the emergence of 'Fordism'. Marxism and Leninism are not dependent on Fordism for their strength. Fordism did not automatically provide a breeding ground for a highly unionised, cohesive and disciplined workforce. Indeed Henry Ford's strategy was explicitly directed against the labour movement and as Gramsci noted in his writings on Fordism, was based upon the playing off of skilled workers against the unskilled.

Let us summarise 4 central flaws in the post-Fordist scenario:

1. Firstly it creates a caricature Fordist economy which never really existed.
2. Marxism and Leninism's origins are pre-Fordist. The working class in Marx's time underwent enormous changes. Marxism is not technologically determinist and its analysis of class is not restricted or even mainly based on the particular techniques of capitalist production.
3. Post-Fordism emphasises a selected number of trends such as flexible specialization which it claims will become dominant, it ignores other trends which suggest otherwise.
4. Lastly it is Eurocentric: industrial production is not being abandoned but relocated to developing countries Brazil, Pacific Rim etc.

The economic basis on which the theorists of New Times have based their arguments is therefore tenuous to say the least.

To conclude what is the balance sheet of Post-modernism?

Firstly the term, is unlikely to last too long. But some items of post-modernist art will survive but only because it passes the test of 'good' art and not specifically because it is 'good' Post-modernism. The political implications of Post-modernism are likely to be more important. Firstly because the questions being raised about the changed nature of capitalist production, class politics and the viability of socialist change are important and not all the points raised in the debate can simply be dismissed as reactionary. But in the end Post-modernism does not encourage us to act, merely to watch and enjoy. It is the political philosophy for the couch potato. In the end the question is not whether or not we live in New Times but whose times we live in.

Further reading

Giddens, A. (1971) *Capitalism and Modern Social Theory: an analysis of the writings of Marx, Durkheim and Max Weber*, Cambridge University Press.

Brown, D. and Harrison, M.J. (1978) *A Sociology of Industrialisation: an introduction*, Macmillan.

Honour, T.F. and Mainwaring, R.M. (1982) *Business and Sociology*, Croom Helm, Chapters 1 and 2.

Sarup, M. (1988) *An Introductory Guide to Poststructuralism and Postmodernism*, Harvester Wheatsheaf. (Very good on Foucault and postmodernism.)

Haralambos, M. (1980) *Sociology: Theories and Perspectives*, Unwin Hyman, 3rd edn, 1990. (Particularly pp. 755–64 covering the relationship between science and sociology, methodology and values.)

Hassard, J. and Parker, M. (eds) (1993) *Postmodernism and Organizations*, Sage, Introduction and Chapter 1 by Hassard. (Very difficult, not for the fainthearted, may be more easily understood after reading this volume.)

Issues for discussion

1. To what extent are the processes of specialisation and rationalisation still dominant in contemporary society?
   Readings: Kumar (Chapter 1 – both)
              Foucault (Chapter 1 – both)
              Thompson (Chapter 3)
              Weber (Chapter 3)
              Taylor (Chapter 3)
              Ray (Chapter 5)
2. To what extent does Marx's analysis of social relations stand the test of time?
   Readings: Friedman (Chapter 1)
              Foucault (Chapter 1 – both)
              Campbell (Chapter 1)
              Coyle (Chapter 1)

3. Compare and contrast Foucault and Marx's analysis of the nature of contemporary society.
   Readings: Friedman (Chapter 1)
              Foucault (Chapter 1 – both)
4. What's new, if anything, about 'New Times'?
   Readings: Campbell (Chapter 1)
              Coyle (Chapter 1)

2

The construction
of individuals, identities
and social differences

In this chapter we look at a number of readings on the construction of individuals, identities and social differences. Together they show the complexity of the human organism and the differing ideas that underpin the theories of that construction. First some classic texts identify elements of human personality; these are followed by others which show how individual identity is formed through social experience.

Some consideration must first be given to the context and time in which they were written, the backgound of which is:

(a) the prevailing hegemony of natural science and its methods against which the social sciences (studying human beings) had difficulty in establishing themselves – unless they emulated such methods by aiming for measurement and absolute certainty, and

(b) the lack of any systematic social research which meant that early theorists were working mainly from commonsense assumptions about human experience. Thus many of the ideas and theories have been regarded as contentious.

Debate has also been fuelled by ideological concerns. When the political potential for 'liberation or domestication' (Freire 1972) offered by academic research is sensed there is much political interest. 'Evidence' on social differences in intelligence, for example, has been used to underpin and legitimate social policies in education and immigration. Nevertheless, much of what you will read in the extracts is now part of generally held views which are valuable for the insights they bring in understanding individuals and the construction of their identities. These socially complex personalities eventually come to be workers of all kinds with varied experiences of class, family, education, gender, race etc. After reading the extracts you will have a greater insight into, and understanding of, the necessarily complex interaction that is the basis of all work situations, whether they be presented as consensual or conflictful.

In the first reading Freud delineates his psychoanalytical theory and explains his understanding of the three inner areas of the mind which together make up the personality. He 'names' them for us as the id, ego and superego, basically a teaching device for conceptualising the functions they perform. They refer to the conscious (ego) and subconscious (superego) those areas to which we do have access and the unconscious (id) to which we do not.

Psychoanalytical theory has always been controversial. Freud's insights were obtained from disturbed and depressed patients. Inevitably, they attracted criticism from those wishing to model social sciences on the experimental and quantitative methods found in the natural sciences. Much later the theory was to be roundly criticised by feminists for its questionable assumptions concerning the importance of penis-envy as determining female development. It has to be remembered that most writing at this time would have been from a male perspective which today would be seen as gender-blind and sexist.

We now turn to a discussion by Eysenck of behaviourism and psychology or 'The Rat or the Couch'. While preferring the more scientific and quantitative approach of the early behaviourists E.L. Thorndike, J.W. Watson and B.F. Skinner, he concludes their approach is too limited, although he amusingly points out, 'we do have lots of research on rats'. Despite his misgivings, measurement is important for Eysenck, and the behaviourist arguments, though 'useful and sensible' as far as they go, do not go far enough. He argues that personality is the fundamental unit of psychology and the traits exhibited by people, such as introversion and extroversion, are 'capable of being accurately observed and precisely measured and meaningfully quantified'. These traits then are assumed to be largely innate rather than learnt.

If he is critical of behaviourism he is also critical of psychoanalysis which he sees as a storytelling exercise lacking hard evidence.

The following reading is from G.H. Mead, a social psychologist, who explains the development of individual consciousness with reference to social experience. While language and communication are built up gradually he argues the self only becomes the self by means of 'reflexiveness – the turning back of the experience of the individual upon himself – [in this way] the whole social process is [...] brought into the experience of the individuals involved in it' (1934: p. 134).

Whatever the history, status and perspective of the theories in this chapter, each provides necessary insight to understand how the individual is constructed and how they exhibit a variety of behaviours during their working lives. In the readings which follow we leave behind the theories that purport to explain the basis of the whole individual and move to later research which emphasises aspects of the whole.

Maslow's reasearch alerts us to the possibility of a hierarchy of needs that individuals have and that motivate them, the basic being food and shelter with the 'highest' being fulfilment or 'self-actualisation'. This academic research has been taken up and used by managerialists in their search for ways to shape and control workers (see, for example, Herzberg in the next chapter) though Maslow's own formulation is much more tentative than some of the management tenets which draw on his work would suggest.

Maslow's research of 1943 is referred to by Friedan in 1963 in the era of growing awareness of gender and race blindness in the literature. She asks why the cultural expectations of women are so limited that many appear to be suffering from 'the problem with no name' (a yearning to be fulfilled which appears to go beyond the role of wife, mother and domestic). Surely, she muses, women as individuals have the same needs as men. Self-actualisation cannot only be for males. The Vroom reading from around the same time extends the analysis of motivation by showing how aspects of the cognitive process are the outcome of an individual appraisal of the social situation, where various preferences are evaluated and acted upon.

This picture of the individual weighing choices rationally and reaching a considered decision is examined in the reading from Milgram. Milgram's interest derived from concerns current in the 1950s and 1960s about the power of group pressure – he even widens his discussion to include fascism and the Nazi regime – and his experiments can be read as corroboration of the social processes of conformity. But Milgram is at pains to point out that individuals do not *always* succumb to the pressures of the group and sometimes stand alone. Clearly, the pressures to conform to group norms can have quite disastrous consequences as Janis demonstrates in Chapter 3 when he discusses the Bay of Pigs fiasco in the Kennedy

Administration of the 1960s. The image of the lone individual standing out against the group is a powerful one representative of a hopeful humanism among Western liberal intellectuals.

Pressures of conformity extend beyond the group to the organisation itself where identities, as we saw in Chapter 1, are moulded. The reading from Merton shows how the structure of an organisation, in this case bureaucracy, can act to shape the personality of the individual who may *become* the bureaucrat, bound by rules regardless of the ends to which the rules are directed.

Although separated by 21 years there is much similarity, as well as some fundamental difference in the two readings that follow. Both Whyte and Kanter analyse the way in which values, opportunity and power are geared to produce the 'right' individuals for the organisation. Whyte documents the way in which the 'well-rounded' man is moulded and made in the image of the corporation – a theme taken up by Pascale and Athos and Höpfl in Chapter 5. Kanter, in 1977, locates the source of this making and moulding in the traditional male structure of opportunity and power which continues to select 'organisation men' even if now there are women with the qualifications and desire to be, if not 'organisation' men, then women in the organisation. The effects of the stress that ensues for women in this situation is taken up later in Chapter 6.

Our social identities take specific forms influenced by our family, educational background and the particular culture in which we live and work. The final readings in this chapter provide some insight into these influences.

Stereotyping, or labelling, is part of all cultures and is often used to effect social control, illustrated here most vividly by Tiger and Oakley. Tiger's discussion of the social consequences of female biology is attacked roundly by Oakley who shows that the 'division of labour by sex' and 'motherhood' are myths disguised to control women's behaviour and maintain male dominance. This is further examined by Dex, who provides examples of work segregated along lines of gender amounting to male control (conscious or otherwise) through stereotyping and the manipulation of socially constructed categories of skill, traditionally a male preserve.

The social construction of differences and their use in the legitimation of social control is also examined in the reading from Labov – this time focusing on ethnicity. Labov demonstrates how deprived ghetto children, categorised as lacking in ability by education authorities, are quite capable of demonstrating considerable intellectual capacity and dexterity, greater than their 'educated' counterparts. On this count education is geared to producing socially-valued outcomes as a means of control, rather than recognising individual talent, as illustrated by Bowles and Gintis in their account of the use of IQ (intelligence quotient) measures in America. Bowles and Gintis argue from a Marxist perspective and emphasise the ideological nature of the values of discipline and virtues of hard work imbided in early schooling and later reproduced in the workplace.

This construction and reproduction of socially-valued identities occurs in a specific historical context: industrial capitalism. Mackenzie shows how Marx and Weber attempted to explain the characteristics of the social relations of production and the development of social classes to organise and control production. Here varying levels of worker and manager come together, bringing to the workplace a mish-mash of sometimes contradictory objectives and identities. This provides some space for freedom of action. Nichols and Beynon, for example, show how workers refer to their managers as either bastards or bad bastards showing how, as individuals, managers can interpret and carry out their tasks in different ways. The room for manoeuvre is however limited, as a productive system geared to profit will see workers ultimately reduced to objects, units of production or machinery. Yet these tenacious relations of social class are not the only identities acted out in the productive process.

In Cockburn we look at the gendered element within the workforce which opens up the previous reading. Again class, skill and relationships are discussed, now refracted through the prism of patriarchy (male domination over women) which emphasises the 'double standard' attitude of men to women at work in this case through the union. Here the stereotypes 'siren-temptress' and 'mother-figure' coexist in the minds of the men in contradictory parallel images.

Our final readings deal with professions – the middle-class groupings of contemporary capitalist society. Perkin gives an account of the development of what he calls a professional society, and argues that expertise and merit have come to supplant not only feudal aristocratic privilege but also entrepreneurial and working-class ideals. If Perkin is correct, and professional occupations do exercise powerful controls over the market, this may just be a cause for some concern as Illich demonstrates. Professionals can use the power they have to their own advantage by 'ordaining' what is good and what is right. Illich offers an interesting note of caution amidst the clamour for professional status from ever-more occupational groups including managers.

Bibliography

Freire, P. (1972) *Cultural Action for Freedom*, Penguin, Harmondsworth.

The dissection of the psychical personality

SIGMUND FREUD

Ladies and gentlemen, – I know you are aware in regard to your own relations, whether with people or things, of the importance of your starting-point. This was also the case with psychoanalysis. It has not been a matter of indifference for the course of its development or for the reception it met with that it began its work on what is, of all the contents of the mind, most foreign to the ego – on symptoms. Symptoms are derived from the repressed, they are, as it were, its representatives before the ego; but the repressed is foreign territory to the ego – internal foreign territory – just as reality (if you will forgive the unusual expression) is external foreign territory. The path led from symptoms to the unconscious, to the life of the instincts, to sexuality; and it was then that psychoanalysis was met by the brilliant objection that human beings are not merely sexual creatures but have nobler and higher impulses as well. It might have been added that, exalted by their consciousness of these higher impulses, they often assume the right to think nonsense and to neglect facts.

You know better. From the very first we have said that human beings fall ill of a conflict between the claims of instinctual life and the resistance which arises within them against it; and not for a moment have we forgotten this resisting, repelling, repressing agency, which we thought of as equipped with its special forces, the ego-instincts, and which coincides with the ego of popular psychology. The truth was merely that, in view of the laborious nature of the progress made by scientific work, even psychoanalysis was not able to study every field simultaneously and to express its views on every problem in the same breath. But at last the point was reached when it was possible for us to divert our attention from the repressed to the repressing forces, and we faced this ego, which had seemed so self-evident, with the secure expectation that here once again we should find things for which we could not have been prepared. It was not easy, however, to find a first approach; and that is what I intend to talk to you about today.

The situation in which we find ourselves at the beginning of our enquiry may be expected itself to point the way for us. We wish to make the ego the matter of our inquiry, our very own ego. But is that possible? After all, the ego is in its very essence a subject; how can it be made into an object? Well, there is no doubt that it can be. The ego can take itself as an object, can treat itself like other objects, can observe itself, criticize itself, and do Heaven knows what with itself. In this, one part of the ego is setting itself over against the rest. So the ego can be split; it splits itself during a number

Abridged excerpts reproduced with the permission of Sigmund Freud Copyrights from *The Standard Edition of the Complete Psychological Works of Sigmund Freud*, edited by James Strachey; published by The Institute of Psycho-Analysis and The Hogarth Press, 1964.

of its functions – temporarily at least. Its parts can come together again afterwards. That is not exactly a novelty, though it may perhaps be putting an unusual emphasis on what is generally known. Mental patients are split and broken structures of this same kind. Even we cannot withhold from them something of the reverential awe which peoples of the past felt for the insane. They have turned away from external reality, but for that very reason they know more about internal, psychical reality and can reveal a number of things to us that would otherwise be inaccessible to us.

We describe one group of these patients as suffering from delusions of being observed. They complain to us that perpetually, and down to their most intimate actions, they are being molested by the observation of un-known powers – presumably persons – and that in hallucinations they hear these persons reporting the outcome of their observation: 'now he's going to say this, now he's dressing to go out' and so on. Observation of this sort is not yet the same thing as persecution, but it is not far from it; it presupposes that people distrust them, and expect to catch them carrying out forbidden actions for which they would be punished. How would it be if these insane people were right, if in each of us there is present in his ego an agency like this which observes and threatens to punish, and which in them has merely become sharply divided from their ego and mistakenly displaced into ex-ternal reality?

I cannot tell whether the same thing will happen to you as to me. Ever since, under the powerful impression of this clinical picture, I formed the idea that the separation of the observing agency from the rest of the ego might be a regular feature of the ego's structure, that idea has never left me, and I was driven to investigate the further characteristics and connections of the agency which was thus separated off. The next step is quickly taken. The content of the delusions of being observed already suggests that the observ-ing is only a preparation for judging and punishing, and we accordingly guess that another function of this agency must be what we call our con-science. There is scarcely anything else in us that we so regularly separate from our ego and so easily set over against it as precisely our conscience. I feel an inclination to do something that I think will give me pleasure, but I abandon it on the ground that my conscience does not allow it. Or I have let myself be persuaded by too great an expectation of pleasure into doing something to which the voice of conscience has objected and after the deed my conscience punishes me with distressing reproaches and causes me to feel remorse for the deed. I might simply say that the special agency which I am beginning to distinguish in the ego is conscience. But it is more prudent to keep the agency as something independent and to suppose that conscience is one of its functions and that self-observation, which is an essential pre-liminary to the judging activity of conscience, is another of them. And since when we recognise that something has a separate existence we give it a name of its own, from this time forward I will describe this agency in the ego as the '**super ego**'.

Hardly have we familiarized ourselves with the idea of a super-ego like this which enjoys a certain degree of autonomy, follows its own intentions and is independent of the ego for its supply of energy, than a clinical picture forces itself on our notice which throws a striking light on the severity of this agency and indeed its cruelty, and on its changing relations to the ego. I am thinking of the condition of melancholia,[1] or, more precisely, of melancholic attacks, which you too will have heard plenty about, even if you are not psychiatrists. The most striking feature of this illness, of whose causation and mechanism we know much too little, is the way in which the super-ego – 'conscience', you may call it, quietly – treats the ego. While a melancholic can, like other people, show a greater or lesser degree of severity to himself in his healthy periods, during a melancholic attack his super-ego becomes over-severe, abuses the poor ego, humiliates it and ill-treats it, threatens it with the direst punishments, reproaches it for actions in the remotest past which had been taken lightly at the time – as though it had spent the whole interval in collecting accusations and had only been waiting for its present access of strength in order to bring them up and make a condemnatory judgement on their basis. The super-ego applies the strictest moral standard to the helpless ego which is at its mercy; in general it represents the claims of morality, and we realize all at once that our moral sense of guilt is the expression of the tension between the ego and the super-ego. It is a most remarkable experience to see morality, which is supposed to have been given us by God and thus deeply implanted in us, functioning [in these patients] as a periodic phenomenon. For after a certain number of months the whole moral fuss is over, the criticism of the super-ego is silent, the ego is rehabilitated and again enjoys all the rights of man till the next attack. In some forms of the disease, indeed, something of a contrary sort occurs in the intervals; the ego finds itself in a blissful state of intoxication, it cele-brates a triumph, as though the super-ego had lost all its strength or had melted into the ego; and this liberated, manic ego permits itself a truly uninhibited satisfaction of all its appetites. Here are happenings rich in unsolved riddles!

No doubt you will expect me to give you more than a mere illustration when I inform you that we have found out all kinds of things about the formation of the super-ego – that is to say, about the origin of conscience. Following a well-known pronouncement of Kant's which couples the con-science within us with the starry Heavens, a pious man might well be tempted to honour these two things as the masterpieces of creation. The stars are indeed magnificent, but as regards conscience God has done an uneven and careless piece of work, for a large majority of men have brought along with them only a modest amount of it or scarcely enough to be worth mentioning. We are far from overlooking the portion of psychological truth that is contained in the assertion that conscience is of divine origin; but the thesis needs interpretation. Even if conscience is something 'within us', yet it is not so from the first. In this it is a real contrast to sexual life, which is in

---

[1] [Modern terminology would probably speak of 'depression'.]

fact there from the beginning of life and not only a later addition. But, as is well known, young children are amoral and possess no internal inhibitions against their impulses striving for pleasure. The part which is later taken on by the super-ego is played to begin with by an external power, by parental authority.

Parental influence governs the child by offering proofs of love and by threatening punishments which are signs to the child of loss of love and are bound to be feared on their own account. This realistic anxiety is the precursor of the later moral anxiety.[2] So long as it is dominant there is no need to talk of a super-ego and of a conscience. It is only subsequently that the secondary situation develops (which we are all too ready to regard as the normal one), where the external restraint is internalised and the super-ego takes the place of the parental agency and observes, directs and threatens the ego in exactly the same way as earlier the parents did with the child.

The super-ego, which thus takes over the power, function and even the methods of the parental agency, is however not merely its successor but actually the legitimate heir of its body. It proceeds directly out of it, we shall learn presently by what process. First, however, we must dwell upon a discrepancy between the two. The super-ego seems to have made a one-sided choice and to have picked out only the parents' strictness and severity, their prohibiting and punitive function, whereas their loving care seems not to have been taken over and maintained. If the parents have really enforced their authority with severity we can easily understand the child's in turn developing a severe super-ego. But, contrary to our expectation, experience shows that the super-ego can acquire the same characteristic of relentless severity even if the upbringing had been mild and kindly and had so far as possible avoided threats and punishments. We shall come back later to this contradiction when we deal with the transformations of instinct during the formation of the super-ego.

The basis of the process is what is called an 'identification' – that is to say, the assimilation of one ego to another one, as a result of which the first ego behaves like the second in certain respects, imitates it and in a sense takes it up into itself. Identification has been not unsuitably compared with the oral, cannibalistic incorporation of the other person. It is a very important form of attachment to someone else, probably the very first, and not the same thing as the choice of an object. The difference between the two can be expressed in some such way as this. If a boy identifies himself with his father, he wants to **be like** his father; if he makes him the object of his choice, he wants to **have** him, to possess him. In the first case his ego is altered on the model of his father; in the second case that is not necessary. Identification and object-choice are to a large extent independent of each other; it is however possible to identify oneself with someone whom, for instance, one has taken as a sexual object, and to alter one's ego in his model. It is said that the influencing of the ego by the sexual object occurs

[2] [Literally 'conscience anxiety'.]

particularly often with women and is characteristic of femininity. I must already have spoken to you in my earlier lectures of what is by far the most instructive relation between identification and object-choice. It can be observed equally easily in children and adults, in normal as in sick people. If one has lost an object or has been obliged to give it up, one often compensates oneself by identifying oneself with it and by setting it up once more in one's ego, so that here object-choice regresses, as it were, to identification.

I myself am far from satisfied with these remarks on identification; but it will be enough if you can grant me that the installation of the super-ego can be described as a successful instance of identification with the parental agency. The fact that speaks decisively for this view is that this new creation of a superior agency within the ego is most intimately linked with the destiny of the Oedipus complex, so that the super-ego appears as the heir of that emotional attachment which is of such importance for childhood. With his abandonment of the Oedipus complex a child must, as we can see, renounce the intense object-cathexes which he has deposited with his parents, and it is as a compensation for this loss of objects that there is such a strong intensification of the identifications with his parents which have probably long been present in his ego. Identifications of this kind as precipitates of object-cathexes that have been given up will be repeated often enough later in the child's life; but it is entirely in accordance with the emotional importance of this first instance of such a transformation that a special place in the ego should be found for its outcome. Close investigation has shown us, too, that the super-ego is stunted in its strength and growth if the surmounting of the Oedipus complex is only incompletely successful. In the course of development the super-ego also takes on the influences of those who have stepped into the place of parents – educators, teachers, people chosen as ideal models. Normally it departs more and more from the original parental figures; it becomes, so to say, more impersonal. Nor must it be forgotten that a child has a different estimate of its parents at different periods of its life. At the time at which the Oedipus complex gives place to the super-ego they are something quite magnificent; but later they lose much of this. Identifications then come about with these later parents as well, and indeed they regularly make important contributions to the formation of character; but in that case they only affect the ego, they no longer influence the super-ego, which has been determined by the earliest parental images.

I am sure you have heard a great deal of the sense of inferiority which is supposed particularly to characterise neurotics. In fact 'inferiority complex' is a technical term that is scarcely used in psychoanalysis. For us it does not bear the meaning of anything simple, let alone elementary. The sense of inferiority has strong erotic roots. A child feels inferior if he notices that he is not loved, and so does an adult. But the major part of the sense of inferiority derives from the ego's relation to its super-ego; like the sense of guilt it is an expression of the tension between them. Altogether, it is hard to separate the sense of inferiority and the sense of guilt. It would perhaps be right to regard the former as the erotic complement to the moral sense of inferiority. Little attention has been given in psychoanalysis to the question of the delimitation of the two concepts.

But let us return to the super-ego. We have allotted it the functions of self-observation, of conscience and of [maintaining] the ideal. It follows from what we have said about its origin that it presupposes an immensely important biological fact and a fateful psychological one: namely, the human child's long dependence on its parents and the Oedipus complex, both of which, again, are intimately interconnected. The super-ego is the representative for us of every moral restriction, the advocate of a striving towards perfection – it is, in short, as much as we have been able to grasp psychologically of what is described as the higher side of human life. Since it itself goes back to the influence of parents, educators and so on, we learn still more of its significance if we turn to those who are its sources. As a rule parents and authorities analogous to them follow the precepts of their own super-egos in educating children. Whatever understanding their ego may have come to with their super-ego, they are severe and exacting in educating children. They have forgotten the difficulties of their own childhood and they are glad to be able now to identify themselves fully with their own parents who in the past laid such severe restrictions upon them. Thus a child's super-ego is in fact constructed on the model not of its parents but of its parents' super-ego; the contents which fill it are the same and it becomes the vehicle of tradition and of all the time-resisting judgements of value which have propagated themselves in this manner from generation to generation. You may easily guess what important assistance taking the super-ego into account will give us in our understanding of the social behaviour of mankind – in the problem of delinquency, for instance – and perhaps even what practical hints on education. It seems likely that what are known as materialistic views of history sin in under-estimating this factor. They brush it aside with the remark that human 'ideologies' are nothing other than the product and superstructure of their contemporary economic conditions. That is true, but very probably not the whole truth. Mankind never lives entirely in the present. The past, the tradition of the race and of the people, lives on in the ideologies of the super-ego, and yields only slowly to the influences of the present and to new changes; and so long as it operates through the super-ego it plays a powerful part in human life, independently of economic conditions.

Now, however, another problem awaits us – at the opposite end of the ego, as we might put it. We should long ago have asked the question: from what part of his mind does an unconscious resistance like this arise? The beginner in psychoanalysis will be ready at once with the answer: it is, of course, the resistance of the unconscious. An ambiguous and unserviceable answer! If it means that the resistance arises from the repressed, we must rejoin: certainly not! We must rather attribute to the repressed a strong upward drive, an impulsion to break through into consciousness. The resistance can only be a manifestation of the ego, which originally put the repression into force and now wishes to maintain it. That, moreover, is the view we always took. Since we have come to assume a special agency in the ego, the super-ego, which represents demands of a restrictive and rejecting character, we may say that repression is the work of this super-ego and that it is carried out either by itself or by the ego in obedience to its orders. In face of the doubt whether the ego and super-ego are themselves unconscious or merely produce unconscious effects, we have, for good reasons, decided in favour of the former possibility. And it is indeed the case that large portions of the ego and super-ego can remain unconscious and are normally unconscious. That is to say, the individual knows nothing of their contents and it requires an expenditure of effort to make them conscious. It is a fact that ego and conscious, repressed and unconscious do not coincide.

There is no need to discuss what is to be called conscious: it is removed from all doubt. The oldest and best meaning of the word 'unconscious' is the descriptive one; we call a psychical process unconscious whose existence we are obliged to assume – for some such reason as that we infer it from its effect –, but of which we know nothing. If we want to be still more correct, we shall modify our assertion by saying that we call a process unconscious if we are obliged to assume that it is being activated **at the moment**, though **at the moment** we know nothing about it. This qualification makes us reflect that the majority of conscious processes are conscious only for a short time; very soon they become **latent**, but can easily become conscious again. In order to explain a slip of the tongue, for instance, we find ourselves obliged to assume that the intention to make a particular remark was present in the subject. We infer it with certainty from the interference with his remark which has occurred; but the intention did not put itself through and was thus unconscious. If, when we subsequently put it before the speaker, he re-cognizes it as one familiar to him, then it was only temporarily unconscious to him; but if he repudiates it as something foreign to him, then it was permanently unconscious.

A consideration of these dynamic relations permits us now to distinguish two kinds of unconscious – one which is easily, under frequently occurring circumstances, transformed into something conscious, and another with which this transformation is difficult and takes place only subject to a considerable expenditure of effort or possibly never at all. We call the unconscious which is only latent, and thus easily becomes conscious, the 'preconscious' and retain the term 'unconscious' for the other. We now have three terms, 'conscious', 'preconscious' and 'unconscious', with which we can get along in our description of mental phenomena. Once again: the preconscious is also unconscious in the purely descriptive sense, but we do not give it that name, except in talking loosely or when we have to make a defence of the existence in mental life of unconscious processes in general.

You will admit, I hope, that so far that is not too bad and allows of convenient handling. Yes, but unluckily the work of psychoanalysis has found itself compelled to use the word 'unconscious' in yet another, third, sense, and this may, to be sure, have led to confusion. Under the new and powerful impression of there being an extensive and important field of mental life which is normally withdrawn from the ego's knowledge so that the processes occurring in it have to be regarded as unconscious in the truly dynamic sense, we have come to understand the term 'unconscious' in a topographical or systematic sense as well; we have come to speak of a 'system' of the preconscious and a 'system' of the unconscious, of a conflict between the ego and the system *Ucs.*, and have used the word more and more to denote a mental province rather than a quality of what is mental. The discovery, actually an inconvenient one, that portions of the ego and super-ego as well are unconscious in the dynamic sense, operates at this point as a relief – it makes possible the removal of a complication. We perceive that we have no right to name the mental region that is foreign to the ego 'the system *Ucs.*', since the characteristic of being unconscious is not restricted to it. Very well; we will no longer use the term 'unconscious' in the systematic sense and we will give what we have hitherto so described a better name and one no longer open to misunderstanding. Following a verbal usage of Nietzsche's and taking up a suggestion by Georg Groddeck [1923], we will in future call it the 'id'.[3] This impersonal pronoun seems particularly well suited for expressing the main characteristic of this province of the mind – the fact of its being alien to the ego. The super-ego, the ego and the id – these, then, are the three realms, regions, provinces, into which we divide an individual's mental apparatus, and with the mutual relations of which we shall be concerned in what follows.

You will not expect me to have much to tell you that is new about the id apart from its new name. It is the dark, inaccessible part of our personality; what little we know of it we have learnt from our study of the dream-work and of the construction of neurotic symptoms, and most of that is of a negative character and can be described only as a contrast to the ego. We approach the id with analogies: we call it a chaos, a cauldron full of seething excitations. We picture it as being open at its end to somatic influences, and as there taking up into itself instinctual needs which find their psychical expression in it. It is filled with energy reaching it from the instincts, but it has no organization, produces no collective will, but only a striving to bring about the satisfaction of the instinctual needs subject to the observance of the pleasure principle. The logical laws of thought do not apply in the id. Contrary impulses exist side by side, without cancelling each other out or diminishing each other: [T]here is nothing in the id that corresponds to the idea of time; there is no recognition of the passage of time, and – a thing that is most remarkable and awaits consideration in philosophical thought – no alteration in its mental processes is produced by the passage of time. Wishful impulses which have never passed beyond the id, but impressions, too, which have been sunk into the id by repression, are virtually immortal; after the passage of decades they behave as though they had just occurred. They can only be recognised as belonging to the past, can only lose their importance and be deprived of their cathexis of energy, when they have

[3] [In German '*Es*', the ordinary word for 'it'.]

been made conscious by the work of analysis, and it is on this that the therapeutic effect of analytic treatment rests to no small extent.

The id of course knows no judgements of value: no good and evil, no morality. The economic or, if you prefer, the quantitative factor, which is intimately linked to the pleasure principle, dominates all its processes. Instinctual cathexes seeking discharge – that, in our view, is all there is in the id.

We can best arrive at the characteristics of the actual ego, in so far as it can be distinguished from the id and from the super-ego, by examining its relation to the outermost superficial portion of the mental apparatus. This system is turned towards the external world, it is the medium for the perceptions arising thence, and during its functioning the phenomenon of consciousness arises in it. It is the sense-organ of the entire apparatus; moreover it is receptive not only to excitations from outside but also to those arising from the interior of the mind. The relation to the external world has become the decisive factor for the ego; it has taken on the task of representing the external world to the id – fortunately for the id, which could not escape destruction if, in its blind efforts for the satisfaction of its instincts, it disregarded that supreme external power. In accomplishing this function, the ego must observe the external world, must lay down an accurate picture of it in the memory-traces of its perceptions, and by its exercise of the function of 'reality-testing' must put aside whatever in this picture of the external world is an addition derived from internal sources of excitation. The ego controls the approaches to motility under the id's orders; but between a need and an action it has interposed a postponement in the form of the activity of thought, during which it makes use of the mnemic residues of experience. In that way it has dethroned the pleasure principle which dominates the course of events in the id without any re-striction and has replaced it by the reality principle, which promises more certainty and greater success.

But what distinguishes the ego from the id quite especially is a tendency to synthesis in its contents, to a combination and unification in its mental processes which are totally lacking in the id. To adopt a popular mode of speaking, we might say that the ego stands for reason and good sense while the id stands for the untamed passions.

So far we have allowed ourselves to be impressed by the merits and capabilities of the ego.

[I]t is now time to consider the other side as well. The ego is after all only a portion of the id, a portion that has been expediently modified by the proximity of the external world with its threat of danger. From a dynamic point of view it is weak, it has borrowed its energies from the id, and we are not entirely without insight into the methods – we might call them dodges – by which it extracts further amounts of energy from the id. One such method, for instance, is by identifying itself with actual or abandoned objects. The object-cathexes spring from the instinctual demands of the id. The ego has in the first instance to take note of them. But by identifying itself with the object it recommends itself to the id in place of the object and seeks to divert the id's libido on to itself. The ego must on the whole carry out the id's intentions, it fulfils its task by finding out the circumstances in which those intentions can best be achieved. The ego's relation to the id might be compared with that of a rider to his horse. The horse supplies the locomotive energy, while the rider has the privilege of deciding on the goal and of guiding the powerful animal's movement. But only too often there arises between the ego and the id the not precisely ideal situation of the rider being obliged to guide the horse along the path by which it itself wants to go.

There is one portion of the id from which the ego has separated itself by resistances due to repression. But the repression is not carried over into the id: the repressed merges into the remainder of the id.

We are warned by a proverb against serving two masters at the same time. The poor ego has things even worse: it serves three severe masters and does what it can to bring their claims and demands into harmony with one another. These claims are always divergent and often seem incompatible. No wonder that the ego so often fails in its task. Its three tyrannical masters are the external world, the super-ego and the id. When we follow the ego's efforts to satisfy them simultaneously – or rather, to obey them simultaneously – we cannot feel any regret at having personified this ego and having set it up as a separate organism. It feels hemmed in on three sides, threatened by three kinds of danger, to which, if it is hard pressed, it reacts by generating anxiety. Owing to its origin from the experiences of the perceptual system, it is earmarked for representing the demands of the external world, but it strives too to be a loyal servant of the id, to remain on good terms with it, to recommend itself to it as an object and to attract its libido to itself. In its attempts to mediate between the id and reality, it is often obliged to cloak the *Ucs.* commands of the id with its own *Pcs.* rationalizations, to conceal the id's conflicts with reality, to profess, with diplomatic disingenuousness, to be taking notice of reality even when the id has remained rigid and unyielding. On the other hand it is observed at every step it takes by the strict super-ego, which lays down definite standards for its conduct, without taking any account of its difficulties from the direction of the id and the external world, and which, if those standards are not obeyed, punishes it with tense feelings of inferiority and of guilt. Thus the ego, driven by the id, confined by the super-ego, repulsed by reality, struggles to master its economic task of bringing about harmony among the forces and influences working in and upon it; and we can understand how it is that so often we cannot suppress a cry: 'Life is not easy!' If the ego is obliged to admit its weakness, it breaks out in anxiety – realistic anxiety regarding the external world, moral anxiety regarding the super-ego and neurotic anxiety regarding the strength of the passions in the id.

I should like to portray the structural relations of the mental personality, as I have described them to you, in the unassuming sketch which I now present you with:

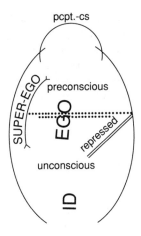

Figure 2.1

As you see here, the super-ego merges into the id; indeed, as heir to the Oedipus complex it has intimate relations with the id; it is more remote than the ego from the perceptual system. The id has intercourse with the external world only through the ego – at least, according to this diagram. It is certainly hard to say today how far the drawing is correct. In one respect it is undoubtedly not. The space occupied by the unconscious id ought to have been incomparably greater than that of the ego or the preconscious. I must ask you to correct it in your thoughts.

And here is another warning, to conclude these remarks, which have certainly been exacting and not, perhaps, very illuminating. In thinking of this division of the personality into an ego, a super-ego and an id, you will not, of course, have pictured sharp frontiers like the artificial ones drawn in political geography. We cannot do justice to the characteristics of the mind by linear outlines like those in a drawing or in primitive painting, but rather by areas of colour melting into one another as they are presented by modern artists. After making the separation we must allow what we have separated to merge together once more. You must not judge too harshly a first attempt at giving a pictorial representation of something so intangible as psychical processes. It is highly probable that the development of these divisions is subject to great variations in different individuals; it is possible that in the course of actual functioning they may change and go through a temporary phase of involution. Particularly in the case of what is phylo-genetically the last and most delicate of these divisions – the differentiation between the ego and the super-ego – something of the sort seems to be true. There is no question but that the same thing results from psychical illness. It is easy to imagine, too, that certain mystical practices may succeed in upsetting the normal relations between the different regions of the mind, so that, for instance, perception may be able to grasp happenings in the depths of the ego and in the id which were otherwise inaccessible to it. It may safely be doubted, however, whether this road will lead us to the ultimate truths from which salvation is to be expected. Nevertheless it may be admitted that the therapeutic efforts of psychoanalysis have chosen a similar line of approach. Its intention is, indeed, to strengthen the ego, to make it more independent of the super-ego, to widen its field of perception and enlarge its organization, so that it can appropriate fresh portions of the id. Where id was, there ego shall be. It is a work of culture – not unlike the draining of the Zuider Zee.

The rat or the couch?

H.J. EYSENCK

I have always been fascinated by humour; jokes, cartoons, satire – these I have found irresistible, and a much more interesting guide to the national consciousness than more weighty tomes and analyses.

There are clearly two sets or classes of jokes current about psychology and psychologists – and I include under this heading psychiatrists and psychoanalysts (not because they know much about psychology – it does not form any major part of their teaching, contrary to common belief, or even to common sense – but because the man in the street does not make this differentiation; after all, he is the person for whom the joke is intended!). These two classes of jokes refer, respectively, to experiments with rats and to psychoanalytic patients on the couch.

Let us begin with the rat joke, and then go on to the couch. [The] famous cartoon of a rat in a box, pressing a lever and saying to another rat: 'I sure got my human well conditioned – whenever I press this lever, he drops a food pellet into the chute!' These jokes and cartoons are legion, and they all make the same point – psychologists believe that they are scientists, but they have only taken over the empty formalism of science; the real essence escapes them, and they play around with pseudo-problems, using rats as an excuse for their failure to work out a proper human psychology which could be of some use to us in our problems. This criticism is of course not confined to jokes; it is often made by more serious writers, and even by psychologists themselves. But of that more anon.

Couch and analyst jokes typically base themselves on the glaring incongruity between claim and performance, fact and fiction. The classic is the cartoon showing two analysts, one young and looking exhausted, the other old but spruce and fresh, emerging from a hospital building. 'How do you manage to listen to them for all these hours, and yet remain so calm?' asks the young man. 'Who listens?' replies the older one. Equally well known is the story of the rich mother who calls in the analyst every time her little boy misbehaves, being unable to deal with his problems herself. One day he refuses to get off his rocking horse, in spite of her entreaties; in despair she calls the analyst. He comes, goes over to the child and whispers a few words in his ear. It works like magic; obediently he gets off the horse, and behaves like an angel all day long. Mother cannot imagine what the analyst said to the boy; father comes home, is told the story, and can't think of an answer either. Finally they ask little Johnny, who bursts out crying and says: 'He told me he'd cut off my tiddler if I didn't behave'. *Sic transit gloria mundi.* Where the rat joke, therefore, attacks the psychologist for doing careful, scientific research but on unimportant, irrelevant topics, the couch joke recognises that the psychologist may deal with important and relevant matters, but does so in an unscientific manner, behaving ultimately in a very common-sense manner, and hiding his ignorance behind a cloak of verbiage and pretence. Apparently you can't win – either you are a remote pedant painstakingly doing ivory tower research that doesn't impinge on life in any way, doesn't lead to any important or interesting discoveries, and is merely 'busy work' type scientism, or you meddle with real problems in your rash exuberance, confuse everybody with pretentious and endless jargon, and finally fail to deliver the goods which you have so rashly promised. Which of these you do depends on whether you are an extravert or an introvert – rat men are introverts, couch men are extraverts, with rare exceptions.

Jokes, cartoons, wit and humour in general require interpretation, according to Freud; can we interpret these results? Freud has no doubt, of course; aggression is repressed because of fear of the consequences of expressing it, and humour (like dreams and 'accidental' error in speech) allows it to escape from this repression, producing laughter and amusement as a consequence of this escape.

My own theory of humour is quite the opposite of Freud's; it might be called a trait theory, or even a 'state and trait' theory. According to this view, people are ranged along a continuum of 'aggressiveness', or 'sexuality' – going from the very aggressive, or very actively sexual, through average to very non-aggressive and timid, or little concerned with sexual matters. According to Freud, the apparently non-aggressive, non-sexual people have repressed their aggressive and sexual tendencies, and appreciate hostile and sexual jokes because these release their 'unconscious' feelings; aggressive and sexually active people do not need such release and do not appreciate these jokes particularly. The evidence, of which there is quite a lot, clearly disagrees with the Freudian interpretation; Thus both the 'trait' approach and the 'state' approach (i.e. determination of the habitual level of aggressiveness, or experimental manipulation of the present level of aggressiveness) confound Freud's views; as people are in general, so do they react to jokes.

I have pointed out the prevalence of this schizophrenic attitude, which divides psychology into an experimental and a social section – two sections which are hardly on speaking terms, which publish in different journals, and hardly ever read the other side's books!

Allied to this is the problem of the fundamental concepts which underlie a science. Chemistry came of age with the enunciation of the atomic theory by Dalton; what would chemistry be without the atom? Biology is founded securely on the concept of the cell. Genetics is based on the notion of the gene. Examples could be multiplied, but there is no need. It is obvious that a scientific discipline stands in need of such fundamental, underlying concepts; where is psychology's to be found? Some have suggested the reflex, or the conditioned reflex; but this can hardly be considered seriously – perception, or social psychology, or even verbal learning are not obviously based on the laws of conditioning, although these may serve to explain certain phenomena and facts in all these fields. It is the purpose of this [reading] to suggest such a fundamental unit; to show how it can be used to unite the various separate fields of psychology; and to demonstrate how we can harness the power of experimental psychology to the solution of social problems.

Briefly – to be expanded presently – my proposal is that **personality** is the fundamental unit in psychology; that this concept, in order to be scientifically acceptable, requires to be anchored firmly to both antecedent and consequent conditions which are capable of being accurately observed, precisely measured, and meaningfully quantified; and that neither an adequate experimental psychology nor a scientifically acceptable social psychology is possible without the inclusion, at the most fundamental level, of this concept of personality. I hope to be able to demonstrate that a causal chain (see Figure 2.2), can be constructed all the way from a consideration of anatomical and physiological structures in the basal ganglia and the cortex, through neurological concepts like 'arousal' and the 'visceral brain',[1] to individual differences in learning, conditioning, perceiving, sensory thresholds and other topics in experimental psychology; these are the 'antecedent' conditions to which the concept of personality may be linked.

It will be obvious that the concept of 'personality', while crucial to this model, requires careful definition; the term is used in so many different senses, even by psychologists, that any particular definition must to some extent be arbitrary, and can only be defended on heuristic grounds. There are now sufficient facts to demonstrate beyond question that the fundamental fact of uniqueness of personality remains undoubted, it does not necessarily preclude the use of the concept in a scientific framework, provided we use it in a restricted sense, with a precise understanding of the invariances in conduct to which we wish to apply it.

---

[1] 'Arousal' is a property of the cortex which ranges along a continuum from sleepiness and drowsiness, at one extreme, to marked mental excitation, at the other; this is usually measured by means of the electroencephalograph (EEG), which records a person's 'brain waves', i.e. the electrical activity of his cortex, picked up from his scalp. There is some evidence that this arousal is essential for mental activity, and is in turn determined by a brain-stem structure called the reticular formation. EEG patterns characteristic of high arousal are significantly more frequently found in introverted persons. Emotional behaviour is largely controlled by a system somewhat independent of the central nervous system and the cortex, namely the so-called sympathetic and parasympathetic system, often called the 'autonomic system' because of this degree of independence. This system is governed by another brain-stem structure, the so-called 'visceral brain'; evidence suggests that this is over-active in emotional and neurotic persons. The emotional activation system and the cortical arousal system are independent for much of the time, but when a person experiences strong emotion this spills over into the arousal system.

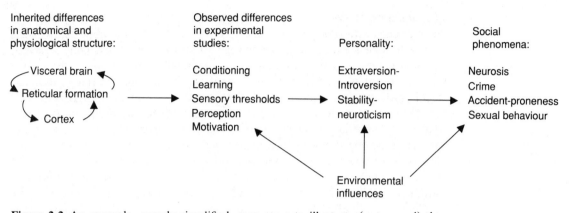

Figure 2.2 An example, grossly simplified, may serve to illustrate (not prove!) the existence of such a chain. Take a person who is endowed with a visceral brain which predisposes him to have strong, long-lasting emotions, particularly of fear and anxiety, and who also possesses a reticular formation which keeps his cortex in a constant state of high arousal. Such arousal facilitates the production of strong conditioned responses, and in the laboratory we will thus find this person giving rise to strong physiological fear reactions when exposed, say, to the threat of an electric shock; he will also be found to produce conditioned responses quickly and strongly. Such a person will tend to develop personality traits characteristic of the introvert and of the potential neurotic, and if circumstances are at all unfavourable he is likely to have a neurotic breakdown, with symptoms of anxiety, phobic fears, obsessive-compulsive symptoms, reactive depression, and so forth. Conversely, the absence of strong cortical arousal leads to poor conditioning, an impulsive personality likely to indulge in anti-social activities. The evidence for such statements as these is reviewed in detail in my book on *The Biological Basis of Personality*; here these assertions are made very dogmatically merely in order to illustrate the meaning of our diagram.

The idiographic[2] point of view lies at one extreme of a continuum at the other extreme of which lies what might be called a neo-behaviouristic point of view, represented explicitly by Skinner and his followers, but implicitly accepted by most experimentalists. According to this point of view, behaviour is a function of certain contingencies which we can manipulate; if pressing a lever in a box is followed by food, the rat will learn to press the lever. By varying the timing of the rewards (regularly after every 100th press, or randomly, or according to some other system) I can gain complete control over the rat's performance. This idea is not always made explicit; it is implicit in the very ways the experimentalist sets up his experiment.

Now the odd thing about most psychological experiments is that the error term, far from being respectably small in comparison with the effects produced by the variables the experimenter has manipulated, such as difficulty level in our example, is in fact enormous – often far greater than the 'main effects' which the experimenter is really interested in. You can get over this difficulty statistically by increasing the number of subjects, or repeating the experiment; in this way you get results which convention enables you to describe as 'statistically significant'. But this legerdemain does not remove

[2] [unique.]

the fundamental weakness of all this work – the fact that different people have reacted differently to identical sets of stimuli! ([R]emember that subjects of psychological experiments are in the vast majority of cases highly selected; random samples of the population are practically never tested. Instead we have a complete reliance on very bright, sophisticated university students, highly motivated and full of ideas as to the purpose of the experiment they are asked to participate in – how can we generalize any findings from such extremely unusual populations?) It has even been suggested that some of the ferocious theoretical struggles between opposing camps in learning theory were due not to any genuine differences, but were due simply to the fact that one group worked with rats bred specially to form an 'emotional' strain, while the other group worked with 'unemotional' rats! Thus does the neglect of individual differences and 'personality' variables avenge itself, even when we are dealing with the humble rat.

If experimental psychologists are guilty, however, so are social psychologists; they commit exactly the same error. The questions asked, and the problems stated, are nearly always phrased in universal terms. The sociologist asks, Do broken homes produce crime? The educationalist asks, Is praise better than blame in motivating children? The psychiatrist asks, Is psychotherapy better than sociodrama? But these are not meaningful questions, and these are not problems which have a unique answer. For some types of people the effects may go one way, for others another. Experiments have suggested that introverted children thrive better when only given praise; extraverted children are more highly motivated by blame. Similarly, anxious children respond differently from non-anxious children. Psychiatric patients react differently to different types of treatment; there is some evidence that phobics with very strong anxieties respond better to so-called **implosion** therapy, while phobics with weaker anxieties respond better to desensitization.[3] Broken homes have different effects on different children; no universal generalization is possible. Social psychologists often pay lip service to these considerations, but their work does not bear witness to any thoroughgoing conversion.

In spite of all we have said so far, there is of course a basic remainder of good sense in the behaviouristic argument. Certain experimental effects are so broad and universal that individual differences do not make very much difference; here general laws based on 'averaging' may be useful and sensible. Hungry people (and rats!) will seek food; thirst will lead to drinking be-

---

[3] Implosion and desensitization therapy are two different varieties of extinction treatment for conditioned emotional fear reactions, such as phobias. In the former, the patient is exposed to the feared object or situation for a long time, and great fear and anxiety are produced; a cure is produced because in the end the patient (or rather his autonomic system!) realizes that nothing fatal or even dangerous is happening to him, in spite of this exposure. Or possibly there is simple habituation; you cannot keep up a state of strong fear for ever. Desensitization gradually exposes the patient to the thing or situation he fears, taking care that he is relaxed; all strong emotional reactions are avoided, and he is trained gradually to encounter the feared object or situation in a more and more threatening form. Both forms of therapy have been shown to work reasonably well, but there is still argument as to when one is to be preferred to the other, and why the one works better in one case, the other on other occasions.

haviour. But such fairly universal generalizations are few and far between, and they are hardly world-shaking discoveries.

The term 'personality' is obviously too broad and general to stand for anything but a programme of research; it has to be analysed in considerable detail before we can make use of it. The usage suggested lies about half-way between the two extremes we have just criticised; personality is neither as unique as the idiographic psychologists suggest, nor is it as universal as the behaviourists would have it. Instead, it is suggested that there are certain dimensions of personality which are important and relevant to the kinds of questions and problems which we are concerned with; dimensions along which people can be ordered from high to low, and which give rise to typologies like that of extraversion-introversion. Thus we break up the total population into groups which are relatively homogeneous with respect to certain attributes which theory suggests are important, relevant and relatively invariant; whether the theories according to which we select our dimensions and our groupings are in fact borne out by experiment is of course an empirical matter.

The theory which seems best to fit the case is one which reaches back to respectable antiquity, although admittedly it has needed some repainting and refurbishing generally. The four temperaments – choleric, sanguinic, phlegmatic, melancholic – go back to the Greek physician Galen, in the second century A.D., and even beyond, Cholerics and sanguinics were both changeable (extraverted we would now say), while phlegmatics and melancholics were unchangeable (introverted); thus people could also be graded along a second dimension of extraversion-introversion, at right angles to the first. In this way we have two continuous dimensions rather than four independent categories; the original four 'types' are now found in the four quadrants generated by this pair of right-angled dimensions, forming as it were a cross, with extremely emotional and unemotional people at the ends of the one dimension, and particularly extraverted or introverted people at the ends of the other, as shown in Figure 2.3 below. Cholerics are thus emotional extraverts, melancholics emotional introverts. This scheme, with minor emendations, has stood the test of time; there are few well conceived investigations of personality, using sufficiently broadly based tests or questionnaires, which do not emerge with these two dimensions prominently displayed. What in fact does the theory say? It suggests that certain traits, such as sociability, impulsiveness, carefreeness, talkativeness, liveliness, activity, and so on, are usually found together; this alleged empirical fact requires us to postulate some supraordinate concept like 'extraversion'. 'Types' are thus based on the observed intercorrelations between traits; it is not implied that everyone must be either a raving extravert or a withdrawn introvert, but merely that everyone can find a place on this particular continuum or dimension. Indeed, it has been shown that most people are in fact between the extremes.

Most investigations use ratings, i.e. scores given to the subjects of the study by observers on the basis of their behaviour, either in life generally,

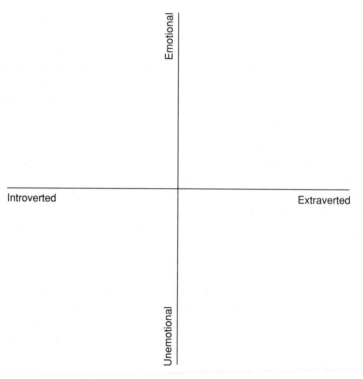

Figure 2.3

or else in experimentally arranged special situations. Thus if you were interested in persistence, you could ask teachers, parents and school friends of a given set of boys of girls about their persistence in everyday life, at school, in sport, etc., or you could rig up special tests which, unbeknown to the children, measured their persistence. For instance you could give them an intelligence test and measure the time taken over each item; if now you introduce an item which is too difficult for the children to do, the length of time taken until they finally gave up would be such a measure.

Description precedes causal analysis; we must know first of all just what it is that we have to account for before we can hope to give a proper developmental or causal account of it. Take sociability: detailed study has shown that there is not one single trait of sociability, but at least three – all quite independent of each other. Introverts are unsociable because they don't particularly care about other people, but they can function perfectly well in a social situation when they feel so inclined. Neurotics are so inclined, but they are afraid of other people, or of making fools of themselves. People with psychotic tendencies are inclined to hate other people, and hence keep away from them. These findings clarify the descriptive situation, and make it possible to now go and state causal hypotheses.

Descriptively, then, we arrive at what might be described as a two-dimensional picture of man, locating his infinite complexity at some point of intersection of the two dimensions of extraversion-introversion and emotionality-stability. The psychologist does not try to rival the artist in portraying life. His aim is analysis, however much that may be anathema to the artist; analysis means to grasp one strand out of an infinitely varied twist and follow it all the way. A two-dimensional theory like that here developed does not of course do all one would like it to do; however, as we shall see, it does a few things, quite important ones at that, and it may improve and do even better in due course. Provided that the theory is in line with the known facts, can predict previously unknown facts, and suggests manipulations of the environment which ultimately turn out to be helpful in controlling it, we may say that the theory has done all that can be expected of it, and may be allowed to flourish until displaced by a better, truer, more inclusive one. But just wishing will not give us such a better theory; it has to be worked for. All scientific theories had to go through stages where their accomplishments were very modest. Chemistry in its early days had the alchemists to contend with, who made tremendous claims for their art; in the same way astronomers had to fight off the inflated claims of the astrologers. What alchemists and astrologers were to chemists and astronomers, psychoanalysts are to psychologists; every science has to pass through its ordeal by quackery.

This is strong language; is it justified? I have discussed the evidence for such a belief so often that I hesitate to devote much space to it for fear of wearying the reader who may have looked at one or other of my Pelican books, or who has dipped into my more serious writings. However, a brief résumé of the main criticisms of Freudian beliefs may be interpolated here, for those not familiar with the argument.

The theory has undergone many subtle changes, and I shall assume it to be too well known to require restatement except in the very briefest outline. To the psychoanalyst neurotic symptoms are merely the observable signs of underlying complexes, repressed well into the unconscious but too strong to remain completely suppressed. These complexes date back to childhood years and are associated with the Oedipus complex which is their *fons et origo*. Treatment consists in **uncovering** the original infantile experience which laid the basis for the later neurosis.

What psychoanalysts have usually done has been to publish individual cases, almost invariably cases in which the patient got better, and to argue from these illustrative examples to the general case. The argument may be formally stated in a way that exposes it as one of the classical examples of the *post hoc ergo propter hoc* fallacy. The fact that a patient, John Doe, who is suffering from a phobia, gets better four years after psychoanalytic treatment has been initiated, is not proof that John Doe has got better **because** of such psychoanalytic treatment, and to reason thus, even by implication, is so obviously absurd that I will not waste space by arguing the case.

To prove its efficacy, psychoanalysis would clearly have to do better than this. If people treated by psychoanalysis did not recover more quickly or in greater numbers than when left untreated, then clearly the claims of psychoanalysis, as far as curative powers are concerned, would have to be rejected. Actually one might anticipate a positive showing for psychoanalysis even though the method was not in fact efficacious. The reasons for this are as follows. Psychoanalysts, by and large, only treat the better-off and more intelligent types of patient, and furthermore they tend to select their patients very stringently in terms of their likelihood to benefit from treatment. On these grounds their patients should have a better recovery rate than the more unselected groups on which the spontaneous recovery base line was established. In actual fact the data suggest very strongly that, if anything, patients treated by psychoanalysis **take longer to recover** and **recover to a lesser extent** than do patients left untreated. This conclusion is arrived at by averaging the claims made by various psychoanalysts and psychoanalytic institutions with respect to their patients.

One might have thought that, with respect to children, psychoanalysis might be more positively placed, as these might be considered to be more impressionable and more easily cured. Here also, however, an extensive review of the literature shows a picture almost identical in every detail with that found in adults. There is no evidence that psychoanalysis of children produces any kind of effect on the neurotic symptoms of these children.

Why is it, the reader may ask, that in spite of its apparent uselessness, psychotherapy is so widely praised by people who have undergone it, and who claim they have been cured by it? The answer I think lies in a famous experiment, reported by the American psychologist, B.F. Skinner. He left a group of pigeons alone in their cage for twelve hours but arranged for an automatic hopper to throw out a few grains of corn at intervals to the hungry animals. When Skinner returned in the morning, he found that the animals were behaving in a very odd manner. Some were jumping up and down on one leg, some were pirouetting about with one wing in the air; others again were stretching the neck as high as it would go. What had happened? The animals, in the course of their explorations, had happened to make that particular movement when the hopper had released some corn. The pigeon, not being a slouch at the *post hoc ergo propter hoc* argument, imagined that the movement **preceding** the corn had, in fact, **produced** the corn, and immediately began to repeat the same movement again and again. When finally another reward came tumbling out of the hopper, the pigeon became more firmly convinced of the causal consequences, so throughout the twelve hours the pigeon performed the movement and the hopper, at irregular intervals, dispensed the corn. To leave out the anthropomorphic terminology, and to put it in slightly more respectable language, we may say that the pigeon became conditioned to make a particular response in order to receive a particular reward. Neurotics get better regardless of treatment; this improvement constitutes the reinforcement, and is equivalent to the corn received by the pigeon. The actions of the psychotherapist are as irrelevant as is the behaviour of the pigeon in the experimental situation.

It may be said altogether that for Freud there was a distinct failure to comprehend a distinction between a fact and the interpretation of that fact. This failure is rendered less obvious than it would otherwise be by Freud's excellent command of language and by his skill in presenting his case to its best advantage. But woe betide the reader who tries to separate the facts from the interpretations, in order to discover whether or not the former can in truth be said to give rise in any unequivocal manner to the latter! He will find his task made almost impossible by the skilful way in which Freud has hidden and glossed over important facts, and the brilliant way in which he has highlighted his interpretive account of what may, should, or ought to have happened, but which, as far as one can discover, probably never did happen. As a supreme example of this, the reader is urged to go back to Freud's original writings and reread his 'Analysis of a Phobia in a Five-year-old Boy' – the famous case of little Hans. This has achieved considerable historical importance and has been universally praised by psychoanalysts as the inauguration of all child analyses. Let us have a look at little Hans, who developed a fear of horses after having seen a horse, which was pulling a bus along the street, fall down in front of his eyes. It is noteworthy that Freud only had one short interview with little Hans; all the rest of the material was provided by the father of little Hans, who, we are told, was an ardent follower of Freud. The father, as will be seen by anyone reading through the account, is constantly telling little Hans what he wants him to say, and usually continues until little Hans (who after all was only five years old) gave some kind of consent. When even this produced no results, the father had no hesitation in saying that Hans really meant exactly the opposite of what he actually said, then treating this, in itself, as an established fact. Freud seems to have realized this to some extent and says: 'It is true that during the analysis Hans had to be told many things which he could not say himself, that he had to be presented with thoughts which he had so far shown no signs of possessing and that his attention had to be turned in the direction from which his father was expecting something to come. This detracts from the evidential value of the analysis but the procedure is the same in every case. For a psychoanalysis is not an impartial scientific investigation but a therapeutic measure.' Freud, himself, followed exactly the same procedure as the father because in his interview with the boy he told him 'that he was afraid of his father because he himself nourished jealous and hostile wishes against him'. The boy, his introspections, his sayings and his thoughts, are never really in the picture; what we always get is what either his father or Freud told him he should think or feel on the basis of their particular hypothesis. And whether the child could finally be made to agree or not, the result was always interpreted as being a vindication of the theory. No one who has a scientist's almost instinctive veneration for facts can regard this psychoanalytic classic as anything but a straightforward attempt to fit the child's testimony into the limits of a cut-and-dried theory, previously determined upon; it is difficult to imagine anything little Hans could have said or done that could not in this manner have been transfused into support of the theory. Even so, however, there are glaring cases of inconsistency in the account; thus little Hans was afraid of the 'black things on the horses' mouths and the things in front of their eyes'; Freud claimed that this fear was based on moustaches and eyeglasses, and had been 'directly transposed from his father on to the horses'. In actual fact the child was thinking of the muzzle and the blinkers which had been worn by the horse that fell. Again Freud interpreted the agoraphobic element of Hans's neurosis 'as a means of allowing him to stay at home with his beloved mother'. Nevertheless, both the horse phobia and the general agoraphobia were present even when little Hans went out with his mother!

There is of course a very simple explanation of little Hans and his phobia – his fear of horses is a conditioned fear response acquired on the occasion when he saw the horse fall. Just as in Pavlov's experiments the bell, when paired a number of times with the saliva-producing food, finally gives rise to salivation when presented by itself, so the pairing of the horse with a situation producing fear caused a conditioned connection which persisted – particularly as little Hans had already had two fear-producing experiences with horses. This explanation is parsimonious; it is based on mechanisms of learning well established in the laboratory; it does not require the suppression and even inversion of little Hans's testimony, as does Freud's own account. Nevertheless, most people seem to prefer Freud's story – perhaps because it has all the attraction of one of the tales from Scheherazade. In comparison with such inventive, almost poetic genius science seems prosaic, boring, simple. The fact that these prosaic, boring and simple theories actually produce methods of therapy that work (as we shall see later), whereas Freud's fairy tales do not, does not seem to influence many people; the charm of Freud the story-teller has convinced many people of the truth of the doctrines peddled by Freud the theorist. It hardly needs pointing out that this a *non sequitur*, but will doing so persuade artists of the falsity of the message of a fellow artist?

Let us now turn to the promised attempt to link personality so defined and described to its antecedents, i.e. the biological, innate aspects of temperament.

I have reviewed the evidence in detail in *The Biological Basis of Personality*, and the outcome of the many dozens of investigations which have been done in this field, notably with identical and fraternal twins, brought up together or in isolation from each other, has been quite unanimously that heredity plays a very important, indeed central, part in making each of us occupy his particular position on the two dimensions of extraversion-introversion and emotionality-stability. Numerically the contribution of heredity to these two type-constructs is about the same as that which has been found to characterise intelligence, i.e. about $\frac{3}{4}$; this leaves $\frac{1}{4}$ of the total variance to be accounted for by environmental differences. This generalization of course must be restricted to our own time, to our own type of culture, and it must also be understood to be an average applying to a whole population; the proportion just quoted may not apply to particular individual.

[It] is never meaningful to think of heredity in the abstract, and apart from a particular type of environment. But given these restrictions, there is no doubt that here and now heredity plays an immensely important part in making us what we are. This does not imply any neglect of, or discourtesy to, environmental influences; these have been so overemphasized in the past fifty years that a slight swing of the pendulum seems only reasonable and just. There is no intention on my part of making this swing go too far in the opposite direction; neglect of environmental determinants is as unscientific and as foolish as neglect of heredity.

What then are the structures in our nervous system which underlie the individual differences in extraversion and stability which we observe? Emotionality-stability seems indissolubly linked with the **autonomic** nervous system, which regulates the expression of the emotions, and which in turn is organized and governed by the 'visceral brain'; it is well known, from animal and human studies, that differences in these structures, and in their functioning, are largely determined by heredity, and indeed animal experiments have shown that we can breed rats selectively for high or low emotionality. There seems to be little doubt that we could do the same for humans, if there were no ethical objections. We might characterize that which is inherited as individual differences in the strength of emotional arousal, and the duration of that arousal, consequent upon certain types of stimulation which either genetically or through learning and conditioning produce autonomic reactions. A person who is high on 'emotionality' is not of course necessarily a neurotic, but there is a certain predisposition to neurosis; in the same way a person with brittle bones is not a fracture case, but he is more likely to break his leg, or his arm, than a person with thick, strong bones – provided both encounter the same environmental hazards. Hence the term 'neuroticism'; it refers to the predisposition, and does not imply an actual neurotic breakdown.

The physiological distinction between introverts and extraverts seems to be related to a particular property of the cerebral cortex often referred to as **arousal**. This term came into use first of all when it was discovered that brain waves, as they appear on the electroencephalograph, are more synchronized when the person is drowsy; alert states of mind are characterized by desynchronization. Anatomico-physiologico-neurological structures like the visceral brain and the reticular formation, the strength of whose functioning in responding to environmental stimulation is largely determined by heredity, give rise to stronger or weaker autonomic reactions, and to greater or less arousal; these emotional and arousal reactions, according to their strength, determine the habitual behaviour pattern of the individual – and this habitual behaviour pattern is what we call 'personality' – and measure in detail as extraversion-introversion, or neuroticism-stability.

Most of the time these personality factors are independent of each other, but this is not always so. We are not often in a state of high emotion – fortunately perhaps; in peace time, at least, experiences of paralysing fear or strong anger are relatively rare, and even somewhat milder emotions occupy no more than perhaps five per cent of our time.

Now states of high emotional excitement are the unfortunate rule for people high on neuroticism, and low on stability; they tend to live in a world of constant crisis, eternal anxiety, recurring emotion. These people then suffer not only from constant stimulation of the visceral brain, but through this they are also typically in a state of high arousal. For them the independence of introversion (high arousal) and emotionality (strong visceral reactions) has broken down, and they are chronically dysthymic – highly aroused and highly emotional. It would seem that extraverts and introverts, emotional and stable subjects, would behave quite differently on psychological experiments, and that unless such differences are taken into account, the whole experiment becomes pretty worthless. Such effects are indeed often found, but to predict exactly what might happen calls for some thorough understanding of the psychological theory underlying the phenomena in question. I will give just one example, to make clear what is involved.

Suppose that I ask you to predict whether extraverts or introverts will remember better a series of paired nonsense syllables, like the following: SIP – WOL; VIL – MUF; SEL – PON. The list of seven such pairs is repeated until it is performed perfectly; all 14 syllables are given accurately, by the subject writing down without prompting all 7 stimulus words, and all 7 response words, in the correct pairing. Groups are now formed of extraverts and introverts respectively; some are tested almost immediately, others after one minute, others after five minutes, others yet after 30 minutes, and a last set after 24 hours. Care is taken to prevent rehearsal by giving subjects some other task to do during the waiting periods (except the 24-hour one, of course). Which group would remember the syllables better, the introverts or the extraverts?

At first blush one might say – the introverts, of course. They have the higher degree of arousal, and cortical arousal or alertness must facilitate remembering. True, but incomplete. What actually goes on when we learn something – nonsense syllables or Shakespeare's poetry? Experimental evidence suggests that we have two kinds of memory; at first new material enters into short-term memory, which is envisaged as consisting of reverberating circuits in the brain. These quickly die out, unless transformed into chemical traces, probably the outcome of some form of protein synthesis, and involving ribonucleic acid. This transformation into long-term memory is called consolidation of the memory trace, and there is evidence to suggest that the length and strength of consolidation is a function, among other things, of the degree of cortical arousal present at the time. So far, one would still consider it likely that introverts would do better; there is, however, one more complication. The process of consolidation of the memory trace interferes with reproduction – possibly because the same sets of neurons or cell assemblies are involved, and can only serve one purpose or the other; consequently, while consolidation is still in process, memory will not be available for reproduction (remembering). This means that extraverts (poor arousal, little consolidation) would remember better shortly after learning than introverts (strong arousal, long consolidation) whose neurons would still be busy with consolidation, and therefore not in a state to produce the learned material ready for remembering. Conversely, after a longer period of time extraverts (poor consolidation, little remembering) would be expected to do rather poorly; introverts, whose strong consolidation would have furnished them with a strong memory trace, would be expected to remember particularly well now.

Consider another interesting feature of this experiment. Improvement of performance during a rest pause has been widely studied by psychologists under the heading of 'reminiscence'; yet the outcome of numerous studies of verbal reminiscence has been so varied, some people finding evidence of such improvement, others not, that it became known as the 'now you see it, now you don't' phenomenon. Introverts show a beautiful instance of reminiscence; over a 24-hour period the score almost doubles! Extraverts instead show a beautiful instance of forgetting; over a 24-hour period the score is almost halved! Take both groups together, and the score does not change at all. No wonder 'reminiscence' became so difficult to pin down; results depended entirely on the personality make-up of your group. Include a majority of introverts, and you get it; include a majority of extraverts, and you don't.

Through the concept of personality, we have thus been enabled to trace a path from the physiological to the experimental side; this path leads on of course to the social side. The greater learning potential of the introvert so demonstrated would obviously be expected to influence his success at school and university, and indeed there is much evidence to show that introversion correlates positively with scholastic achievement beyond the primary school. This particular cause is almost certainly not the only one to produce this effect, but it is very likely one of a whole set of different causes.

I have argued that the ease of conditioning which characterises the introvert makes him more vulnerable to neurotic disorders, which may be conceived as conditioned emotional reactions. Similarly, the failure of the extravert to generate quick and strong conditioned responses makes the development of a 'conscience' in him more difficult – conscience in terms of psychological theory being simply the sum of conditioned anxiety reactions to doing things labelled 'wrong' or 'naughty' in childhood and adolescence.

Yet a third link can be made through the concept of preferred level of sensory stimulation. There is a general law in psychology which states that the best-liked level of stimulation is intermediate between sensory deprivation (i.e. too little stimulation) and too strong stimulation, which produces pain. The latter point is obvious; extremely bright lights, extremely loud noises, very heavy pressures all end up by being painful, and hence avoided. Sensory deprivation is a rather more recent field of experimentation, largely due to the need of knowing what might happen to astronauts shut off from many sources of ordinary stimulation. Put crudely, the subject of the experiment is shut up in a room which is soundproofed and dark; he wears padding over his hands and feet, so that he cannot feel anything. Or else he may be submerged under water, breathing through a tube; the water is of skin temperature, so that he can feel nothing whatever. Conditions such as these become unbearable very soon; the absence of stimulation is no more supportable than the presence of unduly strong stimulation – hence the terror of solitary confinement.

How is this linked with personality? Sensory thresholds are linked with cortical arousal – under conditions of high arousal you hear soft sounds, see subdued light, feel light touches more easily than when in a state of low arousal. Hence introverts would be expected to have lower thresholds than extraverts; an expectation amply borne out by many experimental studies. From this we would expect introverts to be more tolerant of sensory deprivation, extraverts to be more tolerant of pain – to the former the slight stimulation provided by the restricted environment is well above the low threshold of their sense organs, but to the latter it is below that threshold, and nothing is felt. Strong sensory stimulation is so far above the threshold of the introvert that pain is felt, when to the more robust extravert the stimulation is only a little above threshold value, and no pain is felt. These deductions have in fact been verified quite a number of times, and thus lend support to this particular chain.

We can go one step farther and argue that as the optimum point of stimulation lies towards stronger sensory stimuli for the extravert, and towards weaker sensory stimuli for the introvert, and as behaviour would normally be directed to establishing an equilibrium at or near the optimum point of balance, so extraverts would be characterised by what has been called 'stimulus hunger', i.e. they would search for and enjoy strong sensory stimulation, whereas introverts would shy away from it and prefer weak stimuli. In one illustrative experiment introverted and extraverted subjects, tested singly, were isolated in a dark room, and instructed to press a key against a spring. First the mean strength of their press was established; then they were 'rewarded' for strong presses by three seconds of loud juke-box music coming on, and bright coloured lights illuminating the scene. If subjects kept pressing strongly, lights and music stayed on; if not, they went off again. As predicted, extraverts started pressing harder and harder, while introverts pressed less and less hard – the former to enjoy the strong sensory stimulation, the latter to get away from it! Thus even the Skinnerian notion of 'reinforcement' is clearly tied to personality; one man's meat is another man's poison.

Wundt called the extraverted person 'changeable'; the evidence certainly supports him there. Extraverts move their homes more frequently, they change their jobs more frequently, they have less 'brand loyalty' – and in addition, they change their sexual partners more frequently (and have divorces more readily). Why is the extravert more changeable? The answer may lie in a kind of behaviour studied in the laboratory under the heading of 'alternation'. Let a rat loose at the bottom of a T-maze, and put pieces of food at the two arms of the T, in such a way that the rat cannot see them when he reaches the top of the stem, and has to move right or left. Suppose he goes right, finds and eats his meat, and is put back again to the starting point. Will he go right or left next time? You might think that having been rewarded for going right, he will go right again, but this is not so; he is more likely to go the other way. In human terms you might say he was driven by 'curiosity' to find out what lay along the other arm of the T which he hadn't explored yet, but such an anthropomorphic term does not help us very much. There is much evidence that any perceptual or motor experience sets up some form of reactive inhibition, i.e. some tendency which works against that type of behaviour being immediately repeated. This inhibition weakens the tendency to go right, and is stronger than the reinforcement which would otherwise pull the rat to the right; consequently the rat goes left. This is the essence of alternation behaviour; its putative cause is some form of reactive inhibition (which can of course be studied in many other situations, suitably quantified, and is no *deus ex machina* to get us out of our difficulties).

There are of course other conflicts, such as approach-approach (you want to buy a hat and a dress, but you have enough money only for one or the other), or avoidance-avoidance (you don't want to do your homework, and you don't want to be punished, but if you don't do the one, you will get the other). But there is no point in entering into these complexities here.

So much then for this very brief account of some of the links which a theory of personality can forge between the two opposite sides of psychology; there do seem to be connections between electrophysiological measures, such as the EEG, on the one hand, and social activities, like criminal acts or neurotic breakdowns, on the other. Such connections would not be intelligible except through the mediation of such hypothetical constructs (or intervening variables) as extraversion-introversion, or emotionality-stability. It is of course not suggested that these are the only such intervening personality variables; undoubtedly there are many others which in due course will be unearthed by patient research. But a beginning must be made somewhere, and beyond any doubt these two dimensions of personality are important and relevant to much that is being done in experimental psychology and in social psychology.

[H]owever important and fundamental the work of the biologist, psychology requires the concept of the intact organism; the notion of 'behaviour' goes beyond segmental analysis and postulates such notions as 'personality'.

Experimental psychologists aim to discover the laws of learning, or of remembering, or of perceiving, without paying heed to the organism which learns, or remembers, or perceives. They attempt to do this by controlling the environment as much as possible, but of course such control is at best only partial. Any experiment on persons, or rats, inevitably brings into the laboratory the person, or the rat; you cannot control or eliminate this disturbing factor. And the person, or the rat, brings into the experimental laboratory a cortex which works at a predetermined level of arousal, an autonomic system which is overtly reactive, or sluggish, or average, and a brain which is efficient, or poor, or mediocre. We have seen how memory works quite differently in extraverts and introverts; you do not get rid of these differences by averaging. We have seen how learning works quite differently in emotional and unemotional people; you do not get rid of these differences by averaging. And we have seen how neurotic and criminal rats differ in their reactions to our laboratory experiment; even with such very simple organisms personality obtrudes to a very marked extent. It would seem to be the course of wisdom to give in and accept the impossibility of eradicating in the laboratory all the myriad individual differences which interfere with our 'perfect' performance on experimental tasks; instead of treating such factors as 'error' we should accept them as fact and study them in their own right. In this way we may hope to learn something about personality, and incidentally gain some measure of experimental control over this recalcitrant thing called 'human nature'. This message seems so obvious, and so reasonable, yet it is more honoured in the breach than the observance.

Social psychologists, too, although they often pay lipservice to the virtues of personality research, do not often include it in their research designs. I have already drawn attention to the marked tendency of psychologists to ask 'general' questions answers to which would presuppose the existence of some universal notion of 'human nature', uniform and unvaried, instead of the markedly heterogeneous and variable article which we see in the market place.

It would be wrong to think that the traffic between personality study and experimental psychology is one way; this is not so. If experimental psychology needs to take into account personality variables, so equally personality theory would be impossible in any realistic sense without the concepts of experimental psychology, physiology, neurology, and even anatomy and genetics and biochemistry. Such notions as arousal were after all introduced by the experimentalists, and no rational predictions in the field of re-membering could be made if we did not have such theories as those regarding consolidation of the memory trace, short-term and long-term memory, and the interference of consolidation with reproduction. In other words, I am not suggesting that in any sense personality theory is superior to, or independent of, experimental psychology; I am suggesting that only by working closely together, and seeking to establish a unified, unitary science can both hope to live up to their pretensions. And similarly, only by drawing on the accumulated knowledge of experimental and personality study can social psychology hope to become a true science and contribute in its turn to the development of general psychology. For here too the traffic is not all one way; people clearly do not live in isolation, and the concept of personality has little meaning outside its social context.

Psychology is the study of behaviour of persons, or it is nothing; personality is at the very root of its subject matter. We must combine the careful, step-by-step, experimental approach of those who work with rats with the far-reaching social interests, the concern with social issues, which characterize those who use the couch; if we link up these fields through modern concepts of personality theory, then psychology may really be said to be 'on its way'.

The self

G.H. MEAD

A child plays at being a mother, at being a teacher, at being a policeman; that is, it is taking different rôles, as we say. When a child does assume a rôle he has in himself the stimuli which call out that particular response or group of responses. He may, of course, run away when he is chased, as the dog does, or he may turn around and strike back just as the dog does in his play. But that is not the same as playing at something. Children get together to 'play Indian.' This means that the child has a certain set of stimuli which call out in itself the responses that they would call out in others, and which answer to an Indian. In the play period the child utilises his own responses to these stimuli which he makes use of in building a self. The response which he has a tendency to make to these stimuli organizes them. He plays that he is, for instance, offering himself something, and he buys it; he gives a letter to himself and takes it away; he addresses himself as a parent, as a teacher; he has a set of stimuli which call out in himself the sort of responses they call out in others. He takes this group of responses and organizes them into a certain whole. Such is the simplest form of being another to one's self. It involves a temporal situation. The child says something in one character and responds in another character, and then his responding in another character is a stimulus to himself in the first character, and so the conversation goes on. A certain organized structure arises in him and in his other which replies to it, and these carry on the conversation of gestures between themselves.

If we contrast play with the situation in an organized game, we note the essential difference that the child who plays in a game must be ready to take the attitude of everyone else involved in that game, and that these different rôles must have a definite relationship to each other.

[W]here a number of individuals are involved, then the child taking one rôle must be ready to take the rôle of everyone else. If he gets in a ball nine he must have the responses of each position involved in his own position. He must know what everyone else is going to do in order to carry out his own play. He has to take all of these rôles. They do not all have to be present in consciousness at the same time, but at some moments he has to have three or four individuals present in his own attitude, such as the one who is going to throw the ball, the one who is going to catch it, and so on. These responses must be, in some degree, present in his own make-up. In the game, then, there is a set of responses of such others so organized that the attitude of one calls out the appropriate attitudes of the other. The child reacts to a certain stimulus; and the reaction is in himself that is called out in others, but he is not a whole self. In his game he has to have an organization

Abridged excerpt reproduced from Mead, G.H. *Mind, Self and Society*, pp. 150–65; published by University of Chicago Press, Chicago, 1934.

of these rôles; otherwise he cannot play the game. The game represents the passage in the life of the child from taking the rôle of others in play to the organized part that is essential to self-consciousness in the full sense of the term.

This organization is put in the form of the rules of the game. Children take a great interest in rules. They make rules on the spot in order to help themselves out of difficulties. Part of the enjoyment of the game is to get these rules. Now, the rules are the set of responses which a particular attitude calls out. You can demand a certain response in others if you take a certain attitude. These responses are all in yourself as well.

The fundamental difference between the game and play is that in the latter the child must have the attitude of all the others involved in that game. The attitudes of the other players which the participant assumes organize into a sort of unit, and it is that organization which controls the response of the individual. The illustration used was of a person playing baseball. Each one of his own acts is determined by his assumption of the action of the others who are playing the game. What he does is controlled by his being everyone else on that team, at least in so far as those attitudes affect his own particular response. We get then an 'other' which is an organization of the attitudes of those involved in the same process.

The organized community or social group which gives to the individual his unity of self may be called 'the generalized other.' The attitude of the generalized other is the attitude of the whole community. Thus, for example, in the case of such a social group as a ball team, the team is the generalized other in so far as it enters – as an organized process or social activity – into the experience of any one of the individual members of it.

If the given human individual is to develop a self in the fullest sense, it is not sufficient for him merely to take the attitudes of other human individuals toward himself and toward one another within the human social process, and to bring that social process as a whole into his individual experience merely in these terms: he must also, in the same way that he takes the attitudes of other individuals toward himself and toward one another, take their attitudes toward the various phases or aspects of the common social activity or set of social undertakings in which, as members of an organized society or social group, they are all engaged; and he must then, by gener-alizing these individual attitudes of that organized society or social group itself, as a whole, act toward different social projects which at any given time it is carrying out, or toward the various larger phases of the general social process which constitutes its life and of which these projects are specific manifestations. This getting of the broad activities of any given social whole or organized society as such within the experiential field of any one of the individuals involved or included in that whole is, in other words, the essential basis and prerequisite of the fullest development of that individual's self: only in so far as he takes the attitudes of the organized social group to which he belongs toward the organized, co-operative social activity or set of such activities in which that group as such is engaged, does he develop a complete self or possess the sort of complete self he has developed. And on the other hand, the complex co-operative processes and activities and institutional functionings of organized human society are also possible only in so far as every individual involved in them or belonging to that society can take the general attitudes of all other such individuals with reference to these processes and activities and institutional functionings, and to the organized social whole of experiential relations and interactions thereby constituted – and can direct his own behavior accordingly.

It is in the form of the generalized other that the social process influences the behavior of the individuals involved in it and carrying it on, i.e., that the community exercises control over the conduct of its individual members; for it is in this form that the social process or community enters as a determining factor into the individual's thinking. In abstract thought the individual takes the attitude of the generalized other toward himself, without reference to its expression in any particular other individuals; and in concrete thought he takes that attitude in so far as it is expressed in the attitudes toward his behavior of those other individuals with whom he is involved in the given social situation or act. But only by taking the attitude of the generalized other toward himself, in one or another of these ways, can he think at all; for only thus can thinking – or the internalized conversation of gestures which constitutes thinking – occur. And only through the taking by individuals of the attitude or attitudes of the generalized other toward themselves is the existence of a universe of discourse, as that system of common or social meanings which thinking presupposes at its context, rendered possible.

The self-conscious human individual, then, takes or assumes the organized social attitudes of the given social group or community (or of some one section thereof) to which he belongs, toward the social problems of various kinds which confront that group or community at any given time, and which arise in connection with the correspondingly different social projects or organized co-operative enterprises in which that group or community as uch is engaged; and as an individual participant in these social projects or co-operative enterprises, he governs his own conduct accordingly. In politics, for example, the individual identifies himself with an entire political party and takes the organized attitudes of that entire party toward the rest of the given social community and toward the problems which confront the party within the given social situation; and he consequently reacts or responds in terms of the organized attitudes of the party as a whole. He thus enters into a special set of social relations with all the other individuals who belong to that political party; and in the same way he enters into various other special sets of social relations, with various other classes of individuals respectively, the individuals of each of these classes being the other members of some one of the particular organized subgroups (determined in socially functional terms) of which he himself is a member within the entire given society or social community.

In the most highly developed, organized, and complicated human social communities – those evolved by civilized man – these various socially functional classes or subgroups of individuals to which any given individual belongs (and with the other individual members of which he thus enters into a special set of social relations) are of two kinds. Some of them are concrete social classes or subgroups, such as political parties, clubs, corporations, which are all actually functional social units, in terms of which their individual members are directly related to one another. The others are abstract social classes or subgroups, such as the class of debtors and the class of creditors, in terms of which their individual members are related to one another only more or less indirectly, and which only more or less indirectly function as social units, but which afford or represent unlimited possibilities for the widening and ramifying and enriching of the social relations among all the individual members of the given society as an organized and unified whole. The given individual's membership in several of these abstract social classes or subgroups makes possible his entrance into definite social relations (however indirect) with an almost infinite number of other individuals who also belong to or are included within one or another of these abstract social classes or subgroups cutting across functional lines of demarcation which divide different human social communities from one another, and including individual members from several (in some cases from all) such communities.

I have pointed out, then, that there are two general stages in the full development of the self. At the first of these stages, the individual's self is constituted simply by an organization of the particular attitudes of other individuals toward himself and toward one another in the specific social acts in which he participates with them. But at the second stage in the full development of the individual's self that self is constituted not only by an organization of these particular individual attitudes, but also by an organization of the social attitudes of the generalized other or the social group as a whole to which he belongs. These social or group attitudes are brought within the individual's field of direct experience, and are included as elements in the structure or constitution of his self, in the same way that the attitudes of particular other individuals are; and the individual arrives at them, or succeeds in taking them, by means of further organizing, and then generalizing, the attitudes of particular other individuals in terms of their organized social bearings and implications. So the self reaches its full development by organizing these individual attitudes of others into the organized social or group attitudes, and by thus becoming an individual reflection of the general systematic pattern of social or group behavior in which it and the others are all involved – a pattern which enters as a whole into the individual's experience in terms of these organized group attitudes which, through the mechanism of his central nervous system, he takes toward himself, just as he takes the individual attitudes of others.

The game has a logic, so that such an organization of the self is rendered possible: there is a definite end to be obtained; the actions of the different individuals are all related to each other with reference to that end so that they do not conflict; one is not in conflict with himself in the attitude of another man on the team. If one has the attitude of the person throwing the ball he can also have the response of catching the ball. The two are related so that they further the purpose of the game itself. They are interrelated in a unitary, organic fashion. There is a definite unity, then, which is introduced into the organization of other selves when we reach such a stage as that of the game, as over against the situation of play where there is a simple succession of one rôle after another, a situation which is, of course, characteristic of the child's own personality. The child is one thing at one time and another at another, and what he is at one moment does not determine what he is at another. That is both the charm of childhood as well as its inadequacy. You cannot count on the child; you cannot assume that all the things he does are going to determine what he will do at any moment. He is not organized into a whole. The child has no definite character, no definite personality.

The game is then an illustration of the situation out of which an organized personality arises. In so far as the child does take the attitude of the other and allows that attitude of the other to determine the thing he is going to do with reference to a common end, he is becoming an organic member of society. He is taking over the morale of that society and is becoming an essential member of it. He belongs to it in so far as he does allow the attitude of the other that he takes to control his own immediate expression. What is involved here is some sort of an organized process. That which is expressed in terms of the game is, of course, being continually expressed in the social life of the child, but this wider process goes beyond the immediate experience of the child himself. The importance of the game is that it lies entirely inside of the child's own experience, and the importance of our modern type of education is that it is brought as far as possible within this realm. The different attitudes that a child assumes are so organized that they exercise a definite control over his response, as the attitudes in a game control his own immediate response. In the game we get an organized other, a generalized other, which is found in the nature of the child itself, and finds its expression in the immediate experience of the child. And it is that organized activity in the child's own nature controlling the particular response which gives unity, and which builds up his own self.

What goes on in the game goes on in the life of the child all the time. He is continually taking the attitudes of those about him, especially the rôles of those who in some sense control him and on whom he depends. He gets the function of the process in an abstract sort of a way at first. It goes over from the play into the game in a real sense. He has to play the game. The morale of the game takes hold of the child more than the larger morale of the whole community. The child passes into the game and the game expresses a social situation in which he can completely enter; its morale may have a greater hold on him than that of the family to which he belongs or the community in which he lives. There are all sorts of social organizations, some of which are fairly lasting, some temporary, into which the child is entering, and he is playing a sort of social game in them. It is a period in which he likes 'to belong,' and he gets into organizations which come into existence and pass out of existence. He becomes a something which can function in the organized whole, and thus tends to determine himself in his relationship with the group to which he belongs. That process is one which is a striking stage in the development of the child's morale. It constitutes him a self-conscious member of the community to which he belongs.

Such is the process by which a personality arises. I have spoken of this as a process in which a child takes the rôle of the other, and said that it takes place essentially through the use of language. Language is predominantly based on the vocal gesture by means of which co-operative activities in a community are carried out. Language in its significant sense is that vocal gesture which tends to arouse in the individual the attitude which it arouses in others, and it is this perfecting of the self by the gesture which mediates the social activities that gives rise to the process of taking the rôle of the other. The latter phrase is a little unfortunate because it suggests an actor's attitude which is actually more sophisticated than that which is involved in our own experience. To this degree it does not correctly describe that which I have in mind. We see that process most definitely in a primitive form in those situations where the child's play takes different rôles. Here the very fact that he is ready to pay out money, for instance, arouses the attitude of the person who receives money; the very process is calling out in him the corresponding activities of the other person involved. The individual stimulates himself to the response which he is calling out in the other person, and then acts in some degree in response to that situation. In play the child does definitely act out the rôle which he himself has aroused in himself. It is that which gives, as I have said, a definite content in the individual which answers to the stimulus that affects him as it affects somebody else. The content of the other that enters into one personality is the response in the individual which his gesture calls out in the other.

We may illustrate our basic concept by a reference to the notion of property. If we say 'This is my property, I shall control it,' that affirmation calls out a certain set of responses which must be the same in any community in which property exists. It involves an organized attitude with reference to property which is common to all the members of the community. One must have a definite attitude of control of his own property and respect for the property of others. Those attitudes (as organized sets of responses) must be there on the part of all, so that when one says such a thing he calls out in himself the response of the others. He is calling out the response of what I have called a generalized other. That which makes society possible is such common responses, such organized attitudes, with reference to what we term property, the cults of religion, the process of education, and the relations of the family. Of course, the wider the society the more definitely universal these objects must be. In any case there must be a definite set of responses, which we may speak of as abstract, and which can belong to a very large group. Property is in itself a very abstract concept. It is that which the individual himself can control and nobody else can control. The attitude is different from that of a dog toward a bone. A dog will fight any other dog trying to take the bone. The dog is not taking the attitude of the other dog. A man who says 'This is my property' is taking an attitude of the other person. The man is appealing to his rights because he is able to take the attitude which everybody else in the group has with reference to property, thus arousing in himself the attitude of others.

What goes to make up the organized self is the organization of the attitudes which are common to the group. A person is a personality because he belongs to a community, because he takes over the institutions of that community into his own conduct. He takes its language as a medium by which he gets his personality, and then through a process of taking the different rôles that all the others furnish he comes to get the attitude of the members of the community. Such, in a certain sense, is the structure of a man's personality. There are certain common responses which each individual has toward certain common things, and in so far as those common responses are awakened in the individual when he is affecting other persons he arouses his own self. The structure, then, on which the self is built is this response which is common to all, for one has to be a member of a community to be a self. Such responses are abstract attitudes, but they constitute just what we term a man's character. They give him what we term his principles, the acknowledged attitudes of all members of the community toward what are the values of that community. He is putting himself in the place of the generalized other, which represents the organized responses of all the members of the group. It is that which guides conduct controlled by principles, and a person who has such an organized group of responses is a man whom we say has character, in the moral sense.

It is a structure of attitudes, then, which goes to make up a self, as distinct from a group of habits. We all of us have, for example, certain groups of habits, such as the particular intonations which a person uses in his speech. This is a set of habits of vocal expression which one has but which one does not know about. The sets of habits which we have of that sort mean nothing to us; we do not hear the intonations of our speech that others hear unless we are paying particular attention to them. The habits of emotional expression which belong to our speech are of the same sort. We may know that we have expressed ourselves in a joyous fashion but the detailed process is one which does not come back to our conscious selves. There are whole bundles of such habits which do not enter into a conscious self, but which help to make up what is termed the unconscious self.

After all, what we mean by self-consciousness is an awakening in ourselves of the group of attitudes which we are arousing in others, especially when it is an important set of responses which go to make up the members of the community. It is unfortunate to fuse or mix up consciousness, as we ordinarily use that term, and self-consciousness. Consciousness, as frequently used, simply has reference to the field of experience, but self-consciousness refers to the ability to call out in ourselves a set of definite responses which belong to the others of the group. Consciousness and self-consciousness are not on the same level. A man alone has, fortunately or unfortunately, access to his own toothache, but that is not what we mean by self-consciousness.

I have so far emphasized what I have called the structures upon which the self is constructed, the framework of the self, as it were. Of course we are not only what is common to all: each one of the selves is different from everyone else; but there has to be such a common structure as I have sketched in order that we may be members of a community at all. We cannot be ourselves unless we are also members in whom there is a community of attitudes which control the attitudes of all. We cannot have rights unless we have common attitudes. That which we have acquired as self-conscious persons makes us such members of society and gives us selves. Selves can only exist in definite relationships to other selves. No hard-and-fast line can be drawn between our own selves and the selves of others, since our own selves exist and enter as such into our experience only in so far as the selves of others exist and enter as such into our experience also. The individual possesses a self only in relation to the selves of the other members of his social group; and the structure of his self expresses or reflects the general behavior pattern of this social group to which he belongs, just as does the structure of the self of every other individual belonging to this social group.

The essence of the self lies in the internalised conversation of gestures which constitutes thinking, [a]nd hence, the origin and foundations of the self, like those of thinking, are social.

A theory of human motivation

A.H. MASLOW

The basic needs

The 'physiological' needs

The needs that are usually taken as the starting point for motivation theory are the so-called physiological drives. Two recent lines of research make it necessary to revise our customary notions about these needs, first, the development of the concept of homeostasis, and second, the finding that appetites (preferential choices among foods) are a fairly efficient indication of actual needs or lacks in the body.

Homeostasis refers to the body's automatic efforts to maintain a constant, normal state of the blood stream. Cannon (2) has described this process for (1) the water content of the blood, (2) salt content, (3) sugar content, (4)

Abridged excerpt reproduced from Maslow, A.H. (1943) A Theory of Human Motivation. *Psychological Review*, **50**, 372–96.

protein content, (5) fat content, (6) calcium content, (7) oxygen content, (8) constant hydrogen-ion level (acid-base balance) and (9) constant temperature of the blood. Obviously this list can be extended to include other minerals, the hormones, vitamins, etc.

Young (21) has summarized the work on appetite in its relation to body needs. If the body lacks some chemical, the individual will tend to develop a specific appetite or partial hunger for that food element.

Thus it seems impossible as well as useless to make any list of fundamental physiological needs for they can come to almost any number one might wish, depending on the degree of specificity of description. We can not identify all physiological needs as homeostatic. That sexual desire, sleepiness, sheer activity and maternal behavior in animals, are homeostatic, has not yet been demonstrated. Furthermore, this list would not include the various sensory pleasures (tastes, smells, tickling, stroking) which are probably physiological and which may become the goals of motivated behavior.

In a previous paper (13) it has been pointed out that these physiological drives or needs are to be considered unusual rather than typical because they are isolable, and because they are localizable somatically. That is to say, they are relatively independent of each other, of other motivations and of the organism as a whole, and secondly, in many cases, it is possible to demonstrate a localized, underlying somatic base for the drive. This is true less generally than has been thought (exceptions are fatigue, sleepiness, maternal responses) but it is still true in the classic instances of hunger, sex, and thirst.

It should be pointed out again that any of the physiological needs and the consummatory behavior involved with them serve as channels for all sorts of other needs as well. That is to say, the person who thinks he is hungry may actually be seeking more for comfort, or dependence, than for vitamins or proteins. Conversely, it is possible to satisfy the hunger need in part by other activities such as drinking water or smoking cigarettes. In other words, relatively isolable as these physiological needs are, they are not completely so.

Undoubtedly these physiological needs are the most prepotent of all needs. What this means specifically is, that in the human being who is missing everything in life in an extreme fashion, it is most likely that the major motivation would be the physiological needs rather than any others. A person who is lacking food, safety, love, and esteem would most probably hunger for food more strongly than for anything else.

If all the needs are unsatisfied, and the organism is then dominated by the physiological needs, all other needs may become simply non-existent or be pushed into the background. It is then fair to characterize the whole organism by saying simply that it is hungry, for consciousness is almost completely preempted by hunger. All capacities are put into the service of hunger-satisfaction, and the organization of these capacities is almost entirely determined by the one purpose of satisfying hunger. The receptors and effectors, the intelligence, memory, habits, all may now be defined simply as hunger-gratifying tools. Capacities that are not useful for this purpose lie dormant, or are pushed into the background. The urge to write poetry, the desire to acquire an automobile, the interest in American history, the desire for a new pair of shoes are, in the extreme case, forgotten or become of secondary importance. For the man who is extremely and dangerously hungry, no other interests exist but food. He dreams food, he remembers food, he thinks about food, he emotes only about food, he perceives only food and he wants only food. The more subtle determinants that ordinarily fuse with the physiological drives in organizing even feeding, drinking or sexual behavior, may now be so completely overwhelmed as to allow us to speak at this time (but **only** at this time) of pure hunger drive and behavior, with the one unqualified aim of relief.

Another peculiar characteristic of the human organism when it is dominated by a certain need is that the whole philosophy of the future tends also to change. For our chronically and extremely hungry man, Utopia can be defined very simply as a place where there is plenty of food. He tends to think that, if only he is guaranteed food for the rest of his life, he will be perfectly happy and will never want anything more. Life itself tends to be defined in terms of eating. Anything else will be defined as unimportant. Freedom, love, community feeling, respect, philosophy, may all be waved aside as fripperies which are useless since they fail to fill the stomach. Such a man may fairly be said to live by bread alone.

It cannot possibly be denied that such things are true but their **generality** can be denied. Emergency conditions are, almost by definition, rare in the normally functioning peaceful society. That this truism can be forgotten is due mainly to two reasons. First, rats have few motivations other than physiological ones, and since so much of the research upon motivation has been made with these animals, it is easy to carry the rat-picture over to the human being. Secondly, it is too often not realized that culture itself is an adaptive tool, one of whose main functions is to make the physiological emergencies come less and less often. In most of the known societies, chronic extreme hunger of the emergency type is rare, rather than common. In any case, this is still true in the United States. The average American citizen is experiencing appetite rather than hunger when he says 'I am hungry.' He is apt to experience sheer life-and-death hunger only by accident and then only a few times through his entire life.

Obviously a good way to obscure the 'higher' motivations, and to get a lopsided view of human capacities and human nature, is to make the organism extremely and chronically hungry or thirsty. Anyone who attempts to make an emergency picture into a typical one, and who will measure all of man's goals and desires by his behavior during extreme physiological deprivation is certainly being blind to many things. It is quite true that man lives by bread alone – when there is no bread. But what happens to man's desires when there is plenty of bread and when his belly is chronically filled?

At once other (and 'higher') needs emerge and these, rather than physiological hungers, dominate the organism. And when these in turn are satisfied, again new (and still 'higher') needs emerge and so on. This is what we mean by saying that the basic human needs are organized into a hierarchy of relative prepotency.

One main implication of this phrasing is that gratification becomes as important a concept as deprivation in motivation theory, for it releases the organism from the domination of a relatively more physiological need, permitting thereby the emergence of other more social goals. The physiological needs, along with their partial goals, when chronically gratified cease to exist as active determinants or organizers of behavior. They now exist only in a potential fashion in the sense that they may emerge again to dominate the organism if they are thwarted. But a want that is satisfied is no longer a want. The organism is dominated and its behavior organized only by unsatisfied needs. If hunger is satisfied, it becomes unimportant in the current dynamics of the individual.

This statement is somewhat qualified by a hypothesis to be discussed more fully later, namely that it is precisely those individuals in whom a certain need has always been satisfied who are best equipped to tolerate deprivation of that need in the future, and that furthermore, those who have been deprived in the past will react differently to current satisfactions than the one who has never been deprived.

The safety needs

If the physiological needs are relatively well gratified, there then emerges a new set of needs, which we may categorize roughly as the safety needs. All that has been said of the physiological needs is equally true, although in lesser degree, of these desires. The organism may equally well be wholly dominated by them. They may serve as the almost exclusive organizers of behavior, recruiting all the capacities of the organism in their service, and we may then fairly describe the whole organism as a safety-seeking mechanism. Again we may say of the receptors, the effectors, of the intellect and the other capacities that they are primarily safety-seeking tools. Again, as in the hungry man, we find that the dominating goal is a strong determinant not only of his current world-outlook and philosophy but also of his philosophy of the future. Practically everything looks less important than safety, (even sometimes the physiological needs which being satisfied, are now underestimated). A man, in this state, if it is extreme enough and chronic enough, may be characterized as living almost for safety alone.

Although in this paper we are interested primarily in the needs of the adult, we can approach an understanding of his safety needs perhaps more efficiently by observation of infants and children, in whom these needs are much more simple and obvious. One reason for the clearer appearance of the threat or danger reaction in infants, is that they do not inhibit this reaction at all, whereas adults in our society have been taught to inhibit it at all costs. Thus even when adults do feel their safety to be threatened we may not be able to see this on the surface. Infants will react in a total fashion and as if they were endangered, if they are disturbed or dropped suddenly, startled by loud noises, flashing light, or other unusual sensory stimulation, by rough handling, by general loss of support in the mother's arms, or by inadequate support.

In infants we can also see a much more direct reaction to bodily illnesses of various kinds. Sometimes these illnesses seem to be immediately and *per se* threatening and seem to make the child feel unsafe. For instance, vomiting, colic or other sharp pains seem to make the child look at the whole world in a different way. At such a moment of pain, it may be postulated that, for the child, the appearance of the whole world suddenly changes from sunniness to darkness, so to speak, and becomes a place in which anything at all might happen, in which previously stable things have suddenly become unstable. Thus a child who because of some bad food is taken ill may, for a day or two, develop fear, nightmares, and a need for protection and reassurance never seen in him before his illness.

Another indication of the child's need for safety is his preference for some kind of undisrupted routine or rhythm. He seems to want a predictable, orderly world. For instance, injustice, unfairness, or inconsistency in the parents seems to make a child feel anxious and unsafe. This attitude may be not so much because of the injustice *per se* or any particular pains involved, but rather because this treatment threatens to make the world look unreliable, or unsafe, or unpredictable. Young children seem to thrive better under a system which has at least a skeletal outline of rigidity, in which there is a schedule of a kind, some sort of routine, something that can be counted upon, not only for the present but also far into the future. Perhaps one could express this more accurately by saying that the child needs an organized world rather than an unorganized or unstructured one.

The central role of the parents and the normal family setup are indisputable. Quarreling, physical assault, separation, divorce or death within the family may be particularly terrifying. Also parental outbursts of rage or threats of punishment directed to the child, calling him names, speaking to him harshly, shaking him, handling him roughly, or actual physical punishment sometimes elicit such total panic and terror in the child that we must assume more is involved than the physical pain alone. While it is true that in some children this terror may represent also a fear of loss of parental love, it can also occur in completely rejected children, who seem to cling to the hating parents more for sheer safety and protection than because of hope of love.

Confronting the average child with new, unfamiliar, strange, unmanageable stimuli or situations will too frequently elicit the danger or terror reaction, as for example, getting lost or even being separated from the parents for a short time, being confronted with new faces, new situations or new tasks, the sight of strange, unfamiliar or uncontrollable objects, illness or death. Particularly at such times, the child's frantic clinging to his parents is eloquent testimony to their role as protectors (quite apart from their roles as food-givers and love-givers).

From these and similar observations, we may generalize and say that the average child in our society generally prefers a safe, orderly, predictable, organized world, which he can count on, and in which unexpected, unmanageable or other dangerous things do not happen, and in which, in any case, he has all-powerful parents who protect and shield him from harm.

That these reactions may so easily be observed in children is in a way a proof of the fact that children in our society feel too unsafe (or, in a word, are badly brought up). Children who are reared in an unthreatening, loving family do not ordinarily react as we have described above. In such children the danger reactions are apt to come mostly to objects or situations that adults too would consider dangerous.

The healthy, normal, fortunate adult in our culture is largely satisfied in his safety needs. The peaceful, smoothly running, 'good' society ordinarily makes its members feel safe enough from wild animals, extremes of temperature, criminals, assault and murder, tyranny, etc. Therefore, in a very real sense, he no longer has any safety needs as active motivators. Just as a sated man no longer feels hungry, a safe man no longer feels endangered. If we wish to see these needs directly and clearly we must turn to neurotic or near-neurotic individuals, and to the economic and social underdogs. In between these extremes, we can perceive the expressions of safety needs only in such phenomena as, for instance, the common preference for a job with tenure and protection, the desire for a savings account, and for insurance of various kinds (medical, dental, unemployment, disability, old age).

Other broader aspects of the attempt to seek safety and stability in the world are seen in the very common preference for familiar rather than unfamiliar things, or for the known rather than the unknown. The tendency to have some religion or world-philosophy that organizes the universe and the men in it into some sort of satisfactorily coherent, meaningful whole is also in part motivated by safety-seeking. Here too we may list science and philosophy in general as partially motivated by the safety needs (we shall see later that there are also other motivations to scientific, philosophical or religious endeavor).

Otherwise the need for safety is seen as an active and dominant mobiliser of the organism's resources only in emergencies, e.g., war, disease, natural catastrophes, crime waves, societal disorganization, neurosis, brain injury, chronically bad situation.

Some neurotic adults in our society are, in many ways, like the unsafe child in their desire for safety, although in the former it takes on a somewhat special appearance. Their reaction is often to unknown, psychological dangers in a world that is perceived to be hostile, overwhelming and threatening. Such a person behaves as if a great catastrophe were almost always impending, i.e., he is usually responding as if to an emergency. His safety needs often find specific expression in a search for a protector, or a stronger person on whom he may depend, or perhaps, a Fuehrer.

The neurotic individual may be described in a slightly different way with some usefulness as a grown-up person who retains his childish attitudes toward the world. That is to say, a neurotic adult may be said to behave 'as if' he were actually afraid of a spanking, or of his mother's disapproval, or of being abandoned by his parents, or having his food taken away from him. It is as if his childish attitudes of fear and threat reaction to a dangerous world had gone underground, and untouched by the growing up and learning processes, were now ready to be called out by any stimulus that would make a child feel endangered and threatened.

The neurosis in which the search for safety takes its clearest form is in the compulsive-obsessive neurosis. Compulsive-obsessives try frantically to order and stabilize the world so that no unmanageable, unexpected or unfamiliar dangers will ever appear. They hedge themselves about with all sorts of ceremonials, rules and formulas so that every possible contingency may be provided for and so that no new contingencies may appear. They are much like the brain injured cases, described by Goldstein, who manage to maintain their equilibrium by avoiding everything unfamiliar and strange and by ordering their restricted world in such a neat, disciplined, orderly fashion that everything in the world can be counted upon. They try to arrange the world so that anything unexpected (dangers) cannot possibly occur. If, through no fault of their own, something unexpected does occur, they go into a panic reaction as if this unexpected occurrence consituted a grave danger. What we can see only as a none-too-strong preference in the healthy person, e.g., preference for the familiar, becomes a life-and-death necessity in abnormal cases.

The love needs

If both the physiological and the safety needs are fairly well gratified, then there will emerge the love and affection and belongingness needs, and the whole cycle already described will repeat itself with this new center. Now the person will feel keenly, as never before, the absence of friends, or a sweetheart, or a wife, or children. He will hunger for affectionate relations with people in general namely, for a place in his group, and he will strive with great intensity to achieve this goal. He will want to attain such a place more than anything else in the world and may even forget that once, when he was hungry, he sneered at love.

In our society the thwarting of these needs is the most commonly found core in cases of maladjustment and more severe psychopathology. Love and affection, as well as their possible expression in sexuality, are generally looked upon with ambivalence and are customarily hedged about with many restrictions and inhibitions. Practically all theorists of psychopathology have stressed thwarting of the love needs as basic in the picture of maladjustment. Many clinical studies have therefore been made of this need and we know more about it perhaps than any of the other needs except the physiological ones.

One thing that must be stressed at this point is that love is not synonymous with sex. Sex may be studied as a purely physiological need. Ordinarily sexual behavior is multi-determined, that is to say, determined not only by sexual but also by other needs, chief among which are the love and affection needs. Also not to be overlooked is the fact that the love needs involve both giving and receiving love.

The esteem needs

All people in our society (with a few pathological exceptions) have a need or desire for a stable, firmly based, (usually) high evaluation of themselves, for self-respect, or self-esteem, and for the esteem of others. By firmly based self-esteem, we mean that which is soundly based upon real capacity, achievement and respect from others. These needs may be classified into two subsidiary sets. These are, first, the desire for strength, for achievement, for adequacy, for confidence in the face of the world, and for independence and freedom. Secondly, we have what we may call the desire for reputation or prestige (defining it as respect or esteem from other people), recognition, attention, importance or appreciation. These needs have been relatively stressed by Alfred Adler and his followers, and have been relatively neglected by Freud and the psychoanalysts. More and more today however there is appearing widespread appreciation of their central importance.

Satisfaction of the self-esteem need leads to feelings of self-confidence, worth, strength, capability and adequacy of being useful and necessary in the world. But thwarting of these needs produces feelings of inferiority, of weakness and of helplessness. These feelings in turn give rise to either basic discouragement or else compensatory or neurotic trends. An appreciation of the necessity of basic self-confidence and an understanding of how helpless people are without it, can be easily gained from a study of severe traumatic neurosis.

The need for self-actualization

Even if all these needs are satisfied, we may still often (if not always) expect that a new discontent and restlessness will soon develop, unless the individual is doing what he is fitted for. A musician must make music, an artist must paint, a poet must write, if he is to be ultimately happy. What a man **can** be, he **must** be. This need we may call self-actualization.

This term, first coined by Kurt Goldstein, is being used in this paper in a much more specific and limited fashion. It refers to the desire for self-fulfillment, namely, to the tendency for him to become actualized in what he is potentially. This tendency might be phrased as the desire to become more and more what one is, to become everything that one is capable of becoming.

The specific form that these needs will take will of course vary greatly from person to person. In one individual it may take the form of the desire to be an ideal mother, in another it may be expressed athletically, and in still another it may be expressed in painting pictures or in inventions. It is not necessarily a creative urge although in people who have any capacities for creation it will take this form.

The clear emergence of these needs rests upon prior satisfaction of the physiological, safety, love and esteem needs. We shall call people who are satisfied in these needs, basically satisfied people, and it is from these that we may expect the fullest (and healthiest) creativeness. Since, in our society, basically satisfied people are the exception, we do not know much about self-actualization, either experimentally or clinically. It remains a challenging problem for research.

The preconditions for the basic need satisfactions

There are certain conditions which are immediate prerequisites for the basic need satisfactions. Danger to these is reacted to almost as if it were a direct danger to the basic needs themselves. Such conditions as freedom to speak, freedom to do what one wishes so long as no harm is done to others, freedom to express one's self, freedom to investigate and seek for information, freedom to defend one's self, justice, fairness, honesty, orderliness in the group are examples of such preconditions for basic need satisfactions. Thwarting of these freedoms will be reacted to with a threat or emergency response. These conditions are not ends in themselves but they are **almost** so since they are so closely related to the basic needs, which are apparently the only ends in themselves. These conditions are defended because without them the basic satisfactions are quite impossible, or at least, very severely endangered.

If we remember that the cognitive capacities (perceptual, intellectual, learning) are a set of adjustive tools, which have, among other functions, that of satisfaction of our basic needs, then it is clear that any danger to them, any deprivation or blocking of their free use, must also be indirectly threatening to the basic needs themselves. Such a statement is a partial solution of the general problems of curiosity, the search for knowledge, truth and wisdom, and the ever-persistent urge to solve the cosmic mysteries.

We must therefore introduce another hypothesis and speak of degrees of closeness to the basic needs, for we have already pointed out that **any** conscious desires (partial goals) are more or less important as they are more or less close to the basic needs. The same statement may be made for various behavior acts. An act is psychologically important if it contributes directly to satisfaction of basic needs. The less directly it so contributes, or the weaker this contribution is, the less important this act must be conceived to be from the point of view of dynamic psychology. A similar statement may be made for the various defense or coping mechanisms. Some are very directly related to the protection or attainment of the basic needs, others are only weakly and distantly related. Indeed if we wished, we could speak of more basic and less basic defense mechanisms, and then affirm that danger to the more basic defenses is more threatening than danger to less basic defenses (always remembering that this is so only because of their relationship to the basic needs).

The desires to know and to understand

So far, we have mentioned the cognitive needs only in passing. Acquiring knowledge and systematizing the universe have been considered as, in part, techniques for the achievement of basic safety in the world, or, for the intelligent man, expressions of self-actualization. Also freedom of inquiry and expression have been discussed as preconditions of satisfactions of the basic needs. True though these formulations may be, they do not constitute definitive answers to the question as to the motivation role of curiosity, learning, philosophising, experimenting, etc. They are, at best, no more than partial answers.

This question is especially difficult because we know so little about the facts. Curiosity, exploration, desire for the facts, desire to know may certainly be observed easily enough. The fact that they often are pursued even at great cost to the individual's safety is an example of the partial character of our previous discussion. In addition, the writer must admit that, though he has sufficient clinical evidence to postulate the desire to know as a very strong drive in intelligent people, no data are available for unintelligent people. It may then be largely a function of relatively high intelligence. Rather tentatively, then, and largely in the hope of stimulating discussion and research, we shall postulate a basic desire to know, to be aware of reality, to get the facts, to satisfy curiosity, or as Wertheimer phrases it, to see rather than to be blind.

This postulation, however, is not enough. Even after we know, we are impelled to know more and more minutely and microscopically on the one hand, and on the other, more and more extensively in the direction of a world philosophy, religion, etc. The facts that we acquire, if they are isolated or atomistic, inevitably get theorized about, and either analyzed or organized or both. This process has been phrased by some as the search for 'meaning.' We shall then postulate a desire to understand, to systematize, to organize, to analyze, to look for relations and meanings.

Once these desires are accepted for discussion, we see that they too form themselves into a small hierarchy in which the desire to know is prepotent over the desire to understand. All the characteristics of a hierarchy of prepotency that we have described above, seem to hold for this one as well.

We must guard ourselves against the too easy tendency to separate these desires from the basic needs we have discussed above, i.e., to make a sharp dichotomy between 'cognitive' and 'conative' needs. The desire to know and to understand are themselves conative, i.e., have a striving character, and are as much personality needs as the 'basic needs' we have already discussed.

Further characteristics of the basic needs

The degree of fixity of the hierarchy of basic needs

We have spoken so far as if this hierarchy were a fixed order but actually it is not nearly as rigid as we may have implied. It is true that most of the people with whom we have worked have seemed to have these basic needs in about the order that has been indicated. However, there have been a number of exceptions.

1. There are some people in whom, for instance, self-esteem seems to be more important than love. This most common reversal in the hierarchy is usually due to the development of the notion that the person who is most likely to be loved is a strong or powerful person, one who inspires respect or fear, and who is self confident or aggressive. Therefore such people who lack love and seek it, may try hard to put on a front of aggressive, confident behavior. But essentially they seek high self-esteem and its behavior expressions more as a means-to-an-end than for its own sake; they seek self-assertion for the sake of love rather than for self-esteem itself.
2. There are other, apparently innately creative people in whom the drive to creativeness seems to be more important than any other counter-determinant. Their creativeness might appear not as self-actualization released by basic satisfaction, but in spite of lack of basic satisfaction.
3. In certain people the level of aspiration may be permanently deadened or lowered. That is to say, the less prepotent goals may simply be lost, and may disappear forever, so that the person who has experienced life at a very low level, i.e. chronic unemployment, may continue to be satisfied for the rest of his life if only he can get enough food.
4. The so-called 'psychopathic personality' is another example of permanent loss of the love needs. These are people who, according to the best data available, have been starved for love in the earliest months of their lives and have simply lost forever the desire and the ability to give and to receive affection (as animals lose sucking or pecking reflexes that are not exercised soon enough after birth).
5. Another cause of reversal of the hierarchy is that when a need has been satisfied for a long time, this need may be underevaluated. People who have never experienced chronic hunger are apt to underestimate its effects and to look upon food as a rather unimportant thing. If they are dominated by a higher need, this higher need will seem to be the most important of all. It then becomes possible, and indeed does actually happen, that they may, for the sake of this higher need, put themselves into the position of being deprived in a more basic need. We may expect that after a long-time deprivation of the more basic need there will be a tendency to reevaluate both needs so that the more prepotent need will actually become consciously prepotent for the individual who may have given it up very lightly. Thus, a man who has given up his job rather than

lose his self-respect, and who then starves for six months or so, may be willing to take his job back even at the price of losing his self-respect.

6. Another partial explanation of **apparent** reversals is seen in the fact that we have been talking about the hierarchy of prepotency in terms of consciously felt wants or desires rather than of behavior. Looking at behavior itself may give us the wrong impression. What we have claimed is that the person will **want** the more basic of two needs when deprived in both. There is no necessary implication here that he will act upon his desires. Let us say again that there are many determinants of behavior other than the needs and desires.

7. Perhaps more important than all these exceptions are the ones that involve ideals, high social standards, high values and the like. With such values people become martyrs; they will give up everything for the sake of a particular ideal, or value. These people may be understood, at least in part, by reference to one basic concept (or hypothesis) which may be called 'increased frustration-tolerance through early gratification.' People who have been satisfied in their basic needs throughout their lives, particularly in their earlier years, seem to develop exceptional power to withstand present or future thwarting of these needs simply because they have strong, healthy character structure as a result of basic satisfaction. They are the 'strong' people who can easily weather disagreement or opposition, who can swim against the stream of public opinion and who can stand up for the truth at great personal cost. It is just the ones who have loved and been well loved, and who have had many deep friendships who can hold out against hatred, rejection or persecution.

I say all this in spite of the fact that there is a certain amount of sheer habituation which is also involved in any full discussion of frustration tolerance. For instance, it is likely that those persons who have been accustomed to relative starvation for a long time, are partially enabled thereby to withstand food deprivation. What sort of balance must be made between these two tendencies, of habituation on the one hand, and of past satisfaction breeding present frustration tolerance on the other hand, remains to be worked out by further research. Meanwhile we may assume that they are both operative, side by side, since they do not contradict each other. In respect to this phenomenon of increased frustration tolerance, it seems probable that the most important gratifications come in the first two years of life. That is to say, people who have been made secure and strong in the earliest years, tend to remain secure and strong thereafter in the face of whatever threatens.

Degrees of relative satisfaction

So far, our theoretical discussion may have given the impression that these five sets of needs are somehow in a step-wise, all-or-none relationships to each other. We have spoken in such terms as the following: 'If one need is satisfied, then another emerges.' This statement might give the impression that a need must be satisfied 100 per cent before the next need emerges. In actual fact, most members of our society who are normal, are partially satisfied in all their basic needs and partially unsatisfied in all their basic needs at the same time. A more realistic description of the hierarchy would be in terms of decreasing percentages of satisfaction as we go up the hierarchy of prepotency. For instance, if I may assign arbitrary figures for the sake of illustration, it is as if the average citizen is satisfied perhaps 85 per cent in his physiological needs, 70 per cent in his safety needs, 50 per cent in his love needs, 40 per cent in his self-esteem needs, and 10 per cent in his self-actualization needs.

As for the concept of emergence of a new need after satisfaction of the prepotent need, this emergence is not a sudden, saltatory phenomenon but rather a gradual emergence by slow degrees from nothingness. For instance, if prepotent need A is satisfied only 10 per cent then need B may not be visible at all. However, as this need A becomes satisfied 25 per cent, need B may emerge 5 per cent, as need A becomes satisfied 75 per cent need B may emerge 90 per cent, and so on.

Unconscious character of needs

These needs are neither necessarily conscious nor unconscious. On the whole, however, in the average person, they are more often unconscious rather than conscious. It is not necessary at this point to overhaul the tremendous mass of evidence which indicates the crucial importance of unconscious motivation. It would by now be expected, on a priori grounds alone, that unconscious motivations would on the whole be rather more important than the conscious motivations. What we have called the basic needs are very often largely unconscious although they may, with suitable techniques, and with sophisticated people become conscious.

Cultural specificity and generality of needs

This classification of basic needs makes some attempt to take account of the relative unity behind the superficial differences in specific desires from one culture to another. Certainly in any particular culture an individual's conscious motivational content will usually be extremely different from the conscious motivational content of an individual in another society. However, it is the common experience of anthropologists that people, even in different societies, are much more alike than we would think from our first contact with them, and that as we know them better we seem to find more and more of this commonness. We then recognize the most startling differences to be superficial rather than basic, e.g. differences in style of hair-dress, clothes, tastes in food, etc. Our classification of basic needs is in part an attempt to account for this unity behind the apparent diversity from culture to culture. No claim is made that it is ultimate or universal for all cultures. The claim is made only that it is relatively **more** ultimate, more universal, more basic, than the superficial conscious desires from culture to culture, and makes a somewhat closer approach to common-human characteristics. Basic needs are **more** common-human than superficial desires or behaviors.

Multiple motivations of behavior

These needs must be understood **not** to be **exclusive** or single determiners of certain kinds of behavior. An example may be found in any behavior that seems to be physiologically motivated, such as eating, or sexual play or the like. The clinical psychologists have long since found that any behavior may be a channel through which flow various determinants. Or to say it in another way, most behavior is multi-motivated. Within the sphere of motivational determinants any behavior tends to be determined by several or **all** of the basic needs simultaneously rather than by only one of them. The latter would be more an exception than the former. Eating may be partially for the sake of filling the stomach, and partially for the sake of comfort and amelioration of other needs. One may make love not only for pure sexual release, but also to convince one's self of one's masculinity, or to make a conquest, to feel powerful, or to win more basic affection. As an illustration. I may point out that it would be possible (theoretically if not practically) to analyze a single act of an individual and see in it the expression of his physiological needs, his safety needs, his love needs, his esteem needs and self-actualization. This contrasts sharply with the more naive brand of trait psychology in which one trait or one motive accounts for a certain kind of act, i.e. an aggressive act is traced solely to a trait of aggressiveness.

Multiple determinants of behavior

Not all behavior is determined by the basic needs. We might even say that not all behavior is motivated. There are many determinants of behavior other than motives. For instance, one other important class of determinants is the so-called 'field' determinants. Theoretically, at least, behavior may be determined completely by the field, or even by specific isolated external stimuli, as in association of ideas, or certain conditioned reflexes. If in response to the stimulus word 'table,' I immediately perceive a memory image of a table, this response certainly has nothing to do with my basic needs.

Secondly, we may call attention again to the concept of 'degree of closeness to the basic needs' or 'degree of motivation.' Some behavior is highly motivated, other behavior is only weakly motivated. Some is not motivated at all (but all behavior is determined).

Another important point is that there is a basic difference between expressive behavior and coping behavior (functional striving, purposive goal seeking). An expressive behavior does not try to do anything; it is simply a reflection of the personality. A stupid man behaves stupidly, not because he wants to, or tries to, or is motivated to, but simply because he **is** what he is. The same is true when I speak in a bass voice rather than tenor or soprano. The random movements of a healthy child, the smile on the face of a happy man even when he is alone, the springiness of the healthy man's walk, and the erectness of his carriage are other examples of expressive, non-functional behavior. Also the **style** in which a man carries out almost all his behavior, motivated as well as unmotivated, is often expressive.

We may then ask, is **all** behavior expressive or reflective of the character structure? The answer is 'No.' Rote, habitual, automatized, or conventional behavior may or may not be expressive. The same is true for most 'stimulus-bound' behaviors.

It is finally necessary to stress that expressiveness of behavior, and goal-directedness of behavior are not mutually exclusive categories. Average behavior is usually both.

Goals as centering principle in motivation theory

It will be observed that the basic principle in our classification has been neither the instigation nor the motivated behavior but rather the functions, effects, purposes, or goals of the behavior. It has been proven sufficiently by various people that this is the most suitable point for centering in any motivation theory.

Animal- and human-centering

This theory starts with the human being rather than any lower and presumably 'simpler' animal. Too many of the findings that have been made in animals have been proven to be true for animals but not for the human being. There is no reason whatsoever why we should start with animals in order to study human motivation. The logic or rather illogic behind this general fallacy of 'pseudo-simplicity' has been exposed often enough by philosophers and logicians as well as by scientists in each of the various fields. It is no more necessary to study animals before one can study man than it is to study mathematics before one can study geology or psychology or biology.

We may also reject the old, naive, behaviorism which assumed that it was somehow necessary, or at least more 'scientific' to judge human beings by animal standards. One consequence of this belief was that the whole notion of purpose and goal was excluded from motivational psychology simply because one could not ask a white rat about his purposes. Tolman has long since proven in animal studies themselves that this exclusion was not necessary.

Motivation and the theory of psychopathogenesis

The conscious motivational content of everyday life has, according to the foregoing, been conceived to be relatively important or unimportant accordingly as it is more or less closely related to the basic goals. A desire for an ice cream cone might actually be an indirect expression of a desire for love. If it is, then this desire for the ice cream cone becomes an extremely important motivation. If however the ice cream is simply something to cool the mouth with, or a casual appetitive reaction, then the desire is relatively unimportant. Everyday conscious desires are to be regarded as symptoms, as **surface indicators of more basic needs**. If we were to take these superficial desires at their face value we would find ourselves in a state of complete confusion which could never be resolved, since we would be dealing seriously with symptoms rather than with what lay behind the symptoms.

Thwarting of unimportant desires produces no psychopathological results; thwarting of a basically important need does produce such results. Any theory of psychopathogenesis must then be based on a sound theory of motivation. A conflict or a frustration is not necessarily pathogenic. It becomes so only when it threatens or thwarts the basic needs, or partial needs that are closely related to the basic needs.

The role of gratified needs

It has been pointed out above several times that our needs usually emerge only when more prepotent needs have been gratified. Thus gratification has an important role in motivation theory. Apart from this, however, needs cease to play an active determining or organizing role as soon as they are gratified.

What this means is that, e.g. a basically satisfied person no longer has the needs for esteem, love, safety, etc. The only sense in which he might be said to have them is in the almost metaphysical sense that a sated man has hunger, or a filled bottle has emptiness. If we are interested in what **actually** motivates us, and not in what has, will, or might motivate us, then a satisfied need is not a motivator. It must be considered for all practical purposes simply not to exist, to have disappeared. This point should be emphasised because it has been either overlooked or contradicted in every theory of motivation I know. The perfectly healthy, normal, fortunate man has no sex needs or hunger needs, or needs for safety, or for love, or for prestige, or self-esteem, except in stray moments of quickly passing threat. If we were to say otherwise, we should also have to aver that every man had all the pathological reflexes, because if his nervous system were damaged, these would appear.

It is such considerations as these that suggest the bold postulation that a man who is thwarted in any of his basic needs may fairly be envisaged simply as a sick man. This is a fair parallel to our designation as 'sick' of the man who lacks vitamins or minerals. Who is to say that a lack of love is less important than a lack of vitamins? Since we know the pathogenic effects of love starvation, who is to say that we are invoking value-questions in an unscientific or illegitimate way, any more than the physician does who diagnoses and treats pellagra or scurvy? If I were permitted this usage, I should then say simply that a healthy man is primarily motivated by his needs to develop and actualize his fullest potentialities and capacities. If a man has any other basic needs in any active, chronic sense, then he is simply an unhealthy man. He is as surely sick as if he had suddenly developed a strong salt-hunger or calcium hunger.

If this statement seems unusual or paradoxical the reader may be assured that this is only one among many such paradoxes that will appear as we revise our ways of looking at man's deeper motivations. When we ask what man wants of life, we deal with his very essence.

Summary

1. There are at least five sets of goals, which we may call basic needs. These are briefly physiological, safety, love, esteem, and self-actualization. In addition, we are motivated by the desire to achieve or maintain the various conditions upon which these basic satisfactions rest and by certain more intellectual desires.
2. These basic goals are related to each other, being arranged in a hierarchy of prepotency. This means that the most prepotent goal will monopolize consciousness and will tend of itself to organize the recruitment of the various capacities of the organism. The less prepotent needs are minimized, even forgotten or denied. But when a need is fairly well satisfied, the next prepotent ('higher') need emerges, in turn to dominate the conscious life and to serve as the center of organization of behavior, since gratified needs are not active motivators.

    Thus man is a perpetually wanting animal. Ordinarily the satisfaction of these wants is not altogether mutually exclusive, but only tends to be. The average member of our society is most often partially satisfied and partially unsatisfied in all of his wants. The hierarchy principle is usually empirically observed in terms of increasing percentages of non-satisfaction as we go up the hierarchy. Reversals of the average order of the hierarchy are sometimes observed. Also it has been observed that an individual may permanently lose the higher wants in the hierarchy under special conditions. There are not only ordinarily multiple motivations for usual behavior, but in addition many determinants other than motives.
3. Any thwarting or possibility of thwarting of these basic human goals, or danger to the defenses which protect them, or to the conditions upon which they rest, is considered to be a psychological threat. With a few exceptions, all psychopathology may be partially traced to such threats. A basically thwarted man may actually be defined as a 'sick' man, if we wish.
4. It is such basic threats which bring about the general emergency reactions.
5. Certain other basic problems have not been dealt with because of limitations of space. Among these are (a) the problem of values in any definitive motivation theory, (b) the relation between appetites, desires, needs and what is 'good' for the organism, (c) the etiology of the basic

needs and their possible derivation in early childhood, (d) redefinition of motivational concepts, i.e. drive, desire, wish, need, goal, (e) implication of our theory for hedonistic theory, (f) the nature of the uncompleted act, of success and failure, and of aspiration-level, (g) the role of association, habit and conditioning, (h) relation to the theory of inter-personal relations, (i) implications for psychotherapy, (j) implication for theory of society, (k) the theory of selfishness, (l) the relation between needs and cultural patterns, (m) the relation between this theory and Allport's theory of functional autonomy. These as well as certain other less important questions must be considered as motivation theory attempts to become definitive.

References

1. Adler, A. (1938) *Social interest*, London: Faber & Faber.
2. Cannon, W.B. (1932) *Wisdom of the body*, New York: Norton.
3. Freud, A. (1937) *The ego and the mechanisms of defense*, London: Hogarth.
4. Freud, S. (1933) *New introductory lectures on psychoanalysis*, New York: Norton.
5. Fromm, E. (1941) *Escape from freedom*, New York: Farrar and Rinehart.
6. Goldstein, K. (1939) *The organism*, New York: American Book Co.
7. Horney, K. (1937) *The neurotic personality of our time*, New York: Norton.
8. Kardiner, A. (1941) *The traumatic neuroses of war*, New York: Hoeber.
9. Levy, D.M. (1937) Primary affect hunger. *Amer. J. Psychiat.*, vol. 94, pp. 643–52.
10. Maslow, A.H. (1943) Conflict, frustration, and the theory of threat. *J. abnorm. (soc.) Psychol.*, vol. 38, pp. 81–6.
11. — (1939) Dominance, personality and social behavior in women. *J. soc. Psychol.*, vol. 10, pp. 3–39.
12. — (1942) The dynamics of psychological security-insecurity. *Character & Pers.*, vol. 10, pp. 331–44.
13. — (1943) A preface to motivation theory. *Psychosomatic Med.*, vol. 5, pp. 85–92.
14. — and Mittelmann, B. (1941) *Principles of abnormal psychology*, New York: Harper & Bros.
15. Murray, H.A., *et al.* (1938) *Explorations in personality*, New York: Oxford University Press.
16. Plant, J. (1937) *Personality and the cultural pattern*, New York: Commonwealth Fund.
17. Shirley, M. (1942) Children's adjustments to a strange situation. *J. abnorm. (soc.) Psychol.*, vol. 37, pp. 201–17.
18. Tolman, E.C. (1932) *Purposive behavior in animals and men*, New York: Century.
19. Wertheimer, M. Unpublished lectures at the New School for Social Research.
20. Young, P.T. (1936) *Motivation of behavior*, New York: John Wiley & Sons.
21. — (1941) The experimental analysis of appetite. *Psychol. Bull.*, vol. 38, pp. 129–64.

The forfeited self

BETTY FRIEDAN

Scientists of human behaviour have become increasingly interested in the basic human need to grow, man's will to be all that is in him to be. He must take his existence seriously enough to make his own commitment to life, and to the future; he forfeits his existence by failing to fulfil his entire being.

What they are describing as unseen self-destruction in man, is, I think, no less destructive in women who never make a commitment of their own to society or to the future, who never realize their human potential. For the problem that has no name, from which so many women in America suffer today, is caused by adjustment to an image that does not permit them to become what they now can be. It is the growing despair of women who have forfeited their own existence.

> Anxiety occurs at the point where some emerging potentiality or possibility faces the individual, some possibility of fulfilling his existence; but this very possibility involves the destroying of present security, which thereupon gives rise to the tendency to deny the new potentiality.[1]

It is surely as true of women's whole human potential that if she is barred from realizing her true nature, she will be sick. Her anxiety can be soothed by therapy, or tranquillized by pills, or evaded temporarily by busywork. But her unease, her desperation, is nonetheless a warning that her human existence is in danger.

Only recently have we come to accept the fact that there is an evolutionary scale or hierarchy of needs in man (and thus in woman).

In our culture, the development of women has been blocked, the need for self-respect, for self-esteem, and for the esteem of others – 'the desire for strength, for achievement, for adequacy, for mastery and competence, for confidence in the face of the world, and for independence and freedom' – is not clearly recognized for women. Self-esteem in woman, as well as in man, can only be based on real capacity, competence, and achievement; on deserved respect from others rather than unwarranted adulation. But women in America are not encouraged, or expected, to use their full capacities. In the name of femininity, they are encouraged to evade human growth.

In the late thirties, Professor Maslow began to study the relationship between sexuality and what he called 'dominance feeling' or 'self-esteem' or 'ego level' in women. He found, contrary to what one might expect from the psychoanalytical theories and the conventional images of femininity, that the

Abridged excerpt reproduced from Friedan, Betty *The Feminine Mystique*, pp. 269–83; published by Penguin, Harmondsworth, 1963.

[1] Rollo, May (1958) Contributions of Existential Psychotherapy in *Existence, a New Dimension in Psychiatry and Psychology* (eds Rollo, May, Angel, Ernest and Ellenberger, Henri F.), New York, p.52.

more 'dominant' the woman, the greater her enjoyment of sexuality – and the greater her ability to 'submit' in a psychological sense, to give herself freely in love, to have orgasm. It was not that these women higher in 'dominance' were more 'highly sexed', but they were, above all, more completely themselves, more free to be themselves.

Professor Maslow found that the higher the dominance, or strength of self in a woman, the less she was self-centred and the more her concern was directed outward to other people and to problems of the world. On the other hand, the main preoccupation of the more conventionally feminine low-dominance women was themselves and their own inferiorities. From a psychological point of view, a high-dominance woman was more like a high-dominance man than she was like a low-dominance woman. Thus Professor Maslow suggested that either you have to describe as 'masculine' both high-dominance men and women or drop the terms 'masculine' and 'feminine' altogether because they are so 'misleading'. Above all, the high-dominance woman was more psychologically free – more autonomous. The low-dominance woman was not free to be herself, she was other-directed.

[In] this context, Professor Maslow later set about to study people, dead and alive; who, in his view, showed positive evidence of 'self-actualisation', which he defined as 'the full use and exploitation of talents, capacities, potentialities. Such people seem to be fulfilling themselves and to be doing the best that they are capable of doing. . . . They are people who have developed or are developing to the full stature of which they are capable.' [He found] only two women – Eleanor Roosevelt and Jane Addams[!]

The new theorists of the self, who are men, have usually evaded the question of self-realization for a woman. Bemused themselves by the feminine mystique, they assume that there must be some strange 'difference' which permits a woman to find self-realization by living through her husband and children, while men must grow to theirs. It is still very difficult, even for the most advanced psychological theorist, to see woman as a separate self, a human being who, in that respect, is no different in her need to grow than is a man.

Motivation: a cognitive approach

V. VROOM

Contemporary approaches

Two groups of psychologists each carrying out important work have helped to translate the hedonistic doctrine from the realm of philosophical discourse to that of testable psychological theory. These two groups have focused on

Abridged excerpt reproduced with permission from Vroom, V. *Work and Motivation*, pp. 10–19; published by John Wiley and Sons Inc., New York, 1964.

different problems and have developed different types of models to guide their research and interpret their findings. The first group has focused on the problem of **learning** and has approached this problem with a strong behavioristic emphasis. The theories which they have constructed are **historical** in the sense that they assert lawful relations between the behavior of organisms at one point in time and events which have occurred at earlier points in time. The empirical foundation for much of their work is the law of effect, which Thorndike originally stated as follows:

> Of several responses made to the same situation, those which are accompanied or closely followed by satisfaction to the animal will, other things being equal, be more firmly connected with the situation, so that, when it recurs, they will be more likely to recur; those which are accompanied or closely followed by discomfort to the animal will, other things being equal, have their connections with that situation weakened, so that when it recurs, they will be less likely to occur. The greater the satisfaction or discomfort, the greater is the strengthening or weakening of the bond.   (*1911, p. 244*)

The experiments on which the law was based provided tangible evidence that behavior was directed **toward** certain outcomes and **away** from other outcomes. Those outcomes increasing the probability of responses which lead to them were often referred to as satisfiers or rewards, terms implying that their attainment was pleasurable. Similarly, outcomes decreasing the probability of responses which lead to them were referred to as dissatisfiers or punishments.

Gordon Allport (1954) has noted theories based on the law of effect or on the principle of reinforcement imply a 'hedonism of the past.' They assume that the explanation of the present choices of an organism is to be found in an examination of the consequences of his past choices. Responses to a stimulus which have been rewarded in the past will be repeated in the present, whereas those which have not been rewarded or have been punished in the past will not be repeated.

Although the law of effect helped to answer one of the classical problems of hedonism (i.e. how behavior came to be directed toward pleasure and away from pain), it was silent in regard to the question of which outcomes are pleasurable and which are painful. Unless one was willing to rely on the subject's report of his experience of pleasure or pain, there was, in the statement of the law, no mention of an independent criterion by which one could distinguish in advance the class of outcomes which would strengthen responses and those which would weaken them. Without such a criterion the law of effect was difficult to test conclusively and was accused of circularity.

A number of attempts have been made to define more completely the classes of outcomes which act as rewards and as punishments. Hull's conception of need, as a condition in which 'any of the commodities or conditions necessary for individual or species survival are lacking' (p. 17), represented an early attempt in this direction. Satisfaction, or reinforcement to use

Hull's term, occurred when a condition of need was reduced. This use of changes in states of physiological needs was justly criticized on a number of grounds, and subsequently Hull (1951) and many of his associates changed their conception of the basis for reinforcement from changes in tissue conditions to changes in aversive states called drives. Reinforcement resulted not from the reduction of a biological need but from drive reduction. Although Hull was never very explicit about the defining properties of a drive, Miller and Dollard (1941) have anchored it in the intensity of stimulation. A drive was 'a strong stimulus which impels action' (p. 18) on the part of the organism. Increases in stimulation, e.g., from an electric shock or loud noise, constituted increases in drive and were predicted to decrease the probability of responses preceding them. On the other hand, decreases in stimulation constituted drive reduction and were predicted to increase the probability of responses preceding them.

The concept of drive reduction as the basis of reinforcement has achieved greater currency than that of need reduction, but it too has been criticized. There is considerable evidence that organisms, under many conditions, do not seek to avoid stimulation but to attain it. The optimal state does not appear to be the absence of stimulation as drive reduction theory would imply. Sensory deprivation studies indicate that humans find very low levels of stimulation highly unpleasant and disruptive (Bexton, Heron, and Scott, 1954). Work by Harlow on manipulation (1953), by Berlyne on curiosity (1960), and by Montgomery on exploration (1954) indicates that, at least under some circumstances, stimulation is rewarding and can strengthen responses. A similar conclusion is suggested by everyday observations of the frequency with which people engage in highly stimulating activities such as riding roller coasters, driving sports cars, and reading detective stories.

Although there are clearly many unsolved problems in explaining behavior in terms of reinforcement principles, definite progress has been made. The empirical validity of the proposition that the probability of occurrence of a wide range of behaviors can be altered by the outcomes of those behaviors has been supported by a wealth of research using both animals and humans as subjects. Without a doubt the law of effect or principle of reinforcement must be included among the most substantiated findings of experimental psychology and is at the same time among the most useful findings for an applied psychology concerned with the control of human behavior.

A second group of psychologists has accepted the empirical evidence underlying the law of effect but has asserted that the stimulus-response-reinforcement theories of Hull and his followers are not sufficient to account for the more complex aspects of choice behavior. Tolman (1932) and Lewin (1938) were among the early advocates of **cognitive** theories of behavior. Although Tolman's work was mainly with animals and Lewin's was with humans, they both attributed to their subjects internalized representations of their environment. The organism was assumed to have beliefs, opinions, or expectations concerning the world around him. To Tolman, learning consisted not of changes in the strength of habits (i.e., stimulus-response connections) but of changes in beliefs (i.e. stimulus-stimulus or stimulus-response-stimulus connections). He attributed the results of reinforcement studies to learning, but he did not regard reinforcement as a necessary condition for learning to take place.

Although reinforcement was accorded a much less central role, the models of Lewin and Tolman also reflect the influence of hedonism. Both investigators viewed behavior as purposeful or goal-directed, with organisms striving to attain positively valent objects or events and to avoid negatively valent objects or events.

Lewin (1935) distinguished between historical and ahistorical explanations of behavior. He pointed out that the former had its roots in Aristotelian thinking and the latter in Galilean thinking. From an ahistorical point of view behavior at a given time is viewed as depending only on events existing at that time. The problem is one of accounting for the actions of a person from a knowledge of the properties of his life space at the time the actions are occurring. From an historical standpoint, behavior is dependent on events occurring at an earlier time. The historical problem is to determine the way in which the behavior of a person at one point in time is affected by past situations he has experienced and the responses he has made to them. Freud's constant emphasis on the dependence of adult behavior on events which occurred in childhood and Hull's stress on reinforcement of previous responses provide us with good examples of historical explanations.

Lewin's own theorizing was ahistorical, but he noted the complementary nature of ahistorical and historical approaches. Past events can only have an effect on behavior in the present by modifying conditions which exist in the present. If a particular childhood experience is to have any effect on adult behavior, it must do so by changing some property of the person which persists through adulthood. Historical explanations are consequently explanations of the process of change, i.e., of the ways in which properties of persons are modified by events. Ahistorical explanations, on the other hand, concern the effects on behavior of conditions existing at the time the behavior is occurring, and say nothing about how these conditions were established.

Ahistorical models of choice behavior bypass many of the problems that concern the psychologist interested in learning. The choices made by a person in a given situation are explained in terms of his motives and cognitions at the time he makes the choice. The process by which these motives or cognitions were acquired is not specified nor is it regarded as crucial to a consideration of their present role in behavior.

Although bypassing the problem of the origins of psychological properties, an ahistorical approach to motivation is confronted with another set of problems, i.e., problems of operational definition or measurement. In order to test ahistorical models, we must develop methods of measuring or experimentally manipulating these variables. The strategy of the learning theorist, creating carefully controlled training conditions, is supplanted by the use of psychometric assessment devices or the manipulation of situational conditions which are assumed to have some relationship to the constructs in the model.

An outline of a cognitive model

In the remainder of this [reading], we outline a conceptual model which will guide our discussion and interpretation of research.

The model to be described is similar to those developed by other investigators including Lewin (1938), Rotter (1955), Peak (1955), Davidson, Suppes, and Siegel (1957), Atkinson (1958), and Tolman (1959). It is basically ahistorical in form. We assume that the choices made by a person among alternative courses of action are lawfully related to psychological events occurring contemporaneously with the behavior. We turn now to consider the concepts in the model and their interrelations.

The concept of valence

We shall begin with the simple assumption that, at any given point in time, a person has preferences among outcomes or states of nature. For any pair of outcomes, x and y, a person prefers x to y, prefers y to x, or is indifferent to whether he receives x or y. Preference, then, refers to a relationship between the strength of a person's desire for, or attraction toward, two outcomes.

For the sake of consistency, we use the term valence in referring to affective orientations toward particular outcomes. In our system, an outcome is positively valent when the person prefers attaining it to not attaining it (i.e. he prefers x to not x). An outcome has a valence of zero when the person is indifferent to attaining or not attaining it (i.e. he is indifferent to x or not x), and it is negatively valent when he prefers not attaining it to attaining it (i.e. he prefers not x to x). It is assumed that valence can take a wide range of both positive and negative values.

We use the term motive whenever the referent is a preference for a class of outcomes. A positive (or approach) motive signifies that outcomes which are members of the class have positive valence, and a negative (or avoidance) motive signifies that outcomes in the class have negative valence.

It is important to distinguish between the valence of an outcome to a person and its value to that person. An individual may desire an object but derive little satisfaction from its attainment – or he may strive to avoid an object which he later finds to be quite satisfying. At any given time there may be a substantial discrepancy between the anticipated satisfaction from an outcome (i.e. its valence) and the actual satisfaction that it provides (i.e. its value).

There are many outcomes which are positively or negatively valent to persons, but are not in themselves anticipated to be satisfying or dissatisfying. The strength of a person's desire or aversion for them is based not on their intrinsic properties but on the anticipated satisfaction or dissatisfaction associated with other outcomes to which they are expected to lead. People may desire to join groups because they believe that membership will enhance their status in the community, and they may desire to perform their jobs effectively because they expect that it will lead to a promotion.

In effect, we are suggesting that means acquire valence as a consequence of their expected relationship to ends. Peak (1955) has discussed this relationship in some detail. She hypothesises that attitudes, i.e., affective orientations toward objects, are 'related to the ends which the object serves' (p. 153). From this general hypothesis it is possible for Peak to distinguish two types of determinants of attitudes: (1) The cognized instrumentality of the object of the attitude for the attainment of various consequences; and (2) the intensity and the nature of the effect expected from these consequences. If an object is believed by a person to lead to desired consequences or to prevent undesired consequences, the person is predicted to have a positive attitude toward it. If, on the other hand, it is believed by the person to lead to undesired consequences or to prevent desired consequences, the person is predicted to have a negative attitude toward it.

We do not mean to imply that all the variance in the valence of outcomes can be explained by their expected consequences. We must assume that some things are desired and abhored 'for their own sake.' Desegregation may be opposed 'on principle' not because it leads to other events which are disliked, and people may seek to do well on their jobs even though no externally mediated rewards are believed to be at stake.

The concept of expectancy

The specific outcomes attained by a person are dependent not only on the choices that he makes but also on events which are beyond his control. For example, a person who elects to buy a ticket in a lottery is not certain of winning the desired prize. Whether or not he does so is a function of many chance events. Similarly, the student who enrolls in medical school is seldom certain that he will successfully complete the program of study; the person who seeks political office is seldom certain that he will win the election; and the worker who strives for a promotion is seldom certain that he will triumph over other candidates. Most decision-making situations involve some element of risk, and theories of choice behavior must come to grips with the role of these risks in determining the choices that people do make.

Whenever an individual chooses between alternatives which involve uncertain outcomes, it seems clear that his behavior is affected not only by his preferences among these outcomes but also by the degree to which he believes these outcomes to be probable. Psychologists have referred to these beliefs as expectancies (Tolman, 1959; Rotter, 1955; Atkinson, 1958) or subjective probabilities (Edwards, 1954; Davidson, Suppes, and Siegel, 1957). We use the former term. An expectancy is defined as a momentary belief concerning the likelihood that a particular act will be followed by a particular outcome. Expectancies may be described in terms of their strength.

Maximal strength is indicated by subjective certainty that the act **will** be followed by the outcome while minimal (or zero) strength is indicated by subjective certainty that the act **will** not be followed by the outcome.

The differences between the concepts of expectancy, discussed in this section, and instrumentality, discussed in the previous section, should be noted.

Expectancy is an action-outcome association. It takes values ranging from zero, indicating no subjective probability that an act will be followed by an outcome, to 1, indicating certainty that the act will be followed by the outcome. Instrumentality, on the other hand, is an outcome-outcome association. It can take values ranging from -1, indicating a belief that attainment of the second outcome is certain without the first outcome and impossible with it, to $+1$, indicating that the first outcome is believed to be a necessary and sufficient condition for the attainment of the second outcome.

The concept of force

It remains to be specified how valences and expectancies combine in determining choices. The directional concept in our model is the Lewinian concept of force. Behavior on the part of a person is assumed to be the result of a field of forces each of which has direction and magnitude.

There are many possible ways of combining valences and expectancies mathematically to yield these hypothetical forces. On the assumption that choices made by people are subjectively rational, we would predict the strength of forces to be [directly related to] the **product** of valences and expectancies.

It is also assumed that people choose from among alternative acts the one corresponding to the strongest positive (or weakest negative) force. This formulation is similar to the notion in decision theory that people choose in a way that maximizes subjective expected utility.

Expressing force as [directly related to] the product of valence and expectancy has a number of implications which should be noted. An outcome with high positive or negative valence will have no effect on the generation of a force unless there is some expectancy (i.e. some subjective probability greater than zero) that the outcome will be attained by some act. As the strength of an expectancy that an act will lead to an outcome increase, the effect of variations in the valence of the outcome on the force to perform the act will also increase. Similarly, if the valence of an outcome is zero (i.e. the person is indifferent to the outcome), neither the absolute value nor variations in the strength of expectancies of attaining it will have any effect on forces.

References

Allport, G. (1954) The historical background of modern social psychology. In Lindzey, G. (ed.) *Handbook of social psychology*, Cambridge, Mass.: Addison-Wesley, pp. 3–56.

Atkinson, J.W. (1958) Towards experimental analysis of human motivation in terms of motives, expectancies, and incentives. In Atkinson, J.W. (ed.) *Motives in fantasy, action, and society*, Princeton: Van Nostrand, pp. 288–305.

Berlyne, D.E. (1960) *Conflict arousal and curiosity*, New York: McGraw-Hill.

Bexton, W.H., Heron, W., and Scott, T.H. (1954) Effects of decreased variation in the sensory environment. *Canad. J. Psychol.*, vol. 8, pp. 70–6.

Davidson, D., Suppes, P., and Siegel, S. (1957) *Decison making: An experimental approach*, Stanford: Stanford University Press.

Edwards, W. (1954) The theory of decision making. *Psychol. Bull.*, vol. 51, pp. 380–417.

Harlow H.F. (1953) Mice, monkeys, men and motives. *Psychol. Rev.*, vol. 60, pp. 23–32.

Hull, C.L. (1943) *Principles of behavior*, New York: Appleton-Century.

—1 (1951) *Essentials of behavior*, New Haven: Yale University Press.

Lewin, K. (1935) *A dynamic theory of personality*, New York: McGraw-Hill.

—1 (1938) The conceptual representation and the measurement of psychological forces. *Contr. psychol. Theory*, Durham, N.C.: Duke University Press, vol. 1, no. 4.

Miller, N.E. and Dollard, J. (1941) *Social learning and imitation*, New Haven: Yale University Press.

Montgomery, K.C. (1954) The role of the exploratory drive in learning. *J. comp. physiol. Psychol.*, vol. 47, pp. 60–4.

Peak, Helen. (1955) Attitude and motivation. In Jones, M.R. (ed). *Nebraska symposium on motivation*, Lincoln: University of Nebraska Press, pp. 149–88.

Rotter, J.B. (1955) The role of the psychological situation in determining the direction of human behavior. In Jones, M.R. (ed.) *Nebraska symposium on motivation*, Lincoln: University of Nebraska Press, pp. 245–68.

Tolman, E.C. (1959) Principles of purposive behavior. In Koch, S. (ed.) *Psychology: A study of a science*, vol. 2. New York: McGraw-Hill, pp. 92–157.

Thorndike, E.L. (1911) *Animal intelligence: experimental studies*, New York: Macmillan.

Conformity and independence

STANLEY MILGRAM

In laboratory research, the effect of group pressure has most often been studied in its negative aspect; the conspiratorial group is shown to limit, constrain, and distort the individual's responses (Asch, 1951: Blake and Brehm, 1954; Milgram, 1964). Edifying effects of the group, although acknowledged, have rarely been demonstrated with the clarity and force of its destructive potential. Particularly in those areas in which a morally relevant choice is at issue, experimentalists typically examine pressures that diminish the scope of individual action. They have neglected effects that

Abridged excerpt reproduced with permission from Milgram, Stanley (1965) Liberating Effects of Group Pressure. *Journal of Personality and Social Psychology*, **1**, no. 2, 127–34. Copyright © by The American Psychological Association.

enhance the individual's sense of worth, enlarge the possibilities for action, and help the subject resolve conflicting feelings in a direction congruent with his ideals and values. Although in everyday life occasions arise when conformity to group pressures is constructive, in the laboratory 'thinking and investigation have concentrated almost obsessively on conformity in its most sterile forms (Asch, 1959).'

There are technical difficulties to demonstrating the value enhancing potential of group pressure. They concern the nature of the base line from which the group effect is to be measured. The problem is that the experimental subject ordinarily acts in a manner that is socially appropriate. If he has come to the laboratory to participate in a study on the perception of lines, he will generally report what he sees in an honest manner. If one wishes to show the effects of group influence by producing a change in his performance, the only direction open to change is that of creating some deficiency in his performance, which can then be attributed to group influences.

If men tend to act constructively under usual circumstances, the obvious direction of an induced and measurable change is toward inappropriate behavior. It is this technical need rather than the inherently destructive character of group forces that has dictated the lines of a good deal of laboratory research. The experimental problem for any study of **constructive** conformity is to create a situation in which undesirable behavior occurs with regularity and then to see whether group pressure can be applied effectively in the direction of a valued behavior outcome.

Experiment I: Base-line condition

A technique for the study of destructive obedience (Milgram, 1963, in press) generates the required base line. In this situation a subject is ordered to give increasingly more severe punishment to a person. Despite the apparent discomfort, cries, and vehement protests of the victim, the experimenter instructs the subject to continue stepping up the shock level.

Technique

Two persons arrive at a campus laboratory to take part in a study of memory and learning. (One of them is a confederate of the experimenter.) Each subject is paid $4.50 upon arrival, and is told that payment is not affected in any way by performance. The experimenter provides an introductory talk on memory and learning processes and then informs the subjects that in the experiment one of them will serve as teacher and the other as learner. A rigged drawing is held so that the naive subject is always assigned the role of teacher and the accomplice becomes the learner. The learner is taken to an adjacent room and is strapped into an electric chair.

The naive subject is told that it is his task to teach the learner a list of paired associates, to test him on the list, and to administer punishment whenever the learner errs in the test. Punishment takes the form of electric shock, delivered to the learner by means of a shock generator controlled by the naive subject. The teacher is instructed to increase the intensity of the electric shock one step on the generator on each error. The generator contains 30 voltage levels ranging from 15 to 450 volts, and verbal designations ranging from Slight Shock to Danger: Severe Shock. The learner, according to plan, provides many wrong answers, so that before long the naive subject must give him the strongest shock on the generator. Increases in shock level are met by increasingly insistent demands from the learner that the experiment be stopped because of growing discomfort to him. However, the experimenter instructs the teachers to continue with the procedure in disregard of the learner's protests.

A quantitative value is assigned to the subject's performance based on the maximum intensity shock he administered before breaking off. Thus any subject's score may range from 0 (for a subject unwilling to administer the first shock level) to 30 (for a subject who proceeds to the highest voltage level on the board).

Subjects

The subjects used in the several experimental conditions were male adults residing in the greater New Haven area, aged 20–50 years, and engaged in a wide variety of occupations. Each experimental condition described here employed 40 fresh subjects and was carefully balanced for age and occupational types (see Milgram, 1963, Table 2.1, for details).

Results and discussion

In this situation a subject is instructed to perform acts that are in some sense incompatible with his normal standards of behavior. In the face of the vehement protests of an innocent individual, many subjects refuse to carry out the experimenter's orders to continue with the shock procedure. They reject the role assignment of **experimental subject**, assert themselves as persons, and are unwilling to perform actions that violate personal standards of conduct. The distribution of break-off points for this condition is shown in Table 2.1 Column 1. Fourteen of the 40 subjects withdraw from the experiment at some point before the completion of the command series.

The majority of subjects, however, comply fully with the experimenter's commands, despite the acute discomfort they often experience in connection with shocking the victim. Typically these obedient subjects report that they do not wish to hurt the victim, but they feel obligated to follow the orders of the experimenter. On questioning they often state that it would have been 'better' not to have shocked the victim at the highest voltage levels. Consider, for example, the remarks of the following obedient subject. He has completed the experiment and is now questioned by an interviewer (who is not the experimenter).

Table 2.1 Distribution of break-off points by condition

Shock level	Verbal designation and voltage level	Base-line condition (n = 40) (1)	Hypothetical subjects (n = 40) (2)	Disobedient groups (n = 40) (3)	Obedient groups (n = 40) (4)
	Slight shock		3*		
1	15	0	0	0	0
2	30	0	0	0	0
3	45	0	1	0	0
4	60	0	1	0	0
	Moderate shock				
5	75	0	7	0	1
6	90	1	1	0	0
7	105	0	1	1	1
8	120	0	3	0	0
	Strong shock				
9	135	0	2	0	0
10	150	6	9	3←	2
11	165	0	2	4	0
12	180	1	3	1	1
	Very strong shock				
13	195	0	1	4	0
14	210	0	0	12←	0
15	225	0	1	0	0
16	240	0	1	0	0
	Intense shock				
17	255	0	1	0	0
18	270	2	0	4	4
19	285	0	0	0	0
20	300	1	3	2	0
	Extreme intensity shock				
21	315	1	0	3	2
22	330	1	0	0	0
23	345	0	0	0	0
24	360	0	0	1	0
	Danger: severe shock				
25	375	1	0	0	0
26	390	0	0	1	0
27	405	0	0	0	0
28	420	0	0	0	0
	XXX				
29	435	0	0	0	0
30	450	26	0	4	29
	Mean maximum shock	24.55	9.00	16.45	25.70
	Percentage defiant subjects	35.0%	100.0%	90.0%	27.5%

* These three subjects indicated they would refuse to administer even the lowest shock.

I'd like to ask you a few questions. How do you feel? I feel all right, but I don't like what happened to that fellow in there [the victim]. He's been hollering and we had to keep giving him shocks. I didn't like that one bit. I mean he wanted to get out but he [the experimenter] just kept going, he kept throwing 450 volts. I didn't like that.

Who was actually pushing the switch? I was, but he kept insisting. I told him 'No,' but he said you got to keep going. I told him it's time we stopped when we get up to 195 or 210 volts.

Why didn't you just stop? He wouldn't let me. I wanted to stop. I kept insisting to stop, but he said 'No.' . . . I figured the voltage we were giving him was quite a bit. I wanted to stop but he [the experimenter] kept insisting not to stop. I mean the fellow in there is hollering 'I don't want to do it. I want to get out of here. I want to get out of here!'

Why didn't you just disregard what the experimenter said? He says it's got to go on, the experiment.

Do you feel a little upset? Well, I mean I feel concerned about the gentleman in there, I do sir . . . I was getting ready to walk out . . . I couldn't see the point of going on when the guy is suffering in there. I figured he was having a heart attack or something. That's the reason I wanted to stop . . .

The subject was then dehoaxed carefully and had a friendly reconciliation with the victim.

There is additional evidence that, in shocking the victim to the end of the command series, subjects are engaging in behavior which they disvalue and see as antithetical to personal and social ideals.

Spontaneous shock levels. In an experimental control reported elsewhere (Milgram, 1964), subjects administer any voltage level they wish in the absence of group or authoritarian pressure. Under this condition the mean maximum shock for 40 subjects is 82.5 volts (level = 5.50); in contrast, under command of the experimenter (in the base-line condition described above) the mean maximum shock is 368.25 volts (levels = 24.55). When left on their own, subjects administer far lower shock levels than when under command.

Self-image. When persons who have not performed in the experiment are provided with a description of the experimental situation, and are asked to predict their own performance, almost all subjects see themselves as defying the experimenter at some point in the command series. Moreover, they justify their hypothetical behavior in terms of positive qualities of character, employing such statements as 'I'm not the kind of person who is willing to hurt others even for the cause of science.'

Column 2 of Table 2.1 shows the anticipated break-off points of 40 adult respondents who were asked to predict their own experimental performance. Hypothetical subjects respond in terms of ideals, values, and positive self-conceptions; these values are frequently overridden by the forces engendered in the concrete laboratory situation.

Moral judgment. Twenty undergraduates were asked to render a moral judgment on the issue of obeying or disobeying the experimenter. After describing the experiment to the respondents in concrete detail, the experimenter asked:

> In terms of the moral and ethical values most important to you, and taking into account the scientific goals served by the research, how **should** you perform in the experimental situation? Should you go through to the end of the experiment or should you break off at some point?

Valued break-off points ranged from 0 to 255 volts with the median at 150 volts. Subjects were also asked to explain at length the values that should guide their behavior in the laboratory situation. A sample statement is given below:

> I would say that one should not even start the shocks, but rather, forcibly withdraw the moment that the outline of the experiment becomes evident. My reasons for saying this are very complex . . . The first is that the society's morals, which I have absorbed, teach that it is wrong to hurt a man. Morals are usually tied in with religion and this is especially true with Christianity. Having been raised, then, in an old fashioned, staunchly Lutheran family I have internalized the view that hurting a man is wrong, and no amount of intellectual reasoning can shake this belief.

Thus, there is a clear consensus that the only behavior consistent with social values and individual conscience is to defy the experimenter at some point before the completion of the command series. Yet there is a marked discrepancy between this value judgment and the actual performance of subjects in the laboratory. Despite their protests and obvious conflict in shocking the victim, a substantial number of subjects are unable to defy the experimenter's authority, and proceed to administer the highest shock levels commanded by him.

Experiment II: Groups for disobedience

We may now examine in what degree group influence can release the subject from authoritarian control, and allow him to act in a direction congruent with his values and personal standards.

The strategy is to replicate Experiment I, but with this difference: the subject is placed in the midst of two peers who defy the experimenter and refuse to punish the victim against his will. In what degree will the pressure created by their action affect the naive subject's behavior?

Technique

Forty fresh subjects were studied in this condition. The procedure is identical to Experiment I with these exceptions: Four persons appear at the laboratory to take part in an experiment on 'the effects of collective teaching and punishment on memory and learning.' Three subjects are confederates of the experimenter and one is a naive subject. The experimenter explains that three teachers and one learner are to be used in the study, and by means of a rigged drawing, the naive subject is assigned the position of Teacher 3. The roles of Teacher 1, Teacher 2, and learner are filled by the confederates. The learner is strapped into the electric chair and the three teachers are seated before the shock generator. Teacher 1 is told to read the list of word pairs, Teacher 2 informs the subject if he is correct or incorrect in his answers, and Teacher 3 (the naive subject) administers punishment. As in Experiment I, the subjects are instructed to raise the shock level one step each time the learner makes an error. (More detailed descriptions of the group technique can be found in Milgram, 1964.)

Behavior of confederates. The confederates comply with the experimenter through the 150-volt shock. After the 150-volt level is administered Teacher 1 informs the experimenter that he does not wish to participate further, because of the learner's complaints. (It is at the 150-volt shock level that the learner makes his first vehement protest.) The experimenter insists that the subject continue. However, Teacher 1 is not swayed by the experimenter's commands, gets up from his chair in front of the shock generator, and takes a seat in another part of the room. Since the experimenter's efforts to get the subject to return to the generator are futile, the experimenter instructs the remaining two subjects to continue with the experiment. Teacher 3 (the naive subject) is to handle the reading of word pairs, in addition to his regular job of administering electric shock to the learner.

After Shock Level 14 (210 volts) is administered, Teacher 2, expressing concern for the learner, refuses to participate further. The experimenter makes strong efforts to have him continue, but he too leaves his chair in front of the generator and seats himself at an opposite corner of the room, saying 'I'm willing to answer any of your questions, but I'm not willing to shock that man against his will; I'll have no part of it.''

At this point the naive subject is seated alone in front of the shock generator. He has witnessed the defiant actions of two peers. The experimenter orders the naive subject to continue with the experimental procedure by himself, indicating that it is essential that the experiment be completed.

Results and discussion

The break-off points of the naive subjects in Experiment II are shown in Table 2.1, Column 3. The arrows at Shock Levels 10 and 14 indicate the points at which each of the confederates defied the experimenter.

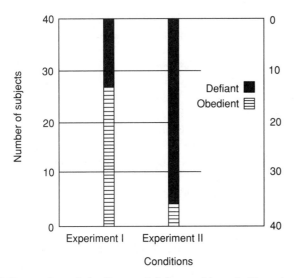
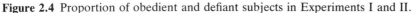

Figure 2.4 Proportion of obedient and defiant subjects in Experiments I and II.

Comparing the proportion of obedient to defiant subjects in Experiments I and II, we see that the effect of the confederates' pressure was substantial. In Experiment I, 26 subjects proceeded to the end of the command series; less than one-sixth of this number obeyed fully in the group setting (obedient versus defiant subjects $x^2 = 25.81$, df $= 1$, $p < .001$). These results are presented graphically in Fig. 2.4. The mean maximum shock in Experiment II (16.45) was also significantly lower than in Experiment II (16.45) was also significantly lower than in Experiment I (24.55, $p < .001$).

After Shock Level 14 the second confederate defies the experimenter. Before Level 15 is administered, 25 naive subjects have followed the defiant group, while at the corresponding point in Experiment I only 8 subjects have refused to follow the experimenter's orders. The confederates appear to exert some influence, however, even on those subjects who do not follow them immediately. Between Voltage Levels 17 and 29, 11 subjects in Experiment II break off, while only 6 subjects do so in Experiment I.

In sum, in the group setting 36 of the 40 subjects defy the experimenter while the corresponding number in the absence of group pressure is 14. The effects of peer rebellion are most impressive in undercutting the experimenter's authority. Indeed, of the score of experimental variations completed in the Yale study on obedience none was so effective in undermining the experimenter's authority as the manipulation reported here.

How should we account for the powerful effect of the experimental manipulation? It is probable that in Experiment I many subjects come near to performing the defiant action but cannot quite bring themselves to the point of disobedience. The additional pressure of the group members leads to an increment in the forces oriented toward defiance; the increment is of sufficient strength so that, in combination with pressures for defiance already present, many subjects are carried over the threshold of disobedience.

The strong liberating effect of the peers brings to mind the powerful effect of a partner in Asch's (1951) study. In that experiment negative pressures originated within the group itself so that the conflicting agents (partner versus majority) were internal to the group boundary; in the present study the peers free the subject from an influence that is **external** to the group. Additionally, the partner's support in Asch's study leads to a response that is fundamentally similar in form but different in value from that of the erring majority. In the present study the peers initiate a radically different order of response, one which has no antecedent in the course of the laboratory hour, and which destroys the very framework of the experiment.

Reactions to the confederates. The reactions of naive subjects to the defiant confederates varied considerably and were in part dependent on the exact point where the subject himself defied the experimenter. A subject who quit simultaneously with the first confederate stated, 'Well, I was already thinking about quitting when the guy broke off.' Most defiant subjects praised the confederates with such statements as, 'I thought they were men of good character, yet I do. When the victim said "Stop," they stopped [Shock Level 11].' 'I think they were very sympathetic people . . . and they were totally unaware of what was in store for them [Shock Level 14].'

A subject who defied the experimenter at Level 21 qualified his approval: 'Well I think they should continue a little further, but I don't blame them for backing out when they did.'

A few subjects acknowledged the importance of the confederates in leading to their own defiance: 'The thought of stopping didn't enter my mind until it was put there by the other two [Shock Level 14].' 'The reason I quit was that I did not wish to seem callous and cruel in the eyes of the other two men who had already refused to go on with the experiment [Shock Level 14].' The majority of subjects, however, denied that the confederates' action was the critical factor in their own defiance.

The fact that obedient subjects failed to follow the defiant group should not suggest that they did not feel the pressure of the confederates' action. One obedient subject stated:

> I felt that I would just look like a real Simon Legree to these guys if I just went on coolly and just kept administering lashes. I thought they reacted normally, and the first thing that came to my mind was to react as they did. But I didn't, because, if they reacted normally, and stopped the experiment, and I did the same, I don't know how many months and days you'd have to continue before you got done.

Thus this subject felt the burden of the group judgment, but sensed that in the light of two defections he had a special obligation to help the experimenter complete his work. Another obedient subject, when asked about the nervousness he displayed in the experiment, replied:

> I think it was primarily because of their actions. Momentarily I was ready to go along with them. Then suddenly I felt that they were just being ridiculous. What was I doing following the crowd? . . . They certainly had a right to stop, but I felt they lost all control of themselves.

And a third obedient subject criticized the confederates more directly, stating:

> I don't think they should have quit. They came here for an experiment, and I think they should have stuck with it.

A closer analysis of the experimental situation points to a number of specific factors that may contribute to the group's effectiveness:

1. The peers instill in the subject the **idea** of defying the experimenter. It may not have occurred to some subjects as a response possibility.
2. The lone subject has no way of knowing whether, in defying the experimenter, he is performing in a bizarre manner or whether this action is a common occurrence in the laboratory. The two examples of disobedience he sees suggest that defiance is a natural reaction to the situation.
3. The reactions of the defiant confederates define the act of shocking the victim as improper. They provide social confirmation to the naive subjects's suspicion that it is wrong to punish a man against his will, even in the context of a psychological experiment.
4. The defiant confederates remain in the laboratory even after withdrawing from the experiment (they have agreed to answer post-experimental questions). Each additional shock administered by the naive subject now carries with it a measure of social disapproval from the two confederates.
5. As long as the two confederates participate in the experimental procedure there is a dispersion of responsibility among the group members for shocking the victim. As the confederates withdraw, responsibility becomes focused onto the naive subject.
6. The naive subject is a witness to two instances of disobedience and observes the **consequences** of defying the experimenter to be minimal.
7. There is identification with the disobedient confederates and the possibility of falling back on them for social support when defying the experimenter.
8. Additionally, the experimenter's power may be diminished by the very fact of failing to keep the two confederates in line, following the general rule that every failure of authority to exact compliance to its commands weakens the perceived power of the authority (Homans, 1961).

Hypothesis of arbitrary direction of group effects

The results examined thus far show that group influence serves to liberate individuals effectively from submission to destructive commands. There are some who will take this to mean that the direction of group influence is arbitrary, that it can be oriented toward destructive or constructive ends with equal impact, and that group pressure need merely be inserted into a social situation on one side of a standard or the other in order to induce movement in the desired direction.

This view ought to be questioned. Does the fact that a disobedient group alters the behavior of subjects in Experiment II necessarily imply that group pressure can be applied in the other direction with similar effectiveness? A competing view would be that the direction of possible influence of a group is not arbitrary, but is highly dependent on the general structure of the situation in which influence is attempted.

To examine this issue we need to undertake a further experimental variation, one in which the group forces are thrown on the side of the experimenter, rather than directed against him. The idea is simply to have the members of the group reinforce the experimenter's commands by following them unfailingly, thus adding peer pressures to those originating in the experimenter's commands.

Experiment III: Obedient groups

Forty fresh subjects, matched to the subjects in Experiments I and II for sex, age, and occupational status, were employed in this condition. The procedure was identical to that followed in Experiment II with this exception: at all times the two confederates followed the commands of the experimenter; at no point did they object to carrying out the experimental instructions. Nor did they show sympathy for or comment on the discomfort of the victim. If a subject attempted to break off they allowed the experimenter primary responsibility for keeping him in line, but contributed background support for the experimenter; they indicated their disapproval of the naive subject's attempts to leave the experiment with such remarks as: 'You can't quit **now**; this experiment has got to get done.' As in Experiment II the naive subject was seated between the two confederates, and in his role of Teacher 3, administered the shocks to the victim.

Results and discussion

The results, presented in Table 2.1, Column 4, show that the obedient group had very little effect on the overall performance of subjects. In Experiment I, 26 of the 40 subjects complied fully with the experimenter's commands; in the present condition this figure is increased but 3, yielding a total of 29 obedient subjects. This increase falls far short of statistical significance ($x^2 = .52$, df = 1, $p > .50$). Nor is the difference in mean maximum shocks statistically reliable. The failure of the manipulation to produce a significant change cannot be attributed to a ceiling artifact since an obedient shift of even 8 of the 14 defiant subjects would yield the .05 significance level by chi square.

Why the lack of change when we know that group pressure often exerts powerful effects? One interpretation is that the authoritarian pressure already present in Experiment I has preempted subjects who would have submitted to group pressures. Conceivably, the subjects who are fully obedient in Experiment I are precisely those who would be susceptible to group forces, while those who resisted authoritarian pressure were also immune to the pressure of the obedient confederates. The pressures applied in Experiment III do not show an effect because they overlap with other pressures having the same direction and present in Experiment I; all persons responsive to the initial pressure have already been moved to the obedient criterion in Experiment I. This possibility seems obvious enough in the present study. Yet every other situation in which group pressure is exerted also possesses a field structure (a particular arrangement of stimulus, motive, and social factors) that limits and controls potential influence within that field. Some structures allow group influence to be exerted in one direction but not another. Seen in this light, the hypothesis of the arbitrary direction of group effects is inadequate.

In the present study Experiment I defines the initial field: the insertion of group pressure in a direction opposite to that of the experimenter's commands (Experiment II) produces a powerful shift toward the group. Changing the direction of group movement (Experiment III) does not yield a comparable shift in the subject's performance. The group success in one case and failure in another can be traced directly to the configuration of motive and social forces operative in the starting situation (Experiment I).

Given any social situation, the strength and direction of potential group influence is predetermined by existing conditions. We need to examine the variety of field structures that typify social situations and the manner in which each controls the pattern of potential influence.

References

Asch, S.E. (1951) Effects of group pressure upon the modification and distortion of judgment. In Guetzkow H. (ed.), *Groups, leadership, and men*, Pittsburgh: Carnegie Press.

Asch, S.E. (1959) A perspective on social psychology. In Koch, S. (ed.), *Psychology: A study of a science*, vol. 3, *Formulations of the person and the social context*, New York: McGraw-Hill, pp. 363–383.

Blake, R.R. and Brehm, J.W. (1954) The use of tape recording to simulate a group atmosphere. *Journal of Abnormal and Social Psychology*, vol. 49, pp. 311–3.

Cartwright, D. and Zander, A. (1960) *Group dynamics*, Evanston, Ill.: Row, Peterson.

Homans, G.C. (1961) *Social behavior: Its elementary forms*, New York: Harcourt, Brace.

Jones, E.E., Wells, H.H., and Torrey, R. (1958) Some effects of feedback from the experimenter on conformity behavior. *Journal of Abnormal and Social Psychology*, vol. 57, pp. 207–13.

Milgram, S. (1963) Behavioral study of obedience. *Jounal of Abnormal and Social Psychology*, vol. 67, pp. 371–78.

Milgram S. (1964) Group pressure and action against a person. *Journal of Abnormal and Social Psychology*, vol. 69, pp. 137–43.

Milgram, S. Some conditions of obedience and disobedience to authority. *Human Relations*, in press.

Wallach, M.A., Kogan, N., and Bem, D.J. (1962) Group influence on individual risk taking. *Journal of Abnormal and Social Psychology*, vol. 65, 75–86.

Bureaucratic structure and personality

ROBERT K. MERTON

A formal, rationally organized social structure involves clearly defined patterns of activity in which, ideally, every series of actions is functionally related to the purposes of the organization. In such an organization there is integrated a series of offices, of hierarchized statuses, in which inhere a number of obligations and privileges closely defined by limited and specific rules. Each of these offices contains an area of imputed competence and responsibility. Authority, the power of control which derives from an acknowledged status, inheres in the office and not in the particular person who performs the official role. Official action ordinarily occurs within the framework of preexisting rules of the organization. The system of prescribed relations between the various offices involves a considerable degree of formality and clearly defined social distance between the occupants of these positions. Formality is manifested by means of a more or less complicated social ritual which symbolises and supports the pecking order of the various offices. Such formality, which is integrated with the distribution of authority within the system, serves to minimize friction by largely restricting (official) contact to modes which are previously defined by the rules of the organization. Ready calculability of others' behavior and a stable set of mutual expectations is thus built up. Moreover, formality facilitates the interaction of the occupants of offices despite their (possibly hostile) private attitudes toward one another. In this way, the subordinate is protected from the arbitrary action of his superior, since the actions of both are constrained by a mutually recognized set of rules. Specific procedural devices foster objectivity and restrain the 'quick passage of impulse into action.'

The structure of bureaucracy

The ideal type of such formal organization is bureaucracy and, in many respects, the classical analysis of bureaucracy is that by Max Weber. Most bureaucratic offices involve the expectation of life-long tenure, in the absence of disturbing factors which may decrease the size of the organization. Bureaucracy maximizes vocational security. The function of security of tenure, pensions, incremental salaries and regularized procedures for promotion is to ensure the devoted performance of official duties, without regard for extraneous pressures. The chief merit of bureaucracy is its technical efficiency, with a premium placed on precision, speed, expert control, continuity, discretion, and optimal returns on input. The structure is one which approaches the complete elimination of personalized relationships and nonrational considerations (hostility, anxiety, affectual involvements, etc.).

With increasing bureaucratization, it becomes plain to all who would see that man is to a very important degree controlled by his social relations to the instruments of production. This can no longer seem only a tenet of Marxism, but a stubborn fact to be acknowledged by all, quite apart from their ideological persuasion. Bureaucratization makes readily visible what was previously dim and obscure. More and more people discover that to work, they must be employed. For to work, one must have tools and equipment. And the tools and equipment are increasingly available only in bureaucracies, private or public.

Bureaucracy is administration which almost completely avoids public discussion of its techniques, although there may occur public discussion of its policies. This secrecy is confined neither to public nor to private bureaucracies. It is held to be necessary to keep valuable information from private economic competitors or from foreign and potentially hostile political groups. And though it is not often so called, espionage among competitors is perhaps as common, if not as intricately organized, in systems of private economic enterprise as in systems of national states. Cost figures, lists of clients, new technical processes, plans for production – all these are typically regarded as essential secrets of private economic bureaucracies which might be revealed if the bases of all decisions and policies had to be publicly defended.

The dysfunctions of bureaucracy

In these bold outlines, the positive attainments and functions of bureaucratic organization are emphasized and the internal stresses and strains of such structures are almost wholly neglected. The community at large, however, evidently emphasizes the imperfections of bureaucracy, as is suggested by the fact that the 'horrid hybrid,' bureaucrat, has become an epithet, a *Schimpfwort*.

The transition to a study of the negative aspects of bureaucracy is afforded by the application of Veblen's concept of 'trained incapacity,' Dewey's notion of 'occupational psychosis' or Warnotte's view of 'professional deformation.' Trained incapacity refers to that state of affairs in which one's abilities function as inadequacies or blind spots. Actions based upon training and skills which have been successfully applied in the past may result in inappropriate responses **under changed conditions**. An inadequate flexibility in the application of skills, will, in a changing milieu, result in more or less serious maladjustments. Thus, to adopt a barnyard illustration used in this connection by Burke, chickens may be readily conditioned to interpret the sound of a bell as a signal for food. The same bell may now be used to summon the trained chickens to their doom as they are assembled to suffer decapitation. In general, one adopts measures in keeping with one's past training and, under new conditions which are not recognized as **significantly** different, the very soundness of this training may lead to the adoption of the wrong procedures. Again, in Burke's almost echolalic phrase, 'people may be unfitted by being fit in an unfit fitness'; their training may become an incapacity.

Dewey's concept of occupational psychosis rests upon much the same observations. As a result of their day to day routines, people develop special preferences, antipathies, discriminations and emphases. (The term psychosis is used by Dewey to denote a 'pronounced character of the mind.') These psychoses develop through demands put upon the individual by the particular organization of his occupational role.

The concepts of both Veblen and Dewey refer to a fundamental ambivalence. Any action can be considered in terms of what it attains or what it fails to attain. 'A way of seeing is also a way of not seeing – a focus upon object A involves a neglect of object B.'

In his discussion, Weber is almost exclusively concerned with what the bureaucratic structure attains: precision, reliability, efficiency. This same structure may be examined from another perspective provided by the ambivalence. What are the limitations of the organizations designed to attain these goals?

For reasons which we have already noted, the bureaucratic structure exerts a constant pressure upon the official to be 'methodical, prudent, disciplined.' If the bureaucracy is to operate successfully, it must attain a high degree of reliability of behavior, an unusual degree of conformity with prescribed patterns of action. Hence, the fundamental importance of discipline which may be as highly developed in a religious or economic bureaucracy as in the army. Discipline can be effective only if the ideal patterns are buttressed by strong sentiments which entail devotion to one's duties, a keen sense of the limitation of one's authority and competence, and methodical performance of routine activities. The efficacy of social structure depends ultimately upon infusing group participants with appropriate attitudes and sentiments. But this very emphasis leads to a transference of the sentiments from the **aims** of the organization onto the particular details of behavior required by the rules. Adherence to the rules, originally conceived as a means, becomes transformed into an end-in-itself; there occurs the familiar process of **displacement of goals** whereby 'an instrumental value becomes a terminal value.' Discipline, readily interpreted as conformance with regulations, whatever the situation, is seen not as a measure designed for specific purposes but becomes an immediate value in the life-organization of the bureaucrat. This emphasis, resulting from the displacement of the original goals, develops into rigidities and an inability to adjust readily. Formalism, even ritualism, ensues with an unchallenged insistence upon punctilious adherence to formalized procedures. This may be exaggerated to the point where primary concern with conformity to the rules interferes with the achievement of the purposes of the organization, in which case we have the familiar phenonenon of the technicism or red tape of the official. An extreme product of this process of displacement of goals is the bureaucratic virtuoso, who never forgets a single rule.

Structural sources of overconformity

Such inadequacies in orientation which involve trained incapacity clearly derive from structural sources. The process may be briefly recapitulated. (1) An effective bureaucracy demands reliability of response and strict devotion to regulations. (2) Such devotion to the rules leads to their transformation into absolutes; they are no longer conceived as relative to a set of purposes. (3) This interferes with ready adaptation under special conditions not clearly envisaged by those who drew up the general rules. (4) Thus, the very elements which conduce toward efficiency in general produce inefficiency in specific instances. Full realization of the inadequacy is seldom attained by members of the group who have not divorced themselves from the meanings which the rules have for them. These rules in time become symbolic in cast, rather than strictly utilitarian.

Thus far, we have treated the ingrained sentiments making for rigorous discipline simply as data, as given. However, definite features of the bureaucratic structure may be seen to conduce to these sentiments. The bureaucrat's official life is planned for him in terms of a graded career, through the organizational devices of promotion by seniority, pensions, incremental salaries, etc., all of which are designed to provide incentives for disciplined action and conformity to the official regulations. The official is tacitly expected to and largely does adapt his thoughts, feelings and actions to the prospect of this career. But **these very devices** which increase the probability of conformance also lead to an over-concern with strict adherence to regulations which induces timidity, conservatism, and technicism. Displacement of sentiments from goals onto means is fostered by the tremendous symbolic significance of the means (rules).

Another feature of the bureaucratic structure tends to produce much the same result. Functionaries have the sense of a common destiny for all those who work together. They share the same interests, especially since there is relatively little competition in so far as promotion is in terms of seniority. In-group aggression is thus minimized and this arrangement is therefore conceived to be positively functional for the bureaucracy. However, the *esprit de corps* and informal social organization which typically develops in such situations often leads the personnel to defend their entrenched interests rather than to assist their clientele and elected higher officials.

It would be much too facile and partly erroneous to attribute such resistance by bureaucrats simply to vested interests. Vested interests oppose any new order which either eliminates or at least makes uncertain their differential advantage deriving from the current arrangements. This is undoubtedly involved in part in bureaucratic resistance to change but another process is perhaps more significant. As we have seen, bureaucratic officials affectively identify themselves with their way of life. They have a pride of craft which leads them to resist change in established routines; at least, those changes which are felt to be imposed by others.

Primary vs. secondary relations

Another feature of the bureaucratic structure, the stress on depersonalization of relationships, also plays its part in the bureaucrat's trained incapacity. The personality pattern of the bureaucrat is nucleated about this norm of impersonality. Both this and the categorizing tendency, which develops from the dominant role of general, abstract rules, tend to produce conflict in the bureaucrat's contacts with the public or clientele. Since functionaries minimize personal relations and resort to categorization, the peculiarities of individual cases are often ignored. But the client who, quite understandably, is convinced of the special features of **his** own problem often objects to such categorical treatment. Stereotyped behavior is not adapted to the exigencies of individual problems. The impersonal treatment of affairs which are at times of great personal significance to the client gives rise to the charge of 'arrogance' and 'haughtiness' of the bureaucrat.

Still another source of conflict with the public derives from the bureaucratic structure. The bureaucrat, in part irrespective of his position within the hierachy, acts as a representative of the power and prestige of the entire structure. In his official role he is vested with definite authority. This often leads to an actually or apparently domineering attitude, which may only be exaggerated by a discrepancy between his position within the hierarchy and his position with reference to the public.[1] Protest and recourse to other officials on the part of the client are often ineffective or largely precluded by the previously mentioned *esprit de corps* which joins the officials into a more or less solidary ingroup. [W]ith the monopolistic nature of the public organization, no such alternative is possible. Moreover, in this case, tension is increased because of a discrepancy between ideology and fact: the governmental personnel are held to be 'servants of the people,' but in fact they are

---

[1] In this connection, note the relevance of Koffka's comments on certain features of the pecking-order of birds. 'If one compares the behavior of the bird at the top of the pecking list, the despot, with that of one very far down, the second or third from the last, then one finds the latter much more cruel to the few others over whom he lords it than the former in his treatment of all members. As soon as one removes from the group all members above the penultimate, his behavior becomes milder and may even become very friendly. . . It is not difficult to find analogies to this in human societies, and therefore one side of such behavior must be primarily the effects of the social groupings, and not of individual characteristics.' K. Koffka, *Principles of Gestalt Psychology* (New York: Harcourt, Brace, 1935), 668–9.

often superordinate. Thus, with respect to the relations between officials and clientele, one structural source of conflict is the pressure for formal and impersonal treatment when individual, personalized consideration is desired by the client. The conflict may be viewed, then, as deriving from the introduction of inappropriate attitudes and relationships. Conflict with**in** the bureaucratic structure arises from the converse situation, namely, when personalized relationships are substituted for the structurally required impersonal relationships.

The organization man

WILLIAM H. WHYTE

This [reading] is about the organization man. They are not the workers, nor are they the white-collar people in the usual, clerk sense of the word. These people only work for The Organization. The ones I am talking about **belong** to it as well. They are the ones of our middle class who have left home, spiritually as well as physically, to take the vows of organization life. Listen to them talk to each other over the front lawns of their suburbia and you cannot help but be struck by how well they grasp the common denominators which bind them. Whatever the differences in their organization ties, it is the common problems of collective work that dominate their attentions. They are wry about it, to be sure; they talk of the 'treadmill', the 'rat race', of the inability to control one's direction. But they have no great sense of plight; between themselves and organization they believe they see an ultimate harmony and, more than most elders recognize, they are building an ideology that will vouchsafe this trust. When a young man says that to make a living these days you must do what somebody else wants you to do, he states it not only as a fact of life that must be accepted but as an inherently good proposition.

The organization man seeks a redefinition of his place on earth – a faith that will satisfy him that what he must endure has a deeper meaning than appears on the surface. I am going to call it a Social Ethic. With reason it could be called an organization ethic, or a bureaucratic ethic:

[· · · · ·]

The union between the world of organization and the college has been so cemented that today's seniors can see a continuity between the college and

Abridged extracts reproduced with permission from Whyte, W.A. *The Organisation Man*, pp. 8–11, 62–3, 76–7, 85–6, 97, 128–30, 197, 253–5; proprietors Simon & Schuster, Inc., published by Pelican, Harmondsworth, 1963.

the life thereafter that we never did. Come graduation, they do not go outside to a hostile world; they transfer.

For the senior who is headed for the corporation it is almost as if it were part of one master scheme. The locale shifts; the training continues, for at the same time that the colleges have been changing their curriculum to suit the corporation, the corporation has responded by setting up its own campuses and classrooms. By now the two have been so well moulded that it's difficult to tell where one leaves off and the other begins. Whatever their many differences, in one great respect they are all of a piece: more than any generation in memory, theirs will be a generation of bureaucrats.

How did he get that way? His elders taught him to be that way. [W]hat he has been getting is more and more a training in the minutiae of the organization skills, and while it is hardly news that the US inclines to the vocational, the magnitude of the swing has been much greater than is generally recognised. Only three out of every ten college graduates are now majoring in anything that could be called a fundamental discipline – in the liberal arts **or** in the sciences. Figures also indicate that this trend has been gathering force for a long time and that it is not to be explained away as a freak of current supply and demand or a hang-over from the disruptions of the Second World War. [E]xecutives of many of our best-known corporations have been arguing in print and speech that for the corporation's own good, the value of fundamental education needs to be restressed. Looking at all these signs, some people hopefully conclude that at last we are now on the verge of a great resurgence in the humanities.

I do not believe any such thing is going to happen. All these agitations for fundamental education are welcome and necessary, but they are minute, I submit, to the forces working in the other direction.

Each year more and more of those who will replace them [the liberal and science student] will be vocational graduates.

[· · · · ·]

I return to my pessimistic forecast. Look ahead to 1985. Those who will control a good part of the educational plant will be products themselves of the most stringently anti-intellectual training in the country. Nor will the layman be out of tune with the vocationalists; to judge by the new suburbia the bulk of middle-class parents of 1985 will know no other standards to evaluate education of their children than those of the social-adjustment type of schooling. And who will be picking the schools to endow and sitting on the boards of trustees? More and more it will be the man of The Organization, the graduate of the business school – the 'modern man', in sum, that his education was so effectively designed to bring about.

The rough-and-tumble days are over

Since the job is to keep things going, more than pioneering, the leader must be the professional manager, 'the man who knows how to elicit participative consultation, how to motivate groups and individuals, how to enhance job satisfactions . . . how to conduct problem-solving meetings.' He will be a generalist who will not think in terms of specific work but in the science of making other people work.

In the old sense of work, he does not work; he encourages others to work. He does not create; he moderates and adjusts those who do create. 'Primarily he is the balance wheel on the tendency of the professional-type individual to wander into new, unexplored, and perhaps dangerous territory.'

Unorthodoxy can be dangerous to The Organization

The pro-administrators sometimes conceded that the administrator could have unconventional ideas himself at times. But, they were in haste to add, he ought to be rather sober about it, and it was on the dangers rather than on the advantages of such unorthodox thinking that they dwelt.

Unorthodoxy is dangerous to The Organization

Some personnel men didn't simply omit mention of inner qualities such as 'drive' and 'imagination'; they went out of their way to warn against them. 'Any progressive employer', said one personnel director, 'would look askance at the individualist and would be reluctant to instil such thinking in the minds of trainees.' Another personnel man put it in more direct terms: 'Men of strong personal convictions, willing to make unorthodox decisions, are more frequently given to the characteristics of 'drive' **rather than** "leadership".' (Italics mine.) This invidious pairing of qualities once thought congenial with each other was not restricted entirely to personnel men. 'We used to look primarily for brilliance' said one president. 'Now that much-abused word 'character' has become very important. We don't care if you're a Phi Beta Kappa or a Tau Beta Phi. We want a well-rounded person who can handle well-rounded people.'

Ideas come from the group, not from the individual

The well-rounded man is one who does not think up ideas himself but mediates other people's ideas and so democratically that he never lets his own judgement override the decisions of the group. 'The decisions should be made by the group,' says a personnel director, 'and agreement reached after discussion and consultation prior to action.' 'The leaders must be attentive and receptive to the ideas of his followers,' says another personnel man, 'and he must adjust his ideas accordingly.'

If the corporation concentrates on getting people who will process other people's ideas, where will it get the other people – that is, the people with ideas?

But even if the 'well-rounded' ideal were no more than rationalization, the concept would still be powerful. It is self-proving. As an example of one very practical consequence we have only to note that in many large corporations the junior executives help out on the interviewing and selecting necessary to restock the cadres. As the trainees go back to the campus to search for their own image, they go back strengthened more than ever in their anti-intellectualism, and in a great Mendelian selection process well-rounded men who were chosen by well-rounded men in turn chose more well-rounded men.

From company to company, trainees express the same impatience. All the great ideas, they explain, have already been discovered and not only in physics and chemistry but in practical fields like engineering. The basic creative work is done, so the man you need – for every kind of job – is a practical, team-player who will do a good shirt-sleeves job. 'I would sacrifice brilliance'. one trainee said, 'for human understanding every time.'

And they do too.

Thus, searching for their own image, management men look for the 'well-rounded' scientists. They don't expect them to be quite as 'well rounded' as junior-executive trainees; they generally note that scientists are 'different'. They do it, however, in a patronising way that implies that the difference is nothing that a good indoctrination programme won't fix up.

Management has tried to adjust the scientist to The Organization rather than The Organization to the scientist. It can do this with the mediocre and still have a harmonious group. It cannot do it with the brilliant; only freedom will make them harmonious. Most corporations sense this, but, unfortunately, the moral they draw from it is something else [again].

Men and women of the corporation

ROSABETH MOSS KANTER

It is not the consciousness of men that determines their existence, but, on the contrary, their social existence determines their consciousness.

(*Karl Marx, A Contribution to the Critique of Political Economy*)

But the understandings of the greater part of men are necessarily formed by their ordinary employments.

(*Adam Smith, The Wealth of Nations*)

The shift in the structure and character of work has created a demand that work produce more than purely economic benefits. To make a living is no longer enough. Work also has to make a life.

(*Peter Drucker, Management*)

Abridged extracts reproduced from Kanter, R.M. *Men and Women of the Corporation*, pp. 1–257; published by Basic Books, Harper Collins, USA, 1977.

The most distinguished advocate and the most distinguished critic of modern capitalism were in agreement on one essential point: the job makes the person. Adam Smith and Karl Marx both recognized the extent to which people's attitudes and behaviors take shape out of the experiences they have in their work.

If jobs 'create' people, then the corporation is the quintessential contemporary people-producer. It employs a large proportion of the labor force, and its practices often serve as models for the organization of other systems. How people-production happens in all large bureaucracies, but especially in one manufacturing firm, is the subject of this [reading]. The case of the organization I have named Industrial Supply Corporation (Indsco) provides the context for illuminating the ways in which organization structure forms people's sense of themselves and of their possibilities.

My focus is on the people who work in offices, who run the administrative apparatus of the large organization. They consist of two major groups. First are the managers, professionals, and technical personnel who make up what Norman Birnbaum called the 'new middle class,' those who are 'workers in all but name and consciousness' and whose 'very careers entail not only acceptance of hierarchy but factural complicity in its maintenance, in the actual exercise of power.' At the very top of this group are the corporate executives Birnbaum termed the 'new elite,' who have effective control of the collective property represented in the corporation, along with privileged access to stock ownership. Far below in status and class position but contiguous in office space are the corps of paper-handlers, record-keepers, and data-manipulators – the clerical and service personnel who make up 'an army of those skilled in one or another organizational technique, or in more specific techniques placed at the service of organizations. They are subordinate, even if the possibility of ascent is open.' In both of these organisational classes, my concern is with individuals and their work experiences rather than with the conflict between classes or the operation of interest groups. The ideologies and theories that legitimate the position and define the characteristics of managers and clericals are described.

The problems of power and powerlessness are taken up [here]. If power is defined as efficacy (the ability to mobilize resources) rather than domination, then the importance of power to the lives of people in organizations makes sense. In the large bureaucracy, power is a virtual requisite for effective performance in jobs with accountability for others, and subordinates have good reasons to prefer to work for the more powerful leaders. The specifically organizational ways in which power accumulates are examined: through activities (often made possible by job attributes) and through alliances with sponsors, peers, and even subordinates. But the several sources of bureaucratic powerlessness (accountability without power) are also made clear; the struggles of people to operate in a powerless situation leads them to tend toward rigid, rules-minded, controlling, and possessive styles. So a major cause of ineffective, stereotypically 'bureaucratic' behavior is seen to lie in the extent to which too few people are empowered in large organizations; the solution becomes a wider sharing of power. Indeed, the problems of women in managerial roles (a preference for male bosses, an image of women's controlling style) spring into focus as problems of powerlessness, not sex.

[I] consider how relative numbers – social composition of groups – affect relationships between men and women (or any two kinds of people). Wherever occupational sex segregation has been in effect, as it has in the managerial and professional ranks of corporations like Indsco, those women who do break into men's territories find themselves in the position of the very few among the very many. This position as 'tokens' (representatives of their category rather than independent individuals) accounts for many of the difficulties such numerically scarce people face in fitting in, gaining peer acceptance, and behaving 'naturally.' The existence of tokens encourages social segregation and stereotyping and may lead the person in that position to overcompensate through either overachievement or hiding successes, or to turn against people of his or her own kind. Thus, numbers – proportional representation – are important not only because they **symbolize** the presence or absense of discrimination but also because they have real consequences for performance.

Some of the context behind my analysis is unique to the administrative ranks of profit-making, shareholder-owned, manufacturing corporations: the high salaries and luxurious fringe benefits for top people; the emphasis on upward mobility and increasing status as a measure of achievement; the frequency of executive transfer among geographic areas and the stringency of constraints on executive wives; the preeminence of sales and marketing functions; a strong technical orientation and a non-intellectual (or even anti-intellectual) culture; and an official political ideology that is pro-capitalist, antiregulation, barely tolerant of unions, and generally conservative. In short, many details of life and behavior inside Indsco reflect the culture, language, and style of mainstream American industry three-quarters of the way through the century.

The women's issue also appears as an important sub-theme in this book. Why is the women's issue joined with examination of the effects of organization structure? There are several important reasons. First, no study of human behavior can any longer be considered complete that ignores the special roles, positions, and constraints affecting women in the public arena, as well as the men who have traditionally peopled organizational research. At the same time, the fate of women is inextricably bound up with organizational structure and processes in the same way that men's life-at-work is shaped by them. Differences based on sex retreat into the background as the people-creating, behavior-shaping properties of organizational locations become clear. Findings about the 'typical' behavior of women in organizations that have been assumed to reflect either biologically based psychological attributes or characteristics developed through a long socialization to a 'female sex role' turn out to reflect very reasonable – and very universal – responses to current organizational situations. Even discrimination itself emerges as a consequence of organizational pressures as much as individual prejudice. Thus, specific attention to women as well as men is one way to demonstrate the utility of the perspective that 'the job makes the person.' And, in turn, to help women.

[I locate] a large measure of the responsibility for the behaviors people engage in at work and their fate inside organizations in the structure of work systems themselves. Life does not consist of infinite possibility because situations do not make all responses equally plausible or equally available. But the limits are not as much internal, rooted in the person, as they are structural and situational. In the view advanced here, people are capable of more than their organizational positions ever give them the tools or the time or the opportunity to demonstrate.

There is both tragedy and hope embodied in this perspective.

Tragedy lies in the self-defeating traps into which individuals fall when they try to make the most of a disadvantaged situation, only to sink further into 'failure' and to generate a cycle that makes rescue increasingly unlikely. Some of the ways people choose to gain recognition and value and to fight for a piece of autonomy, when their situations greatly constrain their bargaining tools, only bind them further to the constraining situation. Or, the dilemmas people confront can provide them with a set of choices that are equally restricting, from which there is no escape.

Behavior in organizations can only be fully understood when there is adequate appreciation of the self-perpetuating cycles and inescapable dilemmas posed by the contingencies of social life: Managers who solve the 'trust' problem inherent in delegating decision-making discretion by insisting on outward, social conformity, only to put themselves in a conformist box, and one where outward appearance becomes manipulated so that it is even less a sign of trustworthiness, and conformity must be even more tightly controlled.

Secretaries who do work that is so lowskill and replaceable that their only way to get recognition and perhaps advancement is to develop a relationship of personal service with a boss, only to find themselves tied further to that boss and rewarded for things that are not generalizable or useful anywhere else in the organization. Wives who must choose how to handle a formal exclusion from the company and an informal set of restrictive social demands. People at dead ends who lower their aspirations, stop trying, disengage, and make it less likely that they will ever get unstuck. 'Token' women who are always different from their peers, no matter what they do, so that they can never be just normal members of the organization but always symbols of their kind. The people with advantage, for whom the cycles are always upward (opportunity creating more opportunity, power generating power), are equally responding to their situations, but they are fortunate in being provided with more of the tools that make success possible. New tools can be provided. The people who are stuck can be offered challenges. The powerless can be given more discretion, more influence over decisions. Tokens can be provided with allies. And more if it is organization structure rather than intrinsic character that determines organizational behavior, then self-defeating, self-perpetuating cycles can be interrupted. The fabric of job relationships can be changed.

Managers: Roles and images

The new career managers lacked a class position buttressed by tradition that would provide grounds for legitimation of their authority. After all, they were neither owners nor a traditional 'ruling class.' (Reinhard Bendix discussed the concerns about authority this evokes in *Work and Authority in Industry*.) Managers had to seek legitimation instead in the increasing professionalization of management, in the development of a 'spirit of managerialism' that gave ideological coherence to the control of a relatively small and exclusive group of men over a large group of workers, and that also differentiated the viewpoint of managers from that of owner-entrepreneurs. The managerial viewpoint stressed rationality and efficiency as the *raison d'être* for managerial control. Without the power of property to back them, the new managers created and relied, instead, on a claim of 'efficiency,' in order to 'justify the unilateral exercise of power by management.' Control by managers was held to provide the most 'rational' way to run an enterprise, and, as Michel Crozier pointed out, in *The Bureaucratic Tradition* (1964), rationality represents one of the best grounds for challenging entrenched power groups. On their claims to hold the keys to efficiency, then, and to know the 'one best way' to organize work, managers provided a basis for their ever-extending role. A review of the origins of modern management theory shows just how 'masculinized' and paternalistic the definition of this role was. To paraphrase Max Weber's classic title, the evolving 'spirit of managerialism' was infused with a 'masculine ethic.'

Although the history of management theory, from scientific management through the human relations school, has been recounted many times, it is worth examining again in the light of its implications for the stratification of organizations by sex.

Management found its first prophet in Frederick Winslow Taylor, the steel company engineer turned management consultant, and its theory in Taylor's 'scientific management.' Taylor gave a name and rationale to the concept of the rational manager who made decisions based on logical, passionless analysis. Although the specifics of Taylor's thought were not necessarily adopted, his general ideas influenced managerial thinking and helped create what has become known as 'classical' administrative theory, a set of theories of organization that 'operate on the principle of establishing in advance of performance the methods of work and areas of responsibility for each position in the structure. . . . The manifest intention of this rationalization is to direct energy in quantity, time, and place according to an overall plan of organization function.

[· · · · ·]

Managers at Indsco had to look the part. They were not exactly cut out of the same mold like paper dolls, but the similarities in appearance were striking. Even this relatively trivial matter revealed the extent of conformity pressures on managers. Not that there were formal dress rules in this enlightened company, like the legendary IBM uniforms, but there was an informal understanding all the same. The norms were unmistakable, after a visitor saw enough managers, invariably white and male, with a certain shiny, clean cut look. The only beards, even after beards became merely daring rather than radical, were the results of vacation-time experiments on camping trips, except (it was said), for a few in R&D – 'but we know that scientists do strange things,' a sales manager commented. An inappropriate appearance could be grounds for complaint to higher management. A new field supervisor was visited by his boss for a 'chat about setting a good example for the guys' after his longish hair, curling the slightest way down the nape of his neck, caused comment. 'Appearance makes a big difference in the response you get around this company,' the boss insisted. Another executive was upset because a staff expert he frequently called upon for help seemed to change his appearance or hairstyle with each fashion wind. 'What are you trying to do now?' he once asked the staffer exasperatedly. 'We get used to you one way, then you have to change. Why must you always be changing?'

If differences in appearance were not easily tolerated in the ranks of those called managers, neither were a wide range of other sorts of difference. It is not news that social conformity is important in managerial careers. There is ample evidence from organizational studies that leaders in a variety of situations are likely to show preference for socially similar subordinates and help them get ahead. As Clark Kerr and his colleagues wrote, 'Incumbents in the managerial hierarchy seek as new recruits those they can rely upon and trust. They demand that the newcomers be loyal, that they accept authority, and that they conform to a prescribed pattern of behavior.'

Unlike a more communal environment, where eccentrics can be lovingly tolerated because trust is based on mutual commitments and deep personal knowledge, those who run the bureaucratic corporation often rely on outward manifestations to determine who is the 'right sort of person.' Managers tend to carefully guard power and privilege for those who fit in, for those they see as 'their kind.' Wilbert Moore was commenting on this phenomenon when he used the metaphor of a 'bureaucratic kinship system' to describe the corporation – but a kinship system based on 'homosexual reproduction,' in which men reproduce themselves in their own image. The metaphor is apt. Because of the **situation** in which managers function, because of the position of managers in the corporate structure, social similarity tends to become extremely important to them. The structure sets in motion forces leading to the replication of managers as the same kind of social individuals. And the men who manage reproduce themselves in kind. In one industrial organization, managers who moved ahead needed to be members of the

Masonic Order and the local yacht club; not Roman Catholic; Anglo-Saxon or Germanic in origin; and Republican.

It is the uncertainty quotient in managerial work, as it has come to be defined in the large modern corporation, that causes management to become so socially restricting: to develop tight inner circles excluding social strangers; to keep control in the hands of socially homogeneous peers; to stress conformity and insist upon a diffuse, unbounded loyalty; and to prefer ease of communication and thus social certainty over the strains of dealing with people who are 'different.' Situational pressures, then, place a great emphasis on personal relations and social homogeneity as functional elements in the carrying out of managerial tasks. And privilege is also kept within a small circle.

The social homogeneity of big business leaders from the early-to-middle twentieth century has been noted frequently by critics such as C. Wright Mills as well as business historians. Their class background and social characteristics tended to be similar: largely white, Protestant men from elite schools.

At Indsco, until ten years ago, top executives in the corporation were traceable to the founders of the company or its subsidiaries – people who held stock or were married to people who did. There was a difference between who did well in the divisions, where performance tended to account for more, and who got into top positions in the corporation itself. To get ahead in the corporation, social connections were known to be very important. Indeed, corporate staff positions became a place to put people who were nonmovers, whose performance was not outstanding, but were part of the 'family.' The social homogeneity of corporate executives was duly noted by other managers. One asked a consultant, 'Do all companies have an ethnic flavor? Our top men all seem to be Scotch-Irish.' (But as management has become more rationalized, and the corporation has involved itself more heavily in divisional operations, there has also been a trend, over the past five years, toward more 'objective' criteria for high-level corporate positions.)

We expect a direct correlation, then, between the degree of uncertainty in a position – the extent to which organizations must rely on personal discretion – and a reliance on 'trust' through 'homosocial reproduction' – selection of incumbents on the basis of social similarity. People who do not 'fit in' by **social** characteristics to the homogeneous management group tend to be clustered in those parts of management with least uncertainty. They are in places where what to do and how to judge its doing tend to be more routine. They are found in increasing numbers away from the top, and they are found in staff positions where they serve as technical specialists. Some women have succeeded in management because of their membership in the ruling family; they were already part of the inner circle. However, most women in business have found their management opportunities in low uncertainty, non-discretionary positions that bear the least pressure to close the circle: closer to the bottom, in more routinised in functions, and in 'expert' rather than decision-making roles. They are also found in those areas where least social contact and organizational communication are required: in staff roles that are administrative rather than line management and in functions such as public relations, where they are removed from the interdependent social networks of the corporation's principal operations.

If the desire for social homogeneity is fostered by organizational uncertainty, the need for smooth communication sets up another set of exclusionary pressures.

If pressures for total dedication sometimes serve to **include** wives in peripheral and auxiliary roles, they also serve to **exclude** many other women from employment as managers. Women have been assumed not to have the dedication of men to their work, or they have been seen to have conflicting loyalties, competing pulls from their other relationships. Successful women executives, as Margaret Hennig showed in her interviews with a hundred of them, have often put off marriage until rather late so that they could devote their time during the important ladder-climbing years to a single-minded pursuit of their careers.

Concerns expressed by men in management about the suitability of women for managerial roles reflect these themes. Questions about turnover, absenteeism, and ambition are frequently raised in meetings at Indsco, when affirmative action officers try to enlist the support of other managers. Sets of statistics and information countering prevalent myths have been prepared to hand out in response to such likely questions. The issue behind them often has to do with marriage.

The question of marriage is experienced by some women in professional, managerial, or sales ladders at Indsco as full of contradictory injunctions. Sometimes they got the message that being single was an advantage, five women reported, sometimes that it was just the opposite. Two single women, one of them forty, in quite different functions, were told by their managers that they could not be given important jobs because they were likely to get married and leave. One male manager said to a female subordinate that he would wait about five years before promoting a competent woman to see if she 'falls into marriage.' On the other hand, they were also told in other circumstances that married women cannot be given important jobs because of their family responsibilities: their children, if they are working mothers; their unborn children and the danger they will leave with pregnancy, if currently childless. One woman asked her manager for a promotion, to which he replied, 'You're probably going to get pregnant.' So she pointed out to him that he told her that eight years ago, and she hadn't. A divorced woman similarly discussed promotion with her manager and was asked 'How long do you want the job? Do you think you'll get married again?' One working mother who had heard that 'married women are absent more,' had to prove that she had taken only one day off in eleven years at Indsco.

A male manager in the distribution function who supervised many women confirmed the women's reports. He said that he never even considered asking a married woman to do anything that involved travel, even if this was in the interests of her career development, and therefore he could not see how he could recommend a woman for promotion into management.

[Secretaries]

The secretarial ladder was short, and rank was determined by bosses' statuses. A secretary with three to four years' experience was eligible for promotion to Secretary II, working for a PRO (person-reporting-to-officer). Secretary IIIs had seven to twelve years' experience and worked for divisional vice-presidents. Secretary IVs worked for division presidents and executive vice-presidents. At the top were executive secretaries of corporate officers. Sometimes these women took on some supervisory responsibility for the secretaries of lower-level managers, distributing extra work or discussing personnel problems. A survey of eighty-eight nonexempt[1] women at one location in 1974 indicated just how limited the secretarial-clerical opportunity structure was. Though 25 per cent of the women had worked for the company over fifteen years, only 12 per cent had held more than three jobs in the corporation. An old hand recalled: 'A person used to be forty-five before becoming an executive secretary and stayed there for fifteen to twenty years. Now they move much faster. They get there at twenty-nine and have no place else to go.' Salaries were also not high. Over half of the nonexempt women earned less than $11,000 a year, despite so many with long service. The executive secretarial position was the peak for nonexempt women. The ceiling for secretaries was set by how high a boss they could snare.

The secretary–boss relationship is the most striking instance of the retention of patrimony within the bureaucracy. Fewer bureaucratic 'safeguards' apply here than in any other part of the system. When bosses make demands at their own discretion and arbitrarily choose secretaries on grounds that enhance their own personal status rather than meeting organizational efficiency tests; expect personal service with limits negotiated privately; exact loyalty; and make the secretary a part of their private retinue, moving when they move – then the relationship has elements of patrimony.

Even more important was the fact that the **boss's status determined the power of the secretary**. Even on the lowest levels, secretaries had some influence through their bosses, mostly in terms of people: the secretaries' assessment of other people in the office or their evaluation of new candidates for clerical jobs. Higher up, secretaries' power derived from control of bosses' calendars. They could make it easy or difficult to see a top executive. They could affect what managers read first, setting priorities for them without their knowing it. They could help or hurt someone's career by the ease with which they allowed that person access.

If the secretary reflected the status of the boss, she also contributed in

[1] [Nonexempt women were relatively junior secretaries working in secretarial pools with little career prospects – Editors]

minor ways to his status. Some people have argued that **secretaries function as 'status symbols'** for executives, holding that the traditional secretarial role is developed and preserved because of its impact on managerial egos, not its contribution to organizational efficiency. One writer was quite explicit about the meaning of a secretary: 'In many companies a secretary outside your door is the most visible sign that you have become an executive; a secretary is automatically assigned to each executive, whether or not his work load requires one . . . When you reach the vice-presidential level, your secretary may have an office of her own, with her name on the door. At the top, the president may have two secretaries . . .' A woman professional at Indsco agreed with the idea that secretaries were doled out as rewards rather than in response to job needs, as she talked about her own problems in getting enough secretarial help.

At Indsco, the secretary's function as a status symbol increased up the ranks as she became more and more bound to a specific boss. 'It's his image, his status, sitting out in front,' a personnel administrator said. 'She's the first thing people see about him.' For this reason, personal appearance – attractiveness and social skills – was a factor in the career prospects of secretaries, with task-related skills again playing a smaller role as secretaries moved up the ranks. 'We have two good secretaries with first-rate skills who can't move up because they dress like grandmothers or housewives,' another official complained. 'Even those executive secretaries who are hitting sixty don't look like mothers. Maybe one or two dowdy types slipped in at that level, but if the guy they work for moves, they couldn't be sold elsewhere at the same grade.' Appearance was so important that secretaries would be sent to Katharine Gibbs as much as for the personal side as for the skills training. Gibbs taught posture, hand care, the use of deodorants, and the importance of clean underwear in addition to filing methods and telephone responses; only recently has Gibbs stopped insisting on the wearing of hats and gloves. This was all designed to make the secretary into a 'pretty package.' Herbert Marcuse, in *One-Dimensional Man*, even considered the secretary to represent a touch of 'managed sex' in the office, a part of the 'large-scale sexual manipulation' of the modern employee: 'Without ceasing to be an instrument of labor, the body is allowed to exhibit its sexual features in the everyday work world and in work relations . . . The sexy office and sales girls, the handsome, virile junior executive . . . are highly marketable commodities . . . Sex is introduced into work and public relations and is thus made more susceptible to (controlled) satisfaction.'

Indsco personnel administrators also found that bosses tended to want highly skilled, highly educated secretaries, whether or not the work load demanded it, as a way of inflating their own importance and deriving status from a secretary. One manager, looking for a new secretary for his department, described the job in glowing terms, stressing the amount of intelligence and independent decision-making it required. The actual job content turned out to be largely typing, filing, and recording material on standardized forms according to a highly routinized procedure. 'Managers don't level about what a job really is,' reported an executive secretary. There was a story circulated among top-level secretaries about a co-worker who did nothing but type from written material, with no opportunity to use initiative, let alone technical skills like shorthand. She soon left the job, and the manager put out a request for a replacement, asking for a 'very experienced secretary,' to the amusement of those reporting the incident. [B]osses had the power to make decisions about the category into which time off fell, being thus able to punish or reward a secretary. [B]y and large, the job was characterized by a degree of availability for unpredictable orders. Power could not be rendered impersonal by the use of routinized schedules.

[Wives!]

The existence of wives also had implications for women officially employed by the company. Just as the image of the secretary spilled over and infused expectations about other women workers, the image of the wife affected responses to career women at Indsco. Because corporate wives were generally seen to be content to operate behind the scenes and to be ambitious for their husbands rather than themselves and because they made use of social rather than intellectual skills in their hostess role, the image of women that emerged for some management men from knowing their own and other wives reinforced the view that career women were an anomaly, that they were unusual or could not really be ambitious, or that their talents must be primarily social and emotional rather than cognitive and managerial. Some men, especially those who had attended engineering schools and were accustomed to an all-male colleague environment, explicitly said they took their sense of how to treat professional and management women from their wives' preferences – often leading to awkward and uncomfortable situations. Such men were then also likely to resent the career women who made them feel uncomfortable, wishing they were more like their wives. (This process of translation could also work **for** employed women, as in the case of a senior executive married to a prominent professional woman, a man who was a strong and public supporter of affirmative action for women). Professional women sometimes said they felt pressure from male managers to live up to the expectations clearly stemming from what the wives were expected to do.

Some of the expectations stemming from the existence of wives had another, more general, effect. Men could bring two people with them to the organization, and indeed, preferential hiring of married men and occasional attention to the wives own characteristics frequently ensured that this was so. But career women, especially in the managerial ranks, did not have this advantage. There was no 'corporate husband' role equivalent to that of corporate wife. Husbands of higher-ranking women who were not themselves part of Indsco sometimes resisted having anything at all to do with the company. One husband refused to attend official dinners or social events with his wife, a marketing executive. At the same time, married women employed by the company were also reminded by their managers of their responsibilities as wives and mothers – or managers expressed concerns that these responsibilities would deflect energy or lower commitment. Thus, while men symbolically brought two people to their jobs, women were seen as perhaps bringing less than one full worker.

The corporate wife as a social role captured public attention in the early 1950s when William H. Whyte, Jr., wrote a series of articles in *Fortune* and elsewhere revealing the extent to which corporations looked over and made rules for wives of men they were considering for executive positions. The corporate wife's acceptance of her fate was taken by Whyte as another sign of the rise of 'groupmindedness,' which he later documented in *The Organization Man*. Whyte's picture, as well as that presented by later journalists and psychiatrists, tended to show the corporate wife as a helpless casualty, even when a willing one. Moving from place to place frequently, subject to rules and constraints, excluded from the office world, stuck with almost exclusive household responsibilities, and lacking their husbands' opportunities for learning and adventure, corporate wives were portrayed as victims of a too-demanding system. And with reason. Alcoholism, unwanted pregnancies, divorce, and bouts of depression in women have all been attributed to features of the managerial lifestyle.

Feminist writings also pointed out the costs of reflected identity or vicarious achievement for wives, and through them, for children. Lack of an independent sense of self was considered a cause of depression. One wife told Robert Seidenberg, 'I bask in my husband's reflected glory. I don't have to be anything myself. His status is my status. Sometimes I feel he's living his life to the fullest, and I'm living his life to the fullest.' However, no one disagreed that marriage to successful men was constraining, shaped role demands for wives, and often put the family last in the men's priorities. William Henry had this to say after a study of the personalities of successful executives: 'They are . . . corporate men, not family men. Wives must actively subordinate themselves to the husbands' work aims or, at the very least, not interfere with them. The key to an effective partnership, and we use this neutral word intentionally, would in fact be the degree to which the wife actively adopted the corporate goals and skillfully aided the husband in that direction. This makes of the wife a kind of highclass assistant, bound by marriage rather than salary but otherwise facilitating the work goals with the same sense of efficiency the husband would expect of his secretary and other office personnel. The all-embracing demands of corporate life do not permit distractions.' As Whyte summarized these latter functions, the wife was a 'wailing wall, a sounding board, and a refuelling station.' She was an important adjunct to the company's motivational apparatus but was never rewarded directly by it for her services.

[The changes required]

Something has been holding women back. That something was usually assumed to be located in the differences between men and women as individuals: their training for different worlds; the nature of sexual relationships, which make women unable to compete with men and men unable to aggress against women; the 'tracks' they were put on in school or at play; and even, in the most biologically reductionist version of the argument, 'natural' dispositions of the sexes. Conclusions like these have become standard explanations for familiar statistics about discrimination. They form the basis for the 'individual' model of work behavior. Whether one leans toward the more social or the more biological side of the argument, both add up to an assumption that the factors producing inequities at work are somehow carried inside the individual person. [The changes] require attention to structures of opportunity and power commitment seems clearly tied to the increasing rewards and chance for growth implied in high opportunity. Furthermore, giving more discretion and autonomy to workers and work groups in formally hierarchical systems creates questions about the role of their immediate supervisors and, eventually, questions about the operation of power in management up the whole line.

These efforts will not work any better than yesterday's, as long as individual models of behavior and change remain in full force. In fact, many change programs in organizations are **not** working. They are using the wrong model and drawing the wrong conclusions. Use of versions of the individual model inevitably leads to the conclusion that 'women are different' and serves to reinforce the present structure of organizations and the one-down position of women within them. Individual model-thinking leads women to believe that the problem lies in their own psychology, and it gives organizations a set of excuses for the slow pace of change. But the whole thrust of this [reading] is to present an alternative model, one that demonstrates that responses to work are a function of basic structural issues, such as the constraints imposed by role and the effects of opportunity, power, and numbers. Attention to **these** issues would require organizations – not people – to change.

References

Hennig, Margaret (1970) 'Career Development of Women Executives' *Ph.D. dissertation, Harvard Business School.*

Henry, William, E. (1967) 'Executive Personality' in Lloydwarne and Darab B. Unwalla (eds), *The Emergent American Society: Large-Scale Organizations*, pp. 241–75. New Haven: Yale University Press.

Kerr, Clark; Dunlop, John T.; Harbison, Frederick H.; and Hyers, Charles A (1960) *Industrialism and Industrial Man*, Cambridge, Mass: Harvard University Press.

Moore, Wilbert (1962) *The Conduct of the Corporation*, New York: Random House, Vintage.

Seidenberg, Robert (1973) *Corporate Wives – Corporate Casualties?* New York: Amacom.

Taylor, Frederick W. (1947) *Scientific Management*, New York: Harper & Row.

The possible biological origins of sexual discrimination

LIONEL TIGER

The biological basis of behaviour

For too long many social scientists have paid inadequate attention not only to the work and thought of behavioural biologists but also to the biological aspects of human behaviour. Sociologists, political scientists and economists have used a model of man in which biological factors were unimportant, or at least residual; no ready means of assimilating information about other living systems than the human has been available to researchers into human social action.

It thus remains the case that undergraduate and post-graduate students in the social sciences almost never are required to demonstrate any serious proficiency in biology. Though they may be subjected to an immense and sophisticated burden of methodological and mathematical instruction and they will learn very well indeed how to collect and handle data, they are hardly likely to learn what data to gather in the first place – in the sense that students of other animals are guided by biological principles to determine what behaviour patterns and what events in the lives of animals reflect a species' central problems, concerns and adaptations.

One serious social and scientific consequence of this is that – as usual – women have suffered particular deprivation. Because of the blurring of biological distinctions, even the categories 'maleness' and 'femaleness' have been inadequately treated – perhaps much less than the less significant and less provocative categories 'rich' and 'poor'. The over and surprising reason for this is that it has been tacitly assumed that in all spheres except the explicitly reproductive males and females are much the same. To suggest otherwise implies biases of a quasi-racial kind. Moreover, there was also an implication that female equality in practice might be eroded by the assumption of female difference in theory.

My argument is that it is necessary to see biological factors as of prime importance in discussing maleness and femaleness. This involves understanding human evolution, human neurophysiology, cross-cultural regularities – in general, the biological infrastructure of human social relationships. Knowing as we do the importance of socio-sexual differences in many mammalian reproductive systems, perhaps it will not surprise if, employing this perspective, we learn that we are a species boasting considerable male-female differences which extend and ramify more widely through our human societies than many of our theories of socialization, organization and action in general would have us recognize and predict.

Abridged excerpts reproduced with permission from Tiger, L. The Possible Origins of Sexual Discrimination. *Impact of Science on Society*, vol. XX, no. 70, 1970, 29–44.

Hunting, the master pattern

It could be said that our most elaborate biological adaptation is to create culture. But if culture is our most complex concoction, it remains unchallenged by anthropologists and biologists that hunting is the master pattern of the human species. It is the organizing activity which integrated the morphological, physiological, genetic and intellectual aspects of the individual human organisms and of the population who compose our single species. Hunting is a way of life, not simply a 'subsistence technique', and it involves commitments, correlates and consequences spanning the entire biobehavioural continuum of the individual and of the entire species of which he is a member.

[O]ur practice of hunting was the infra-structural condition of our specialized evolution, and though it is tempting to see in this only a confirmation of theories of human bloodiness and evil, it remains the case that hunting was a co-operative activity and that in the acts of pursuit and slaughter there was selective advantage to those individuals able to work together, attuned to each others' needs, resources and states, and willing to mould their individual behaviour to the collective pattern of the group.

The critical subordinate section of this argument (for our purpose here) is that hunting was an all-male enterprise and that just as there was selection **for** co-operative hunting males, there was selection **against** both those females willing to hunt and those males agreeable to female participants in their hunts. The reasons for this proposition depend on a variety of individually disputable bits of evidence. But their over-all implications seem to point forcefully in the direction of an increased differentiation of male-female behaviour through evolution at the same time as there was probably a decreased physical differentiation.

How theoretical equality causes factual inequality

My basic proposition takes the form of a paradox; that the understandable and universally acceptable notion that males and females are equal and should have all equal rights of law, economy, politics, etc., has contributed to the practical inequality of females.

Theoretical sexual equality has forced rejection of any concern about sexual differences. The practical result of this has been the continued deprivation of females and the slowing-up of a process of opening opportunities to women in present structures, of changing the structures and of adding new ones to accommodate women. At the moment, it is women who must accommodate themselves, and they are being asked to compete with men in male-oriented institutions. The net result of this is their continued deprivation and a recently increased resentment and anxiety.

A number of obvious examples come quickly to mind. A variety of researches have confirmed what many other less-sophisticated communities have known all along – that the female menstrual cycle has some appreciable and predictable effects on female social, psychological and even technical behaviour. Crime rates, industrial accident rates and incidence of illness, for example, have been correlated with the regular cycle.

A recent report by K. Dalton of the University College Hospital, London, reveals that young women writing examinations are affected by as much as 14 per cent by the time of their cycle at which they undertake some tests. The implications of this simple finding are of course enormous. For example, persons wishing to enter graduate school in the United States of America must take special examinations on a national standard. Should a woman write these during her low-performance time, she begins with virtually a second-class result and the work of her previous years in the educational system and her own personal qualities and skills may be severely devalued. In good part this is because she participates in a system which does not formally recognize her femininity, admitting that it may be the cause of changes in behaviour or performance of direct pertinence to the educational system which has so expensively provided her the opportunity for seeking graduate training.

[I]t seems inevitable that should women become airline pilots it will be necessary for their work schedules to conform to their biological rhythms – not because accidents are inevitable, but because they become somewhat more likely and hence a risk subject to control by conscientious managers.

Male bonds and female exclusion

Menstrual cycles and child-rearing are very obvious factors in any effort to assess the reality and possibility of female participation in what we can call the 'macro-structures of society' – those involving large-scale organization and the major corporate enterprises. More subtle but perhaps even more significant influence are the essentially primate valences – bonding tendencies.

I mean by this that the tendency for males to form bonds in work, fighting, politics, etc., and the more obvious but equally pervasive propensity for males and females to form at least ephemeral bonds centring round the process of sexual titillation and consummation, may be as formidable barriers to egalitarian female employment as the obvious ones directly related to reproduction. And an additional factor which has been often overlooked both by ethnographers and students of contemporary politics and economics is the apparent difficulty females have in forming the bonds necessary in order to manage structures involving power and wealth. Let us explore these factors in turn.

It should by now be clear that the proposition here is that if males bond because it is 'in the nature of the beast' to do so, then this places a considerable burden both on women seeking to join these bonds, and on those men willing to allow females into groups when this may signally affect the groups and the relations between group members.

One intriguing example of this phenomenon is the secret society; only exceptionally are these heterosexual. They are mostly all-male and when women do join them, this appears to mark the end of the society's particular drama and effect on its surroundings. This is, again, not to recommend a particular attitude or policy towards secret societies. But it is to suggest that they express certain effective propensities of the human male and that we can observe in these curious and unpredictable organizations a feature of male behaviour in the voluntary world which may find more formal expression in the more overt and legislated worlds of business, politics, etc.

Team sport is another example of this phenomenon; with the exception of tennis and skating, team sports are overwhelmingly unisexual. Except for the most violent of sports, there is no reason why rules governing female participation could not be introduced and appropriate numbers of women join teams. But I suggest that team sports depend on the bonding process and that female participation is anathema to this and would severely curtail the enjoyment of both players and spectators because of the disturbance of the male socio-dramaturgy of sport.

Perhaps both secret societies and sports will be seen by some as a wretched and retrogressive failure of males to embrace a modern and wholesome sexual egalitarianism. It may also be sensible to see them as rather complex projections of species-wide (and their incidence is species-wide) propensities for male bonding. In any event, they do exist (though secret societies are under considerable pressure, particularly in the United States) and represent a clue to what many men are concerned about and to the ways in which they willingly choose to spend their time.

If we apply the principles of these forms of association to other areas we can see that the rejection of female co-workers by males may stem from more than retrogressive pique, prejudice, lack of sympathy for females, or some other impetus regarded as malignant and uninformed. This means that coping with this rejection may involve dealing with subconscious processes which are possibly of ancient primate origin and which have for several million years and until just recently served very well for political and economic survival. What we may call 'the anti-female tradition', has its origins, then, not only in belligerent male chauvinist ideology and, in economic exploitation of females, but in a genetic process which evolved because pre-hominids found they could survive and reproduce better if they excluded females from the processes of political dominance, with survival further aided by the exclusion of females from the hunting party.

Myths of woman's place

A. OAKLEY

Industrial capitalism is the economic and social system in which the present alienation and oppression of women as housewives has arisen. But other forces also act to maintain the home-centredness of women's identity. A set of myths about woman's place in society provides the rationale for the ideology of gender roles in which femininity and domesticity are equated.

A myth is 'a purely fictitious narrative ... embodying some popular idea concerning natural or historical phenomena' (*Oxford English Dictionary*). In the ideology of woman's place, two statements popularly believed to be true, but actually untrue, are these: 'Only women are, ever have been, or can be housewives,' and 'Only women as mothers are, ever have been, or can be the proper people to rear children.' The former can be called the 'myth of the division of labour by sex' and the latter the 'myth of motherhood'. Both myths are referred to directly and indirectly by housewives particularly when discussing the participation of men in domestic tasks, and also in considering the question of gender-role reversal in the family.

As anthropologists have discovered in the study of small-scale societies, the function of myth is not only or even chiefly symbolic or explanatory. The primary function of myth is to validate an existing social order. Myth enshrines conservative social values, raising tradition on a pedestal. It expresses and confirms, rather than explains or questions, the sources of cultural attitudes and values. The notions expressed in myth are always held as sacred – they are perceived and transmitted as sacred – and it is through its sacred aspect that myth justifies the claim that the conservation of the status quo is the all-important social task; it supports the view of the world held by people who say that 'it has always been and should always remain as they know it' (Mair, 1965). Because myth anchors the present in the past it is a sociological charter for a future society which is an exact replica of the present one.

The myth of the division of labour by sex and the myth of motherhood are myths because as statements of fact they are untrue, and because, despite this lack of veracity, they are powerful forces acting to conserve the tradition of women's domestic identity. Myth stated as fact becomes fact: what is mythological appears real. Authenticity triumphs despite (or because of) the concealment of bias.

The myth of the division of labour by sex describes the relegation of women to a domestic role in the family group as natural, universal and necessary. It states that women are naturally housewives in all societies, and that women need to assume this role for society to survive. The myth does not always make these assertions categorically, but imprecise reiterations of necessity, universality and naturalness abound (just as they do in popular discussions on the subject of gender roles). Reference is usually made in the myth to scientific or academic work which is held to prove the point – in other words, to contain a detailed version of the myth and to present the pseudo-evidence for its credibility.

Three different sorts of 'expert' promulgate the myth of the division of labour by sex. There are the ethologists, whose self-conferred mission is to sketch in those parts of the myth which document the naturalness of woman's domestic role. Anthropologists, with data on the division of labour by sex in different societies, provide the evidence for its universality; and, finally, the sociological contribution is a stake in the necessity of the division of labour by sex which confines women to the home. To survive, it is said, society requires the restriction of women to the housewife-wife-mother roles. Of these three, the anthropological contribution is probably the most influential. Ethology is concerned with the study of unlearned, species-specific behaviour. It emphasises the **biological** substratum of human social behaviour: what is natural rather than merely social.

The ethologist claims that the division of labour by sex, with women as housewives and men as non-housewives, has 'direct biological roots' (Tiger, 1969). Such a claim enables the myth of the division of labour by sex to take on the quality of a 'myth of origin', and hence to gain in persuasive power. What the ethologist contributes is that part of the myth which 'explains' how it all started, which links the division of labour between female and male in industrial societies with the division of labour between female and male in animal societies both today and millennia ago.

Proponents and popularisers of the myth of origin related to the division of labour by sex include Desmond Morris (*The Naked Ape*), Lionel Tiger (*Men in Groups*), Lionel Tiger and Robin Fox (*The Imperial Animal*), and Robert Ardrey (*African Genesis*). This is the sort of assertion they make about the division of labour by sex:

> The evidence is sufficiently extensive and heterogeneous in its theoretical, disciplinary and natural origin to lend confidence to the notion that the sexual division of labour is a cross-cultural constant . . . we are involved here with a phenomenon deeply rooted in the nature of human social life . . . It is a feature of social life at the heart of man's survival, the understanding of which must involve an approach to 'behavioural bedrock' – to the fundaments of the behavioural process.
>
> (*Tiger, 1969*)

> One of the few general rules about human cultures that anthropologists can safely affirm is that in all known societies a distinction is made between 'women's work' and 'men's work' . . . this goes back to the evolution of the hunting animal, where male and female were assigned

radically different tasks . . . This basic pattern evolved in a hunting context that molded its content and direction.

(*Tiger and Fox, 1972*)

These verbose statements conceal an essentially false chain of reasoning. Tiger, Fox *et al.* look around at human society, make a (false) generalization about it, and then search around in evolution and animal societies for evidence to support it. Hence Tiger observes that the 'sexual division of labour is a cross-cultural constant'. Since the book in which he proclaims this is one about male bonding, he continues by saying 'the crux of my argument is that male bonding patterns reflect and arise out of man's history as a hunter' (Tiger, 1969). This boils down to the argument that the sexual division of labour is determined by the fact that once-upon-a-time (supposedly) men went hunting and women stayed at home.

The argument has two basic weaknesses. Firstly, it assumes that we know exactly how evolution occurred and that it was a more or less unilinear process. Neither of these statements is in fact true. The second obvious weakness inheres in the generalizations from animals to humans, and from humans back to animals. Very specific differences mark human beings off from their animal ancestors and counterparts, not least of which is the enormous dependence of the human species on learning processes: the human capacity to invent, perpetuate and change culture.

In outline the ethologists assert that 'man' began as a vegetarian tree-dwelling hairy ape. About 15 million years ago, with the climatic changes of the Pliocene, the environment changed and lush vegetation was replaced by scrub and grassland. The ape had to come down from the trees and adapt his capacities to a ground-based search for animal food. Hunting and house-wifery were the adaptive capacities required by these changes, and therefore acquired by male and female respectively.

The animal species whose behaviour bears some relation to the aggressive, meat-eating, ground-dwelling ape of the myth are **not** those who, in evolutionary terms, could be called 'man's' closest relatives. The ethologist cites macaques and baboons, but these are monkeys, not apes. The ape species of chimpanzees and gorillas are much more closely related to *Homo sapiens*. While baboons and macaques are largely ground-dwellers and are aggressive and bloodthirsty animals, chimpanzees and gorillas are mild-mannered vegetarians. Female-male differences in size and strength are greater among the former than among the latter. As a matter of fact, if the sexual division of labour between hunting males and babysitting females was as rigid as the myth claims among animals who were the ancestors of *Homo sapiens*, then the female-male difference in size and strength among humans today would be very much greater than it is. According to Björn Kúrten in *Not From the Apes*, even the descent of man from the apes is in question: 'It would be more correct to say that apes and monkeys descended from early ancestors of man' (Kúrten, 1972).

[T]he whole argument about the traditional division of labour by sex being natural subverts the oppression of women to domesticity as a masculine convenience. For the prehominid male home is 'a place to come back to with the spoils, where the females and young will be waiting . . . ': we are left to imagine what home might mean to the prehominid female. This description has immediate parallels with the place of men in the family today. The male, as Elaine Morgan puts it

> sees himself quite unconsciously as the main line of evolution with a female satellite revolving around him as the moon revolves around the earth. This not only causes him to overlook valuable clues to our ancestry, but sometimes leads him into making statements that are arrant and demonstrable nonsense.

If the picture of the aggressive male striding out across the savannah for game is a fable,

> the man who is reading the book (to say nothing of the man who is writing it) gets no end of a kick out of thinking that all that power and passion and brutal virility is seething within him, just below the skin . . . so he averts his eyes from the primate family tree, forgets that he descended from apes, and identifies with the baboon, even if it means making a monkey of himself.
>
> (*Morgan, 1972*)

The anthropological contention that 'women-housewife and man-non-housewife' is a pattern reproduced in the social structure of all human communities is probably the most influential part of the whole division-of-labour-by-sex myth. For this reason, the arguments deserve some factual contradictions:

Like ethology, anthropology not only describes what (mythically) occurs, but answers the question as to why it occurs. Biology is held ultimately responsible. The female's more extensive and burdensome reproductive role and the male's 'superior' size and strength are the two biological bases, according to Murdock's (1965) account, of the traditional division of labour.

A close look at how childbearing and childrearing are managed in many small-scale societies produces the perception that pregnancy and lactation are burdensome occupations only in a culture that views them as such – which many do not. Activity during pregnancy and lactation is not ruled out by the 'facts' of biology, but variously prescribed or prohibited according to cultural custom. What nature (or biology) decrees is not gender-role differentiation, but reproductive specialization. Females conceive children, gestate and give birth to them, and – in pre-industrial cultures – enable them to survive by feeding them on human milk. Males impregnate females. But the fact that females bear children, while males only impregnate females, does not determine the division of labour between female and male in society at large. The web of cultural beliefs about masculine and feminine parenthood roles intervenes as a variable factor.

Among the Mbuti pygmies of the Congo forest gender differentiation is minimal. Childbirth is treated casually, and the mother's tie to her child imposes no restraints on her ordinary activity.

> The mother is likely to be off on the hunt, or on the trail somewhere when birth takes place; there is no lessening of activity for her during pregnancy. Childbirth is said to be effected easily, with complications rarely happening. Any woman may act as midwife . . . Within two hours of delivery, if birth took place in the camp, the mother is apt to appear in the doorway of her hut, with a bundle wrapped in bark cloth held in her arms. Within the same period of time, if birth took place on the trail she will continue her journey.
>
> (*Turnbull, 1965*)

Both Mbuti parents have to obey certain food taboos until the child can crawl. Beyond this, the only other restriction on normal activity for either parent is the taboo on sexual intercourse between mother and father during the lactation period – a common (but not universal) means of 'family planning' in small-scale societies.

For the people of Alor, an Indonesian island, childbirth is integrated in a similar way with the normal daily activities of women. The subsistence economy is in women's hands: women are responsible for the cultivation and collection of all vegetable foods – the staple diet of the community. The most prized characteristic in a woman is her industriousness, her thorough commitment to the agricultural work which requires her absence from the home for a major part of each day. The reluctance of women to take on the responsibilities of childbearing as well as their other duties is accepted as normal. 'We men are the ones who want children. Our wives don't. They just want to sleep with us.' Childbirth takes place in a corridor off the family living room. When the baby is born, the mother wraps it up and joins her relatives and friends. Birth is 'an easy and casual procedure'.[1] Ten to fourteen days after childbirth, a woman returns to regular field work, leaving her baby in the care of the father, an older sibling, or a grandmother (Dubois, 1944).

The impact of childbirth on the roles of parents is clearly a cultural construct. In both cases the variable which intervenes between the biological 'fact' of reproductive specialization and the cultural fact of gender-role differentiation is the complex of beliefs and values attached to the reproductive roles of female and male. Each culture may have its own validating myth.

The anthropological myth which validates our social pattern not only asserts that childbearing and childrearing are burden-some occupations but that they restrict women's activity so as to rule out any extra-domestic role. This is manifestly untrue. In most cultures all over the world, and in our

---

[1] Mortality from childbirth is not necessarily higher in small-scale societies than in modern industrial society, and there is evidence that it may be lower. Hospitalized childbirth carries a risk of infection which 'primitive' childbirth does not. (See Ford, *A Comparative Study of Human Reproduction*, p. 58.)

own before industrialization, women have engaged in productive work, which has required travel away from the home base and the expenditure of substantial physical energy. Where cultural beliefs sanction the participation of women in productive work, this activity has been made compatible with childcare. Sometimes childcare has been seen as the husband-father's responsibility, sometimes older children are relied on to care for younger ones, sometimes a whole kinship network is the childcare context, sometimes the women of the community evolve a system of communal childrearing. Often a combination of methods is used. The assertion that childrearing restricts women to the home is a duplication of that other myth, the myth of motherhood. It reproduces the values of one culture rather than describing the conditions of all human cultures.

The same is true of those characteristics of the division of labour by sex supposedly based on the male's superior size and strength. The myth merely repeats the belief of one culture about the biologically-based incapacity of the female to carry out heavy or demanding work. It distorts the contrary evidence which can be found in many other cultures.

The aborigines of Tasmania are one society in which the division of labour by sex deviates from this mythical pattern. These people assigned seal-hunting, fishing, and the catching of opossums to the women of the community. Opossum-catching was a particularly skilled and dangerous task. The pursued opossum retired to a hollow in a decayed branch at the top of a smooth-trunked gum tree: the women had to climb the tree using only a rope and a sharp flint or hatchet, and then walk out along the projecting branch to extract the opossum from its retreat, flinging it to the ground below. The task was reported to be carried out with ease by a healthy woman, but 'one who had been out of health . . . could not get many steps off the ground, so that not only skill, but a considerable measure of strength appears necessary to ascend the gigantic gum trees' (Roth, 1899).

For fishing, the Tasmanian women slung baskets round their waists and then dived down to prise crayfish off the underwater rocks with wooden chisels. They seemed 'quite at home in the water' and pursued their task with expertise, efficiency and perseverance.

Women as hunters and warriors are commonplace in some cultures. In the old African kingdom of Dahomey, Amazons were women enrolled as regular members of the king's army. In 1845 the Dahomean army consisted of 5000 women and 7000 men.

This participation of women in armies is, of course, also found in modern times. In the Second World War, millions of women served in every branch of the regular armed services. That few saw actual combat is due, not to their physical unsuitability for it, but to the belief that war 'should be the one impregnable male bastion' (Laffin, 1967).

Building and heavy agricultural work – the remaining purportedly masculine activities – are other areas in which the myth of the division of labour by sex distorts the truth.

In Britian, heavy agricultural work was performed by women until the last century, when technology began to reduce the need for heavy manual labour. Over much of the world, but particularly in Africa, the cultivation of the land has been a feminine role either predominantly or (often) exclusively. Forty years ago female farming with no male help (except with the felling of trees) characterized the whole of the Congo region, large parts of South-East and East Africa, and areas of West Africa too. The situation is much the same today, with women performing between 50 per cent and 80 per cent of the total agricultural work in a wide sample of communities all over Africa.

In many societies, men are not considered superior in strength, in any case.

As [an] anthropologist reported to an American conference on 'The Potential of Women', Burundi people could not understand how it was that the practice of allotting heavy work to the female was reversed in her (the anthropologist's) own culture – as she told them it was. 'My African neighbours,' she said,

> had become accustomed to the idea that my country engaged in all manner of nonsensical practices. They were usually tactfully tolerant, but when I said that in my country, it was the men who did the heavy work . . . they did not conceal disapproval. This was a mistake, they maintained. Everybody knows that men are not suited **by nature** to heavy work . . . Men drink too much and do not eat enough to keep up their strength; they are more tense and travel about too much to develop the habits or the muscles needed for sustained work on the farms.
>
> (Albert, 1963)

The sociological myth, like the ethological and anthropological ones, is underpinned by the assumption that biology necessarily determines the place of women in society – and thus, by derivation, the place of women in the family.

The myth is that **someone** has to take care of the children, and since fathers have to work, **mothers** must do the childrearing. 'Mother' here means not the biological mother role but the social childrearer role. The truth of the matter is the reverse of the myth: **because** women take care of children men are free to be away from the home, involved in their employment work.

In practice the sociological argument means that the restriction of women to the family is a matter of convenience – not to women, but to men, to children, and to the institution of marriage and the family itself. It means that the family oppresses women, because the oppression of women is convenient, whilst their liberation would be inconvenient: a disruptive and destructive force. In particular their oppression in the housewife role is belied by the assertion that the family role is an 'expressive' one, concerned with the abstract qualities of emotional warmth and supportive love. There is no mention of anything so prosaic, so instrumental as housework. The washing of dirty dishes and dirty clothes, the cooking of meals, the emptying of rubbish, the removal of dirt, the cleansing of excrement-stained cloth and bathroom equipment, are these really 'expressive' tasks – channels for the expression of emotional warmth and love? Do they actually provide an opportunity for the expressive leader of the family (the woman-housewife) to care for the emotional interior of the family, to integrate the family as a group? Are they not instead directly antagonistic to the expression of caring emotions?

Because the housewife role is a family role the myth of the division of labour by sex validates the institution of the family and makes its preservation mandatory. For the sociologist, and for the anthropologist and ethologist, the myth of the division of labour by sex is essentially the myth of the family. These stereotyped figures which people the myth are always pair-bonded, like the family, and the young are **their** young, as in the family. The family, like the division of labour by sex, is universal and natural. Yet since it is actually not universal or natural, these claims simply reiterate the premises on which our own family system is based. They spring from the intellectual's internalization of his[2] own cultural milieu: he hopes that what he believes in – the family and marriage – is more than a mere figment of his imagination. The family 'must' exist.

References

Albert, Ethel M. (1963) 'Women of Burundi: A Study of Social Values', Paulme (ed.).

Ardrey, Robert (1961) *African Genesis*, Fontana Books, London.

Douglas, Mary (1954) 'The Lele of Kasai' in Daryll Forde (ed.), *African Worlds*, University Press, Oxford.

Dubois, Cora (1944) *People of Alor*, University of Minnesota Press, Minneapolis.

Ford, C.S. (1945) *A Comparative Study of Human Reproduction*, Yale University Press.

Kúrten, Björn (1972) *Not From the Apes*, Gollancz, London.

Laffin, John (1967) *Women in Battle*, Abelard-Schuman, London.

Mair, Lucy (1965) *An Introduction to Social Anthropology*, Clarendon Press, Oxford.

Moore, Barrington Jr. (1969) 'Thoughts on the Future of the Family', in Edwards.

Morgan, Elaine (1972) *The Descent of Woman*, Souvenir Press, London.

Morris, Desmond (1968) *The Naked Ape*, Corgi, London.

Murdock, George P. (1965) *Social Structure*, Free Press, New York.

Roth, H. Ling (1899) *The Aborigines of Tasmania*, F. King & Son, Halifax.

Tiger, Lionel (1969) *Men in Groups*, Random House, New York.

— and Fox, Robin (1972) *The Imperial Animal*, Secker & Warburg, London.

Turnbull, Colin (1965) *Wayward Servants*, Eyre & Spottiswoode, London.

[2] The androcentricity is a critical source of bias. See Barrington Moore, 'Thoughts on the Future of the Family'.

The sexual division of work

SHIRLEY DEX

A number of mainly British feminist writers have now started to ask questions about the meaning of 'skill'. In some cases the work has been stimulated by Braverman's (1974) account of a deskilling process, but it stands independently of Braverman's much criticised work. The answers to this question about the nature of skill have illustrated that the notion is far from being clear or unambiguously defined, and more importantly, the meaning of 'skill' is integrally bound up with the sexual division of labour. An understanding of the sexual division of labour requires as a precondition, therefore, a thorough understanding of the meaning and generation of skill distinctions in labour markets.

Some of the empirical work illustrates these issues clearly. A study of the process of producing paper boxes in Britain by Craig *et al.* (1979) found that women who worked on hand-fed machines were considered, classified and paid as unskilled workers. Men who produced cartons on a more automated process which required less individual concentration were classified at a higher level of skill, semi-skilled. Drawing attention to this example, Phillips and Taylor (1980, p. 84) point out that there is a sense in this case study in which the work that women do must, of necessity, be thought of as unskilled, just because it is done by women: 'The women producing paper boxes are simply women producing paper boxes, and however much the work itself might seem to qualify for upgrading, it remains unskilled because it is done by typically unskilled workers – women'.

Studies cited by Phillips and Taylor and a study by Coyle (1982), both of the clothing industry in Britain, reach similar conclusions; that the skill divisions between men and women in that industry have been generated through the struggle of unionised men in often craft-based unions to retain their craft dominance, at the expense of women. Men have retained control and excluded women from working on certain jobs traditionally thought to be more skilled; for example, cutting. Whether they are technically more skilled than women's sewing jobs is highly [contentious]. The fact that one job has had a lengthy apprenticeship scheme whilst the other has not should not necessarily be the criterion on which a decision is made, especially when the nature of the job has changed. Similarly, it is difficult to accept that machining done by men is so clearly skilled, when machining done by women is labelled as semi-skilled. The doubtful nature of skill divisions in this industry can be seen most vividly through the changes which have occurred through the introduction of new technology. In Birnbaum's study, when men were forced to take on machining work usually done by women and labelled as semi-skilled they fought to redefine the job as skilled. Coyle

Abridged excerpt reproduced from Dex, S. *The Sexual Division of Work*, pp. 100–2; published by Wheatsheaf Books, Brighton, 1985.

(1982) demonstrated that men had retained their skilled status as cutters, and the associated pay differential, even after the introduction of new machinery which did all the skilled cutting and which in effect made the men into machine minders. It would seem to be the case within the clothing industry, for a women to become skilled she would have to change her sex.

This process takes on a slightly different form outside the manufacturing industry, where craft-based unions are not present. On the whole, the non-manufacturing sector has been the one which has grown and offered the growing women's workforce new jobs. The idea that women's work is unskilled or semi-skilled can be built in from the start, and this tertiery sector has created, therefore, a whole set of low-skilled women's jobs, often white-collar semi-skilled and certainly low-paid jobs. The outcome is the same; that the work is categorised as less skilled because women are doing these jobs. The cost advantages to employers are obvious. Crompton, Jones and Reid (1982) and Davies (1975) have started to document these distinctions in clerical occupations. At a more general level, part-time jobs are often regarded as lower in status than full-time jobs when it is the same job. The caring occupations, like child-care, nursery nurses and the whole array of social service jobs done by women (e.g. homehelps) are also thought to be generally fairly unskilled. What this means is that the skills involved are not recognised as skills by either the employers or society – and certainly the remuneration would tend to identify such jobs as low skilled. Of course, the ultimate area of women's low-skilled work is in the home in unwaged child-rearing and domestic responsibilities.

References

Braverman, H. (1974) *Labor and Monopoly Capital*, Monthly Review Press.
Craig, C., Rubery, J., Tarling, R., and Wilkinson F. (1982) *Labour Market Structure, Industrial Organization and Low Pay*, Cambridge University Press.
Davies, M. (1975) 'Women's place is at the typewriter: The feminization of the clerical labor force' in Edwards. Reich and Gordon (eds).
Phillips, A. and Taylor B. (1980) 'Sex and skill: Notes towards a feminist economics' in *Feminist Review*.

The logic of nonstandard English

W. LABOV

The traditional view of nonstandard English held by many public school teachers is that it is an illogical form of speech; that when children are

Abridged excerpts reproduced from Labov, W. (1969) The Logic of Nonstandard English in *Report of The Twentieth Annual Round Table Meeting on Linguistics and Language Studies: Linguistics and The Teaching of Standard English to Speakers of Other Languages or Dialects (Monograph Series on Language and Linguistics, no. 22)* edited by Alatis, James E. pp. 1–2 and 12–18.

taught the standard forms they are also being taught to think logically. Linguists have endeavored for many years to show that differences in language are matters of social convention established by historical processes which shift continually the social prestige of dialect variants.

Recent programs for teaching the 'culturally disadvantaged', particularly those of Karl Bereiter and his associates, have revived the notion that nonstandard dialects are illogical, attributing poor educational performance to cognitive disabilities reflected in language.

The educational programs proposed are based upon sociological and linguistic misinterpretations of the data. The linguistic behavior reported by Bereiter is merely the product of a defensive posture which children adopt in an alien and threatening situation. Such behavior can be produced at will in any group of children and can be altered by changing the relevant sociolinguistic variables.

There are many important questions concerning the cognitive correlates of syntactic complexity which current research technique has not yet answered. At present, there is no basis for attributing poor educational performance to the grammatical and phonological characteristics of any nonstandard dialect of English.

In the past decade, a great deal of federally-sponsored research has been devoted to the educational problems of children in ghetto schools. In order to account for the poor performance of children in these schools, educational psychologists have attempted to discover what kind of disadvantage or defect they are suffering from. The viewpoint which has been widely accepted, and used as the basis for large-scale intervention programs, is that the children show a cultural deficit as a result of an impoverished environment in their early years. Considerable attention has been given to language. In this area, the deficit theory appears as the concept of 'verbal deprivation': Negro children from the ghetto area receive little verbal stimulation, are said to hear very little well-formed language, and as a result are impoverished in their means of verbal expression: they cannot speak complete sentences, do not know the names of common objects, cannot form concepts or convey logical thoughts.

Unfortunately, these notions are based upon the work of educational psychologists who know very little about language and even less about Negro children. The concept of verbal deprivation has no basis in social reality: in fact, Negro children in the urban ghettos receive a great deal of verbal stimulation, hear more well-formed sentences than middle-class children, and participate fully in a highly verbal culture; they have the same basic vocabulary, possess the same capacity for conceptual learning, and use the same logic as anyone else who learns to speak and understand English.

The notion of 'verbal deprivation' is a part of the modern mythology of educational psychology, typical of the unfounded notions which tend to expand rapidly in our educational system. In past decades linguists have been as guilty as others in promoting such intellectual fashions at the expense of both teachers and children. But the myth of verbal deprivation is particularly dangerous, because it diverts attention from real defects of our educational system to imaginary defects of the child; and as we shall see, it leads its sponsors inevitably to the hypothesis of the genetic inferiority of Negro children which it was originally designed to avoid.

The most useful service which linguists can perform today is to clear away the illusion of 'verbal deprivation' and provide a more adequate notion of the relations between standard and nonstandard dialects.

Our work in the speech community makes it painfully obvious that in many ways working-class speakers are more effective narrators, reasoners and debaters than many middle-class speakers who temporize, qualify, and lose their argument in a mass of irrelevant detail. Many academic writers try to rid themselves of that part of middle-class style that is empty pretension, and keep that part that is needed for precision. But the average middle-class speaker that we encounter makes no such effort; he is enmeshed in verbiage, the victim of sociolinguistic factors beyond his control.

I will not attempt to support this argument here with systematic quantitative evidence, although it is possible to develop measures which show how far middle-class speakers can wander from the point. I would like to contrast two speakers dealing with roughly the same topic – matters of belief. The first is Larry H., a 15-year-old core member of the Jets, being interviewed by John Lewis. Larry is one of the loudest and roughest members of the Jets, one who gives the least recognition to the conventional rules of politeness. For most readers of this paper, first contact with Larry would produce some fairly negative reactions on both sides: it is probable that you would not *like* him any more than his teachers do. Larry causes trouble in and out of school; he was put back from the eleventh grade to the ninth, and has been threatened with further action by the school authorities.

JL: What happens to you after you die? Do you know?
Larry: Yeah, I know.
JL: What?
Larry: After they put you in the ground, your body turns into – ah – bones, an' shit.
JL: What happens to your spirit?
Larry: Your spirit – soon as you die, your spirit leaves you.
JL: And where does the spirit go?
Larry: Well, it all depends . . .
JL: On what?
Larry: You know, like some people say if you're good an' shit, your spirit goin' t'heaven . . . 'n' if you bad, your spirit goin' to hell. Well, bullshit! Your spirit goin' to hell anyway, good or bad.
JL: Why?
Larry: Why? I'll tell you why. 'Cause, you see, doesn' nobody really know that it's a God, y'know, 'cause I mean I have seen black gods, pink gods, white gods, all color gods, and don't nobody know it's really a God. An' when they be sayin' if you good, you goin' t'heaven, tha's

bullshit, 'cause you ain't goin' to no heaven, 'cause it ain't no heaven for you to go to.

Larry is a paradigmatic speaker of nonstandard Negro English (NNE) as opposed to standard English (SE). His grammar shows a high concentration of such characteristic NNE forms as negative inversion [**don't nobody know** . . .], negative concord [**you ain't goin' to no heaven** . . .], invariant **be** [**when they be sayin'** . . .], dummy **it** for SE **there** [**it ain't no heaven** . . .], optional copula deletion [**if you're good** . . . **if you bad** . . .], and full forms of auxiliaries [**I have seen** . . .]. The only SE influence in this passage is the one case of **doesn't** instead of the invariant **don't** of NNE. Larry also provides a paradigmatic example of the rhetorical style of NNE: he can sum up a complex argument in a few words, and the full force of his opinions comes through without qualification or reservation. He is eminently quotable, and his interviews give us many concise statements of the NNE point of view. One can almost say that Larry **speaks** the NNE culture.

It is the logical form of this passage which is of particular interest here. Larry presents a complex set of interdependent propositions which can be explicated by setting out the SE equivalents in linear order. The basic argument is to deny the twin propositions.

(A) If you are   (B) then your spirit will go to heaven.
      good,
(−A) If you are bad,   (C) then your spirit will go to hell.

Larry denies (B), and asserts that **if (A) or (−A), then (C).** His argument may be outlined as follows:

1. Everyone has a different idea of what God is like.
2. Therefore nobody really knows that God exists.
3. If there is a heaven, it was made by God.
4. If God doesn't exist, he couldn't have made heaven.
5. Therefore heaven does not exist.
6. You can't go somewhere that doesn't exist.
−B. Therefore you can't go to heaven.
C. Therefore you are going to hell.

The argument is presented in the order: (C), because (2) because (1), therefore (2), therefore (−B) because (5) and (6). Part of the argument is implicit: the connection (2) therefore (−B) leaves unstated the connecting links (3) and (4), and in this interval Larry strengthens the propositions from the form (2) **Nobody knows if there is** . . . to (5) **There is no** . . . Otherwise, the case is presented explicitly as well as economically. The complex argument is summed up in Larry's last sentence, which shows formally the dependence of (−B) on (5) and (6):

An' when they be sayin' if you good, you goin' t'heaven,
[The proposition, if A, then B]
Tha's bullshit,

[is absurd]
'cause you ain't goin' to no heaven
[because −B]
'cause it ain't no heaven for you to go to.
[because (5) and (6)].

This hypothetical argument is not carried on at a high level of seriousness. It is a game played with ideas as counters, in which opponents use a wide variety of verbal devices to win. There is no personal commitment to any of these propositions, and no reluctance to strengthen one's argument by bending the rules of logic as in the (2–5) sequence. But if the opponent invokes the rules of logic, they hold. In John Lewis' interviews, he often makes this move, and the force of his argument is always acknowledged and countered within the rules of logic. In this case, he pointed out the fallacy that the argument (2–3–4–5–6) leads to (−C) as well as (−B), so it cannot be used to support Larry's assertion (C):

JL: Well, if there's no heaven, how could there be a hell?
Larry: I mean–ye-eah. Well, let me tell you, it ain't no hell, 'cause this is hell right here, y'know!
JL: This is hell?
Larry: Yeah, this is hell right here!

Larry's answer is quick, ingenious and decisive. The application of the (3–4–5) argument to hell is denied, since hell is here, and therefore conclusion (C) stands. These are not ready-made or preconceived opinions, but new propositions devised to win the logical argument in the game being played. The reader will note the speed and precision of Larry's mental operations. He does not wander, or insert meaningless verbiage. The only repetition is (2), placed before and after (1) in his original statement. It is often said that the nonstandard vernacular is not suited for dealing with abstract or hypothetical questions, but in fact speakers from the NNE community take great delight in exercising their wit and logic on the most improbable and problematical matters. Despite the fact that Larry H. does not believe in God, and has just denied all knowledge of him, John Lewis advances the following hypothetical question:

JL: . . . But, just say that there is a God, what color is he? White or black?
Larry: Well, if it is a God . . . I wouldn' know what color, I couldn' say, – couldn' nobody say what color he is or really **would** be.
JL: But now, jus' suppose there was a God –
Larry: Unless'n they say . . .
JL: No, I was jus' sayin' jus' suppose there is a God, would he be white or black?
Larry: . . . He'd be white, man.
JL: Why?
Larry: Why? I'll tell you why. 'Cause the average whitey out here got every-

thing, you dig? And the nigger ain't got shit, y'know? Y'understan'?
So–um–for–in order for **that** to happen, you know it ain't no black
God that's doin' that bullshit.

No one can hear Larry's answer to this question without being convinced
that they are in the presence of a skilled speaker with great 'verbal presence
of mind', who can use the English language expertly for many purposes.
Larry's answer to John Lewis is again a complex argument. The formulation
is not SE, but it is clear and effective even for those not familiar with the
vernacular. The nearest SE equivalent might be: 'So you know that God
isn't black, because if he was, he wouldn't have arranged things like that'.

The reader will have noted that this analysis is being carried out in
standard English, and the inevitable challenge is: why not write in NNE,
then, or in your own nonstandard dialect? The fundamental reason is, of
course, one of firmly fixed social conventions. All communities agree that
SE is the 'proper' medium for formal writing and public communication.
Furthermore, it seems likely that SE has an advantage over NNE in explicit
analysis of surface forms, which is what we are doing here.

[I]t will be helpful to examine SE in its primary natural setting, as the
medium for informal spoken communication of middle-class speakers.

Let us now turn to the second speaker, an upper-middle-class, college
educated Negro man being interviewed by Clarence Robins in our survey of
adults in Central Harlem.

CR: Do you know of anything that someone can do, to have someone
who has passed on visit him in a dream?

Chas. M.: Well, I even heard my parents say that there is such a thing as
something in dreams some things like that, and sometimes dreams
do come true. I have personally never had a dream come true.
I've never dreamt that somebody was dying and they actually
died, (Mhm) or that I was going to have ten dollars the next day
and somehow I got ten dollars in my pocket. (Mhm). I don't
particularly believe in that, I don't think it's true. I do feel,
though, that there is such a thing as–ah–witchcraft. I do feel
that in certain cultures there is such a thing as witchcraft, or
some sort of **science** of witchcraft; I don't think that it's just a
matter of believing hard enough that there is such a thing as
witchcraft. I do believe that there is such a thing that a person
can put himself in a state of **mind** (Mhm), or that–er–something
could be given them to intoxicate them in a certain–to a certain
frame of mind–that–that could actually be considered witchcraft.

Charles M. is obviously a 'good speaker' who strikes the listener as well-
educated, intelligent and sincere. He is a likeable and attractive person – the
kind of person that middle-class listeners rate very high on a scale of 'job
suitability' and equally high as a potential friend. His language is more
moderate and tempered than Larry's; he makes every effort to qualify his

opinions, and seems anxious to avoid any misstatements or over-statements. From these qualities emerge the primary characteristic of this passage – its **verbosity**. Words multiply, some modifying and qualifying, others repeating or padding the main argument. The first half of this extract is a response to the initial question on dreams, basically:

1. Some people say that dreams sometimes come true.
2. I have never had a dream come true.
3. Therefore I don't believe (1).

Some characteristic filler phrases appear here: **such a thing as, some things like that, particularly.** Two examples of dreams given after (2) are after-thoughts that might have been given after (1). Proposition (3) is stated twice for no obvious reason. Nevertheless, this much of Charles M.'s response is well-directed to the point of the question. He then volunteers a statement of his beliefs about witchcraft which shows the difficulty of middle-class speakers who (a) want to express a belief in something but (b) want to show themselves as judicious, rational and free from superstitions. The basic proposition can be stated simply in five words:

But I believe in witchcraft.

However, the idea is enlarged to exactly 100 words, and it is difficult to see what else is being said. In the following quotations, padding which can be removed without change in meaning is shown in brackets.

(1) 'I [do] feel, though, that there is [such a thing as] witchcraft.' **Feel** seems to be a euphemism for 'believe'.

(2) '[I do feel that] in certain cultures [there is such a thing as witchcraft.]' This repetition seems designed only to introduce the word **culture**, which lets us know that the speaker knows about anthropology. Does **certain cultures** mean 'not in ours' or 'not in all'?

(3) '[or some sort of **science** of witchcraft.]' This addition seems to have no clear meaning at all. What is a 'science' of witchcraft as opposed to just plain witchcraft? The main function is to introduce the word 'science', though it seems to have no connection to what follows.

(4) 'I don't think that it's just [a matter of] believing hard enough that [there is such a thing as] witchcraft.' The speaker argues that witchcraft is not merely a belief; there is more to it.

(5) 'I [do] believe that [there is such a thing that] a person can put himself in a state of **mind** . . . that [could actually be considered] witchcraft.' Is witchcraft as a state of mind different from the state of belief denied in (4)?

(6) 'or that something could be given them to intoxicate them [to a certain frame of mind] . . .' The third learned word, **intoxicate**, is introduced by this addition. The vacuity of this passage becomes more evident if we remove repetitions, fashionable words and stylistic decorations:

But I believe in witchcraft.
I don't think witchcraft is just a belief.
A person can put himself or be put in a state of mind that is witchcraft.

Without the extra verbiage and the O.K. words like **science**, **culture**, and **intoxicate**, Charles M. appears as something less than a first-rate thinker. The initial impression of him as a good speaker is simply our long-conditioned reaction to middle-class verbosity: we know that people who use these stylistic devices are educated people, and we are inclined to credit them with saying something intelligent. Our reactions are accurate in one sense: Charles M. is more educated than Larry. But is he more rational, more logical, or more intelligent? Is he any better at thinking out a problem to its solution? Does he deal more easily with abstractions? There is no reason to think so. Charles M. succeeds in letting us know that he is educated, but in the end we do not know what he is trying to say, and neither does he.

Schooling in capitalist America

S. BOWLES and H. GINTIS

The genetic interpretation of inequality had regained much of its tarnished academic respectability and has come to command the attention of social scientists and policy-makers alike. The first major shot was Arthur Jensen's argument in the *Harvard Educational Review* that the failure of compensatory education to raise scholastic achievement levels must be attributed to the heritability of IQ. Jensen's survey of the heredity research of Burt and others was embraced and extended by Harvard psychologist Richard Herrnstein. The distribution of wealth, privilege, and social status, asserted Herrnstein, is determined to a major and increasing extent by the distribution of IQ. Because IQ is highly heritable, economic and social status is passed on within families from one generation to the next.

These assertions by Jensen, Herrnstein, and others constituted a fundamental attack on the liberal reformist position. Yet the liberal defense has been curiously superficial: The putative economic importance of IQ has remained undocumented by the genetic school and unchallenged by their critics. Amidst a hundred-page statistical barrage relating to the genetic and environmental components of intelligence, Jensen saw fit to devote only three sparse and ambiguous pages to this issue. Later advocates of the 'genetic school' have considered this 'elemental fact,' if anything, even less necessary of support. Nor has their choice of battleground proved injudicious; to our knowledge, not one of their environmentalist critics has taken the economic importance of IQ any less for granted.

This glaring lapse in the liberal defense is itself instructive. 'The most important thing . . . that we can know about a man,' says Louis Wirth, 'is what he takes for granted, and the most elemental and important facts about

Abridged excerpts reproduced from Bowles, S. and Gintis, H. *Schooling in Capitalist America*, pp. 115–20 and 123–4; published by Routledge and Kegan Paul, London, 1976.

a society are those that are seldom debated and generally regarded as settled.' We are questioning here the undisputed assumption underlying both sides of the recently revived IQ controversy: that the distribution of IQ is a basic determinant of the structure of privilege.

Our empirical results reinforce our contention that the emphasis on IQ as the basis for economic success serves to legitimate an authoritarian, hierarchical, stratified, and unequal economic system, and to reconcile individuals to their objective position within this system. Legitimation is enhanced when people merely believe in the intrinsic importance of IQ. This belief is facilitated by the strong associations among all the economically desirable attributes – social class, education, cognitive skills, occupational status, and income – and is integrated into a pervasive ideological perspective. That IQ is not a major determinant of the social class structure also supports our argument that access to a particular job depends on the individual's pattern of noncognitive personality traits (motivation, orientation to authority, discipline, internalization of work norms), as well as on such personal attributes as sex, race, age, and educational credentials. These personality traits and personal attributes aid in legitimating and stabilizing the structure of authority in the modern enterprise itself. Thus, primarily because of the central economic role of the school system, the production of adequate intellectual skills becomes a spin-off, a by-product of a stratification mechanism grounded in the supply, demand, production, and certification of an entirely different set of personal attributes.

We must begin a discussion of genetic transmission of economic status by asking what 'heritability' means. That IQ is highly heritable is merely to say that individuals with similar genes will exhibit similar IQs independent of differences in the social environments they might experience during their mental development. The main support for the genetic school are several studies of individuals with precisely the same genes (identical twins) raised in different environments (i.e. separated at birth and reared in different families). Their IQs tend to be fairly similar. In addition, there are studies of individuals with no common genes (unrelated individuals) raised in the same environment (e.g. the same family) as well as studies of individuals with varying genetic similarities (e.g. fraternal twins, siblings, fathers and sons, aunts and nieces) and varying environments (e.g. siblings raised apart, cousins raised in their respective homes). The difference in IQs for these groups conform roughly to the genetic inheritance model suggested by the identical twin and unrelated individual studies.

Leon Kamin recently presented extensive evidence casting strong doubt on the genetic position. But by and large, environmentalists have been unable to convincingly disprove the central proposition of the genetic school. But then, they have emphasised that it bears no important social implications. They have argued, for example, that the genetic theory says nothing about the 'necessary' degree of racial inequality or the limits of compensatory education. First, environmentalists deny that there is any evidence that the average IQ difference between black and whites (amounting to about fifteen

IQ points) is genetic in origin, and second, they deny that any estimate of heritability tells us much about the capacity of enriched environments to lessen IQ differentials, either within or between racial groups.

But the environmentalists' defense strategy has been costly. In their egalitarian zeal vis-à-vis racial differences, the environmentalists have sacrificed the modern liberal interpretation of social inequality. The modern liberal approach is to attribute social class differences to unequal opportunity. That is, while the criteria for economic success are objective and achievement-oriented, the failures and successes of parents are passed onto their children via distinct learning and cultural environments. From this it follows that the achievement of a more equal society merely requires that all youth be afforded the educational and other social conditions of the best and most successful. But the liberal counterattack against the genetic position represented a significant retreat, for it did not successfully challenge the proposition that IQ differences among whites of differing social class backgrounds are rooted in differences in genetic endowments. Indeed, the genetic school's data come precisely from observed differences in the IQ of whites across socioeconomic levels! The liberal failure to question the causal role of IQ in getting ahead economically completes the rout. The fundamental tenet of modern liberal social theory – that progressive social welfare programs can gradually reduce and eliminate social class differences, cultures of poverty and affluence, and inequalities of opportunity – has been done in to a major extent by its erstwhile advocates. So the old belief – adhered to by present-day conservatives and liberals of past generations – that social classes sort themselves out on the basis of innate individual capacity to cope successfully in the social environment, and hence tend to reproduce themselves from generation to generation has been restored.

[· · · · ·]

The most immediate support for the IQ theory of social inequality which we will call 'IQism' – flows from two substantial relationships. The first is the significant association between socioeconomic background and childhood IQ. Thus, according to our research, having a parent in the top decile in socioeconomic status gives a child a 42 per cent chance of being in the top fifth in IQ, while having a parent in the bottom socioeconomic status decile gives him only a 4.9 per cent chance. The second is the important association between childhood IQ and later economic success: An individual in the top childhood IQ decile is nearly four times as likely to achieve the highest income quintile as an individual from the bottom IQ decile.

The proponent of IQism argues that higher social class leads to higher IQ, which, in turn, leads to a greater chance of economic success. We shall show, however, that this inference is simply erroneous. Specifically, we will demonstrate the truth of the following proposition, which constitutes the empirical basis of our thesis: the fact that economic success tends to run in the family arises almost completely independently from any inheritance of

IQ, whether it be genetic or environmental. Thus, while one's economic status tends to resemble that of one's parents, only a minor portion of this association can be attributed to social class differences in childhood IQ, and a virtually negligible portion to social class differences in genetic endowments even if one were to accept the Jensen estimates of heritability. Thus a perfect (obviously hypothetical) equalization of IQs among individuals of differing social backgrounds would reduce the intergenerational transmission of economic status by only a negligible amount. We conclude that a family's position in the class structure is reproduced primarily by mechanisms operating **independently** of the inheritance, production, and certification of intellectual skills.

$$[\cdot \cdot \cdot \cdot \cdot]$$

The power and privilege of the capitalist class are often inherited, but not through superior genes. (Try asking David Rockefeller to hand over his capital in return for thirty more IQ points!) Differences in IQ, even were they genetically inherited, could not explain the historical pattern of economic and educational inequalities. The intractability of inequality of income and of economic opportunity cannot be attributed to genetically inherited differences in IQ. The disappointing results of the 'War on Poverty' cannot be blamed on the genes of the poor. The failure of egalitarian school reforms reflects the fact that inequality under capitalism is rooted not in individual deficiencies, but in the structure of production and property relations.

[E]ducation should be viewed as reproducing inequality by legitimating the allocation of individuals to economic positions on the basis of ostensibly objective merit. Moreover, the basis for assessing merit – competitive academic performance – is only weakly associated with the personal attributes indicative of individual success in economic life. Thus the legitimation process in education assumes a largely symbolic form.

This legitimation process, however, is fraught with its own contradictions. For the technocratic-meritocratic ideology progressively undermines the overt forms of discrimination which divide the work force into racially, sexually, and ethnically distinct segments. Ironically, the partial success of the meritocratic ideology has helped to create a political basis for working class unity. With the irrationality of these forms of discrimination increasingly exposed, the justification of inequality must increasingly rely on educational inequalities and IQism. Yet workers, minorities, and others have fought hard and to some extent successfully to reduce educational inequality, with little effect on economic inequality itself. This has tended to increase conflicts within education, to cast further doubt on the fairness of the income distribution process, and at the same time undercut traditional educational philosophy. Thus even the symbolism of meritocracy is threatened in the contemporary period.

Yet, as we have suggested, the reproduction function of education goes far beyond symbolic legitimation. [T]he education system plays a central role in preparing individuals for the world of alienated and stratified work relationships. Such a class analysis of education is necessary, we believe, to understand the dynamics of educational change and also the structural relations among social class, education, and economic success – relationships which we have seen to be inexplicable purely in terms of cognitive variables.

Class

G. MACKENZIE

The beginnings of the systematic analysis of social classes are to be found in the works of John Millar and Adam Ferguson. Writing in Scotland in the latter part of the 18th century, both men viewed classes simply as strata ranked hierarchically on the basis of wealth.

It was not until more than half a century later that Marx began to develop his theory of social class and class structure. It has been suggested that John Millar exercised an important influence on Marx. This may be the case. But it must not be allowed to obscure the fact that Marx explicitly eschewed the 'vulgar common sense' explanations of social class, which merely regarded class differences as 'differences in the size of one's purse.' Rather, classes were to be seen as comprising groups of individuals placed in a similar relationship to the means of production.

For Marx, productive activity is the basis of any human society: 'Production is the first historical act and the production of material life is a fundamental condition of all history.' Furthermore, production can only take place insofar as men cooperate with one another. It involves, therefore, a definite set of **social** relations. To the extent that the organisation of production requires a division of labour – which enables the production of an economic **surplus**, and thereby the development of private ownership of the means of production – the stage is set for the emergence of social classes.

Marx's view of class structure is, therefore, essentially dichotomous: focusing on the ownership and non-ownership of property as the basis of class formation and class relations. This does not mean, of course, that Marx denied the existence of 'intermediate classes.' In his analysis of the class struggle in France, for example, he identified no less than six distinct classes. But it does mean that he viewed such classes as temporary, as transitional. With the advancement of capitalist society, they would lose their separate identities, gradually becoming merged with one or the other of the two great classes: the bourgeoisie and the proletariat.

Abridged excerpts reproduced with permission from MacKenzie, G. Class. *New Society*, 19 October 1972, 142–4. Copyright © New Statesman and Society, 1972.

It is important to emphasise at least three points with regard to this concept of class structure.

Firstly, social classes are distinguished not by source or amount of income, but by access or nonaccess to property rights. Income categories are conceptually sterile: they yield a plurality of groupings, but individuals within those groupings may be differentially related to the means of production. A miner, a schoolteacher and a self-employed toolmaker may all be in the same income bracket, but nevertheless they occupy significantly different positions in relation to the means of production.

Secondly, Marx's analysis of social class reflects his primary concern with the explanation of social change – with the discovery of the 'law of motion of modern society.' For that motion is crucially dependent on the relationship between social classes, a relationship which is essentially one of conflict and struggle. It is the class struggle that is the prime agent or mechanism of social change or development – a development which is in the direction of a communist society, where private property and thereby social classes will be eliminated.

Thirdly, Marx's analysis of social class – and thereby of social change – is not 'economically determinist.' Classes do not realise themselves until they develop a level of **class-consciousness**, and thereby begin to participate in political conflict as organised groups. Change becomes possible at the point when objective class interests are transformed into a subjective awareness, and a social class begins to improve its position in the social structure at the expense of another class. It begins, in other words, a move towards the 'revolutionary reconstitution of society at large.' The development of such class-consciousness and class action cannot be regarded as inevitable. It depends on the members of a particular class being placed in a social situation that engenders feelings of class-consciousness and of class solidarity. For Marx, this situation was provided by the development of large-scale industry, which concentrates in one place large numbers of people, all in an identical class situation and with identical class interests. Work situation assumes, therefore, a vital role in the development of class ideology. At the same time as the capitalist brings together wage labourers in order to maximise efficiency and therefore surplus, he sows the seeds of his own destruction.

Unlike Marx, Max Weber was less concerned with linking the analysis of class to a general theory of history. Weber explicitly rejected an attempt to formulate an overall explanation of the development of human society. He pointed out that the analysis of class did not exhaust all the relevant dimensions of social stratification. In fact, two additional components had to be identified: those of **status** and **party**. Class, status and party, Weber maintained, were distinct enough to require separate analysis and description, though they mostly coalesce empirically.

According to Weber, we may speak of a 'class' when a number of people share similar 'life chances' in the market. 'Life chances' means quite simply the ability to gain access to scarce goods and services: goods such as food, a home, consumer durables: services such as medical care, education for one's children, legal protection and representation. This ability is determined by 'the amount and kind of power, or lack of such, to dispose of goods or skills for the sake of income in a given economic order.' Again, '"property" and "lack of property" are, therefore, the basic category of all class situations.'

But unlike Marx, Weber is concerned with differentiating **within** these basic categories, in terms of the amount and kind of property owned, as well as in terms of the kinds of services that the non-propertied can offer in return for income in the market. The doctor is in a more powerful situation than the unskilled labourer, while the owner of a large woollen mill is in a position superior to that occupied by the proprietor of a small building firm. Weber adopted a theoretical position contrary to that of Marx – i.e. he did not, by definition, view middle or intermediate classes as transitional phenomena. He distinguished between at least four main groupings in the class structure of capitalist societies: (a) the dominant ownership and commercial class; (b) the propertyless white-collar workers and intelligentsia; (c) the petty bourgeoise; (d) the manual working class. This latter category, Weber also pointed out, may itself contain divisions based on differing skill-levels. (Writing at the same time, Michels expressed concern at 'the veritable class distinction' that was emerging between German skilled and non-skilled workers.)

Like Marx, Weber stressed the fact that the existence of large numbers of people in a similar class situation, and with similar class interests, did not **automatically** lead to class-consciousness and thereby class conflict. Indeed, to the extent that class differences are seen as legitimate, and are thereby accepted by members of all social classes, class conflict may, in certain periods, be almost totally absent. Again like Marx, Weber saw the large-scale enterprise as particularly conducive to class conflict. Such enterprises made class differences especially visible at the same time as they enabled ideas to be easily disseminated through the workforce – especially if adequate leadership were available.

[· · · · ·]

Marx predicted that the abolition of the division of labour, with the completion of automation, might be accompanied by the disappearance of class differences. On the other hand, as Alain Touraine has hypothesised, automation may widen the gap between skilled and the ever-increasing proportion of non-skilled workers in the labour force. We cannot yet know which (if either) of these two theorists is the more correct. Neither can we know what changes will occur in the structure of white collar occupations. But our ignorance does not invalidate my central thesis: that there is a regular and clear relationship between the system of property ownership and the division of labour, on the one hand, and the class structure of contemporary industrial societies, on the other.

The labour of superintendence: managers

T. NICHOLS and H. BEYNON

There is a theory about a 'managerial revolution'. It holds that it is 'the managers' who control industry now; that either power resides in some ill-defined middle level 'technostructure' or (there are different versions) at the top where, because the new men have arrived, profit is no longer the driving force. This theory seems to appeal to some academics and business commentators. Somewhere, there might just be a middle manager who believes it. But if there is, he isn't to be found at Riverside. None of the managers we talked to there was in any doubt that his job was to make profit and that if he failed in this his future with ChemCo[1] was in jeopardy. For whereas management organisation has often been restructured, so that at Riverside managers and foremen have taken on more responsibility, these additional responsibilities have come in such a form that they make these men more closely accountable to capital. The apparent devolution of decision making, rather than resulting in the middle managers becoming an independent power in the corporation reveals them less and less ambiguously for what, objectively, they are; so much (relatively highly paid) labour.

The very process of rationalisation and bureaucratic control to which the superintendence of labour subjects factory workers (though not only factory workers, the same thing is happening in the service sector) simultaneously serves as an organisational device by means of which these managers are themselves held to account. These managers are driven by the impersonal force of capital. And it is of course this very impersonality which gives some credence to the PR men's slogans about how nobody (or everybody) owns the big corporations. But what we want to stress here is that it is now perhaps as clear as at any time in the history of capitalism that the labour of superintendence – the managers and foremen who are 'responsible' for the plants – is itself a victim of this same impersonal force: is a figure on a balance sheet.

Whether managers work in a small 'backward' factory or for a giant 'progressive' corporation, their lives are structured by the imperative to make profit. But in chemicals plant managers often have to cope with complex technology, and complex organisation as well.

Riverside managers talk a lot about 'the system'. Substantially, their job is to ensure that its component parts are most profitably aligned. The grinder manager, for example, is, as he says, always 'juggling'. Aside from 'man management' and technical innovation – and, given his plant is an old one

---

[1] [Nichols and Beynon make clear in the beginning of their book that, for reasons of confidentiality, ChemCo is not the real name of the company studied, (1977: viii) – Editors.]

Abridged excerpts reproduced from Nichols, T. and Beynon, H. *Living with Capitalism*, pp. 31–4 and 37–43; published by Routledge & Kegan Paul, London, 1977.

and not designed for the job, the inevitable work of 'mend and make do' – he has to plan the week's production run. He has to specify the quantities of various 'mixes' in advance, then keep the plant running. But demand for particular 'mixes' can fluctuate sharply. This can cause him problems, especially since space in his silo is limited. If a ship loaded with potash docks, his store has to be emptied ready. At such times other managers will make very clear to him that an idle ship loses money. But for technical reasons, to meet their demands could mean that he had to drop 30 tons of his currently – and continuously producing – 'mix' on the floor. This will take a bulldozer to clean up. It will also mean lost production, and lost money for his plant. In emergencies he may be able to 'import' particular mixes from ChemCo plants elsewhere – but again this will eat into his plant's profits. It's no real get-out. So, surplus capacity or under capacity he's in trouble. He has to produce continuously for the market. If his plant goes down he's in big trouble, **and**, if his feeder plants go down, **he** is the one who will cry 'Produce! Produce!' to **their** managers.

Ideally, ChemCo in general, and within it the Riverside site, should operate like a computer, with everything programmed in. In monopoly capitalism though, there is still the market to contend with. The working lives of plants can be shortened. They can be technically outmoded in the process of being built. And unplanned shifts in demand can have widespread ramifications for 'the system', even for mundane matters like storage. Take the manager concerned with warehousing:

> 'The selling people tell us they want an order immediately, which means that we've got to completely alter the whole organisation of the job down on the shop floor. It's all part of modern thinking. This is what management, modern management, is all about. Production will want standage, the material handling people will not, so there's a basic incompatibility. The management's job is to be able to come to some compromise, to be able to stand above it all, as it were, and look at things in terms of the overall system. That's why communication comes into it. Modern management therefore is about flexibility and change.
>
> At peak season, like nowadays, in peak season we'll tear ourselves inside out for the customers and that's what Jimmy was doing a minute ago when he rang me ["that's the system working", he beamed happily after Jimmy rang].'

In one important sense, for all these managers the 'juggling' is the job.

Riverside was designed as a technically interdependent system. For example, if certain plants come off line a chain reaction is set up. This not only means that other plants on site have to stop production (or waste their product) but that plants owned by other firms, which the Riverside complex is contracted to supply, also have to stop production. Very obvious economic considerations like these make managers eager to avoid plants coming off line at all, and to get them back on line as soon as possible. Whilst running, given the capital investment at stake, they must run them as efficiently as possible (the same holds for the labour intensive parts of the site. The continuous operation of the capital intensive plants depends on the packing and bagging workers not creating bottlenecks).

'The system', however, is not just a **technical** system. There is also what ChemCo managers call 'the other side'. By this they mean the workers. For just as the plant managers have to work collectively on the technical side of their work, it is essential if the entire mass of labour power on the Riverside site is to be put to the most profitable use that 'the other side' works as one big collectivity too. Short of an explosion or a technical fault which threatens production, 'trouble' – real trouble – means people. Without workers, sophisticated technology counts for nothing.

These managers therefore take 'the other side' seriously. They know that Riverside workers aren't militant but they want to keep things this way. They also want an actively involved and 'flexible' workforce to prevent waste and to make the system run efficiently. This is one reason why NWA[2] came in. Because a workforce which just plodded along and did what it was told to do was no longer good enough. Not if workers **had** to be told.

A by-product of the coming of the NWA was that these managers had to acquaint themselves with a new technical literature – on the psychosociology of work. 'You scientific buggers. You're suckers for middle range technical sounding theories', a visiting consultant told them. 'Plenty of diagrams and "theories". You like that don't you?' They do indeed. But they don't get it all from books and courses and they like to add a few embellishments of their own – Army life and experience with their own children are both grist for this particular mill. Moreover their 'theories' make evident both these men's essentially technical frame of reference, and their essentially economic function. 'Human beings', as one put it, 'are our most important piece of machinery. And like machines, if you don't keep them running men will go rusty. You've got to jump on them now and then to make sure they don't seize up.' One manager, pointing to a maintenance marker board, followed the people – machines analogy right through.

> 'Pity we haven't got one for labour. You know, with a column here to tell you which ones are defective, one for those completely u/s, one for replacements . . .'

For the most part this view of workers as things – as people-objects, to be worked on – takes more subtle forms. But that managers think like this is not surprising, in view of these men's technical training and the job they are paid to do, which involves thinking in terms of 'labour costs' and treating the labour power of other men as a commodity.

On the shop floor it's said, about a couple of Riverside managers in particular, that 'They aren't bad blokes. Given that they're managers, that is. They'd do anything for you **personally**.' 'Personally' means letting a bloke borrow your car spraying equipment, or talking to him about what it would

---

[2][NWA stands for New Working Agreement – Editors.]

be like for his son to do O-level Chemistry, or, providing things aren't too tight, helping him to get time off. It also means not driving it home unnecessarily that you are a manager. But 'personally' or not, these men **are** still managers. The theories of psycho-sociology notwithstanding, they've had to learn the hard way about 'man-management' and how to defend their 'right to manage'. And this means that 'in this game you can either be a bastard or a bad bastard'. ('Bad bastards' are managers who behave like bastards because they **are** bastards. Common or garden 'bastards' are men who find that, as managers, there are unpleasant things they have to do.)

Yet whatever their satisfactions and regrets, and whatever they feel, and whatever they think about it, one thing is certain: the 'economising' which came to ChemCo in the 1960s had very real effects upon these managers' lives at work.

For one thing the management structure has been 'flattened out'. The jobs which used to exist above theirs in the management hierarchy have been removed. As a result, many of them know that their careers have 'come to a halt in the middle'. Too old now to rate as 'whiz kids', they have no place to go.

We noted earlier that the technical interdependence of the production process created pressures, and that managers were thereby impelled to control each other. But the performance records which today's manager keeps on his subordinates are a further source of control. By means of these bureaucratic devices the manager himself can ultimately be further exposed to the chill wind of the market. Each manager has a job description and formally specified objectives. Such predefined expectations of performance make failure all the more glaring and cost consciousness all the more important. Moreover, just as each manager holds regular reviews of progress with his foremen, and the foremen with their workers, so he too is subject to regular reviews of progress, about **his** performance with his boss. The 'system' is a bureaucratic system – a system of control. It programmes, monitors and processes the 'performance' of labour, including that of the labour of superintendence, which itself is concerned with programming, monitoring, and processing in order to control.

Of course, barring bottlenecks, labour troubles, unanticipated shifts in supply and demand, leaks and emissions, and urgent phone calls in the middle of the night to say that plant's 'gone down', the manager should lead a programmed, well planned life – one in fact which allows him to plan further. Indeed to 'juggle' successfully, to be able to say 'that's the system working', can spell real satisfaction. But clearly the list of things which can 'upset the system' is by no means short. On any given day few managers can afford to relax, to be confident, as they put it, that 'the system knows what it's doing'. And should a manager make a mistake it can cost him dear.

Today, his 'performance' is indelibly recorded on a personal record card, to be scrutinised and reviewed by managers at the Central Career Planning Department. Any weakness or failure, any 'unnecessary' labour disputes or technical breakdown will be recorded. It will be marked down on his card.

These managers are well aware what this can mean. They watched as Edward Blunsen expanded plant capacity but increasingly antagonised the men on the plant – an antagonism that blew up into 'a mess' during spring 1972:

> 'It will go down on his record. One day when he's being considered for a higher job, someone will see it. It may be five years, may be tomorrow, may be twenty years' time, but it will go down on his record. And that will go with him.'

Such are the controls to which the labour of superintendence is now subjected.

Seeing such things, indeed – as part of 'the economising' – reluctantly being instrumental in bringing them about, can turn a manager in on himself. 'Say it happens to me', says George.

> 'I'm 48 years old. I joined ChemCo at the age of 24. I've got 24 years' service too. Say I go for an interview. "Ah! Mr Smith, you're a chemist", they say. "A chemist are you?" And there I am, I took my degree in 1947 . . . there are young people just taken their degrees, 25 to 30 years old, can ask for a much lower salary than I'm used to.
>
> "Ah!" they say, "well, you're a manager are you, Mr Smith? and what do you manage?" And I say, "Well, I've managed this plant now for seven years." "Ah!" they say, "well, where have you managed your plant?" "At ChemCo I say." Now I know the ChemCo system but what about modern innovations they think. "And what salary do you get, Mr Smith? I see, X thousand pounds. Thank you. . . ." So I can understand these blokes when they're 50, when they are sitting in front of the fire, when they don't want to go back north. "Is it going to happen to me?" they think. And then it does. The letter comes. It must be fucking awful.'

Where personal morality and economics collide, George Smith is given to show you he is doubtful and a little confused, even about what his own motives are. 'I don't think I'm like **that**', he says. 'But . . .' Or 'I don't honestly know.' Or, talking about decisions made higher up, 'I **think** that that's why we did it.' Or, a favourite expression this, 'If you put it in cynical terms of course . . .'

Yet it would be wrong to think that all ChemCo managers are racked by moral torment. Anyway, whether like some of the 'whiz kids' they delight in quantification and are in love with capitalist rationality or whether like George they dislike 'counting numbers' and hesitatingly inspect themselves for cynicism, they still have a job to do. They are still part of 'the system'. Which is perhaps why, sitting side by side with the site manager, George contains his ambivalence and puts things rather differently. Dr Jones, talking to us with George, was very concerned about production, and about the new human relations:

> 'I would say we have been very involved, perhaps over-involved, with this sort of thing. We have had innumerable Consultants on the plants. To my

mind I don't doubt the theory at all, the theory of Herzberg for example makes a deal of sense. What I doubt is the **application** of it, its applicability to industrial situations. Sometimes you know, I think we spend no time in this place on **work**. We have tried the lot here. T Groups, Job Enlargement, the lot. And I think very few of them, or very few of them we have tried, have made a real impact on **production**. I think the only one that has helped in any way has been Methods Change.'

At this point George joined in:

'James liked Methods Change because it was orientated toward profit, or more obviously oriented toward profit. And he has a point there. Sometimes you do have the impression that we are not here to make fertiliser or chemical or cement at all but to be experimenting with new types of human relations techniques.

The first thing to remember is that we are in business to make money and that management's job is basically production. If all these techniques help then well and good . . .'

But let's go back to George thinking aloud about redundancy; about the question of who is responsible.

'The thing is I don't think they think it's **me**. I don't think they think it's **my boss**. They think it's "**them**". But we're "**them**". But it's not **us**. It's something **above us**. Something up there.'

As he finished this complex soliloquy he gazed up at the ceiling – and lifted up his arms. His sense of confusion is perfectly understandable. In a big corporation like ChemCo business is a complicated business. Yet in a big corporation like ChemCo, business is in some ways still very simple. For when men fail to find any one individual responsible for their fate, and when managers have to make distasteful decisions which conflict with their own often humane inclinations, it can be for one and the same reason: because they are subject to the dictates of an impersonal force – capital.

Male dominance and technological change

CYNTHIA COCKBURN

[You are referred to the wealth of historical and statistical material which appears in the Cockburn book omitted here because of lack of space.]

Among the many divisions and tensions within the working class in printing, the rift between men and women has been one of the most deep and

Abridged excerpt reproduced from Cockburn, C. *Brothers – Male Dominance and Technological Change*, pp. 151–90; published by Pluto Press, London, 1983.

destructive. The aggressiveness of craftsmen and their unions towards women as potential rivals for work is often represented in union history (and even today) as an unfortunate but inevitable by-product of the men's class struggle with the employer. 'They were only defending themselves against the employer's exploitation of women as cheap labour.' The conflict cannot be reduced to this single dimension of class, however. Had nothing but class interest been at stake, the men would have found women acceptable as apprentices, would have fought whole-heartedly for equal pay for women **and** for the right of women to keep their jobs at equal pay. As it was, the men and their unions sought to have the women removed from the trade. The arguments used by men against women differed from those used against male rivals. They expressed the interests of men in the social and sexual subordination of women. There is no doubt that, in the last resort, the craft work of composition for print was men's work **because men said it was**. The typographical associations did not stop at rhetoric: they organised to exclude women and were not ashamed to say so. 'If it were not for the union in London I venture to think that women would be all over the London trade,' said Naylor.[1] Fortunately, the London Union has been strong enough to keep them entirely out.' It was in very similar vein that men said to me only last year, 'It has been the policy of our union: keep them out.' 'Women will only come into the news trade if the union loses its grip.'

It was not until 1909 that the Edinburgh comps launched the big crusade against women for which the trade had been waiting. In the meantime, the monotype machine method of typesetting was spreading fast in the book trade. It separated the processes of setting and casting, making the typesetting occupation, on a typewriter-style of keyboard, highly compatible with contemporary views of women's employment. The Edinburgh men were now in competition with women for both hand and machine composing.

Towards the end of 1909 a 'memorial' was sent to the masters by the Edinburgh branch of the STA: get rid of the women. The members were determined to back it with action. 'What course that action will take is today the agitating thought in Edinburgh printing circles.' The compositors were receiving particular support from the unskilled men of the Warehousemen and Cutters' Union and the National Society of Operative Printers' Assistants to whom they offered thanks 'for invaluable services rendered'. Jonathan Zeitlin has pointed out how the craftsmen gained the allegiance of the unskilled men by promising to lend their own muscle to the struggle of the unskilled for recognition by employers.

A curious memorial was received by the masters individually and the Master Printers' Association, their trade body. A copy also reached the STA. It became known as the 'We Women' memorial and was signed by 300 women. It read:

> That up to the time in Edinburgh the Monotype machines have been largely, if not chiefly, operated by women, and that women have proved

[1] General Secretary of the London Society of Compositors in 1907.

themselves entirely competent to work these machines, so that it seems a great hardship that women should be debarred from working at them in future. That since we have realised the position of women in the printing trade is seriously threatened, **we women** have been trying to organise ourselves with a view to securing justice for ourselves and for the women who may in future desire to practice the business of compositors or monotypists.

We urge the Masters' Association to delay any decision hurtful to the interests of women compositors until the women's case has been given full consideration.

The STA hit back energetically. 'The vast majority of girls', it contended, 'knew absolutely nothing either of the memorial or its authors'. It was certainly the product of a small coterie of outside feminists 'engaged in political warfare'. It is worth noting that 'The Woman Question' pulled out unprecedented numbers of men into active union participation. The meetings in Edinburgh at this time 'for size and solidarity of feeling . . . beat all records within the personal knowledge of its members'.

[T]he employers conceded: no new female learners would be taken into composing departments for a period of six years, i.e. up to 30 June 1916. All keyboards of composing machines installed in future would be operated by male labour. The temporary stop became a permanent ban on female apprentices in Scotland. The ban was still in effect in 1953, by which time the few female compositors remaining in the city were all elderly, having been apprenticed before the agreement of 1910.

The newspaper industry, which is our special concern, has always had a worse record with regard to women's participation and segregation than other parts of the printing industry. In 1976 the Arbitration Service demonstrated the confinement of women to clerical, canteen and cleaning jobs in the national newspaper industry, with a small proportion finding work as journalists, publicity artists and in the administration. If we see the industry as producing a fat 'wage packet' for the working class, women have by no means received their fair share of it.

It was not, of course, a matter of mere choice for women. Job markets get segmented by the actions of employers and unions in such a way that occupations tend to become 'men's work' or 'women's work', with little overlap. Throughout the working world, women tend to be clustered into certain occupations and industries rather than spread evenly among them. This **occupational segregation** has a horizontal aspect, in which women cluster into certain types of work, and a vertical aspect, in which they cluster into the lower ranks in terms of seniority and pay. There has been surprisingly little change in the degree of sexual segregation of either kind in Britain between 1901 and 1971.

In particular, women are 'segmented out' of the more rewarding jobs. This general picture is reflected in print where, as the Printing and Publishing Industry Training Board point out, 'The occupations of women mirror those followed by women in the economy overall. Throughout this century men in printing have been higher earners relative to other manufacturing workers, but they have neglected to bring their female colleagues along in their wake.

What is happening under the impact of new technology and developments within capital in the printing industry, is the break-up of old structures within the working class, and the dissolution of some of the patriarchal forms.

The traditional compositor, however, takes these things hard. This disquiet of skilled men who have long been sheltered by their organisation from the competition of women at work and long accustomed to possessing an un-questioned, if often benign, authority over a woman in the home, echoes in some ways the disquiet of men as they saw their women and children drawn into industrial work for the first time in the early years of the Industrial Revolution. Many of the men I interviewed in the London news trade in 1980 represented women **as a problem**. 'I think there is a resentment about girls coming into the industry. It is a threat, a definite threat in that sense.'

Why do men feel as they do? What do they stand to lose and what meanings are they making, what ideologies are they constructing and de-ploying, to stave off their loss? It is interesting to compare the case that men were making out against women at the turn of the century and the case they make today. The similarities are striking. But what is more striking than the similarities revealed in the men's consciousness is the contrast in their circum-stances and prospects, then and now. Their arguments were threadbare then, they are in tatters today. The men are continuing to handle contradic-tion by recourse to the same ideological formula.

But mechanisation of typesetting was one thing and computerised photo-composition quite another. Its introduction coincides with a collapse of national competitiveness – there are no easy pickings of empire this time. It arrives at a time when the printing industry is fighting for survival against do-it-yourself print, cheap foreign print, electronic media and alternative forms of advertising. It is occurring in mid-recession, when unemployment is very high and working-class organisations are under threat. Computerised photo-composition offers productivity gains of a different order of magnitude to those of mechanical typesetting. It implies a revolution in the organisation of print on an altogether different scale to that of the 1890s and 1900s. It has, besides, more striking gender connotations, both ideological and practi-cal. The social and political contexts, too, differ markedly. Cracks have begun to appear in the structure of patriarchal rights, as embodied in law and state policy. The change is being experienced by men in the context of an upsurge of self-expression among women which has charged, if not changed, the climate of opinion since 1970. It is not surprising, then, to find that the men's practised, time-honoured arguments about women and their place in men's world have lost something of their ring of confidence.

'She couldn't do it'

Why were women unsuitable for the skilled work of composition for print? **Physical** reasons are often cited first. The work of hot-metal composition was said to have been too heavy for women. Women are supposed to have weaker spines than men. 'There was too much standing involved for them,' (1980) 'When a girl is made to stand one day, she cannot the next. Her back gives way and she cannot do it. Nature revolts against it herself' (1907). 'At Linotype, too, it takes a degree of heft or knack – to change the magazines for instance' (1980).

It should be noted at once that women **were** capable of the complete range of craft skills. At the Women's Printing Society shop in the late nineteenth century the women did imposition and make-up as well as type-setting. There have also been a number of competent women linotype operators.

The second reason the men put forward why women 'couldn't do a comp's work is that they just don't have the **mental ability**. They are, basically, rather stupid.' One told me that the managing director of his firm had intended to use the typists to break a strike, but the plan had foundered due to the girls' inadequacy. 'You can't expect a **girl** to sit down and remember all the format codes.' Specifically, girls are represented as illiterate. The men like to think of literacy as part of their own exclusive stock-in-trade, something in which they can feel superior even to journalists: The supposed inequality between the male and female intellect underlies some of the arguments in the nineteenth century too. An early typesetting invention was the Hattersley machine, which had a separate mechanism for the tedious job of distributing used type. A Sheffield typographer proposed that the oc-cupation of dissing **must** be seen as women's work because, 'a man's brain would greatly deteriorate until he became very low indeed in the scale if he was stuck at **that**, day after day. He could not understand how any intelligent printer could advocate that any intelligent man should stand playing with a thing like that all day' (1893).[3]

The third essentialism called into play by the men is '**natural temperament**'. One form of this is the portrayal of women as having an innate aversion to machinery. 'Machinery – that's anathema to a woman. They build up a complex about it.' (1980) 'Woman are too temperamental to work with machinery. They aren't happy with machinery like a man is.' (1980) It is true that fewer women than men are at home with technology – printing technology or any other mechanical technology. The history recounted in Chapter 1, however, should have been sufficient to demonstrate that men as a sex have **appropriated** the technology – tools, machinery and know-how – of composing for print. The same thing has happened in every other in-dustrially applied technology. Men have been the designers, developers and maintenance engineers and often, also, the operators, of machines. Besides, a male-dominated society has resulted in an education system, as well as an

[2] Typographical Association Meeting, Dec. 4th.

occupational structure, that forms boys as scientific and technological and dequalifies girls in these respects. Though capital employs women on some machines, and indeed has often displaced men to do so, nonetheless women are characteristically situated in a routine, operational relationship to the equipment. When it needs attention it is a man who is called to fix it. There is a sense in which women are only 'lent' machinery by men (Cockburn, 1981). Given their reliance on arguments concerning women's natural technological passivity, it is particularly embittering for compositors today to find themselves in an inert relationship to computerised photocomposition systems, not dissimilar from that of most women to machinery and a far cry from the total technological grasp of the craft tradition.

'She shouldn't do it'

There have been appeals to two principles in arguing that women **should** not do a compositor's work (even if she could). The first is the principle that it is proper and logical for the male head of the family to be its breadwinner, earning enough on his own efforts to keep a wife and children. The second is that women, visualised as sexual creatures, would be exposed to bad moral influences by entering a male occupation – or indeed any paid work outside the home. The fact is, of course, that many women at the time did work all their lives. Many did not marry. It is interesting to note that only two of the many women printers passing through the Women's Printing Society in London in its first **eighteen** years, married (M. Bateson, 1895).

During the twentieth century, critics have increasingly exposed the illogicality of 'the family wage' as a concept. Not all men have dependents. Eleanor Rathbone calculated, around the time of the first world war, that the 'family wage' was paid on behalf of about three million wives and 16 million children who were mere 'phantoms', the non-existent responsibility of bachelors. Worse, not all women were supported by men, and one-third of all women workers were wholly or partially responsible for the keep of other people. But skilled craftsmen, such as the compositors, continued within the labour movement to resist the introduction of state family allowances which alone could have made a more equal distribution of income. The artisan defended his right 'to keep half the world in purgatory because he enjoys playing redeemer to his own wife and children' (E. Rathbone, 1949).

If 'the family wage and the male breadwinner' is the first principle flouted by women who seek after compositors' employment, the second is **sexual morality**. The historical evidence shows the men arguing that women would be coarsened by working alongside men, they would hear language that was not good for their ears, they would lose their sweet femininity (even perhaps their virginity) in the course of abrasive contact with the masculine world of paid work.

Men appear to have a strong need to visualise and to make meaning of women in two incompatible ways. First, they need to see women as pure and unsullied beings. Women should be clean. A real woman is, 'somebody who looks like a woman, who smells nice, you know, that kind of sexual aura, makes you feel protective towards them.' as one comp put it. No ink under **her** fingernails. On the other hand, however, men want women's sexuality as free currency. They want women to be like the communal bicycles in the Amsterdam of the libertarian revolt of the late sixties: there to be picked up, ridden and laid aside by any one at any time. This is the 'meaning' ascribed to women in compositors' workplace culture. The men's relationship with each other is mediated through the coinage of women, in which women are handled and besmirched routinely.

The separation of work and home is taken to be a feature of capitalist production and capitalist relations alone. Within the context of capitalism, however, it has developed a significance within sex-relations as well. When a women turns up, in the flesh, in the man's workplace demanding and expecting essentially human treatment, that is to say neither being idealised nor defiled, she presents a startling dilemma for men. Implicitly she asserts her own estimate of her worth and her own definition of her sexuality, in defiance of his. In doing this, she spoils both his games: by becoming a competitor she has to be taken seriously, which is incompatible with being a sexual pawn. One comp described to me how he felt himself to be engaged in an escalating struggle as a worker and as a member of a trade union with newspaper owners, the bosses, while holding the lid on a growing rebellion from his wife. Along with other women, she could now use contraception to undermine men's power over procreation, cite the priority of her career over housework and 'wear jeans which she knows don't turn me on'. 'So what can a man do about it? We can't **attack** women!' The way out of this contradiction involves hard choices for men.

References

Bateson, Margaret (1895) *Professional Women upon their Professions.*

Cockburn, Cynthia (1981) 'The Material of Male Power,' *Feminist Review*, no. 9.

Hakim, Catherine (1979) '*Occupational Segregation*', Research Paper, no. 9. Dept. of Employment, HMSO, Nov.

Rathbone, Eleanor (1949) 'The Disinherited Family,' republished as *Family Allowances*, Allen & Unwin.

Zeitlin, Jonathan (1980) 'Craft Regulation and the Division of Labour; Engineers and Compositors in Britain, 1890–1914', *Warwick University Ph.D. Thesis*.

The rise of professional society: England since 1880

H. PERKIN

We live, in fact, in an increasingly professional society. Modern society in Britain, as elsewhere in the developed world, is made up of career hierarchies of specialized occupations, selected by merit and based on trained expertise. Where pre-industrial society was based on passive property in land and industrial society on actively managed capital, professional society is based on human capital created by education and enhanced by strategies of closure, that is, the exclusion of the unqualified. Landed and industrial wealth still exerts power but is increasingly managed by corporate professionals in property companies and business corporations. The professional hierarchies cut across the horizontal solidarities of class in the warp and weft of the social fabric. Both class and hierarchy are an integral part of the fabric and neither ever quite disappears from view.

Professionalism permeates society from top to bottom, in two ways. Firstly, the professional hierarchies – not all of them equal in status or rewards, or stretching as far as the top – reach much further down the social pyramid than ever landlordship or even business capital did, and embrace occupations formerly thought beyond the reach of professional aspiration. As more and more jobs become subject to specialized training and claim expertise beyond the common sense of the layman – and all professionals are laymen to the other professions – their occupants demand the status and rewards of a profession. In these days of increasingly employed professionals – close to the original model of the clergy or the military rather than medicine or the law, though even doctors and lawyers are now mostly salaried employees – this means a secure income, a rising salary scale, fringe benefits such as paid holidays and sick leave, and an occupational pension. Such professional conditions of work are increasingly within reach not merely of non-manual workers but of increasing numbers of the manual working class.

Secondly, a professional society is one permeated by the professional social ideal. A social ideal is a model of how society should be organized to suit a certain class or interest and of the ideal citizen and his contribution to it. Pre-industrial society was permeated by the aristocratic ideal based on property and patronage. Passive property, usually in land, provided the means for the ideal citizen, the leisured gentleman, to offer his unique contribution of political rule, moral leadership and encouragement of art, literature and sport. Patronage enabled him to select the recruits for those positions of power and influence not filled by property alone. Industrial society was permeated by the entrepreneurial ideal based on active capital

Abridged excerpts reproduced from Perkin, H. *The Rise of Professional Society: England since 1880*, pp. 2–4 and 6–8; published by Routledge, London, 1989.

and competition, on business investment as the engine of the economy run by the active owner-manager, ideally the self-made man who rose to wealth and influence by his own intrinsic worth and won out in open competition. The rival ideal of the working class, never achieved in practice, was the collective ideal of labour and co-operation, of labour as the sole source of wealth and co-operative endeavour as the fairest means of harnessing and rewarding it, and of the worker's right to the whole produce of labour. The professional ideal, based on trained expertise and selection by merit, differed from the other three in emphasizing human capital rather than passive or active property, highly skilled and differentiated labour rather than the simple labour theory of value, and selection by merit defined as trained and certified expertise. No more or no less than the rest did it live up to reality. Not all landlords were benevolent gentlemen, not all capitalists self-made men, not all wage earners more concerned with rising with their class rather than out of it. And not all professional men were prepared to let merit rise without help from family wealth or privileged education. Professional society is based on merit, but some acquire merit more easily than others.

The professions live by persuasion and propaganda, by claiming that their particular service is indispensable to the client or employer and to society and the state. By this means they hope to raise their status and through it their income, authority and psychic rewards (deference and self-respect). With luck and persistence they may turn the human capital they acquire into material wealth. In the pre-industrial past individual professionals – royal favourites (in the oldest profession) like George Villiers, Duke of Buckingham or Nell Gwyn, archbishops like Wolsey and Sumner, judges like Lords Eldon and Scott, generals like Marlborough and Wellington, and even lowly solicitors with other incomes like Sir John Hawkins or Sir Walter Scott – were able to buy land and try to found a family. In industrial society even actors and playwrights like Sheridan, Ellen Terry and Bernard Shaw turned human capital into visible wealth. But only in post-industrial society have the professions as a whole been able to establish human capital as the dominant form of wealth.

Property is not, as is commonly believed, an object or a credit instrument, which are just its outward signs. Leaving aside its lesser meaning as the right to immediate use of tangible objects like a car, a house or an owner-occupied farm (each of which, indeed, yields an imputed rent), property in its major meaning of power over resources, which creates relations between members of a society, is **a right to a flow of income**: rent, interest, profits labour service, or goods in kind. It is an acknowledged and legitimated claim to other people's labour.

How could the professions transform a service into income-yielding property? Gary Becker, Pierre Bourdieu, Alvin Gouldner, Anthony Giddens and others have familiarized the concepts of human, educational, cultural and intellectual capital, by which investment in acquired knowledge and expertise yields a rate of return commensurate with that of material capital. Such theories tend to assume that investment in specialized training of **itself** yields a differential return without any control of the market (other than the fortuitous economic or demographic fluctuations in supply and demand for specialized labour). Unfortunately for that analysis, specialized training of itself yields only earned income, payment for immediate services rendered, which may even fall below the cost of production if the service is oversupplied or undervalued. It cannot, except accidentally, create property in the form of vested income without some device to transform it into a scarce resource.

The transforming device is professional control of the market. When a professional occupation has, by active persuasion of the public and the state, acquired sufficient control of the market in a particular service, it creates an artificial scarcity in the supply which has the effect of yielding a rent, in the strict Ricardian sense of a payment for the use of a scarce resource. Some part of the payment, of course, will always accrue to the immediate work performed, but its value will be enhanced by an amount proportional to the scarcity of the service or skill. A natural or 'accidental' example, the fortuitous result of a unique though professionally trained voice, is that of Placido Domingo, who is paid a very large fee for each performance, most of which is rent for the use of the scarce resource, or a Henry Moore sculpture, which is a lump of stone transformed in value by his signature. Monopoly is not a *sine qua non*: scarcity may appear long before outright monopoly – the landlords charged rent long before achieving a monopoly, if they ever did – and the element of rent will be larger or smaller accordingly. But **some** element of rent accrues from any degree of control of the market, which is why organized professions are paid more than equivalent unorganized occupations. Since the essence of property is the right to (some portion of) the flow of income from the resource owned, this professional capital, which is manifestly more tangible than stocks or shares, less destructible than many forms of material property (buildings burn more readily than people), and capable of self-renewal by means of improvement in skills and expertise, is thus in the truest sense a species of property – albeit contingent property, contingent upon the performance of the service.

The importance of such property to the professional is that it gives him what all income-yielding property provides for its possessors: independence, security, the right to criticize without fear of the consequences, and so a secure position from which to defend one's place in society or, if he so wishes, a position of leverage from which to change society or one's own corner of it. Above all, it gives him the psychic security and self-confidence to press his own social ideal, his own vision of society and how it should be organized, upon the other classes. And the gradual triumph of the professional ideal over the last hundred years paved the way for the hegemony of human capital and the emergence of professional society.

Disabling professions

I. ILLICH

Professionalism is one of many forms that the control over work has taken. In former times soldiers of fortune refused to fight until they got the licence to plunder. Lysistrata organized female chattels to enforce peace by refusing sex. Doctors in Cos conspired by oath to pass trade secrets only to their offspring. Guilds set the curriculum, prayers, tests, pilgrimages and hazings through which Hans Sachs had to pass before he was permitted to shoe his fellow burghers. In capitalist countries, unions attempt to control who shall work what hours for what minimum pay. All trade associations are attempts by those who sell their labour to determine how work shall be done, and by whom. Professions also do this, but they go further: they decide what shall be made, for whom and how their decrees shall be enforced. They claim special, incommunicable authority to determine not just the way things are to be made, but also the reason why their services are mandatory. Many professions are now so highly developed that they not only exercise tutelage over the citizen-become-client, but also determine the shape of his world-become-ward.

There is a further distinction between professional power and that of other occupations. Its authority springs from a different source: a guild, a union or a gang forces respect for its interest and rights by strike, blackmail or overt violence. A profession, like a priesthood, holds power by concession from an elite whose interests it props up. As a priesthood provides eternal salvation, so a profession claims legitimacy as the interpreter, protector and supplier of a special, this-worldly interest of the public at large. This kind of professional power exists only in societies in which élite membership itself is legitimized or acquired by professional status. Professional power is a specialized form of the privilege to prescribe. It is this power of prescription that gives control within the industrial state. The profession's power over the work its members do is therefore distinct and new both in scope and in origin.

Merchants sell you the goods they stock. Guildsmen guarantee quality. Some craftspeople tailor their product to your measure or fancy. Professionals tell you what you need and claim the power to prescribe. They not only recommend what is good, but actually ordain what is right.

Some already live, and others are capable of moving, beyond the Age of Disabling Professions and its glittering shopping centres for goods and services. The days of politicians who promise more inclusive packages of welfare are numbered; soon, they will receive the same reception formerly accorded priest-ridden electoral slates and the verbiage of Marxist epigones.

Abridged excerpts reproduced from Illich, I. *et al. Disabling Professions*, pp. 16–17 and 38–9; published by Marion Boyars, London, 1977.

Professional cartels are now as brittle as the French clergy in the age of Voltaire; soon, the still inchoate post-professional ethos will reveal the iron cage of their nakedness. The professional peddlers of health, education, welfare and peace of mind required almost twenty-five years to establish their control over who **ought** to get what and why. For a long time, yet, they might also be able to control who **shall** get what, and at what cost, acting like gangsters. But unbeknownst to them, their credibility fades fast. A post-professional ethos takes shape in the spirit of those who begin to see the emperor's true physiognomy.

Thousands of individuals and groups now challenge professional dominance over themselves and the socio-technical conditions in which they live. They do so by the questions they ask and the style of life which they consciously create.

These non-ideological minorities may turn into a political force. The age of Disabling Professions may very well close when these silent minorities can clarify the philosophical and legal character of what in common **they do not want**. The advantages of self-chosen joyful austerity evidenced by these people will acquire political form and weight only when combined with a general theory that places freedom within publicly chosen limits above claims for ever more costly packages of 'rights'.

We are incapable of imagining what free men can do when equipped with modern tools respectfully constrained. The Post-Professional Ethos will hopefully result in a social panorama more colourful and diverse than all the cultures of past and present taken together.

Further reading

Hayes, N. (1984) *A First Course in Psychology*, Nelson, 2nd edn, 1988.

Ribeaux, P. and Poppleton, S.E. (1978) *Psychology and Work: an introduction*, Macmillan.

Rose, N. (1989) *Governing the Soul: The shaping of the private self*, Routledge, Chapter 5. (See also further reading for Chapters 3 and 5.)

Murphy, J., John, M., and Brown, H. (1984) *Dialogues and Debates in Social Psychology*, Lawrence Erlbaum Associates in conjunction with The Open University. (Has specific reference to ways in which psychology has been conceptualised and acted upon. Uses original material to illustrate this for example, see the nature-nurture debate in education and Milgram's discussion of his experiments as they refer to war criminals.)

Hollway, W. (1991) *Work Psychology and Organizational Behaviour: Managing the Individual at Work*, Sage. (A critical appraisal of the way in which psychology has been used to manage workers.)

Issues for discussion

1. Compare and contrast the behaviourist and psychoanalytical approaches to the understanding of the individual.
   Readings: Freud (Chapter 2)
                   Eysenck (Chapter 2)
2. Critically evaluate Maslow's theory of motivation.
   Readings: Maslow (Chapter 2)
                   Friedan (Chapter 2)
                   Vroom (Chapter 2)
3. To what extent, if at all, do Milgram's experiments illustrate Foucault's ideas on discipline, accommodation and resistance?
   Readings: Milgram (Chapter 2)
                   Foucault (Chapter 1 – both)
4. Examine the causes of women's subordinate position within organisations.
   Readings: Friedan (Chapter 2)

Oakley (Chapter 2)
Tiger (Chapter 2)
Dex (Chapter 2)
Kanter (Chapter 2)
Cockburn (Chapter 2)

5. To what extent are managers part of an increasingly professional society? Is professionalisation desirable?

Readings: MacKenzie (Chapter 2)
Nichols and Beynon (Chapter 2)
Perkin (Chapter 2)
Illich (Chapter 2)

6. To what extent are organisational identities the product of social influences?

Readings: all readings but particularly Mead, Merton, Whyte, Kanter, Tiger, Oakley, Labov, and Bowles and Gintis (all Chapter 2)

3

Discipline, accommodation and resistance

In this chapter the focus of analysis moves from the separate individual identities and social divisions, and begins the exploration of how individuals and groups are brought into various forms of relationship within the organisation. These patterns of relationship are presented here as forms of 'discipline' – this use of the term is controversial, but it is employed here in a broad sense. It covers both the ways in which human behaviour is subject to disciplines which are imposed by others and external to the individual, as well as to the ways in which knowledge and norms are internalised and begin to form the very identities which regulate action. It looks at this issue, however, in what should be seen as a preliminary way. This chapter does not deal with the human consequences of these relations, except in so far as accommodation and resistance are consequences. It does not deal with the issues of flexibility and quality with which much of the contemporary literature is preoccupied and which is dealt with in the final part of the book. Nor does it address the subject of gender or ethnic relations within the organisation. Instead, this chapter reflects the preoccupation and silences of the literature on organisations from the early years of this century through to the early 1980s. This does not mean, however, that this material should be considered irrelevant or out of date. The forms of discipline, accommodation and resistance identified here are still very much with us, and need to be grasped before contemporary issues and debates can properly be understood.

At the risk of oversimplifying, two distinct approaches to the discipline and control of organizational members can be discerned in this chapter. They can be labelled 'classical' and 'human relations' approaches respectively. The first of these is illustrated in the first three readings in this chapter by Thompson, Weber and Taylor. These relate to the historical period from early industrial capitalism in the eighteenth century through to the early part of the twentieth century, though many would see them as having continuing relevance. The classical form of discipline they illustrate is 'rational' and impersonal. Thompson analyses how workers become subjected to the discipline of the clock, while Weber deals with bureaucracy and the rules, hierarchy and division of labour it entails. Taylor advocates direct management control over every detail of the process of production and embraces both time-discipline and elements of bureaucracy (though not, perhaps, the career structure that the latter entails).

The 'human relations' form of discipline emphasises the need for positive social relationships within working groups and between workers and managers. A 'considerate' management style is advocated and job satisfaction for workers is held to be compatible with, if not essential for, high productivity. This approach came to be particularly influential – in the realm of management theory at least – in the period immediately after the Second World War. It is represented here in the readings by Mayo, and Coch and French. Mayo shows how good morale and increased output can result from allowing workers to form into cohesive groups and suggests how 'the company'(i.e. management) may both produce such effects and profit by them. Coch and French take this further, suggesting that a participative approach to managing groups may remove group resistance to change.

The readings by Herzberg and Needham later in this chapter can also be seen as illustrating ways of implementing a 'human relations' approach. Herzberg, it is true, is sometimes labelled a 'neo-human relations' writer and concentrates on the individual and the job rather than the group. He does, however, share many of the assumptions and aspirations of earlier writers in the human relations tradition. In the reading presented here he suggests ways of improving worker motivation through 'enriching' the job and as such he can be seen as advocating the reversal of trends set in train by Taylor's scientific management (or Taylorism). However, the extent to which job enrichment is simply an attenuation of the worst excesses of scientific management rather than a negation of them is debatable. The article by Needham also deals with a mechanism for attempting to create job satisfaction – the use of 'autonomous work groups' (quasi-autonomous might be a more accurate description).

The piece by Brunsson, while not directly in the human relations tradition, can also be read alongside those by Mayo and Coch and French in that he too emhasises the importance of social relations in instilling motivation and commitment among employees. In a highly provocative article he advocates 'irrational' decision making as a way of generating such motivation and commitment – a sentiment once again at odds with those expressed by the rationalising Taylor.

If, however, the human relations approach to discipline rests largely upon the assumption that groups can be made to work in ways which are, from a managerial viewpoint, functional, several readings in this chapter point in the opposite direction. The piece by Roethlisberger and Dickson appears here alongside Mayo's because it, too, is an account of an aspect of the classic 'Hawthorne' studies which began in the Hawthorne plant in Chicago in the 1920s. This reading, too, shows the importance of the group, but here the group acts to restrict production to a level below which a strict Taylorian would aspire. Roethlisberger and Dickson interpret this as the group insulating itself from managerially-initiated change. As such it might be said to illustrate the very 'problem' Coch and French seek to address in the reading which follows. The reading does, however, also suggest how, at any given point of time, individual managers and groups of workers may reach an accommodation which may not be optimal from the standpoint of the logic of efficiency, but is nevertheless satisfactory to all concerned. Of course, though, any such 'equilibrium' is likely to be unstable.

The extract from Janis also presents a picture of a group working in a way which, from a managerial viewpoint again, may be less than reassuring. He analyses why the Kennedy administration in the 1960s made the tremendous blunder of authorising the abortive Bay of Pigs invasion of Cuba and explains it with reference to the 'in-group' pressures in a cohesive decision-making group (there are echoes here of the pressure to conformity in groups discussed by Milgram in Chapter 2). While the particular example of decision making dealt with by Janis may seem remote from day-to-day organisational realities he sees the potential for 'group-think' in decision-making groups at any level. If this is so and if groups are to form the basis of well-regulated organisational life, then the lessons for managers are somewhat disquieting: the prospect for chaos and dysfunction are considerable. The pieces by both Janis and Brunsson also raise doubts as to the extent to which 'rationalisation' is an ongoing process; the reality of organisational life is often profoundly contradictory with pressures towards rational, scientific and rule-governed processes on the one hand, and non-rational processes on the other.

The question of why one disciplinary approach rather than

another one is taken up and used is an important one but is not satisfactorily resolved in this chapter. However, the reading by Fiedler suggests one kind of answer although it is at the level of the relationship between the individual 'leader' (or manager) and the group rather than at the level of the organisation as a whole. He poses the question of which 'leadership style' is best – whether autocratic and task-oriented on one hand or democratic, considerate and people-oriented on the other. His answer is that different approaches are required in different situations, the situation being analysed in terms of the power of the leader, the nature of the task and leader-group relations. Needham suggests other variables that might be important in determining what disciplinary strategy management will adopt. Among others these include conditions in the labour market. Other explanations might, of course, be offered: that a human relations approach for example is better suited to certain positions in the new kind of flexible firm (see the reading by Atkinson in Chapter 4) or that the human relations approach arises from the failure of the classical approach (see Axtell-Ray in Chapter 5).

It would, however, be a mistake to see human relations as replacing classical approaches in any definitive way either historically or theoretically. Both approaches continue to have contemporary relevance both on their own terms and in strange cocktails to be looked at in Part Two of the book when flexibility and quality are examined.

From a Marxist perspective there is, in any case, little to choose between the two approaches, both serving to sustain exploitation and commodification. Indeed, the readings by Coch and French, Herzberg and Needham can be seen as providing evidence of how little change to social relations and the nature of work is brought about by the application of human relations techniques. From a Foucauldian perspective, too, both approaches can be seen as disciplinary technologies – the latter perhaps the more insidious because it rests more on self-disciplining practices. From this perspective, however, these disciplinary technologies need not be used in a calculating way by one individual group or class to control or exploit another. They nevertheless dictate what relationships and identities are to be found within organisations – thus bureaucracy creates bureaucratic relations and personalities (as discussed for example by Merton in Chapter 2), while at one and the same time bureaucrats create bureaucracy.

Whatever form of discipline is adopted, the potential for resistance exists. The reading by Hobsbawm and Rude shows the variety of forms resistance took in early industrial capitalism including rioting, arson and sabotage. This pre-dates the establishment of trade unions but, as the extract from Taylor and Walton illustrates, such forms of relatively spontaneous and unorganised (or covertly organised) resistance are still to be found. Hyman's contribution takes this distinctintion between organised and unorganised conflict as its starting point, and provides a brief look at the strike as a form of resistance.

It will be noted that the examples of resistance provided here are of manual worker resistance to the employer or manager. This is not intended to suggest that resistance is not also found in management and professional circles. Management resistance to new forms of discipline is, in fact, often found, see, for example, the readings by Hill in Chapter 5.

One final point needs to be made and that is that worker resistance is not just the **consequence** of disciplinary regimes. It should become apparent from these readings that the development of particular forms of discipline is itself the **outcome** of resistance and also an attempt to avoid it. This can be seen in Coch and French's article which poses the 'problem' of how to **overcome** resistance but it is also apparent in Taylor's contribution which explicitly is aimed at ending the 'war' between employer and employee. It is apparent, however, that no system of discipline has yet succeeded altogether in preventing resistance arising or recurring. This is also true of the most recent attempts to impose discipline through 'flexibility' and 'culture' which are dealt with in Part Two of the book.

Time and work – discipline

E.P. THOMPSON

[Thompson makes a large number of references to obscure historical documents and secondary sources. These have been omitted here.]

Attention to time in labour depends in large degree upon the need for the synchronization of labour. But in so far as manufacturing industry remained conducted upon a domestic or small workshop scale, without intricate subdivision of processes, the degree of synchronization demanded was slight, and task-orientation was still prevalent. The putting-out system demanded much fetching, carrying, waiting for materials. Bad weather could disrupt not only agriculture, building and transport, but also weaving, where the finished pieces had to be stretched on the tenters to dry. As we get closer to each task, we are surprised to find the multiplicity of subsidiary tasks which the same worker or family group must do in one cottage or workshop. Even in larger workshops men sometimes continued to work at distinct tasks at their own benches or looms, and – except where the fear of the embezzlement of materials imposed stricter supervision – could show some flexibility in coming and going.

Hence we get the characteristic irregularity of labour patterns before the coming of large-scale machine-powered industry. Within the general demands of the week's or fortnight's tasks – the piece of cloth, so many nails or pairs of shoes – the working day might be lengthened or shortened. Moreover, in the early development of manufacturing industry, and of mining, many mixed occupations survived: Cornish tinners who also took a hand in the pilchard fishing; Northern lead-miners who were also smallholders; the village craftsmen who turned their hands to various jobs, in building, carting, joining; the domestic workers who left their work for the harvest; the Pennine small-farmer/weaver.

The work pattern was one of alternate bouts of intense labour and of idleness, wherever men were in control of their own working lives. (The pattern persists among some self-employed – artists, writers, small farmers, and perhaps also with students – today, and provokes the question whether it is not a 'natural' human work-rhythm.) On Monday or Tuesday, according to tradition, the hand-loom went to the slow chant of **Plen-ty of Time, Plen-ty of Time**: on Thursday and Friday, **A day t'lat, A day t'lat**. The temptation to lie in an extra hour in the morning pushed work into the evening, candle-lit hours. There are few trades which are not described as honouring Saint Monday: shoemakers, tailors, colliers, printing workers, potters, weavers, hosiery workers, cutlers, all Cockneys. Despite the full employment of many

The abridged extract from E.P. Thompson, 'Time, Work-Discipline and Industrial Capitalism', *Past and Present*, no. 38 (December 1967), pp. 56–97, is reprinted with kind permission (World Copyright: The Past and Present Society, 175 Banbury Road, Oxford, England).

London trades during the Napoleonic Wars, a witness complained that 'we see Saint Monday so religiously kept in this great city . . . in general followed by a Saint Tuesday also'.

[· · · · ·]

Saint Monday, indeed, appears to have been honoured almost universally wherever small-scale, domestic, and outwork industries existed; was generally found in the pits; and sometimes continued in manufacturing and heavy industry. It was perpetuated, in England, into the nineteenth – and, indeed, into the twentieth – centuries for complex economic and social reasons. In some trades, the small masters themselves accepted the institution, and employed Monday in taking-in or giving-out work. In Sheffield, where the cutlers had for centuries tenaciously honoured the Saint, it had become 'a settled habit and custom' which the steel-mills themselves honoured (1874):

> This Monday idleness is, in some cases, enforced by the fact that Monday
> is the day that is taken for repairs to the machinery of the great
> steelworks.

Where the custom was deeply-established, Monday was the day set aside for marketing and personal business.

This irregular working rhythm is commonly associated with heavy weekend drinking: Saint Monday is a target in many Victorian temperance tracts. But even the most sober and self-disciplined artisan might feel the necessity for such alternations. 'I know not how to describe the sickening aversion which at times steals over the working man and utterly disables him for a longer or shorter period, from following his usual occupation', Francis Place wrote in 1829.

[· · · · ·]

We may, finally, note that the irregularity of working day and week were framed, until the first decades of the nineteenth century, within the larger irregularity of the working year, punctuated by its traditional holidays, and fairs. Still, despite the triumph of the Sabbath over the ancient saints' days in the seventeenth century, the people clung tenaciously to their customary wakes and feasts, and may even have enlarged them both in vigour and extent.

[· · · · ·]

The most arduous and prolonged work of all was that of the labourer's wife in the rural economy. One part of this – especially the care of infants – was the most task-orientated of all. Another part was in the fields, from which she must return to renewed domestic tasks. As Mary Collier complained in a sharp rejoinder to Stephen Duck:

> ... when we Home are come,
> Alas! we find our Work but just begun;
> So many Things for our Attendance call,
> Had we ten Hands, we could employ them all.
> Our Children put to Bed, with greatest Care
> We all Things for your coming Home prepare:
> You sup, and go to Bed without delay,
> And rest yourselves till the ensuing Day;
> While we, alas! but little Sleep can have,
> Because our froward Children cry and rave ...
>
> In ev'ry Work (we) take our proper Share;
> And from the Time that Harvest doth begin
> Until the Corn be cut and carry'd in,
> Our Toil and Labour's daily so extreme,
> That we have hardly ever **Time to dream**.

Such hours were endurable only because one part of the work, with the children and in the home, disclosed itself as necessary and inevitable, rather than as an external imposition. This remains true to this day, and, despite school times and television times, the rhythms of women's work in the home are not wholly attuned to the measurement of the clock. The mother of young children has an imperfect sense of time and attends to other human tides. She has not yet altogether moved out of the conventions of 'pre-industrial' society.

I have placed 'pre-industrial' in inverted commas: and for a reason.

$$[\cdot \cdot \cdot \cdot \cdot]$$

Above all, the transition is not to 'industrialism' *tout court* but to industrial capitalism or (in the twentieth century) to alternative systems whose features are still indistinct. What we are examining here are not only changes in manufacturing technique which demand greater synchronization of labour and a greater exactitude in time-routines in **any** society; but also these changes as they were lived through in the society of nascent industrial capitalism. We are concerned simultaneously with time-sense in its technological conditioning, and with time-measurement as a means of labour exploitation.

There are reasons why the transition was peculiarly protracted and fraught with conflict in England: among those which are often noted, England's was the first industrial revolution, and there were no Cadillacs, steel mills, or television sets to serve as demonstrations as to the object of the operation. Moreover, the preliminaries to the industrial revolution were so long that, in the manufacturing districts in the early eighteenth century, a vigorous and licensed popular culture had evolved, which the propagandists of discipline regarded with dismay. Josiah Tucker, the dean of Gloucester, declared in 1745 that 'the **lower** class of people' were utterly degenerated. Foreigners (he sermonized) found 'the **common people** of our **populous cities** to be the most **abandoned**, and **licentious** wretches on earth':

> Such brutality and insolence, such debauchery and extravagance, such idleness, irreligion, cursing and swearing, and contempt of all rule and authority . . . Our people are **drunk with the cup of liberty**.

The irregular labour rhythms described in the previous section help us to understand the severity of mercantilist doctrines as to the necessity for holding down wages as a preventative against idleness, and it would seem to be not until the second half of the eighteenth century that 'normal' capitalist wage incentives begin to become widely effective. The confrontations over discipline have already been examined by others. My intention here is to touch upon several points which concern time-discipline more particularly. The first is found in the extraordinary Law Book of the Crowley Iron Works. Here, at the very birth of the large-scale unit in manufacturing industry, the old autocrat, Crowley, found it necessary to design an entire civil and penal code, running to more than 100,000 words, to govern and regulate his refractory labour-force. The preambles to Orders Number 40 (the Warden at the Mill) and 103 (Monitor) strike the prevailing note of morally-righteous invigilation. From Order 40:

> I having by sundry people working by the day with the connivence of the clerks been horribly cheated and paid for much more time than in good conscience I ought and such hath been the baseness & treachery of sundry clerks that they have concealed the sloath & negligence of those paid by the day . . .

And from Order 103:

> Some have pretended a sort of right to loyter, thinking by their readiness and ability to do sufficient in less time than others. Others have been so foolish to think bare attendance without being imployed in business is sufficient . . . Others so impudent as to glory in their villany and upbrade others for their diligence . . .

> To the end that sloath and villany should be detected and the just and diligent rewarded, I have thought meet to create an account of time by a Monitor, and do order and it is hereby ordered and declared from 5 to 8 and from 7 to 10 is fifteen hours, out of which take $1\frac{1}{2}$ for breakfast, dinner, etc. There will then be thirteen hours and a half neat service . . .

This service must be calculated 'after all deductions for being at taverns, alehouses, coffee houses, breakfast, dinner, playing, sleeping, smoaking, singing, reading of news history, quarelling, contention, disputes or anything forreign to my business, any way loytering'.

The Monitor and Warden of the Mill were ordered to keep for each day employee a time-sheet, entered to the minute, with 'Come' and 'Run'. In the Monitor's Order, verse 31 (a later addition) declares:

> And whereas I have been informed that sundry clerks have been so unjust as to reckon by clocks going the fastest and the bell ringing before the hour for their going from business, and clocks going too slow and the bell ringing after the hour for their coming to business, and those two black traitors Fowell and Skellerne have knowingly allowed the same; it is therefore ordered that no person upon the account doth reckon by any other clock, bell, watch or dyall but the Monitor's, which clock is never to be altered but by the clock-keeper. . . .

The Warden of the Mill was ordered to keep the watch 'so locked up that it may not be in the power of any person to alter the same'. His duties also were defined in verse 8:

> Every morning at 5 a clock the Warden is to ring the bell for beginning to work, at eight a clock for breakfast, at half an hour after for work again, at twelve a clock for dinner, at one to work and at eight to ring for leaving work and all to be lock'd up.

His book of the account of time was to be delivered in every Tuesday with the following affidavit:

> This account of time is done without favour or affection, ill-will or hatred, & do really believe the persons above mentioned have worked in the service of John Crowley Esq the hours above charged.

We are entering here, already in 1700, the familiar landscape of disciplined industrial capitalism, with the time-sheet, the time-keeper, the informers and the fines. Some seventy years later the same discipline was to be imposed in the early cotton mills (although the machinery itself was a powerful supplement to the time-keeper). Lacking the aid of machinery to regulate the pace of work on the pot-bank, that supposedly-formidable disciplinarian, Josiah Wedgwood, was reduced to enforcing discipline upon the potters in surprisingly muted terms. The duties of the Clerk of the Manufactory were:

> To be at the works the first in the morning, & settle the people to their business as they come in, – to encourage those who come regularly to their time, letting them know that their regularity is properly noticed, & distinguishing them by repeated marks of approbation, from the less orderly part of the workpeople, by presents or other marks suitable to their ages, &c.

> Those who come later than the hour appointed should be noticed, and if after repeated marks to disapprobation they do not come in due time, an account of the time they are deficient in should be taken, and so much of their wages stopt as the time comes to if they work by wages, and if they

work by the piece they should after frequent notice be sent back to breakfast-time.

These regulations were later tightened somewhat:

Any of the workmen forceing their way through the Lodge after the time alow'd by the Master forfeits 2/-d.

and McKendrick has shown how Wedgwood wrestled with the problem at Etruria and introduced the first recorded system of clocking-in. But it would seem that once the strong presence of Josiah himself was withdrawn the incorrigible potters returned to many of their older ways.

It is too easy, however, to see this only as a matter of factory or workshop discipline, and we may glance briefly at the attempt to impose 'time-thrift' in the domestic manufacturing districts, and its impingement upon social and domestic life. Almost all that the masters **wished** to see imposed may be found in the bounds of a single pamphlet, the Rev. J. Clayton's *Friendly Advice to the Poor*, 'written and publish'd at the Request of the late and present Officers of the Town of Manchester' in 1755. 'If the **sluggard hides his hands** in his bosom, rather than applies them to work; if he spends his Time in Sauntring, impairs his Constitution by Laziness, and dulls his Spirit by Indolence . . .' then he can expect only poverty as his reward. The labourer must not loiter idly in the market-place or waste time in market-ing. Clayton complains that 'the Churches and Streets [are] crowded with Numbers of Spectators' at weddings and funerals, 'who in spight of the Miseries of their Starving Condition . . . make no Scruple of wasting the best Hours in the Day, for the sake of gazing . . .'. The tea-table is 'this shameful devourer of Time and Money'. So also are wakes and holidays and the annual feasts of friendly societies. So also is 'that slothful spending the Morning in Bed':

The necessity of early rising would reduce the poor to a necessity of going to Bed betime; and thereby prevent the Danger of Midnight revels.

Early rising would also 'introduce an exact Regularity into their Families, a wonderful Order into their Oeconomy'.

[· · · · ·]

One other non-industrial institution lay to hand which might be used to inculcate 'time-thrift': the school. Clayton complained that the streets of Manchester were full of 'idle ragged children; who are not only losing their Time, but learning habits of gaming', etc. He praised charity schools as teaching Industry, Frugality, Order and Regularity: 'the Scholars here are obliged to rise betimes and to observe Hours with great Punctuality'.

[· · · · ·]

Exhortations to punctuality and regularity are written into the rules of all the early schools:

> Every scholar must be in the school-room on Sundays, at nine o'clock in the morning, and at half-past one in the afternoon, or she shall lose her place the next Sunday, and walk last.

Once within the school gates, the child entered the new universe of disciplined time. At the Methodist Sunday Schools in York the teachers were fined for unpunctuality. The first rule to be learned by the scholars was:

> I am to be present at the School . . . a few minutes before half-past nine o'clock. . . .

Once in attendance, they were under military rule:

> The Superintendent shall again ring, – when, on a motion of his hand, the whole School rise at once from their seats; – on a second motion, the Scholars turn; – on a third, slowly and silently move to the place appointed to repeat their lessons, – he then pronounces the word 'Begin'. . . .

The onslaught, from so many directions, upon the people's old working habits was not, of course, uncontested. In the first stage, we find simple resistance. But, in the next stage, as the new time-discipline is imposed, so the workers begin to fight, not against time, but about it. The evidence here is not wholly clear. But in the better-organized artisan trades, especially in London, there is no doubt that hours were progressively shortened in the eighteenth century as combination advanced. Lipson cites the case of the London tailors whose hours were shortened in 1721, and again in 1768: on both occasions the mid-day intervals allowed for dinner and drinking were also shortened – the day was compressed. By the end of the eighteenth century there is some evidence that some favoured trades had gained something like a ten-hour day.

Such a situation could only persist in exceptional trades and in a favourable labour market. A reference in a pamphlet of 1827 to 'the English system of working from 6 o'clock in the morning to 6 in the evening' may be a more reliable indication as to the general expectation as to hours of the mechanic and artisan outside London in the 1820s. In the dishonourable trades and outwork industries hours (when work was available) were probably moving the other way.

It was exactly in those industries – the textile mills and the engineering workshops – where the new time-discipline was most rigorously imposed that the contest over time became most intense. At first some of the worst masters attempted to expropriate the workers of all knowledge of time. 'I worked at Mr. Braid's mill', declared one witness:

> There we worked as long as we could see in summer time, and I could not say at what hour it was that we stopped. There was nobody but the master

and the master's son who had a watch, and we did not know the time. There was one man who had a watch . . . It was taken from him and given into the master's custody because he had told the men the time of day. . . .

[· · · · ·]

Petty devices were used to shorten the dinner hour and to lengthen the day. 'Every manufacturer wants to be a gentleman at once', said a witness before Sadler's Committee:

and they want to nip every corner that they can, so that the bell will ring to leave off when it is half a minute past time, and they will have them in about two minutes before time . . . If the clock is as it used to be, the minute hand is at the weight, so that as soon as it passes the point of gravity, it drops three minutes all at once, so that it leaves them only twenty-seven minutes, instead of thirty.

A strike-placard of about the same period from Todmorden put it more bluntly: 'if that piece of dirty suet, 'old Robertshaw's engine-tenter', do not mind his own business, and let ours alone, we will shortly ask him how long it is since he received a gill of ale for running 10 minutes over time'. The first generation of factory workers were taught by their masters the importance of time; the second generation formed their short-time committees in the ten-hour movement; the third generation struck for overtime or time-and-a-half. They had accepted the categories of their employers and learned to fight back within them. They had learned their lesson, that time is money, only too well.

We have seen, so far, something of the external pressures which enforced this discipline. But what of the internalisation of this discipline? How far was it imposed, how far assumed? We should, perhaps, turn the problem around once again, and place it within the evolution of the Puritan ethic. One cannot claim that there was anything radically new in the preaching of industry or in the moral critique of idleness. But there is perhaps a new insistence, a firmer accent, as those moralists who had accepted this new discipline for themselves enjoined it upon the working people. Long before the pocket watch had come within the reach of the artisan, Baxter and his fellows were offering to each man his own interior moral time-piece. Thus Baxter, in his *Christian Directory*, plays many variations on the theme of Redeeming the Time: 'use every minute of it as a most precious thing, and spend it wholly in the way of duty'. The imagery of time as currency is strongly marked, but Baxter would seem to have an audience of merchants and of tradesmen in his mind's eye:

Remember how gainful the Redeeming of Time is . . . in Merchandize, or any trading; in husbandry or any gaining course, we use to say of a man that hath grown rich by it, that he hath made use of his Time.

In all these ways – by the division of labour; the supervision of labour; fines; bells and clocks; money incentives; preachings and schoolings; the suppression of fairs and sports – new labour habits were formed, and a new time-discipline was imposed. It sometimes took several generations (as in the Potteries), and we may doubt how far it was ever fully accomplished: irregular labour rhythms were perpetuated (and even institutionalized) into the present century, notably in London and in the great ports.

Throughout the nineteenth century the propaganda of time-thrift continued to be directed at the working people, the rhetoric becoming more debased, the apostrophes to eternity becoming more shop-soiled, the homilies more mean and banal. In early Victorian tracts and reading-matter aimed at the masses one is choked by the quantity of the stuff. But eternity has become those never-ending accounts of pious death-beds (or sinners struck by lightning), while the homilies have become little Smilesian snippets about humble men who by early rising and diligence made good. The leisured classes began to discover the 'problem' (about which we hear a good deal today) of the leisure of the masses. A considerable proportion of manual workers (one moralist was alarmed to discover) after concluding their work were left with

> several hours in the day to be spent nearly as they please. And in what manner . . . is this precious time expended by those of no mental cultivation? . . . We shall often see them just simply annihilating those portions of time. They will for an hour, or for hours together . . . sit on a bench, or lie down on a bank or hillock . . . yielded up to utter vacancy and torpor . . . or collected in groups by the road side, in readiness to find in whatever passes there occasions for gross jocularity; practising some impertinence, or uttering some jeering scurrility, at the expense of persons going by. . . .

This, clearly, was worse than Bingo: non-productivity, compounded with impertinence. In mature capitalist society all time must be consumed, marketed, put to **use**; it is offensive for the labour force merely to 'pass the time'.

But how far did this propaganda really succeed? How far are we entitled to speak of any radical restructuring of man's social nature and working habits? I have given elsewhere some reasons for supposing that this discipline was indeed internalized, and that we may see in the Methodist sects of the early nineteenth century a figuration of the psychic crisis entailed. Just as the new time-sense of the merchants and gentry in the Renaissance appears to find one expression in the heightened awareness of mortality, so, one might argue, the extension of this sense to the working people during the industrial revolution (together with the hazard and high mortality of the time) helps to explain the obsessive emphasis upon death in sermons and tracts whose consumers were among the working-class. Or (from a positive stand-point) one may note that as the industrial revolution proceeds, wage incentives and expanding consumer drives – the palpable rewards for the productive consumption of time and the evidence of new 'predictive' attitudes to the future – are evidently effective. By the 1830s and 1840s it was commonly observed that the English industrial worker was marked off from his fellow Irish worker, not by a greater capacity for hard work, but by his regularity, his methodical paying-out of energy, and perhaps also by a repression, not of enjoyments, but of the capacity to relax in the old, uninhibited ways.

Bureaucracy

MAX WEBER

Domination and legitimacy

Domination [is] the probability that certain specific commands (or all commands) will be obeyed by a given group of persons. It thus does not include every mode of exercising 'power' or 'influence' over other persons. Domination ('authority') in this sense may be based on the most diverse motives of compliance: all the way from simple habituation to the most purely rational calculation of advantage. Hence every genuine form of domination implies a minimum of voluntary compliance, that is, an **interest** (based on ulterior motives or genuine acceptance) in obedience.

Not every case of domination makes use of economic means; still less does it always have economic objectives. However, normally the rule over a considerable number of persons requires a staff, that is, a **special** group which can normally be trusted to execute the general policy as well as the specific commands. The members of the administrative staff may be bound to obedience to their superior (or superiors) by custom, by affectual ties, by a purely material complex of interests, or by ideal (*wertrationale*) motives. The quality of these motives largely determines the type of domination. **Purely** material interests and calculations of advantages as the basis of solidarity between the chief and his administrative staff result, in this as in other connexions, in a relatively unstable situation. Normally other elements, affectual and ideal, supplement such interests. In certain exceptional cases the former alone may be decisive. In everyday life these relationships, like others, are governed by custom and material calculation of advantage. But custom, personal advantage, purely affectual or ideal motives of solidarity, do not form a sufficiently reliable basis for a given domination. In addition there is normally a further element, the belief in **legitimacy**.

Abridged extract reprinted with the permission of The Free Press, a Division of Macmillan, Inc. from *The Theory of Social Economic Organisation* by Max Weber, translated by A.M. Henderson and Talcott Parsons. Edited by Talcott Parsons. Copyright © 1947, renewed 1975 by Talcott Parsons.

Experience shows that in no instance does domination voluntarily limit itself to the appeal to material or affectual or ideal motives as a basis for its continuance. In addition every such system attempts to establish and to cultivate the belief in its legitimacy. But according to the kind of legitimacy which is claimed, the type of obedience, the kind of administrative staff developed to guarantee it, and the mode of exercising authority, will all differ fundamentally. Equally fundamental is the variation in effect. Hence, it is useful to classify the types of domination according to the kind of claim to legitimacy typically made by each.

The three pure types of authority

There are three pure types of legitimate domination. The validity of the claims to legitimacy may be based on:

1. Rational grounds–resting on a belief in the legality of enacted rules and the right of those elevated to authority under such rules to issue commands (legal authority).
2. Traditional grounds–resting on an established belief in the sanctity of immemorial traditions and the legitimacy of those exercising authority under them (traditional authority); or finally,
3. Charismatic grounds–resting on devotion to the exceptional sanctity, heroism or exemplary character of an individual person, and of the normative patterns or order revealed or ordained by him (charismatic authority).

In the case of legal authority, obedience is owed to the legally established impersonal order. It extends to the persons exercising the authority of office under it by virtue of the formal legality of their commands and only within the scope of authority of the office. In the case of traditional authority, obedience is owed to the **person** of the chief who occupies the traditionally sanctioned position of authority and who is (within its sphere) bound by tradition. But here the obligation of obedience is a matter of personal loyalty within the area of accustomed obligations. In the case of charismatic authority, it is the charismatically qualified leader as such who is obeyed by virtue of personal trust in his revelation, his heroism or his exemplary qualities so far as they fall within the scope of the individual's belief in his charisma.

1. The usefulness of the above classification can only be judged by its results in promoting systematic analysis. The concept of 'charisma' ('the gift of grace') is taken from the vocabulary of early Christianity. For the Christian hierocracy Rudolf Sohm, in his *Kirchenrecht*, was the first to clarify the substance of the concept, even though he did not use the same terminology. Others (for instance, Holl in *Enthusiasmus und Bussgewalt*) have clarified certain important consequences of it. It is thus nothing new.

2. The fact that none of these three ideal types, the elucidation of which will occupy the following pages, is usually to be found in historical cases in

'pure' form, is naturally not a valid objection to attempting their conceptual formulation in the sharpest possible form. In this respect the present case is no different from many others.

$$[\cdots\cdots]$$

But even so it may be said of every historical phenomenon of authority that it is not likely to be 'as an open book.' Analysis in terms of sociological types has, after all, as compared with purely empirical historical investigation, certain advantages which should not be minimized. That is, it can in the particular case of a concrete form of authority determine what conforms to or approximates such types as 'charisma,' 'hereditary charisma,' 'the charisma of office,' 'patriarchy,' 'bureaucracy,' the authority of status groups, and in doing so it can work with relatively unambiguous concepts. But the idea that the whole of concrete historical reality can be exhausted in the conceptual scheme about to be developed is as far from the author's thoughts as anything could be.

Legal authority: the pure type

The purest type of exercise of legal authority is that which employs a bureaucratic administrative staff. Only the supreme chief of the organization occupies his position of dominance (*Herrenstellung*) by virtue of appropriation, of election, or of having been designated for the succession. But even **his** authority consists in a sphere of legal 'competence.' The whole administrative staff under the supreme authority then consists, in the purest type, of individual officials (constituting a 'monocracy' as opposed to the 'collegial' type, which will be discussed below) who are appointed and function according to the following criteria:

1. They are personally free and subject to authority only with respect to their impersonal official obligations.
2. They are organized in a clearly defined hierarchy of offices.
3. Each office has a clearly defined sphere of competence in the legal sense.
4. The office is filled by a free contractual relationship. Thus, in principle, there is free selection.
5. Candidates are selected on the basis of technical qualifications. In the most rational case, this is tested by examination or guaranteed by diplomas certifying technical training, or both. They are **appointed**, not elected.
6. They are remunerated by fixed salaries in money, for the most part with a right to pensions. Only under certain circumstances does the employing authority, especially in private organizations, have a right to terminate the appointment, but the official is always free to resign. The salary scale is graded according to rank in the hierarchy; but in addition

to this criterion, the responsibility of the position and the requirements of the incumbent's social status may be taken into account.

7. The office is treated as the sole, or at least the primary, occupation of the incumbent.
8. It constitutes a career. There is a system of 'promotion' according to seniority or to achievement, or both. Promotion is dependent on the judgment of superiors.
9. The official works entirely separated from ownership of the means of administration and without appropriation of his position.
10. He is subject to strict and systematic discipline and control in the conduct of the office.

This type of organization is in principle applicable with equal facility to a wide variety of different fields. It may be applied in profit-making business or in charitable organizations, or in any number of other types of private enterprises serving ideal or material ends. It is equally applicable to political and to hierocratic organizations. With the varying degrees of approximation to a pure type, its historical existence can be demonstrated in all these fields.

Monocratic bureaucracy

Experience tends universally to show that the purely bureaucratic type of administrative organization – that is, the monocratic variety of bureaucracy – is, from a purely technical point of view, capable of attaining the highest degree of efficiency and is in this sense formally the most rational known means of exercising authority over human beings. It is superior to any other form in precision, in stability, in the stringency of its discipline, and in its reliability. It thus makes possible a particularly high degree of calculability of results for the heads of the organization and for those acting in relation to it. It is finally superior both in intensive efficiency and in the scope of its operations, and is formally capable of application to all kinds of administrative tasks.

The development of modern forms of organization in all fields is nothing less than identical with the development and continual spread of bureaucratic administration. This is true of church and state, of armies, political parties, economic enterprises, interest groups, endowments, clubs, and many others. Its development is, to take the most striking case, at the root of the modern Western state. However many forms there may be which do not appear to fit this pattern, such as collegial representative bodies, parliamentary committees, soviets, honorary officers, lay judges, and what not, and however many people may complain about the 'red tape,' it would be sheer illusion to think for a moment that continuous administrative work can be carried out in any field except by means of officials working in offices. The whole pattern of everyday life is cut to fit this framework. If bureaucratic administration is, other things being equal, always the most rational type from a technical point of view, the needs of mass administration make it today completely indispensable. The choice is only that between bureaucracy and dilettantism in the field of administration.

The primary source of the superiority of bureaucratic administration lies in the role of technical knowledge which, through the development of modern technology and business methods in the production of goods, has become completely indispensable. In this respect, it makes no difference whether the economic system is organised on a capitalistic or a socialistic basis. Indeed, if in the latter case a comparable level of technical efficiency were to be achieved, it would mean a tremendous increase in the importance of professional bureaucrats.

When those subject to bureaucratic control seek to escape the influence of the existing bureaucratic apparatus, this is normally possible only by creating an organization of their own which is equally subject to bureaucratization. Similarly the existing bureaucratic apparatus is driven to continue functioning by the most powerful interests which are material and objective, but also ideal in character. Without it, a society like our own – with its separation of officials, employees, and workers from ownership of the means of administration, and its dependence on discipline and on technical training – could no longer function. The only exception would be those groups, such as the peasantry, who are still in possession of their own means of subsistence. Even in the case of revolution by force or of occupation by an enemy, the bureaucratic machinery will normally continue to function just as it has for the previous legal government.

The question is always who controls the existing bureaucratic machinery. And such control is possible only in a very limited degree to persons who are not technical specialists. Generally speaking, the highest-ranking career official is more likely to get his way in the long run than his nominal superior, the cabinet minister, who is not a specialist.

Though by no means alone, the capitalistic system has undeniably played a major role in the development of bureaucracy. Indeed, without it capitalistic production could not continue and any rational type of socialism would have simply to take it over and increase its importance. Its development, largely under capitalistic auspices, has created an urgent need for stable, strict, intensive, and calculable administration. It is this need which is so fateful to any kind of large-scale administration. Only by reversion in every field – political, religious, economic, etc. – to small-scale organization would it be possible to any considerable extent to escape its influence. On the one hand, capitalism in its modern stages of development requires the bureaucracy, though both have arisen from different historical sources. Conversely, capitalism is the most rational economic basis for bureaucratic administration and enables it to develop in the most rational form, especially because, from a fiscal point of view, it supplies the necessary money resources.

Along with these fiscal conditions of efficient bureaucratic administration, there are certain extremely important conditions in the fields of communication and transportation. The precision of its functioning requires the services of the railway, the telegraph, and the telephone, and becomes increasingly dependent on them. A socialistic form of organization would not alter this fact. It would be a question whether in a socialistic system it would be possible to provide conditions for carrying out as stringent a bureaucratic organization as has been possible in a capitalistic order. For socialism would, in fact, require a still higher degree of formal bureaucratization than capitalism. If this should prove not to be possible, it would demonstrate the existence of another of those fundamental elements of irrationality – a conflict between formal and substantive rationality of the sort which sociology so often encounters.

Bureaucratic administration means fundamentally domination through knowledge. This is the feature of it which makes it specifically rational. This consists on the one hand in technical knowledge which, by itself, is sufficient to ensure it a position of extraordinary power. But in addition to this, bureaucratic organizations, or the holders of power who make use of them, have the tendency to increase their power still further by the knowledge growing out of experience in the service. For they acquire through the conduct of office a special knowledge of facts and have available a store of documentary material peculiar to themselves. While not peculiar to bureaucratic organizations, the concept of 'official secrets' is certainly typical of them. It stands in relation to technical knowledge in somewhat the same position as commercial secrets do to technological training. It is a product of the striving for power.

Superior to bureaucracy in the knowledge of techniques and facts is only the capitalist entrepreneur, within his own sphere of interest. He is the only type who has been able to maintain at least relative immunity from subjection to the control of rational bureaucratic knowledge. In large-scale organizations, all others are inevitably subject to bureaucratic control, just as they have fallen under the dominance of precision machinery in the mass production of goods.

In general, bureaucratic domination has the following social consequences:

1. The tendency to 'levelling' in the interest of the broadest possible basis of recruitment in terms of technical competence.
2. The tendency to plutocracy growing out of the interest in the greatest possible length of technical training. Today this often lasts up to the age of thirty.
3. The dominance of a spirit of formalistic impersonality: '*Sine ira et studio*,' without hatred or passion, and hence without affection or enthusiasm. The dominant norms are concepts of straightforward duty without regard to personal considerations. Everyone is subject to formal equality of treatment; that is, everyone in the same empirical situation. This is the spirit in which the ideal official conducts his office.

The development of bureaucracy greatly favors the levelling of status, and this can be shown historically to be the normal tendency. Conversely, every process of social levelling creates a favorable situation for the development of bureaucracy by eliminating the office-holder who rules by virtue of status privileges and the appropriation of the means and powers of administration; in the interests of 'equality,' it also eliminates those who can hold office on an honorary basis or as an avocation by virtue of their wealth. Everywhere bureaucratization foreshadows mass democracy, which will be discussed in another connection.

The 'spirit' of rational bureaucracy has normally the following general characteristics:

1. Formalism, which is promoted by all the interests which are concerned with the security of their own personal situation, whatever this may consist in. Otherwise the door would be open to arbitrariness and hence formalism is the line of least resistance.
2. There is another tendency, which is apparently, and in part genuinely, in contradiction to the above. It is the tendency of officials to treat their official function from what is substantively a utilitarian point of view in the interest of the welfare of those under their authority. But this utilitarian tendency is generally expressed in the enactment of corresponding regulatory measures which themselves have a formal character and tend to be treated in a formalistic spirit.

This tendency to substantive rationality is supported by all those subject to authority who are not included in the group mentioned above as interested in the protection of advantages already secured. The problems which open up at this point belong in the theory of 'democracy.'

Scientific management

F.W. TAYLOR

Fundamentals of scientific management

President Roosevelt, in his address to the Governors at the White House, prophetically remarked that 'The conservation of our national resources is only preliminary to the larger question of national efficiency.'

The whole country at once recognized the importance of conserving our material resources and a large movement has been started which will be effective in accomplishing this object. As yet, however, we have but vaguely appreciated the importance of 'the larger question of increasing our national efficiency.'

We can see our forests vanishing, our water-powers going to waste, our

Abridged from Taylor, F.W. *The Principles of Scientific Management*, Norton Library Edition, 1967, New York (first published in 1911), pp. 5–12, 24, 25, 35–9, 139, 140.

soil being carried by floods into the sea; and the end of our coal and our iron is in sight. But our larger wastes of human effort, which go on every day through such of our acts as are blundering, ill-directed, or inefficient, and which Mr. Roosevelt refers to as a lack of 'national efficiency,' are less visible, less tangible, and are but vaguely appreciated.

We can see and feel the waste of material things. Awkward, inefficient, or ill-directed movements of men, however, leave nothing visible or tangible behind them. Their appreciation calls for an act of memory, an effort of the imagination. And for this reason, even though our daily loss from this source is greater than from our waste of material things, the one has stirred us deeply, while the other has moved us but little.

As yet there has been no public agitation for 'greater national efficiency,' no meetings have been called to consider how this is to be brought about. And still there are signs that the need for greater efficiency is widely felt.

The search for better, for more competent men, from the presidents of our great companies down to our household servants, was never more vigorous than it is now. And more than ever before is the demand for competent men in excess of the supply.

What we are all looking for, however, is the ready-made, competent man; the man whom some one else has trained. It is only when we fully realize that our duty, as well as our opportunity, lies in systematically cooperating to train and to make this competent man, instead of in hunting for a man whom some one else has trained, that we shall be on the road to national efficiency.

In the past the prevailing idea has been well expressed in the saying that 'Captains of industry are born, not made'; and the theory has been that if one could get the right man, methods could be safely left to him. In the future it will be appreciated that our leaders must be trained right as well as born right, and that no great man can (with the old system of personal management) hope to compete with a number of ordinary men who have been properly organized so as efficiently to cooperate.

In the past the man has been first; in the future the system must be first. This in no sense, however, implies that great men are not needed. On the contrary, the first object of any good system must be that of developing first-class men; and under systematic management the best man rises to the top more certainly and more rapidly than ever before.

The principal object of management should be to secure the maximum prosperity for the employer, coupled with the maximum prosperity for each employé.

The words 'maximum prosperity' are used, in their broad sense, to mean not only large dividends for the company or owner, but the development of every branch of the business to its highest state of excellence, so that the prosperity may be permanent.

In the same way maximum prosperity for each employé means not only higher wages than are usually received by men of his class, but, of more importance still, it also means the development of each man to his state of maximum efficiency, so that he may be able to do, generally speaking, the highest grade of work for which his natural abilities fit him, and it further means giving him, when possible, this class of work to do.

It would seem to be so self-evident that maximum prosperity for the employer, coupled with maximum prosperity for the employé, ought to be the two leading objects of management, that even to state this fact should be unnecessary. And yet there is no question that, throughout the industrial world, a large part of the organization of employers, as well as employés, is for war rather than for peace, and that perhaps the majority on either side do not believe that it is possible so to arrange their mutual relations that their interests become identical.

The majority of these men believe that the fundamental interests of employés and employers are necessarily antagonistic. Scientific management, on the contrary, has for its very foundation the firm conviction that the true interests of the two are one and the same; that prosperity for the employer cannot exist through a long term of years unless it is accompanied by prosperity for the employé, and *vice versa*; and that it is possible to give the workman what he most wants – high wages – and the employer what he wants – a low labor cost – for his manufactures.

It is hoped that some at least of those who do not sympathize with each of these objects may be led to modify their views; that some employers, whose attitude toward their workmen has been that of trying to get the largest amount of work out of them for the smallest possible wages, may be led to see that a more liberal policy toward their men will pay them better; and that some of those workmen who begrudge a fair and even a large profit to their employers, and who feel that all of the fruits of their labor should belong to them, and that those for whom they work and the capital invested in the business are entitled to little or nothing, may be led to modify these views.

No one can be found who will deny that in the case of any single individual the greatest prosperity can exist only when that individual has reached his highest state of efficiency; that is, when he is turning out his largest daily output.

The truth of this fact is also perfectly clear in the case of two men working together. To illustrate: if you and your workman have become so skilful that you and he together are making two pairs of shoes in a day, while your competitor and his workman are making only one pair, it is clear that after selling your two pairs of shoes you can pay your workman much higher wages than your competitor who produces only one pair of shoes is able to pay his man, and that there will still be enough money left over for you to have a larger profit than your competitor.

In the case of a more complicated manufacturing establishment, it should also be perfectly clear that the greatest permanent prosperity for the workman, coupled with the greatest prosperity for the employer, can be brought about only when the work of the establishment is done with the smallest combined expenditure of human effort, plus nature's resources, plus the cost for the use of capital in the shape of machines, buildings, etc. Or, to state the same thing in a different way: that the greatest prosperity can exist only as the result of the greatest possible productivity of the men and machines of the establishment – that is, when each man and each machine are turning out the largest possible output; because unless your men and your machines are daily turning out more work than others around you, it is clear that competition will prevent your paying higher wages to your workmen than are paid to those of your competitor. And what is true as to the possibility to paying high wages in the case of two companies competing close beside one another is also true as to whole districts of the country and even as to nations which are in competition. In a word, that maximum prosperity can exist only as the result of maximum productivity. Later in this paper illustrations will be given of several companies which are earning large dividends and at the same time paying from 30 per cent. to 100 per cent. higher wages to their men than are paid to similar men immediately around them, and with whose employers they are in competition. These illustrations will cover different types of work, from the most elementary to the most complicated.

If the above reasoning is correct, it follows that the most important object of both the workmen and the management should be the training and development of each individual in the establishment, so that he can do (at his fastest pace and with the maximum of efficiency) the highest class of work for which his natural abilities fit him.

[· · · · ·]

[Owing] to the fact that the workmen in all of our trades have been taught the details of their work by observation of those immediately around them, there are many different ways in common use for doing the same thing, perhaps forty, fifty, or a hundred ways of doing each act in each trade, and for the same reason there is a great variety in the implements used for each class of work. Now, among the various methods and implements used in each element of each trade there is always one method and one implement which is quicker and better than any of the rest. And this one best method and best implement can only be discovered or developed through a scientific study and analysis of all of the methods and implements in use, together with accurate, minute, motion and time study. This involves the gradual substitution of science for rule of thumb throughout the mechanic arts.

[· · · · ·]

Under the old type of management success depends almost entirely upon getting the 'initiative' of the workmen, and it is indeed a rare case in which this initiative is really attained. Under scientific management the 'initiative' of the workmen (that is, their hard work, their good-will, and their ingenuity) is obtained with absolute uniformity and to a greater extent than is possible under the old system; and in addition to this improvement on the part of the men, the managers assume new burdens, new duties, and responsibilities never dreamed of in the past. The managers assume, for instance, the burden of gathering together all of the traditional knowledge which in the past has been possessed by the workmen and then of classifying, tabulating, and reducing this knowledge to rules, laws, and formulæ which are immensely helpful to the workmen in doing their daily work. In addition to developing a **science** in this way, the management take on three other types of duties which involve new and heavy burdens for themselves.

These new duties are grouped under four heads:

First. They develop a science for each element of a man's work, which replaces the old rule-of-thumb method.

Second. They scientifically select and then train, teach, and develop the workman, whereas in the past he chose his own work and trained himself as best he could.

Third. They heartily cooperate with the men so as to insure all of the work being done in accordance with the principles of the science which has been developed.

Fourth. There is an almost equal division of the work and the responsibility between the management and the workmen. The management take over all work for which they are better fitted than the workmen, while in the past almost all of the work and the greater part of the responsibility were thrown upon the men.

It is this combination of the initiative of the workmen, coupled with the new types of work done by the management, that makes scientific management so much more efficient than the old plan.

Three of these elements exist in many cases, under the management of 'initiative and incentive,' in a small and rudimentary way, but they are, under this management, of minor importance, whereas under scientific management they form the very essence of the whole system.

The fourth of these elements, 'an almost equal division of the responsibility between the management and the workmen,' requires further explanation. The philosophy of the management of 'initiative and incentive' makes it necessary for each workman to bear almost the entire responsibility for the general plan as well as for each detail of his work, and in many cases for his implements as well. In addition to this he must do all of the actual physical labor. The development of a science, on the other hand, involves the establishment of many rules, laws, and formulæ which replace the judgment of the individual workman and which can be effectively used only after having been systematically recorded, indexed, etc. The practical use of scientific data also calls for a room in which to keep the books, records, etc., and a desk for the planner to work at. Thus all of the planning which under the old system was done by the workman, as a result of his personal experience, must of necessity under the new system be done by the management in accordance with the laws of the science; because even if the workman was well suited to the development and use of scientific data, it would be physically impossible for him to work at his machine and at a desk at the same time. It is also clear that in most cases one type of man is needed to plan ahead and an entirely different type to execute the work.

The man in the planning room, whose specialty under scientific management is planning ahead, invariably finds that the work can be done better and more economically by a subdivision of the labor; each act of each mechanic, for example, should be preceded by various preparatory acts done by other men. And all of this involves, as we have said, 'an almost equal division of the responsibility and the work between the management and the workman.'

To summarize: Under the management of 'initiative and incentive' practically the whole problem is 'up to the workman,' while under scientific management fully one-half of the problem is 'up to the management.'

Perhaps the most prominent single element in modern scientific management is the task idea. The work of every workman is fully planned out by the management at least one day in advance, and each man receives in most cases complete written instructions, describing in detail the task which he is to accomplish, as well as the means to be used in doing the work. And the work planned in advance in this way constitutes a task which is to be solved, as explained above, not by the workman alone, but in almost all cases by the joint effort of the workman and the management. This task specifies not only what is to be done but how it is to be done and the exact time allowed for doing it. And whenever the workman succeeds in doing his task right, and within the time limit specified, he receives an addition of from 30 per cent to 100 per cent to his ordinary wages. These tasks are carefully planned, so that both good and careful work are called for in their performance, but it should be distinctly understood that in no case is the workman called upon to work at a pace which would be injurious to his health. The task is always so regulated that the man who is well suited to his job will thrive while working at this rate during a long term of years and grow happier and more prosperous, instead of being overworked. Scientific management consists very largely in preparing for and carrying out these tasks.

Scientific management does not necessarily involve any great invention, nor the discovery of new or startling facts. It does, however, involve a certain **combination** of elements which have not existed in the past, namely, old knowledge so collected, analyzed, grouped, and classified into laws and rules that it constitutes a science; accompanied by a complete change in the mental attitude of the working men as well as of those on the side of the management, toward each other, and toward their respective duties and responsibilities. Also, a new division of the duties between the two sides and intimate, friendly cooperation to an extent that is impossible under the philosophy of the old management. And even all of this in many cases could not exist without the help of mechanisms which have been gradually developed.

It is no single element, but rather this whole combination, that constitutes scientific management, which may be summarized as:

Science, not rule of thumb.
Harmony, not discord.
Cooperation, not individualism.
Maximum output, in place of restricted output.
The development of each man to his greatest efficiency and prosperity.

The work group and 'positive mental attitudes'

ELTON MAYO

Acting in collaboration with the National Research Council, the Western Electric Company in its Hawthorne Works in Chicago had for three years been engaged upon an attempt to assess the effect of illumination upon the worker and his work. [The] inquiry involved in one phase the segregation of two groups of workers, engaged upon the same task, in two rooms equally illuminated. The experimental diminution of the lighting, in ordered quantities, in one room only, gave no sufficiently significant difference, expressed in terms of measured output, as compared with the other still fully illuminated room. Somehow or other that complex of mutually dependent factors, the human organism, shifted its equilibrium and unintentionally defeated the purpose of the experiment.

This interesting failure must be held in part responsible for the provocation to further experiment. But in addition to this problem of method, there were many concrete questions of high importance to which the executive authority desired objective answers, independent of executive opinion. Fatigue, monotony, and their effects upon work and worker were topics of much contemporary discussion. Was it possible to demonstrate clearly the part played by these in industrial situations? Furthermore, any company controlling many thousand workers tends naturally to develop its own methods or 'policies,' but tends also to lack any satisfactory criterion of the actual value of its methods of dealing with people. Whereas a machine will in some way reveal an inefficiency, a method of handling human situations will rarely reveal that it is rooted in mere custom and use rather than wisdom. These various considerations led to the institution of a second inquiry or series of inquiries in April, 1927.

In the institution of this second inquiry full heed was paid to the lesson of the first experiment. A group of workers was segregated for observation of the effect of various changes in the conditions of work. No attempt was made to 'test for the effect of single variables.' Where human beings are concerned one cannot change one condition without inadvertently changing others – so much the illumination experiment had shown. The group was kept small – six operatives – because the company officers had become alert to the possible significance for the inquiry of changes of mental attitude; it was believed that such changes were more likely to be noticed by the official observers if the group were small. Arrangements were made to measure accurately all changes in output; this also meant that the group must be small. An accurate record of output was desired for two reasons: first, changes in production differ from many other human changes in that they lend themselves to exact and continuous determination; second, variations in output do effectively show 'the combined effect' of all the conditions affecting a group. The work of Vernon and Wyatt supports the view that an output curve does indicate the relative equilibrium or disequilibrium of the individual and the group.

The operation selected was that of assembling telephone relays. This consists in 'putting together a coil, armature, contact springs, and insulators in a fixture and securing the parts in position by means of four machine screws'; each assembly takes about one minute, when work is going well. The operation ranks as repetitive; it is performed by women. A standard assembly bench with places for five workers and the appropriate equipment were put into one of the experimental rooms. This room was separated from the main assembly department by a ten-foot wooden partition. The bench was well illuminated; arrangements were made for observation of temperature and humidity changes. An attempt was made to provide for the observation of other changes and especially of unanticipated changes as well as those experimentally introduced. This again reflected the experience gained in the illumination experiments. Thus constituted, presumably for a relatively short period of observation, the experimental room actually ran on from April, 1927, to the middle of 1932, a period of over five years. And the increasing interest of the experiment justified its continuance until the economic depression made further development impossible.

Six female operatives were chosen, five to work at the bench, one to procure and distribute parts for those engaged in assembly. I shall not discuss the method of choosing these operatives, except to say that all were experienced workers. This was arranged by those in charge because they wished to avoid the complications which learning would introduce. Within the first year the two operatives first chosen – numbers one and two at the outset – dropped out, and their places were taken by two other workers of equal or superior skill who remained as numbers one and two until the end. The original number five left the Hawthorne Works for a time in the middle period but subsequently returned to her place in the group. In effect, then, there exist continuous records of the output of five workers for approximately five years. These records were obtained by means of a specially devised apparatus which, as each relay was completed, punched a hole in a moving tape. The tape moved at a constant speed, approximately one-quarter of an inch per minute; it punched five rows of holes, one row for each worker. At the right of each worker's place at the bench was a chute within which was an electric gate. When the worker finished a relay she placed it in the chute; as it passed through, it operated the electric gate and the punching apparatus duly recorded the relay. By measuring the distance on the tape between one hole and the next it is possible to calculate the time elapsing between the completion of one relay and another. The company thus has a record of every relay assembled by every operative in the experimental room for five years and in almost every instance has also a record of the time taken to assemble it. These exceptionally interesting figures are being analyzed by my colleague, T.N. Whitehead (1938).

The transfer of the five workers into the experimental room was carefully arranged. It was clear that changes in output, as measured by the recording device, would constitute the most important series of observations. The continuity and accuracy of this record would obviously make it the chief point of reference for other observations. Consequently, for two weeks before the five operatives were moved into the special room, a record was kept of the production of each one without her knowledge. This is stated as the base output from which she starts. After this, the girls were moved into the experimental room and again for five weeks their output was recorded without the introduction of any change of working conditions or procedures. This, it was assumed, would sufficiently account for any changes incidental to the transfer. In the third period, which lasted for eight weeks, the experimental change introduced was a variation in method of payment. In the department the girls had been paid a group piece rate as members of a group of approximately one hundred workers. The change in the third period was to constitute the five a unitary group for piece-rate payment. 'This meant that each girl would earn an amount more nearly in proportion to her individual effort since she was paid with a group of five instead of a group of one hundred.' (Pennock, 1930). It also meant that each girl was given a strong, though indirect, interest in the achievement of the group. After watching the effect of this change of grouping for eight weeks, the company officers felt that the more significant experimentation might begin.

In the fourth experimental period the group was given two rest pauses of five minutes each, beginning at 10.00 in the midmorning and at 2.00 in the afternoon respectively. The question had been discussed beforehand with the operatives – as all subsequent changes were – and the decision had been in favor of a five minute rather than a ten or fifteen minute pause partly because there was some feeling that, if the break were longer, the lost time would perhaps not be made up. This was continued for five weeks, at which time it was clear that just as total output had increased perceptibly after the constitution of the workers as a group for payment, so also had it definitely risen again in response to the rests. The alternative of the original proposals, two ten-minute rest pauses, was therefore adopted as the experimental change in period five. This change was retained for four weeks, in which time both the daily and weekly output of the group showed a greater rise than for any former change. In the sixth period the group was given six five-minute rests for four weeks. The girl operatives expressed some dislike of the constant interruption and the output curve showed a small recession.

The seventh experimental period was destined to become standard for the remaining years of the experiment. The subsequent changes are, for the most part, some variation of it. It may be regarded as concluding the first phase of the inquiry which was devoted, first, to the transfer of the operative and the establishment of routines of observation and, second, to experiment with rest pauses of varying incidence and length. Period seven was originally intended to discover the effect of giving some refreshment – coffee or soup and a sandwich – to the workers in the midmorning period. The observers in charge had, in process of talking with the girls, found out that they fre-

Relay assembly test room

Western Electric Co.-Hawthorne Works-Chicago

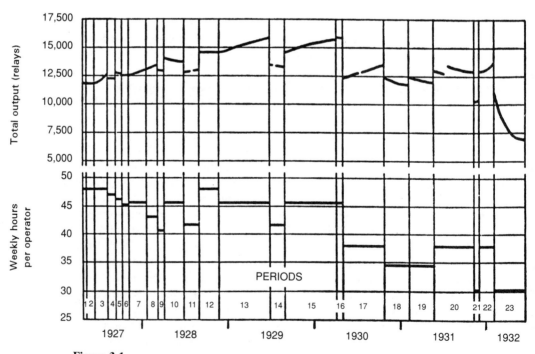

Figure 3.1

quently came to work in the morning after little or no breakfast. They became hungry long before lunch and it was thought that there was an indication of this in a downward trend of the output record before the midday break. It was therefore decided that the company should supply each member of the group with adequate refection in the middle of the working morning and perhaps some slighter refreshment in the midafternoon. This, however, meant an abandonment of the six five-minute rests and a return to the two ten-minute rest pauses. Such a return was in any event justified both by the expressed preference of the workers and by the fact that the output records seemed to indicate it as the better arrangement. The refreshment provided, however, made necessary some extension of the morning break. Period seven accordingly is characterized by a midmorning break of fifteen minutes (9.30 a.m.) with lunch and a midafternoon break of ten minutes (2.30 p.m.). This arrangement persisted in uncomplicated form for eleven weeks, and in that time production returned to its former high level and remained there.

In the second phase of experimentation, periods eight to eleven inclusive, the conditions of period seven are held constant and other changes are introduced. In period eight the group stopped work half an hour earlier every day – at 4.30 p.m. This was attended with a remarkable rise in both daily and weekly output. This continued for seven weeks until the tenth of March, 1928. Early in this period the original numbers one and two dropped out and their places were taken by those who rank as one and two for the greater part of the inquiry. In the ninth period the working day was shortened still further and the group stopped at 4 p.m. daily. This lasted for four weeks and in that time there was a slight fall both in daily and weekly output – although the average hourly output rose. In the tenth period the group returned to the conditions of work of period seven – fifteen-minute morning rest pause with refreshment, ten-minute rest pause in midafternoon, and a full working day to five o'clock. This period lasted for twelve weeks, and in that time the group in respect of its recorded daily and weekly output achieved and held a production very much higher than at any previous time. It was, perhaps, this 'high' of production which brought to expression certain grave doubts which had been growing in the minds of the company officers responsible for the experiment. Many changes other than those in production had been observed to be occurring; up to this time it had been possible to assume for practical purposes that such changes were of the nature of adaptation to special circumstance and not necessarily otherwise significant. Equally it had been possible to assume that the changes recorded in output were, at least for the most part,, related to the experimental changes in working conditions – rest pauses or whatnot – singly and successively imposed. At this stage these assumptions had become untenable – especially in the light of the previously expressed determination 'not to test for single variables' but to study the situation.

Period eleven was a concession to the workers, at least in part. I do not mean that the company had not intended to extend their second experimental phase – observation of the effect of shorter working time – to include a record of the effect of a five-day week. I am convinced that this was intended; but the introduction of a shorter working week – no work on Saturday – at this time refers itself to two facts, first, that the twelve weeks of this period run between the second of July and the first of September in the summer of 1928 and, second, it refers itself also by anticipation to the next experimental change. For it had already been agreed between the workers and the officers in charge that the next experiment, twelve, should be the restoration of the original conditions of work – no rest pauses, no lunch, no shortened day or week. In period eleven – the shortened week in summer – the daily output continued to increase; it did not, however, increase sufficiently to compensate for the loss of Saturday morning's work, consequently the weekly output shows a small recession. It is important to note that although the weekly output shows this recession, it nevertheless remains above the weekly output of all other periods except periods eight and ten.

September, 1928, was an important month in the development of the inquiry. In September, the twelfth experimental change began and, by arrangement with the workers, continued for twelve weeks. In this period, as I have said, the group returned to the conditions of work which obtained in period three at the beginning of the inquiry; rest periods, special refreshments, and other concessions were all abolished for approximately three months. In September, 1928, also began that extension of the inquiry known as 'The Interview Program' which I shall discuss in the next chapter [not included here]. Both of these events must be regarded as having strongly influenced the course of the inquiry.

The history of the twelve-week return to the so-called original conditions of work is soon told. The daily and weekly output rose to a point higher than at any other time, and in the whole period 'there was no downward trend.' At the end of twelve weeks, in period thirteen, the group returned, as had been arranged, to the conditions of period seven with the sole difference that whereas the company continued to supply coffee or other beverage for the midmorning lunch, the girls now provided their own food. This arrangement lasted for thirty-one weeks – much longer than any previous change. Whereas in period twelve the group's output had exceeded that of all the other performances, in period thirteen, with rest pauses and refreshment restored, their output rose once again to even greater heights. It had become clear that the itemized changes experimentally imposed, although they could perhaps be used to account for minor differences between one period and another, yet could not be used to explain the major change – the continually increasing production. This steady increase as represented by all the contemporary records seemed to ignore the experimental changes in its upward development.

The fourteenth experimental period was a repetition of period eleven; it permitted the group to give up work on Saturday between the first of July and the thirty-first of August, 1929. The fifteenth period returned again to the conditions of the thirteenth, and at this point we may regard the conditions of period seven as the established standard for the group.

It had been the habit of the officers in charge to issue reports of the progress of the experiment from time to time. These reports were published privately to the Western Electric Company and certain of its officers. From these documents one can gain some idea of the contemporary attitude to the inquiry of those who were directing it. The third of these reports was issued on August 15, 1928, and consequently did not carry its comment or description beyond period ten. The fourth was issued on May 11, 1929, and in it one finds interesting discussion of the events I have just described. The first allusion to the problem is a remark to the effect that 'although periods seven, ten, and thirteen involve the same length working day, the upward trend has continued through all three of these periods.' Later the report says: 'The increased production during the test has taken the operators from an average weekly output of about 2,400 relays [each] at the beginning to a present average weekly output of about 3,000 relays. [Period 13, which lasted until the end of June, 1929.] Periods seven, ten, and thirteen had the same working conditions; namely, a fifteen-minute rest and lunch in the morning and a ten-minute rest in the afternoon. Yet the average weekly output for the group in period seven was a little over 2,500 relays each, for period ten it was a little over 2,800 relays, and for period thirteen it was about 3,000 relays. Furthermore, period twelve was like period three in working conditions requiring a full day's work without any lunch or rest. Yet the average output for period three was less than 2,500 relays a week and that for period twelve was more than 2,900 relays a week. Period twelve was continued for twelve weeks and there was no downward trend. . . . The hourly output rate was distinctly higher during the full working day of period twelve than during the full working day of period three. Between the comparable periods seven, ten, and thirteen the rate of production also increased.'

[· · · · ·]

'The operators have no clear idea as to why they are able to produce more in the test room; but as shown in the replies to questionnaires . . . there is the feeling that better output is in some way related to the distinctly pleasanter, freer, and happier working conditions. . . .'

The report proceeds to remark that 'much can be gained industrially by carrying greater personal consideration to the lowest levels of employment.'

Mr. G.A. Pennock, in a paper read before a conference of the Personnel Research Federation on November 15, 1929, in New York says: '. . . this unexpected and continual upward trend in productivity throughout the periods, even in period twelve when the girls were put on a full forty-eight hour week with no rest period or lunch, led us to seek some explanation or analysis.' (Pennock, 1930). He goes on to mention three possibilities: first, fatigue which he finds it easy to exclude on the medical evidence, on the basis of certain physiological findings, and on the obvious ground that the 'gradually rising production over a period of two years' precludes such a possibility. He considers that the payment incentive of the higher group earnings may play some small part, but proceeds to state his conviction that the results are mainly due to changes in mental attitude. He proceeds to cite evidence to show the extent of this change.

It will be remembered that one of the avowed intentions of this inquiry was to observe as well as might be the unanticipated changes, including changes of mental attitude. The method overtly adopted at the beginning of the inquiry is stated in an early report as follows:

'C. Pertinent Records

Other records pertinent to the test and of value as an aid in interpreting results and psychological effects are maintained as follows:

1. The temperature and relative humidity, which are recorded each hour and then averaged, are plotted on the daily average hourly curve.

2. A complete report of the daily happenings (history sheets) of the test is made and this records what changes are made; what transpires during the day; operators' remarks; our own observations; and anything that will assist as an explanation when rationalizing the performance curve.

3. A 'Log Sheet' is maintained on each operator upon which her starting and finishing time is entered, and the time at which changes from one type to another are made; also all intervals, or non-productive time, such as personal time out, changes in type, repairs, and anything detracting from the actual production time.

4. An original hospital report, or record of physical examination, is kept. This has been supplemented each time the group is reëxamined which occurs periodically every five or six weeks. . . .

5. An attempt was made to discover the home and social environs of each girl worker. . . .

6. Data have been gathered in the attempt to reflect what in the judgment of the operators themselves is the reason why they do better work under test-room conditions. . . .'

These original provisions were effective largely because the experimental room was in charge of an interested and sympathetic chief observer. He understood clearly from the first that any hint of 'the supervisor' in his methods might be fatal to the interests of the inquiry. So far as it was possible he and his assistants kept the history sheets and the log sheet faithfully posted. In addition to this he took a personal interest in each girl and her achievement; he showed pride in the record of the group. He helped the group to feel that its duty was to set its own conditions of work, he helped the workers to find the 'freedom' of which they so frequently speak.

In the early stages of development, it was inevitable that the group should become interested in its achievement and should to some extent enjoy the reflected glory of the interest the inquiry attracted. As the years passed this abated somewhat, but all the evidence – including the maintenance of a high

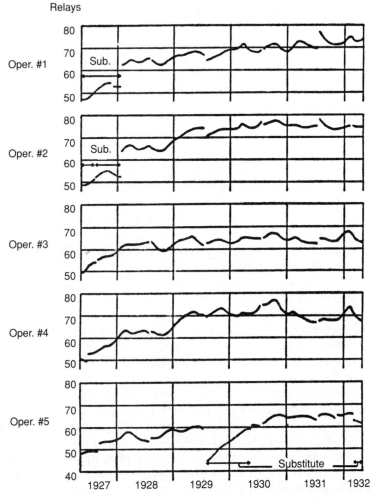

Figure 3.2

output – goes to show that something in the reconditioning of the group must be regarded as a permanent achievement. At no time in the five-year period did the girls feel that they were working under pressure; on the contrary, they invariably cite the absence of this as their reason for preferring the 'test room.'

The reason, then, for Mr. Pennock's claim is plain. Undoubtedly, there had been a remarkable change of mental attitude in the group. This showed in their recurrent conferences with high executive authorities. At first shy and uneasy, silent and perhaps somewhat suspicious of the company's intention, later their attitude is marked by confidence and candor. Before every change of program, the group is consulted. Their comments are listened to and discussed; sometimes their objections are allowed to negative a suggestion. The group unquestionably develops a sense of participation in the critical determinations and becomes something of a social unit. This developing social unity is illustrated by the entertainment of each other in their respective homes, especially operatives one, two, three, and four.

How can a change such as this be assessed? It is a change of mental attitude; it is also far more.

[· · · · ·]

The most significant change that the Western Electric Company introduced into its 'test room' bore only a casual relation to the experimental changes. What the company actually did for the group was to reconstruct entirely its whole industrial situation. Miss May Smith has wisely observed that the repetition work is 'a thread of the total pattern,' but 'is not the total pattern.' The company, in the interest of developing a new form of scientific control – namely, measurement and accurate observation – incidentally altered the total pattern, in Miss Smith's analogy, and then experimented with that thread which, in this instance, was the work of assembling relays. The consequence was that there was a period during which the individual workers and the group had to re-adapt themselves to a new industrial milieu, a milieu in which their own self-determination and their social well-being ranked first and the work was incidental. The experimental changes – rest pauses, food, and talk at appropriate intervals – perhaps operated at first mainly to convince them of the major change and to assist the re-adaptation. But once the new orientation had been established, it became proof against the minor experimental changes. At Hawthorne as the situation developed the experimental changes became minor matters in actuality – whatever the operatives thought. . . . [W]ith respect to period twelve any theory that there was 'a return to original conditions' is non-sensical. At that time the new industrial milieu, the new 'total pattern,' had been sufficiently established and the repetition work, 'the thread,' ran true to this, its chief determinant.

It must not be supposed that the abandonment of rest pauses and other concessions in period twelve was without effect. On the contrary the 'personal time out' reverted to its original dimension; in none of the periods between twelve and three does it bulk as large as in twelve and three. The average hourly output was stated at the time to have diminished. But these minor consequences were obscured by the major achievement, the capacity of the group – unsuspected even by themselves – to ignore an interference and continue their response to the major change – the novel industrial milieu. By strengthening the 'temperamental' inner equilibrium of the workers, the company enabled them to achieve a mental 'steady state' which offered a high resistance to a variety of external conditions.

References

Pennock, G.A. (1930) 'Industrial Research at Hawthorne: An Experimental Investigation of Rest Periods, Working Conditions and Other Influences' *Personnel Journal*, vol. VIII, no. 5, Feb., p. 299.
Whitehead, T.N. (1938) *The Industrial Worker* (Two Volumes) Harvard Univ. Press, Cambridge.

Group restriction of output

F.J. ROETHLISBERGER and WILLIAM J. DICKSON

[This is the report of a study of a group of 14 male workers engaged on wiring, soldering and inspecting banks of telephone switchgear. Of the 14 men, 9 were engaged on wiring, 3 on soldering and there were 2 inspectors (although one of these was replaced in the course of the study). For the purposes of this study they were segregated from other workers in the plant in a separate room and their interactions were recorded by an observer who was located in the room with them – Editors.]

Determinants of clique membership

[I]t is apparent [from our analysis] that th[e] group of operators [we studied] held certain definite ideas as to the way in which an individual should conduct himself. These sentiments, which were connected chiefly with occupation, output, and supervision, may be summarized as follows:

1. You should not turn out too much work. If you do, you are a 'rate-buster.'
2. You should not turn out too little work. If you do, you are a 'chiseler.'
3. You should not tell a supervisor anything that will react to the detriment of an associate. If you do, you are a 'squealer.'
4. You should not attempt to maintain social distance or act officious. If you are an inspector, for example, you should not act like one.

It may be concluded that the individual's position in the group was in large part determined by the extent to which his behavior was in accord with these sentiments. The members of clique A, the people who held the most favored position in the group, conformed to the group's rules of behavior in all respects. Members of clique B conformed to rules (1), (3), and (4). Indeed, they attached more importance to these rules than anyone else. This is easily understood because the higher the output of their associates, the more unfavorable their own output appeared. 'Squealing' was more objectionable to them than to the others because more of their actions were wrong from the standpoint of management. Finally, they resented any show of superiority more than the others did because they were in the most subordinate position.

The function of the group's internal organization

The social organization of the bank wiremen performed a twofold function: (1) to protect the group from internal indiscretions, and (2) to protect it from outside interference. The same mechanism sometimes served to fulfill both functions.

The mechanisms by which internal control was exercised were varied. Perhaps the most important were sarcasm, 'binging,' and ridicule. Through such devices pressure was brought to bear upon those individuals who deviated too much from the group's norm of acceptable conduct. From this point of view, it will be seen that the great variety of activities ordinarily labeled 'restriction of output' represent attempts at social control and discipline and as such are important integrating processes. In addition to overt methods, clique membership itself may be looked upon as an instrument of control. Those persons whose behavior was most reprehensible to clique A were excluded from it. They were, in a sense, socially ostracized. This is one of the universal social processes by means of which a group chastises and brings pressure to bear upon those who transgress its codes.

The operators attempted to protect themselves from outside interference by bringing into line those outsiders, supervisors and inspectors, who stood in a position of being able to interfere in their affairs. The chief mechanism by which they attempted to control these people was that of daywork allowance claims. The manner in which this weapon was brought into play against [the third inspector] shows how formidable it could be. The operators did not use this weapon against [the first inspector] or the group chief because they did not have to; both of these people submitted to group control. [The third inspector], however, refused to be assimilated, and they helped to bring about his removal by charging him with excessive amounts of daywork. This was the most effective device at their command. Interestingly enough, it was a device provided them by their wage incentive plan. The mechanism by which they sought to protect themselves from management was the maintenance of uniform output records, which could be accomplished by reporting more or less output than they produced and by claiming daywork.

It can be seen, therefore, that nearly all the activities of this group may be looked upon as methods of controlling the behavior of its members. The men had elaborated, spontaneously and quite unconsciously, and intricate social organization around their collective beliefs and sentiments. The question as to what gave rise to those sentiments and beliefs, whether they arose from actual or potential threats to their security, as the operators claimed, is an important one and will be dealt with at length in the following [section].

Formal vs. informal organization

It has been shown that the internal function of [the bank wiremen's] organization was to control and regulate the behavior of its members. Externally, however, it functioned as a protective mechanism. It served to protect the group from outside interference by manifesting a strong resistance to change, or threat of change, in conditions of work and personal relations.

The problem, therefore, be comes that of discovering those external factors which gave rise to this resistance.

When stated in these terms, a number of answers to this problem are immediately suggested. Perhaps the wiremen were apprehensive of the investigators. Did not the study situation itself encourage the type of behavior observed? Or were not the operators simply attempting to stave off the effects of the depression, which were becoming noticeable within the factory at that time? Or, finally, were they not, in restricting their output, simply attempting to protect their economic interests? Inasmuch as any of these possibilities might have accounted for the situation, they must be considered at the outset.

*Weekly average hourly output in the observation room
compared with that in the department*

In the case of one operator events associated with his removal to the obser-vation room did have an adverse effect upon his attitude, and indirectly upon his output rate. The output rates of the other eight wiremen were not greatly affected.

*Attitudes of the men while in the observation room
compared with their attitudes while in the department*

Were the attitudes of the operators toward their work, supervision, working conditions, and fellow workmen altered greatly by placing them under observation? In general, no. Their attitudes, as revealed in interviews taken before and after the study began, remained substantially the same.

*Overt behavior in the observation room
compared with overt behavior in the department*

Did the overt behavior of the operators change much in the observation room compared with their behavior in the department? It is true that the men in the observation room were more boisterous and talkative than those in the regular department, but the difference in behavior was more one of degree than of kind.

The relations of the interviewer and observer to the group

Inasmuch as the interviewer and the observer were a part of the situation they were studying, their relations with the operators and supervisors must also be considered. Of the two, the observer was much more closely associated with the operators and therefore was more likely to influence their behavior.

It has already been pointed out that the observer was apparently regarded with distrust at first but that in time he became friendly with all the operators. That they had not the slightest fear of him is attested to by the kind of material he was able to obtain. Many of the incidents he observed would not have taken place had he been regarded with suspicion or distrust.

How did the operators regard the interviewer: as someone who had authority over them, as an equal, or just as someone to talk to? No employee acted in the interview, as though he were trying to create a favorable impression upon the interviewer. [T]hey were not apprehensive of the interviewer. They felt free to talk about many things in the interview which they would not have discussed with their supervisors or co-workers.

It can be concluded that the investigators surely were not observing, a situation of their own making. Their relations with the group were very satisfactory. There was no evidence after the first few weeks that the operators were afraid of them or distrusted them. This is not to say they had no influence on the situation. They probably did have, but it is very unlikely that the investigators were merely observing a situation of their own creation.

The effects of the depression

Did not the situation in the Bank Wiring Observation Room reflect the response of the operators to the business depression? Was this not merely their way of warding off unemployment? In part, yes. There could be no doubt that the depression and fear of layoff occupied an increasingly important place in their thoughts, particularly after the beginning of 1932. In their interviews and in their daily conversations with one another and the observer they speculated endlessly upon when the depression would end, whether they would be laid off, and what would happen to them if they were. All but one of them were in very poor financial condition and if they were unemployed could not escape public support for long.

Although this was true, the investigators believed that fear of unemployment was only one among many factors determining the situation. It is doubtful if their formation into cliques and their attitudes toward their supervision had any relation to it. As for restriction of output, it may have been related to the effects of the depression but even that is doubtful. The output figures available, which stretched back before the depression, did not reflect any major interference.

Restriction of output and economic interest

Perhaps the most common way of interpreting situations like this is to argue that the employee, in acting as he does, is simply protecting his economic interests. It is argued that if he does not restrict his output at some level his piece rate will be cut, the less capable workers will be reprimanded or discharged, or some of his co-workers will be laid off. These reasons are the same as those the worker himself gives for his behavior and are taken as explanatory and self-evident. It is assumed that the worker, from a logical appraisal of his work situation or from his own past experiences, formulates a plan of action which in the long run will be to his own best interests and then acts in accordance with that plan. This theory is based upon two primary assumptions: first, that the worker is primarily motivated by economic interest; and, second, that work behavior is logical and rational. In what follows, these assumptions will be examined in the light of the facts of this study.

Let us begin by examining the reasons the employees gave for their own behavior. These reasons may be summarized in the belief the men held that if output went too high something might happen – the 'bogey'[1] might be raised, the 'rate' might be raised, the 'rate' might be lowered, someone might be laid off, hours might be reduced, or the supervisors might reprimand the slower workers. Now one of the interesting things about these reasons is the confusion they manifest. In talking about 'rates,' for example, many of the employees were not clear as to whether they were talking about piece rates, hourly rates, or rates of working. The consequences of changing a rate would vary depending upon which rate was changed; yet the operators did not discriminate. Again, raising the bogey would have none of the

---

[1] [The bogey represented a level of performance which could be sustained by a skilled and efficient operator – Editors.]

consequences they feared. If it induced them to increase their output, the effect would be to increase their earnings; otherwise, there would be no effect whatsoever. The result would be the opposite of cutting a piece rate; yet some of the operators felt that the result would be the same. It is clear, therefore, that their actions were not based upon a logical appraisal of their work situation.

Another important observation which supports the above conclusion is that not one of the bank wiremen had ever experienced any of the things they claimed they were guarding against. Their bogey had not been raised, their piece rates had not been lowered, nor had their hourly rates; yet they acted and talked as though they had. Their behavior, in other words, was not based upon their own concrete experience with the company. In this connection it might be pointed out that from a logical standpoint the operators should have wanted hourly rates to be flexible. They should have wanted them raised or lowered depending upon changes in the levels of an individual's efficiency, for only in that way could earnings be made to correspond with output. Yet all of them, the highest and lowest alike, were opposed to a lowering of hourly rates.

Another illustration of the nonlogical character of their behavior is found in an incident which occurred before the study began. Hours of work had been shortened from 48 to 44 per week. The supervisors told the men that if they turned out the same amount of work in the shorter time their earnings would remain the same. After a great deal of persuasion, the men agreed to try, and they were very much surprised to find that their earnings did stay the same. Not one of the men who commented upon this in an interview could see how it could be, in spite of the fact that their supervisors had tried to explain it to them.

At this point an objection might be raised. Granted that the employees did not clearly understand their payment system, were they not, nevertheless, acting in accordance with their economic interests? Even though none of them had experienced a reduction of piece rates, was it not a possibility? And were they not at least guarding against that possibility by controlling their output?

In considering this objection, let us assume for the time being that many of their fears were justified. Let us suppose that the piece rate was endangered if their output exceeded their concept of a day's work. Then what would follow from this if we assume that they were motivated primarily by economic interest? It would seem that each and every worker would push his output up to 6,600 connections per day and then hold it at that point. If all of them maintained that level of output consistently, they would be securing the maximum of earnings possible without endangering the piece rate. The facts are, however, that there were wide differences in the outputs of different individuals and that some of the operators were far short of 6,600 connections per day. If earnings had been their chief concern, differences in output levels should not have existed unless the operators were working at top capacity, and that was far from being the case.

Furthermore, in these terms it would be impossible to account for the amount of daywork claimed. Had they been chiefly concerned with earnings, they would have seen to it that there was very little daywork. It follows that this group of operators could not be said to be acting in accordance with their economic interests even if we assume that the reasons they gave for their actions were supportable by experimental evidence, which, of course, was not the case.

[Another] fallacy lies in the assumption that the worker can effectively control the actions of management by acting in certain ways. Changes in piece rates, hours of work, number of people employed, and so on, frequently lie completely outside the control of the worker and even of management. Furthermore, changes in piece rates at the Western Electric Company, for example, are not based upon the earnings of the worker. The company's policy is that piece rates will not be changed unless there is a change in manufacturing process. Changes in process are made by engineers whose duty it is to reduce unit cost wherever the saving will be sufficient to justify the change. In certain instances such changes may be made irrespective of direct labor cost per unit. Again, where labor is a substantial element, increased output tends to lower unit cost and thus tends to obviate the need for a change in process. Restriction works precisely opposite. Restriction tends to increase unit costs and, instead of warding off a change in the piece rate as the worker believes, may actually induce one.

From this analysis it may be concluded that the ideology expressed by the employees was not based upon a logical appraisal of their situation and that they were not acting strictly in accordance with their economic interests. Rather, the situation was as represented in Figure 3.3, in which A stands for the sentiments of the group, B for their behavior in restricting output, and C for the reasons they gave for acting as they did. The economic interest argument which we have been considering assumes a causal relation between

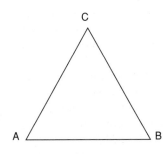

A = sentiments of the group
B = behavior in restricting output
C = reasons given for their behavior

Figure 3.3 Mutually interdependent relations between behaviour, sentiment, and belief.

C and B. It assumes that B follows from C. Actually, we see that for these operators B was an expression of A, the group's sentiments. Their behavior was a way of affirming those sentiments which lay at the root of their group organization. C, far from being the 'cause' of their actions, was merely the way in which they rationalized their behavior. They attempted to give logical reasons for their conduct and to make it appear as though the latter was directed toward some outside interference, whereas in fact B was primarily directed toward and expressed A.

Other misinterpretations of restriction of output

In addition to the three major arguments so far considered, there are a host of other ways of interpreting restriction of output, most of which are based upon an inadequate understanding of human behavior.

One common way of misinterpreting such a situation is to blame the worker on the ground that he is deliberately and willfully opposing management. It is said that for malicious reasons he refuses to co-operate, that he is ungrateful or just plain lazy. This interpretation, however, is not supported by the facts of the situation under discussion. First, there was nothing in the behavior of this group that even faintly resembled conscious, planned opposition to management. The activities of the men in this group were directed inward toward maintaining their own social organization. They were not primarily directed outward toward management, as a casual observer might suppose. Of course, their endeavor to preserve their internal organization did result in a certain amount of opposition to management. This opposition came about indirectly and quite inevitably; there was no conscious intent. Secondly, with the exception of W_9 [wireman 9] these men could hardly be called lazy. As we have shown, the men stopped work earlier than they were supposed to because they felt impelled to and not just to waste time. They were yielding to a pressure far stronger than financial incentive. Instead of saying they were lazy, it would be more accurate to characterize their behavior as abstention from work. This constrained idleness was unsatisfactory to some of the workmen who were aware of a discrepancy between what they should do as members of the group and what they could do if they felt free to work.

Another very common way of misconceiving this situation, one which is closely allied to the above, is to conclude that the behavior of the employees is a manifestation of overt hostility between management and employees. This error arises because of a failure to relate the behavior of the employees to their social situation. Instead, their behavior is judged in terms of what it should be according to the formal organization. It is contrasted with an ideal and, of course, is found wanting. Here it is relevant to point out that the company had a long record of fair dealing with its employees; and its attitude, as reflected in its socially directed employee relations policies, was distinctly sympathetic. Moreover, verbally in the interviewing program and overtly in their continued connection with the company, as shown by an exceptionally low labor turnover, the employees gave ample evidence of their appreciation of, and friendliness toward, the company. In the interviews of 1929, where over 40,000 complaints were voiced, there was not one single unfavorable comment expressed about the company in general.

A third common error is to assume that the immediate supervisor was responsible for the situation. For instance, it might be argued that in the Bank Wiring Observation Room the group chief was to blame because he sided with the workers rather than with management. Supervisory training is inevitably suggested as a remedy. The error here is the assumption that the supervisor, by sheer force of personality, can make his actual situation correspond to what it is theoretically held to be. The logic of industrial organization conceives of the supervisor as management's representative, and hence as having the necessary power to see that the policies of the company are carried out. It is only too clear that the supervisor could be pictured more accurately as victim than as contriver of the situation in the observation room. In the instances studied, the group chief had two alternatives. Either he had to side with his subordinates or he had to try to represent management. Both courses, however, had unpleasant consequences to him. If he tried to represent management, he would lose sympathetic control of his men, and his duties as supervisor would become more difficult. If he chose to side with his subordinates, the job of handling them would become easier, but his relations with his supervisors would become more insecure. The difficulties he encountered resided in the nature of the situation itself, in the interrelations of human beings with different duties, obligations, and interests. Furthermore, these difficulties could not be easily solved by supervisory training.

Still another error lies in assuming that situations in which restriction of output occurs are examples of inefficiency and poor management. In describing human situations of this sort there is always the danger of making them seem worse than they really are; that is, there is a tendency to judge them in terms of a logic of efficiency which is considered an ideal to be sought. Judged by customary standards, the output of the workers was acceptable and satisfactory. In the bank wiring department, output per worker was considered high. According to the foreman, it had risen over a period of years from an average of some 4,000 connections a day to 6,000. The bank wiring department also ranked high when its output was compared with the output of men in other concerns doing the same kind of work. The average output per man in outside concerns was about 4,000 connections per day as compared with 6,000 for this group. The department officials were proud of these accomplishments, and some of them commented that if the men consistently turned out more than 6,000 connections a day they would 'wear their fingers out.' Any outsider watching the men work, especially during the morning hours, would have concurred in this statement. The speeds attained by some of the men were in fact astonishing.

It is well to remember, therefore, that only with reference to an abstract logic of efficiency could the phenomenon described be called 'restriction';

that is to say, the workers were not producing so much as they might have had physiological fatigue been the only factor limiting output. Instead of describing such behavior as "restriction,' it could be described equally well as behavior which was not strictly in accordance with the logic of efficiency. Inasmuch as fewer moral implications attach to the statement that the workers' behavior did not conform to some abstract logic, the latter description is perhaps preferable.

The social organization of the company

Since the preceding considerations do not provide a satisfactory explanation of the situation in the Bank Wiring Observation Room, let us now turn to an examination of the relation between the social organization of the wiring group and the company structure, of which the wiring group was a small part.

[· · · · ·]

It is clear that no simple dichotomous classification of the company's personnel could be made. The personnel could not be divided into an employer and an employee class because there was no employer class. Every person in the company from top to bottom was an employee.

Although the total personnel could not be divided into two classes, this does not mean that certain groups did not have more in common than other groups. In general, five main groups could be distinguished: management, supervisors, technologists, office workers, and shop workers.

The general relations between these four groups are represented in Figure 3.4. Management, by which is meant the group in whom responsibility for the concern as a whole is vested, exercises control through two main subgroups, supervisors and technologists. The supervisory category includes those lower-ranking supervisors whose chief concern is with getting a job done and carrying out the purposes of the managerial group. The

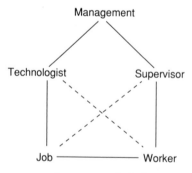

Figure 3.4 Interrelations among four groups in industry.

technologist group includes all people with specialized training, such as the trained engineer, the efficiency expert, the cost accountant, and the rate setter.

The relation between the technologist and the worker

[· · · · ·]

Modern industry has found it necessary to employ a large number of specialists. The primary function of these specialists is to make improvements in machines, technical processes, methods, and products. The indirect result of this activity is a high incidence of change in jobs and related conditions of work.

Perhaps the chief characteristic of the specialist group is that they are experimentally minded. They think in terms of their specialized logics and they scrutinize everything that comes within their scope from the point of view of their specialty. Frequently their attention is directed to the worker himself. For example, when it is found that the employee does not have the best possible work patterns and routines from a logical point of view, a highly logical plan may be introduced in terms of which he is supposed to govern his actions. Technologists frequently devise ingenious procedures to bring the worker's actions into line with a logic of efficiency. If the assumptions upon which such plans are based be granted, the plans themselves are sound. Certainly the technologist has no intention of foisting an arbitrary set of rules upon the worker. In fact, many of his plans are designed to help the worker. Carefully thought-out wage plans are intended to reimburse the worker with a wage proportional to his efforts. The simplification of his job, whether through a change in process, division of labor, or elimination of random movements, is supposed to make his work easier and less fatiguing. If fatigue is eliminated, the worker, theoretically, can produce more and can thereby earn more money. Indeed, some proponents of 'rationalization' in industry see in it the solution of all labor troubles.

Why is it, then, that sometimes these logical plans, as in the case of the Bank Wiring Observation Room, do not work out as intended? The answer would seem to lie in the fact that frequently plans which are intended to promote efficiency have consequences other than their logical ones, and these unforeseen consequences tend to defeat the logical purposes of the plan as conceived. Let us consider some of these possible nonlogical consequences.

First, technical innovations make for changes in the worker's job and through the job may have profound consequences to the employee. For in so far as his job is changed, his position in the social organization, his interpersonal relations, his traditions of craftsmanship, and his social codes which regulate his relations to other people may also be affected.

Secondly, the worker must frequently accommodate himself to changes which he does not initiate. Many of the systems introduced to improve his efficiency and to control his behavior do not take into account his senti-ments. Because of his position in the company structure, at the bottom level of a well-stratified organization, he cannot hold to the same degree the sentiments of those who are instituting the changes.

Thirdly, many of these same systems tend to subordinate the worker still further in the company's social structure. For instance, some of the incentive schemes and the procedures connected with them – job analysis, time and motion studies – apply for the most part only to the shop worker.

In summary, it may be said that the technologist is related to the worker in two ways. First, and more important, he is related to the worker indirectly through the job the worker performs. The indirect effects of technical innovation must be assessed not only in terms of fatigue and monotony but also in terms of their social consequences for the worker as a member of a social organization. Secondly, the technologist is related to the worker directly through those activities, such as time and motion studies, which are intended to supply him with standardized skills. The consequences of these activities must be assessed not only in terms of their logical objective, but also in terms of their effects upon the worker's sentiments of personal integrity. Thus it is seen that the technologist may be unwittingly a source of interference and constraint. Resistance to such interference was the chief external function of the bank wiremen's informal organization.

The relation of the supervisor to the worker

To attribute the formation of the bank wiremen's informal organization solely to the indirect, social consequences of the activity of technical specialists would clearly be an oversimplification. The relation between the supervisory group and the worker must also be considered.

Unlike the technologist, the supervisor is related to the worker in a direct, personal, face-to-face way. He has disciplinary authority over the worker. To say that one person has disciplinary authority over another is a shorthand way of saying that one person is under the obligation of seeing that another person's conduct is in accord with certain generally accepted norms. The father-son relationship resembles the supervisor-employee relationship in that it contains an element of disciplinary authority. But the norms of conduct with reference to which discipline is exercised are of an entirely different nature in these two cases. In the case of the father-son relationship these norms are set by society at large. The father disciplines his son into socially controlled and socially approved modes of behavior, and he is aided in that process by numerous social institutions, such as the church and the school. But in the case of the supervisor-employee relationship no similar social codes exist. The criterion in terms of which the supervisor must exercise discipline is not the convention of ordinary social living but a logic of efficiency. His duty is to see that the worker's behavior corresponds to rules of efficient conduct. It is this insistence upon a logic of efficiency, this continual attempt to force the human organization into logical molds, that creates constraint.

This point was illustrated time and again in the Bank Wiring Observation Room. There it was seen that most of the problems encountered by the supervisors were problems of inducing the workmen to conform to the rules of the technical organization. The worker's conduct was considered right or wrong in so far as it corresponded to these rules. The supervisor's success was evaluated by his superiors in terms of how well he succeeded in achieving this objective. Theoretically, these rules were supposed to promote efficiency, and adherence to them was supposed to redound to the worker's advantage. From the point of view of the worker's sentiments, however, many of them were annoying and seemingly functioned only as subordinating or differentiating mechanisms.

Consider, for example, the unwritten rule that wiremen should not help one another wire. This rule received its sanction from the belief that employees could turn out more work by working only on the equipments to which they were assigned. There would be less opportunity for talking, less likelihood of their getting in one another's way, and less likelihood of their delaying the solderman and the inspector. There was, in other words, no logical reason why workmen should want to help one another in this fashion. To the wiremen, however, this was just another arbitrary rule. Many of them preferred to work together occasionally. It was one of the ways in which they expressed their solidarity; it was one of the integrative mechanisms in their internal organization. Furthermore, they knew that working together did not necessitate slowing down. In fact, the evidence showed that sometimes when they were refused the privilege of helping one another, they became less efficient.

It can be seen that one of the chief sources of constraint in a working group can be a logic which does not take into account the worker's sentiments. Any activity not strictly in accordance with such a logic (and sometimes this means most forms of social activity) may be judged 'wrong.' As a result, such activity can only be indulged in openly within the protection of an informal group, which, in turn, may become organized in opposition to the effective purpose of the total organization.

Summary

In the studies reported it has been shown that in certain departments at the Hawthorne plant there existed informal employee organizations resulting in problems such as have been described. An attempt has been made to point out that to state such problems in terms of 'restriction,' 'faulty supervision,' or 'mismanagement' is to mistake symptoms for causes and to neglect the social factors involved.

The significant problem for investigation appeared to be that of specifying the factors which give rise to such informal organizations. In attempting to answer this question, the external function of one group, the bank wiremen, was examined. This function could be characterized as that of resisting change. Following this lead, the position of the Bank Wiring Observation Room group in relation to the total company structure was then examined.

This analysis led to the general conclusion that the informal organization of the bank wiring group resulted primarily from the position of that group in the total company structure and its consequent relations with other groups within the company.

Overcoming resistance to change using group methods

LESTER COCH and JOHN R.P. FRENCH

Introduction

It has always been characteristic of American industry to change products and methods of doing jobs as often as competitive conditions or engineering progress dictates. This makes frequent changes in an individual's work necessary. In addition, the markedly greater turnover and absenteeism of recent years result in unbalanced production lines which again makes for frequent shifting of individuals from one job to another. One of the most serious production problems faced at the Harwood Manufacturing Corporation has been the resistance of production workers to the necessary changes in methods and jobs. This resistance expressed itself in several ways, such as grievances about the piece rates that went with the new methods, high turnover, very low efficiency, restriction of output, and marked aggression against management. Despite these undesirable effects, it was necessary that changes in methods and jobs continue.

Efforts were made to solve this serious problem by the use of a special monetary allowance for transfers, by trying to enlist the cooperation and aid of the union, by making necessary layoffs on the basis of efficiency, etc. In all cases, these actions did little or nothing to overcome the resistance to change. On the basis of these data, it was felt that the pressing problem of resistance to change demanded further research for its solution. From the point of view of factory management, there were two purposes to the research: (1) Why do people resist change so strongly? and (2) What can be done to overcome this resistance?

Background

The main plant of the Harwood Manufacturing Corporation, where the present research was done, is located in the small town of Marion, Virginia. The plant produces pajamas and, like most sewing plants, employs mostly

Abridged excerpt reproduced from Coch, L. and French, J.R.P. (1948) Overcoming Resistance to Change. *Human Relations*, **1**, 512–32.

women. The plant's population is about 500 women and 100 men. The workers are recruited from the rural, mountainous areas surrounding the town, and are usually employed without previous industrial experience. The average age of the workers is 23; the average education is eight years of grammar school.

The policies of the company in regard to labor relations are liberal and progressive. A high value has been placed on fair and open dealing with the employees and they are encouraged to take up any problems or grievances with the management at any time. Every effort is made to help foremen find effective solutions to their problems in human relations, using conferences and role-playing methods. Carefully planned orientation, designed to help overcome the discouragement and frustrations attending entrance upon the new and unfamiliar situation, is used. Plant-wide votes are conducted where possible to resolve problems affecting the whole working population. The company has invested both time and money in employee services such as industrial music, health services, lunch-room, and recreation programs. In the same spirit, the management has been conscious of the importance of public relations in the local community; they have supported both financially and otherwise any activity which would build up good will for the company. As a result of these policies, the company has enjoyed good labor relations since the day it commenced operations.

Harwood employees work on an individual incentive system. Piece rates are set by time study and are expressed in terms of units. One unit is equal to one minute of standard work: 60 units per hour equal the standard efficiency rating. Thus, if on a particular operation the piece rate for one dozen is 10 units, the operator would have to produce 6 dozen per hour to achieve the standard efficiency rating of 60 units per hour. The skill required to reach 60 units per hour is great. On some jobs, an average trainee may take 34 weeks to reach the skill level necessary to perform at 60 units per hour. Her first few weeks of work may be on an efficiency level of 0.5 to 20 units per hour.

The amount of pay received is directly proportional to the weekly average efficiency rating achieved. Thus, an operator with an average efficiency rating of 75 units per hour (25 per cent more than standard) would receive 25 per cent more than base pay. However, there are two minimum wages below which no operator may fall. The first is the plantwide minimum, the hiring-in wage; the second is a minimum wage based on six months' employment and is 22 per cent higher than the plantwide minimum wage. Both minima are smaller than the base pay for 60 units per hour efficiency rating.

The rating of every piece worker is computed every day and the results are published in a daily record of production which is shown to every operator. This daily record of production for each production line carries the names of all the operators on that line arranged in rank order of efficiency rating, with the highest rating girl at the top of the list. The supervisors speak to each operator each day about her unit ratings. Because of the above procedures, many operators do not claim credit for all the work done in a given day. Instead, they save a few of the piece rate tickets as a 'cushion' against a rainy day when they may not feel well or may have a great amount of machine trouble.

When it is necessary to change an operator from one type of work to another, a transfer bonus is given. This bonus is so designed that the changed operator who relearns at an average rate will suffer no loss in earnings after change. Despite this allowance, the general attitudes toward job changes in the factory are markedly negative. Such expressions as, 'When you make your units (standard production), they change your job,' are all too frequent. Many operators refuse to change, preferring to quit.

The transfer learning curve

An analysis of the after-change relearning curves of several hundred experienced operators rating standard or better prior to change showed that 38 per cent of the changed operators recovered to the standard unit rating of 60 units per hour. The other 62 per cent either became chronically sub-standard operators or quit during the relearning period.

The average relearning curve for those who recover to standard production on the simplest type job in the plant is eight weeks long, and, when smoothed, provides the basis for the transfer bonus. The bonus is the percent difference between this expected efficiency rating and the standard of 60 units per hour.

Interviews with operators who have been transferred to a new job reveal a common pattern of feelings and attitudes which are distinctly different from those of successful non-transfers. In addition to resentment against the management for transferring them, the employees typically show feelings of frustration, loss of hope of ever regaining their former level of production and status in the factory, feelings of failure, and a very low level of aspiration.

[· · · · ·]

[One] factor which seems to affect recovery rates of changed operators is the amount of we-feeling. Observations seem to indicate that a strong psychological sub-group with negative attitudes toward management will display the strongest resistance to change. On the other hand, changed groups with high we-feeling and positive cooperative attitudes are the best relearners. Collections of individuals with little or no we-feeling display some resistance to change but not so strongly as the groups with high we-feeling and negative attitudes toward management. However, turnover for the individual transfers is much higher than in the latter groups. This phenomenon of the relationship between we-feeling and resistance to change is so overt that for years the general policy of the management of the plant was never to change a group as a group but rather to scatter the individuals in different areas throughout the factory.

An analysis of turnover records for changed operators with high we-feeling showed a 4 per cent turnover rate per month at 30 to 34 units per hour, not significantly higher than in unchanged operators but significantly lower than in changed operators with little or no we-feeling. However, the acts of aggression are far more numerous among operators with high we-feeling than among operators with little we-feeling. Since both types of operators experience the same frustration as individuals but react to it so differently, it is assumed that the effect of the in-group feeling is to set up a restraining force against leaving the group and perhaps even to set up driving forces toward staying in the group. In these circumstances, one would expect some alternative reaction to frustration rather than escape from the field. This alternative is aggression. Strong we-feeling provides strength so that members dare to express aggression which would otherwise be suppressed.

One common result in a sub-group with strong we-feeling is the setting of a group standard concerning production. Where the attitudes toward management are antagonistic, this group standard may take the form of a definite restriction of production to a given level. This phenomenon of restriction is particularly likely to happen in a group that has been transferred to a job where a new piece rate has been set; for they have some hope that if production never approaches the standard, the management may change the piece rate in their favor.

A group standard can exert extremely strong forces on an individual member of a small sub-group. That these forces can have a powerful effect on production is indicated in the production record of one presser during a period of forty days.

Table 3.1

In the group	
Days	Production per day
1–3	46
4–6	52
7–9	53
10–12	56
Scapegoating begins	
13–16	55
17–20	48
Becomes a single worker	
21–24	83
25–28	92
29–32	92
33–36	91
37–40	92

For the first twenty days she was working in a group of other pressers who were producing at the rate of about 50 units per hour. Starting on the thirteenth day, when she reached standard production and exceeded the production of the other members, she became a scapegoat of the group. During this time her production decreased toward the level of the remaining members of the group. After twenty days the group had to be broken up and all the other members were transferred to other jobs leaving only the scapegoat operator. With the removal of the group, the group standard was no longer operative; and the production of the one remaining operator shot up from the level of about 45 to 96 units per hour in a period of four days. Her production stabilized at a level of about 92 and stayed there for the remainder of the twenty days. Thus it is clear that the motivational forces induced in the individual by a strong sub-group may be more powerful than those induced by management.

The experiment

On the basis of the preliminary theory that resistance to change is a combination of an individual reaction to frustration with strong group-induced forces it seemed that the most appropriate methods for overcoming the resistance to change would be group methods. Consequently an experiment was designed employing two variations of democratic procedure in handling groups to be transferred. The first variation involved participation through representation of the workers in designing the changes to be made in the jobs. The second variation consisted of total participation by all members of the group in designing the changes. A third control group was also used. Two experimental groups received the total participation treatment. The three experimental groups and the control group were roughly matched with respect to: (1) the efficiency ratings of the groups before transfer; (2) the degree of change involved in the transfer; (3) the amount of we-feeling observed in the groups.

In no case was more than a minor change in the work routines and time allowances made. The control group, the eighteen hand pressers, had formerly stacked their work in one-half dozen lots on a flat piece of cardboard the size of the finished product. The new job called for stacking their work in one half dozen lots in a box the size of the finished product. The box was located in the same place the cardboard had been. An additional two minutes per dozen was allowed (by the time study) for this new part of the job. This represented a total job change of 8.8 per cent.

Experimental group 1, the thirteen pajama folders, had formerly folded coats with pre-folded pants. The new job called for the folding of coats with unfolded pants. An additional 1.8 minutes per dozen was allowed (by time study) for this new part of the job. This represented a total job change of 9.4 per cent.

Experimental groups 2 and 3, consisting of eight and seven pajama examiners respectively, had formerly clipped threads from the entire garment and examined every seam. The new job called for pulling only certain threads off and examining every seam. An average of 1.2 minutes per dozen was subtracted (by time study) from the total time on these two jobs. This represented a total job change of 8 per cent.

The control group of hand pressers went through the usual factor routine when they were changed. The production department modified the job, and a new piece rate was set. A group meeting was then held in which the control group was told that the change was necessary because of competitive conditions, and that a new piece rate had been set. The new piece rate was thoroughly explained by the time study man, questions were answered, and the meeting dismissed.

Experimental group 1 was changed in a different manner. Before any changes took place, a group meeting was held with all the operators to be changed. The need for the change was presented as dramatically as possible, showing two identical garments produced in the factory; one was produced in 1946 and had sold for 100 per cent more than its fellow in 1947. The group was asked to identify the cheaper one and could not do it. This demonstration effectively shared with the group the entire problem of the necessity of cost reduction. A general agreement was reached that a savings could be effected by removing the 'frills' and 'fancy' work from the garment without affecting the folders' opportunity to achieve a high efficiency rating. Management then presented a plan to set the new job and piece rate:

1. Make a check study of the job as it was being done.
2. Eliminate all unnecessary work.
3. Train several operators in the correct methods.
4. Set the piece rate by time studies on these specially trained operators.
5. Explain the new job and rate to all the operators.
6. Train all operators in the new method so they can reach a high rate of production within a short time.

The group approved this plan (though no formal group decision was reached), and chose the operators to be specially trained. A sub-meeting with the 'special' operators was held immediately following the meeting with the entire group. They displayed a cooperative and interested attitude and immediately presented many good suggestions. This attitude carried over into the working out of the details of the new job; and when the new job and piece rates were set, the 'special' operators referred to the resultants as 'our job,' 'our rate,' etc. The new job and piece rates were presented at a second group meeting to all the operators involved. The 'special' operators served to train the other operators on the new job.

Experimental groups 2 and 3 went through much the same kind of change meetings. The groups were smaller than experimental group 1, and a more intimate atmosphere was established. The need for a change was once again made dramatically clear; the same general plan was presented by management. However, since the groups were small, all operators were chosen as 'special' operators; that is, all operators were to participate directly in the designing of the new jobs, and all operators would be studied by the time study man. It is interesting to note that in the meetings with these two groups, suggestions were immediately made in such quantity that the stenographer had great difficulty in recording them. The group approved of the plans, but again no formal group decision was reached.

Results

The results of the experiment are summarized in graphic form in Figure 3.5. The gaps in the production curves occur because these groups were paid on a time-work basis for a day or two. The control group improved little beyond their early efficiency ratings. Resistance developed almost immediately after the change occurred. Marked expressions of aggression against management occurred, such as conflict with the methods engineer, expression of hostility against the supervisor, deliberate restriction of production, and lack of cooperation with the supervisor. There were 16 per cent quits in the first forty days. Grievances were filed about the piece rate, but when the rate was checked, it was found to be a little 'loose.'

Experimental group 1 showed an unusually good relearning curve. At the end of fourteen days, the group averaged 61 units per hour. During the fourteen days, the attitude was cooperative and permissive. They worked well with the methods engineer, the training staff, and the supervisor. (The supervisor was the same person in the cases of the control group and experimental group 1). There were no quits in this group in the first forty

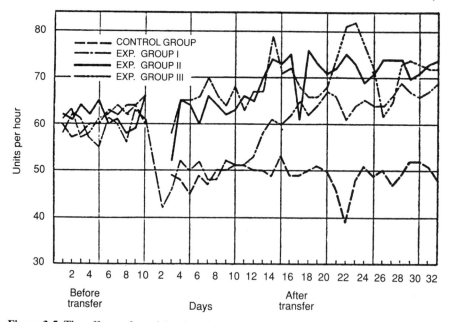

Figure 3.5 The effects of participation through representation (groups 1) and of total participation (groups 2 and 3) on recovery after an easy transfer.

days. This group might have presented a better learning record if work had not been scarce during the first seven days. There was one act of aggression against the supervisor recorded in the first forty days. It is interesting to note that the three special representative operators in experimental group 1 recovered at about the same rate as the rest of their group.

Experimental groups 2 and 3 recovered faster than experimental group 1. After a slight drop on the first day of change, the efficiency ratings returned to a pre-change level and showed sustained progress thereafter to a level about 14 per cent higher than the pre-change level. No additional training was provided them after the second day. They worked well with their supervisors and no indications of aggression were observed from these groups. There were no quits in either of these groups in the first forty days.

A fourth experimental group, composed of only two sewing operators, was transferred by the total participation technique. Their new job was one of the most difficult jobs in the factory, in contrast to the easy jobs for the control group and the other three experimental groups. As expected, the total participation technique again resulted in an unusually fast recovery rate and a final level of production well above the level before transfer. Because of the difficulty of the new job, however, the rate of recovery was slower than for experimental groups 2 and 3, but faster than for experimental group 1.

In the first experiment, the control group made no progress after transfer for a period of 32 days. At the end of this period the group was broken up and the individuals were reassigned to new jobs scattered throughout the factory. Two and a half months after their dispersal, the thirteen remaining members of the original control group were again brought together as a group for a second experiment.

This second experiment consisted of transferring the control group to a new job, using the total participation technique in meetings which were similar to those held with experimental groups 2 and 3. The new job was a pressing job of comparable difficulty to the new job in the first experiment. On the average it involved about the same degree of change. In the meetings no reference was made to the previous behavior of the group on being transferred.

The results of the second experiment were in sharp contrast to the first (see Fig. 3.6). With the total participation technique, the same control group now recovered rapidly to their previous efficiency rating, and, like the other groups under this treatment, continued on beyond it to a new high level of production. There was no aggression or turnover in the group for 19 days after change, a marked modification of their previous behavior after transfer. Some anxiety concerning their seniority status was expressed, but this was resolved in a meeting of their elected delegate, the union business agent, and a management representative. It should be noted in Figure 3.6 that the pre-change level on the second experiment is just above 60 units per hour; thus the individual transfers had progressed to just above standard during the two and a half months between the two experiments.

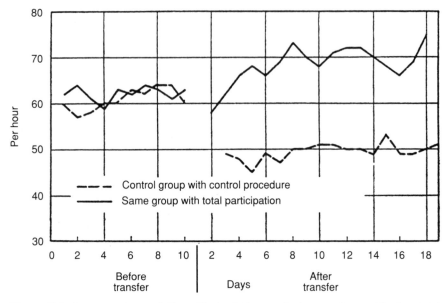

Figure 3.6 A comparison of the effect of the control procedure with the total participation procedure on the same group.

Interpretation

The purpose of this section is to explain the drop in production resulting from transfer, the differential recovery rates of the control and the experimental groups, the increases beyond their former levels of production by the experimental groups, and the differential rates of turnover and aggression.

The first experiment showed that the rate of recovery is directly proportional to the amount of participation, and that the rates of turnover and aggression are inversely proportional to the amount of participation. The second experiment demonstrated more conclusively that the results obtained depended on the experimental treatment rather than on personality factors like skill or aggressiveness, for identical individuals yielded markedly different results in the control treatment as contrasted with the total participation treatment.

Apparently total participation has the same type of effect as participation through representation, but the former has a stronger influence. In regard to recovery rates, this difference is not unequivocal because the experiment was unfortunately confounded. Right after transfer, experimental group number 1 had insufficient material to work on for a period of seven days. Hence their slower recovery during this period is at least in part due to insufficient work. In succeeding days, however, there was an adequate supply of work and the differential recovery rate still persisted. Therefore we are inclined to believe that participation through representation results in slower recovery than does total participation.

The goal of standard production

In considering the negative attitudes toward transfer and the resistance to being transferred, there are several important aspects of the complex goal of reaching and maintaining a level of 60 units per hour. For an operator producing below standard, this goal is attractive because it means success, high status in the eyes of her fellow employees, better pay, and job security. On the other hand, there is a strong force against remaining below standard because this lower level means failure, low status, low pay, and the danger of being fired. Thus it is clear that the upward force corresponding to the goal of standard production will indeed be strong for the transfer who has dropped below standard.

It is equally clear why any operator, who accepts the stereotype about transfer, shows such strong resistance to being changed. She sees herself as becoming a failure, and losing status, pay, and perhaps the job itself. The result is a lowered level of aspiration and a weakened force toward the goal of standard production.

Just such a weakening of the force toward 60 units per hour seems to have occurred in the control group in Experiment I. The participation treatments, on the other hand, seem to have involved the operators in designing the new job and setting the new piece rates in such a way that they did not lose hope of regaining the goal of standard production. Thus the participation resulted in a stronger force toward higher production. However, this force alone can hardly account for the large differences in recovery rate between the control group and the experimental groups; certainly it does not explain why the latter increased to a level so high above standard.

Management pressure

On all operators below standard the management exerts a pressure for higher production. This pressure is no harsh and autocratic treatment involving threats. Rather it takes the form of persuasion and encouragement by the supervisors. They attempt to induce the low rating operator to improve her performance and to attain standard production.

The grievances, aggression, and tension in the control group in Experiment I indicate that they rejected the force toward higher production induced by the management. The group accepted the stereotype that transfer is a calamity, but the control procedure did not convince them that the change was necessary and they viewed the new job and the new piece rates set by management as arbitrary and unreasonable.

The experimental groups, on the contrary, participated in designing the changes and setting the piece rates so that they spoke of the new job as 'our job' and the new piece rates as 'our rates'. Thus they accepted the new situation and accepted the management induced force toward higher production.

From the acceptance by the experimental groups and the rejection by the control group of the management induced forces, we may derive that the former had additional own forces toward higher production whereas the latter had additional own forces toward lower production. This difference helps to explain the better recovery rate of the experimental groups.

Group standards

Probably the most important force affecting the recovery under the control procedure was a group standard, set by the group, restricting the level of production to 50 units per hour. Evidently this explicit agreement to restrict production is related to the group's rejection of the change and of the new job as arbitrary and unreasonable. Perhaps they had faint hopes of demonstrating that standard production could not be attained and thereby obtain a more favorable piece rate. In any case there was a definite group phenomenon which affected all the members of the group.

$$[\cdot \cdot \cdot \cdot \cdot]$$

In the control group, too, we would expect the group to induce strong forces on the members. The more a member deviates above the standard the stronger would be the group-induced force to conform to the standard, for such deviations both negate any possibility of management's increasing the piece rate and at the same time expose the other members to increased pressure from management. Thus individual differences in levels of production should be sharply curtailed in the control group after transfer.

Turnover and aggression

It is now clear that the driving force toward 60 is a complex affair; it is partly a negative driving force corresponding to the negative valence of low pay, low status, failure, and job insecurity. Turnover results not only from the frustration produced by the conflict of these two forces, but also as a direct attempt to escape from the region of these negative valences. For the members of the control group, the group standard to restrict production prevented escape by increasing production, so that quitting their jobs was the only remaining escape. In the participation groups, on the contrary, both the group standards and the additional own forces resulting from the acceptance of management-induced forces combined to make increasing production the distinguished path of escape from this region of negative valence.

In considering turnover as a form of escape from the field, it is not enough to look only at the psychological present; one must also consider the psychological future. The employee's decision to quit the job is rarely made exclusively on the basis of a momentary frustration or an undesirable present situation; she usually quits when she also sees the future as equally hopeless. The operator transferred by the usual factory procedure (including the control group) has in fact a realistic view of the probability of continued failure because, as we have already noted, 62 per cent of transfers do in fact fail to recover to standard production. Thus the higher rate of quitting for transfers as compared to non-transfers results from a more pessimistic view of the future.

The control procedure had the effect for the members of setting up management as a hostile power field. They rejected the forces induced by this hostile power field, and group standards to restrict production developed within the group in opposition to management. In this conflict between the power field of management and the power field of the group, the control group attempted to reduce the strength of the hostile power field relative to the strength of their own power field. This change was accomplished in three ways: (1) the group increased its own power by developing a more cohesive and well-disciplined group, (2) they secured 'allies' by getting the backing of the union in filing a formal grievance about the new piece rate, (3) they attacked the hostile power field directly in the form of aggression against the supervisor, the time study engineer, and the higher management. Thus the aggression was derived not only from individual frustration but also from the conflict between two groups. Furthermore, this situation of group conflict both helped to define management as the frustrating agent and gave the members strength to express any aggressive impulses produced by frustration.

Conclusions

It is possible for management to modify greatly or to remove completely group resistance to changes in methods of work and the ensuing piece rates. This change can be accomplished by the use of group meetings in which management effectively communicates the need for change and stimulates group participation in planning the changes.

For Harwood's management, and presumably for managements of other industries using an incentive system, this experiment has important implications in the field of labor relations. A majority of all grievances presented at Harwood have always stemmed from a change situation. By preventing or greatly modifying group resistance to change, this concomitant to change may well be greatly reduced. The reduction of such costly phenomena as turnover and slow relearning rates presents another distinct advantage.

Harwood's management has long felt that action research such as the present experiment is the only key to better labor-management relations. It is only by discovering the basic principles and applying them to the true causes of conflict that an intelligent, effective effort can be made to correct the undesirable effects of the conflict.

Leadership – a contingency model

FRED E. FIEDLER

[McGrath, 1967] pointed out, that most researchers in this area have gravitated toward two presumably crucial clusters of leadership attitudes and behaviors. These are the critical, directive, autocratic, task-oriented versus the democratic, permissive, considerate, person-oriented type of leadership. While this categorization is admittedly oversimplified, the major controversy in this area has been between the more orthodox viewpoint – reflected in traditional supervisory training and military doctrine that the leader should be decisive and forceful, that he should do the planning and thinking for the group, and that he should coordinate, direct, and evaluate his men's actions – and the other viewpoint – reflected in the newer human-relations-oriented training and in the philosophy behind nondirective and brain-storming techniques – which stresses the need for democratic, permissive, group-oriented leadership techniques. Both schools of thought have strong adherents and there is evidence supporting both points of view (Gibb, 1954; Hare, 1962).

While one can always rationalize that contradictory findings by other investigators are due to poor research design, or different tests and criteria, such problems present difficulties if they appear in one's own research. We have, during the past thirteen years, conducted a large number of studies on leadership and group performance, using the same operational definitions and essentially similar leader attitude measures. The inconsistencies which we obtained in our own research program demanded an integrative theoretical formulation which would adequately account for the seemingly confusing results.

The studies which we conducted used as the major predictor of group performance an interpersonal perception or attitude score which is derived from the leader's description of his most and of his least preferred co-workers. He is asked to think of all others with whom he has ever worked, and then to describe first the person with whom he worked best (his most preferred co-worker) and then the person with whom he could work least well (his least preferred co-worker, or LPC). These descriptions are obtained, wherever possible, before the leader is assigned to his team. However, even where we deal with already existing groups, these descriptions tend to be of individuals whom the subject has known in the past rather than of persons with whom he works at the time of testing.

The descriptions are typically made on 20 eight-point bipolar adjective scales, similar to Osgood's Semantic Differential (Osgood *et al.*, 1957), e.g.,

Abridged excerpt reproduced from Fiedler, F.E. The Contingency Model: A Theory in Proshansky, H. and Seidenberg, B. (eds) *Basic Studies in Social Psychology*, pp. 538–55; published by Holt, Reinhart & Winston, New York, 1969.

Pleasant <u>8</u> : <u>7</u> : <u>6</u> : <u>5</u> : <u>4</u> : <u>3</u> : <u>2</u> : <u>1</u> Unpleasant
Friendly <u>8</u> : <u>7</u> : <u>6</u> : <u>5</u> : <u>4</u> : <u>3</u> : <u>2</u> : <u>1</u> Unfriendly

These items are scaled on an evaluative dimension, giving a score of 8 to the most favorable pole (i.e. Friendly, Pleasant) and a score of 1 to the least favorable pole. Two main scores have been derived from these descriptions. The first one, which was used in our earlier studies, is based on the profile similarity measure D (Cronbach and Gleser, 1953) between the descriptions of the most and of the least preferred co-worker. This score, called the Assumed Similarity between Opposites, or ASo, indicates the degree to which the individual perceives the two opposites on his co-worker continuum as similar or different. The second score is simply based on the individual's description of his least preferred co-worker. LPC, and indicates the degree to which the subject evaluates his LPC in a relatively favorable or unfavorable manner. The two measures are highly correlated (0.80 to 0.95) and will here be treated as interchangeable.

[· · · · ·]

The person with high LPC or ASo, who perceives his least preferred co-worker in a relatively favorable, accepting manner, tends to be more accepting, permissive, considerate, and person-oriented in his relations with group members. The person who perceives his most and least preferred co-workers as quite different, and who sees his least preferred co-worker in a very unfavorable, rejecting manner tends to be directive, controlling, task-oriented, and managing in his interactions.

ASo and LPC scores correlated highly with group performance in a wide variety of studies, although, as mentioned above, not consistently in the same direction. [Groups] with different coaches seemed to require different leader attitudes.

Development of the model

Key definitions

We shall define the leader as the group member who is officially appointed or elected to direct and coordinate group action. In groups in which no one has been so designated, we have identified the informal leader by means of sociometric preference questions such as asking group members to name the person who was most influential in the group, or whom they would most prefer to have as a leader in a similar task.

The leader's effectiveness is here defined in terms of the group's performance on the assigned primary task. Thus, although a company manager may have, as one of his tasks, the job of maintaining good relations with his customers, his main job, and the one on which he is in the final analysis evaluated, consists of the long-range profitability of the company. Good relations with customers, or high morale and low labor turnover may well contribute to success, but they would not be the basic criteria by this definition.

The categorization of group-task situations

Leadership is essentially a problem of wielding influence and power. When we say that different types of groups require different types of leadership we imply that they require a different relationship by which the leader wields power and influence. Since it is easier to wield power in some groups than in others, an attempt to categorize groups might well begin by asking what conditions in the group-task situation will facilitate or inhibit the leader's exercise of power. On the basis of our previous work we postulated three important aspects in the total situation which influence the leader's role.

1. Leader-Member Relations. The leader who is personally attractive to his group members, and who is respected by his group, enjoys considerable power (French, 1956). In fact, if he has the confidence and loyalty of his men he has less need of official rank. This dimension can generally be measured by means of sociometric indices or by group atmosphere scales (Fiedler, 1962) which indicate the degree to which the leader experiences the group as pleasant and well disposed toward him.

2. Task Structure. The task generally implies an order 'from above' which incorporates the authority of the superior organization. The group member who refuses to comply must be prepared to face disciplinary action by the higher authority. For example, a squad member who fails to perform a lawful command of his sergeant may have to answer to his regimental commander. However, compliance with a task order can be enforced only if the task is relatively well structured, i.e. if it is capable of being programmed. One cannot effectively force a group to perform well on an unstructured task such as developing a new product or writing a good play.

Thus, the leader who has a structured task can depend on the backing of his superior organization, but if he has an unstructured task the leader must rely on his own resources to inspire and motivate his men. The unstructured task thus provides the leader with much less effective power than does the highly structured task.

We operationalized this dimension by utilising four of the aspects which Shaw (1962) recently proposed for the classification of group tasks. These are (a) decision **verifiability**, the degree to which the correctness of the solution can be demonstrated objectively; (b) **goal clarity**, the degree to which the task requirements are clearly stated or known to the group; (c) **goal path multiplicity**, the degree to which there are many or few procedures available for performing the task (reverse scoring); and (d) **solution specificity**, the degree to which there is one rather than an infinite number of correct solutions (e.g. solving an equation vs. writing a story). Ratings based on these four dimensions have yielded interrater reliabilities of 0.80 to 0.90.

3. Position Power. The third dimension is defined by the power inherent in the position of leadership irrespective of the occupant's personal relations with his members. This includes the rewards and punishments which are officially or traditionally at the leader's disposal, his authority as defined by the group's rules and bylaws, and the organizational support given to him in dealing with his men. this dimension can be operationally defined by means of a check list (Fiedler, 1964) containing items such as 'Leader can effect promotion or demotion.' 'Leader enjoys special rank and status in real life which sets him apart from, and above, his group members.' The median interrater agreement of four independent judges rating 35 group situations was 0.95.

A three-dimensional group classification

Group-task situations can now be rated on the basis of the three dimensions of leader-member relations, task structure, and position power. This locates each group in a three-dimensional space. A rough categorization can be accomplished by halving each of the dimensions so that we obtain an eight-celled cube (Fig. 3.7). We can now determine whether the correlations between leader attitudes and group performance within each of these eight cells, or octants, are relatively similar in magnitude and direction. If they are, we can infer that the group classification has been successfully accomplished since it shows that groups falling within the same octant require similar leader attitudes.

Consideration of Figure 3.7 suggests a further classification of the cells in terms of the effective power which the group-task situation places at the leader's disposal, or more precisely, the favorableness of the situation for the leader's exercise of his power and influence.

Such an ordering can be accomplished without difficulty at the extreme poles of the continuum. A liked and trusted leader with high rank and a

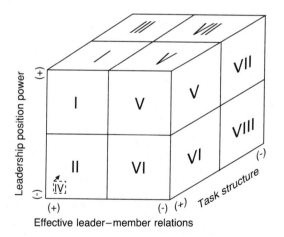

Figure 3.7 A model for the classification of group-task situations.

structured task is in a more favorable position than is a disliked and power-less leader with an ambiguous task. The intermediate steps pose certain theoretical and methodological problems. To collapse a three-dimensional system into an undimensional one implies in Coombs' terms a partial order or a lexicographic system for which there is no unique solution. Such an ordering must, therefore, be done either intuitively or in accordance with some reasonable assumptions. In the present instance we have postulated that the most important dimension in the system is the leader-member relationship since the highly liked and respected leader is less in need of position power or the power of the higher authority incorporated in the task structure. The second most important dimension is the task structure, since a leader with a highly structured task does not require a powerful leader position. (For example, privates or noncommissioned officers in the army are at times called upon to lead or instruct officers in certain highly structured tasks – such as demonstrating a new weapon or teaching medical officers close order drill – though not in unstructured tasks – such as planning new policies on strategy.) This leads us to order the group-task situations first on leader-member relations, then on task structure, and finally on position power. While admittedly not a unique solution, the resulting ordering constitutes a reasonable continuum which indicates the degree of the leader's effective power in the group.

A contingency model for predicting leadership performance

As was already apparent from Table 3.2, the relationship between leader attitudes and group performance is contingent upon the accurate classification of the group-task situation. A more meaningful model of this con-

Table 3.2 Median correlation between leader LPC and group performance in various octants

	Leader-Member Relations	Task Structure	Position Power	Median Correlation	Number of Relations Included in Median
Octant I	Good	Structured	Strong	−.52	8
Octant II	Good	Structured	Weak	−.58	3
Octant III	Good	Unstructured	Strong	−.41	4
Octant IV	Good	Unstructured	Weak	.47	10
Octant V	Mod. Poor	Structured	Strong	.42	6
Octant VI	Mod. Poor	Structured	Weak		0
Octant VII	Mod. Poor	Unstructured	Strong	.05	10
Octant VIII	Mod. Poor	Unstructured	Weak	−.43	12

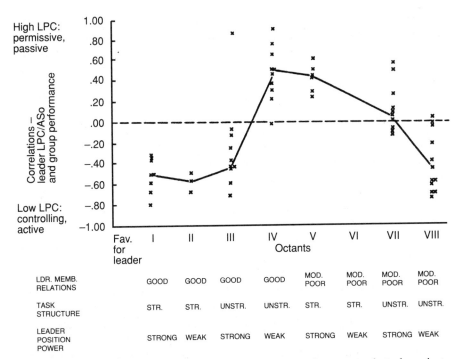

Figure 3.8 Correlations of leader LPC and group performance plotted against octants, that is, favorableness of group-task situation for leader.

tingency relationship emerges when we now plot the correlation between LPC or ASo and group performance on the one hand, against the octants ordered on the effective power or favorableness-for-the-leader dimension on the other. This is shown in Figure 3.8. Note that each point in the plot is a **correlation** predicting leadership performance or group effectiveness. The plot therefore represents 53 **sets of groups** totaling over 800 separate groups.

As Figure 3.8 shows, managing, controlling, directive (low LPC) leaders perform most effectively either under very favorable or under very unfavorable situations. Hence we obtain negative correlations between LPC and group performance scores. Considerate, permissive, accepting leaders obtain optimal group performance under situations intermediate in favorableness. These are situations in which (a) the task is structured, but the leader is disliked and must, therefore, be diplomatic; (b) the liked leader has an ambiguous, unstructured task and must, therefore, draw upon the creativity and cooperation of his members. Here we obtain positive correlations between LPC and group performance scores. Where the task is highly structured and the leader is well liked, non-directive behavior or permissive attitudes (such as asking how the group ought to proceed with a missile count-down) is neither appropriate nor beneficial. Where the situation is quite unfavorable, e.g. where the disliked chairman of a volunteer group faces an ambiguous task, the leader might as well be autocratic and directive since a positive, non-directive attitude under these conditions might result in complete inactivity on the part of the group. This model, thus, tends to shed some light on the apparent inconsistencies in our own data as well as in data obtained by other investigators.

Discussion

The contingency model seeks to reconcile results which up to now had to be considered inconsistent and difficult to understand. We have here attempted to develop a theoretical framework which can provide guidance for further research. While the model will undoubtedly undergo modifications and elaboration as new data become available, it provides an additional step toward a better understanding of leadership processes required in different situations. We have here tried to specify exactly the type of leadership which different group-task situations require.

The model has a number of important implications for selection and training as well as for the placement of leaders and organizational strategy. Our research suggests, first of all, that we can utilize a very broad spectrum of individuals for positions of leadership. The problem becomes one of placement and training rather than of selection since both the permissive, democratic, human-relations-oriented and the managing, autocratic, task-oriented leader can be effectively utilized. Leaders can be trained to recognize their own style of leadership as well as the conditions which are most compatible with their style.

The model also points to a variety of administrative and supervisory strategies which the organisation can adopt to fit the group-task situation to the needs of the leader. Tasks can, after all, be structured to a greater or lesser extent by giving very specific and detailed, or vague and general, instructions: the position power of the group leader can be increased or decreased and even the congeniality of a group and its acceptance of the leader can be affected by appropriate administrative action, e.g. increasing or decreasing the group's homogeneity.

The model also throws new light on phenomena which were rather difficult to fit into our usual ideas about measurement in social psychology. Why, for example, should groups differ so markedly in their performance on nearly parallel tasks? The model – and our data – show that the situation becomes easier for the leader as the group moves from the novel to the already known group-task situations. The leaders who excel under relatively novel and therefore more difficult conditions are not necessarily those who excel under those which are more routine, or better known, and therefore more favorable. Likewise, we find that different types of task structure require different types of leader behavior. Thus, in a research project's early phases the project director tends to be democratic and permissive: everyone is urged to contribute to the plan and to criticise all aspects of the design. This situation changes radically in the more structured phase when the research design is frozen and the experiment is underway. Here the research director tends to become managing, controlling, and highly autocratic and woe betide the assistant who attempts to be creative in giving instructions to subjects, or in his timing of tests. A similar situation is often found in business organization where the routine operation tends to be well structured and calls for a managing, directive leadership. The situation becomes suddenly unstructured when a crisis occurs. Under these conditions the number of discussions, meetings, and conferences increases sharply so as to give everyone an opportunity to express his views.

At best, this model is of course only a partial theory of leadership. The leader's intellectual and task-relevant abilities, and the members' skills and motivation, all play a role in affecting the group's performance. It is to be hoped that these other important aspects of group interaction can be incorporated into the model in the not too distant future.

References

Fiedler, F.E. (1962) Leader attitudes, group climate, and group creativity. *J. abnorm. soc. Psychol.*, vol. 65, pp. 308–18.

— (1964) A contingency model of leadership effectiveness. In Berkowitz, L. (ed.), *Advances in experimental social psychology*, New York: Academic Press.

Gibb, C.A. (1954) Leadership. In Lindzey, G. (ed.), *Handbook of social psychology*, vol. 2. Reading, Mass.: Addison-Wesley.

Hare, A.P. (1962) *Handbook of small group research*, New York: The Free Press of Glencoe.

McGrath, J.E. (1962) *A summary of small group research studies*, Arlington, Va.: Human Sciences Research Inc. (Litho.).

Osgood, C.E., Suci, G.A., and Tannenbaum, P.H. (1957) *The measurement of meaning*, Urbana, Ill.: Univer. of Illinois Press.

Groupthink and poor quality decision making

IRVING L. JANIS

I use the term 'groupthink' as a quick and easy way to refer to a mode of thinking that people engage in when they are deeply involved in a cohesive in-group, when the members' strivings for unanimity override their motivation to realistically appraise alternative courses of action. 'Groupthink' is a term of the same order as the words in the newspeak vocabulary George Orwell presents in his dismaying *1984* – a vocabulary with terms such as 'doublethink' and 'crimethink.' By putting groupthink with those Orwellian words, I realize that groupthink takes on an invidious connotation. The invidiousness is intentional: Groupthink refers to a deterioration of mental efficiency, reality testing, and moral judgment that results from in-group pressures.

A perfect failure: the Bay of Pigs

The Kennedy administration's Bay of Pigs decision ranks among the worst fiascoes ever perpetrated by a responsible government. Planned by an over-ambitious, eager group of American intelligence officers who had little background or experience in military matters, the attempt to place a small brigade of Cuban exiles secretly on a beachhead in Cuba with the ultimate aim of overthrowing the government of Fidel Castro proved to be a 'perfect failure.' The group that made the basic decision to approve the invasion plan included some of the most intelligent men ever to participate in the councils of government. Yet all the major assumptions supporting the plan were so completely wrong that the venture began to founder at the outset and failed in its earliest stages.

[· · · · ·]

Two days after the inauguration in January 1961, President John F. Kennedy and several leading members of his new administration were given a detailed briefing about the proposed invasion by Allen Dulles, head of the CIA, and General Lyman Lemnitzer, chairman of the Joint Chiefs of Staff. During the next eighty days, a core group of presidential advisers repeatedly discussed this inherited plan informally and in the meetings of an advisory committee that included three Joint Chiefs of Staff. In early April 1961, at one of the meetings with the President, all the key advisers gave their approval to the CIA's invasion plan. Their deliberations led to a few modifications of details, such as the choice of the invasion site.

On April 17, 1961, the brigade of about fourteen hundred Cuban exiles, aided by the United States Navy, Air Force, and the CIA, invaded the swampy coast of Cuba at the Bay of Pigs. Nothing went as planned. On the first day, not one of the four ships containing reserve ammunition and supplies arrived; the first two were sunk by a few planes in Castro's air force, and the other two promptly fled. By the second day, the brigade was completely surrounded by twenty thousand troops of Castro's well-equipped army. By the third day, about twelve hundred members of the brigade, comprising almost all who had not been killed, were captured and ignominiously led off to prison camps.

[· · · · ·]

It seems improbable that the shocking number of errors can be attributed to lack of intellectual capability for making policy judgments. The core members of Kennedy's team who were briefed on the Cuban invasion plan included three cabinet members and three men on the White House staff, all of whom were well qualified to make objective analyses of the pros and cons of alternative courses of action on vital issues of government policy.

Dean Rusk, Secretary of State, had been recruited by John F. Kennedy from his high-level position as head of the Rockefeller Foundation because of his solid reputation as an experienced administrator who could be counted on to have good ideas and sound judgment. He had served in policy-making positions in the State Department under Dean Acheson, first as head of the office of political affairs and later as deputy undersecretary in charge of policy coordination. During the Truman administration, Rusk became a veteran policy-maker and exerted a strong influence on a variety of important decisions concerning United States foreign policy in Asia.

Robert McNamara, the Secretary of Defense, was an expert statistician who had worked his way up to the presidency of the Ford Motor Company. He enjoyed a towering reputation for his intellectual brilliance and cold logic combined with personal integrity. Early in his career he had been on the faculty of the Harvard Business School. Later he developed his expertise in the statistical control unit of the United States Air Force, where he helped to work out a successful system for surveillance and control to facilitate decision-making about the flow of materials and production. During his years at Ford Motor Company, McNamara had also devised new techniques for improving rational methods of decision-making.

Then, too, there was Robert Kennedy, the Attorney General, one of the most influential members of the President's team. According to his close associates in the government, the President's brother was a bright young man whose strengths far outweighed his weaknesses. The Attorney General had been briefed on the invasion plan from the beginning. He did not attend the entire series of formal meetings of the advisory committee but was brought in as an active participant about four or five days before the President made his final decision. During that week, according to his memorandum dictated six weeks later, 'I attended some meetings at the White House. Afterwards I said to Jack that I thought that . . . based on the information that had been given to him . . . there really wasn't any alternative to accepting it.' On one occasion during that same crucial week, he used his personal influence to suppress opposition to the CIA plan.

Also on hand was McGeorge Bundy, the President's Special Assistant for National Security Affairs, who had the rank of a cabinet member. A key man on Kennedy's White House team, Bundy was one of the leading intellectuals imported to Washington from Harvard University, where he had been Dean of Arts and Sciences. His background in decision-making was not limited to the problems of a great university; earlier in his career, as a scholar, he had made a close study of Secretary of State Acheson's decisions.

The White House staff also included Arthur Schlesinger Jr., an outstanding Harvard historian whom the President asked to attend all the White House meetings on the invasion plan, and Richard Goodwin, another Harvard man 'of uncommon intelligence.' Goodwin did not attend the policy-making meetings but was informed about the invasion plan, discussed it frequently with Schlesinger, and conferred with Rusk and others during the weeks preceding the final decision.

The President asked five of the six members of this core group to join him at the White House meetings of the ad hoc advisory committee on the Cuban invasion plan. At these meetings, Kennedy's advisers found themselves face-to-face with three Joint Chiefs of Staff, in full, medaled regalia. These military men were carry-overs from the Eisenhower administration; throughout the deliberations, they remained quite detached from the Kennedy team. Also present at the meetings of the advisory committee were five others who had fairly close ties to the President and his main advisers. Two of the most active participants were the director and deputy director of the CIA, Allen Dulles and Richard Bissell. They, too, were carry-overs from the Eisenhower administration, but President Kennedy and his inner circle welcomed them as members of the new administration's team. According to Roger Hilsman (director of the intelligence branch of the State Department), Bissell 'was a brilliant economist and government executive whom President Kennedy had known for years and so admired and respected that he would very probably have made him Director of the CIA when Dulles eventually retired.' Bissell was the most active advocate of the CIA plan; his eloquent presentations did the main job of convincing the conferees to accept it.

Three others who participated in the White House meetings as members of the advisory committee were exceptionally well qualified to appraise the political consequences of the invasion: Thomas C. Mann, assistant secretary of state for inter-American affairs; Adolph A. Berle, Jr., chairman of the Latin American task force; and Paul Nitze, assistant secretary of defense, who had formerly been the director of the policy planning staff in the State Department.

The group that deliberated on the Bay of Pigs decision included men of considerable intellectual talent. Like the President, all the main advisers were shrewd thinkers, capable of objective, rational analysis, and accustomed to speaking their minds. But collectively they failed to detect the serious flaws in the invasion plan.

Six major miscalculations

The President and his key advisers approved the Bay of Pigs invasion plan on the basis of six assumptions, each of which was wrong. In retrospect, the President's advisers could see that even when they first began to discuss the plan, sufficient information was available to indicate that their assumptions were much too shaky. They could have obtained and used the crucial information beforehand to correct their false assumptions if at the group meetings they had been more critical and probing in fulfilling their advisory roles.

Assumption number 1: No one will know that the United States was responsible for the invasion of Cuba. Most people will believe the CIA cover story, and skeptics can easily be refuted.

[· · · · ·]

Assumption number 2: The Cuban air force is so ineffectual that it can be knocked out completely just before the invasion begins.

[· · · · ·]

Assumption number 3: The fourteen hundred men in the brigade of Cuban exiles have high morale and are willing to carry out the invasion without any support from United States ground troops.

[· · · · ·]

Assumption number 4: Castro's army is so weak that the small Cuban brigade will be able to establish a well-protected beachhead.

[· · · · ·]

Assumption number 5: The invasion by the exile brigade will touch off sabotage by the Cuban underground and armed uprisings behind the lines that will effectively support the invaders and probably lead to the toppling of the Castro regime.

[· · · · ·]

Assumption number 6: If the Cuban brigade does not succeed in its prime military objective, the men can retreat to the Escambray Mountains and reinforce the guerrilla units holding out against the Castro regime.

[· · · · ·]

Why did the advisory group fail?

Why so many miscalculations? Couldn't the six false assumptions have been avoided if the advisory group had sought fuller information and had taken it into account? Some of the grossest errors resulted from faulty planning and communication within the CIA: The agency obviously had its own serious defects, but they do not concern us in the present inquiry. Nor are we going to try to unravel the complicated reasons for the Joint Chiefs' willingness to endorse the CIA's plan. The central question is: Why did the President's main advisers, whom he had selected as core members of his team, fail to pursue the issues sufficiently to discover the shaky ground on which the six assumptions rested? Why didn't they pose a barrage of penetrating and embarrassing questions to the representatives of the CIA and the Joint Chiefs of Staff? Why were these men taken in by the incomplete and inconsistent answers they were given in response to the relatively few critical questions they raised?

[· · · · ·]

Symptoms of groupthink among president Kennedy's advisers

According to the groupthink hypothesis, members of any small cohesive group tend to maintain esprit de corps by unconsciously developing a number of shared illusions and related norms that interfere with critical thinking and reality resting. If the available accounts describe the deliberations accurately, typical illusions can be discerned among the members of the Kennedy team during the period when they were deciding whether to approve the CIA's invasion plan.

The illusion of invulnerability An important symptom of groupthink is the illusion of being invulnerable to the main dangers that might arise from a risky action in which the group is strongly tempted to engage. Essentially, the notion is that 'If our leader and everyone else in our group decides that it is okay, the plan is bound to succeed. Even if it is quite risky, luck will be on our side.' A sense of 'unlimited confidence' was widespread among the 'New Frontiersmen' as soon as they took over their high government posts, according to a Justice Department confidant, with whom Robert Kennedy discussed the secret CIA plan on the day it was launched:

> It seemed that, with John Kennedy leading us and with all the talent he had assembled, **nothing could stop us**. We believed that if we faced up to the nation's problems and applied bold, new ideas with common sense and hard work, we would overcome whatever challenged us.

That this attitude was shared by the members of the President's inner circle is indicated by Schlesinger's statement that the men around Kennedy had enormous confidence in his ability and luck: 'Everything had broken right for him since 1956. He had won the nomination and the election against all the odds in the book. Everyone around him thought he had the Midas touch and could not lose.' Kennedy and his principal advisers were sophisticated and skeptical men, but they were, nevertheless, 'affected by the euphoria of the new day.' During the first three months after he took office – despite growing concerns created by the emerging crisis in Southeast Asia, the gold drain, and the Cuban exiles who were awaiting the go-ahead signal to invade Cuba – the dominant mood in the White House, according to Schlesinger, was 'buoyant optimism.' It was centered on the 'promise of hope' held out by the President: '**Euphoria reigned; we thought for a moment that the world was plastic and the future unlimited.**'

All the characteristic manifestations of group euphoria – the buoyant optimism, the leader's great promise of hope, and the shared belief that the group's accomplishments could make 'the future unlimited' – are strongly reminiscent of the thoughts and feelings that arise among members of many different types of groups during the phase when the members become cohesive. At such a time, the members become somewhat euphoric about their newly acquired 'we-feeling'; they share a sense of belonging to a powerful, protective group that in some vague way opens up new potentials for each of them. Often there is boundless admiration of the group leader.

Once this euphoric phase takes hold, decision-making for everyday activities, as well as long-range planning, is likely to be seriously impaired. The members of a cohesive group become very reluctant to carry out the unpleasant task of critically assessing the limits of their power and the real losses that could arise if their luck does not hold. They tend to examine each risk in black and white terms. If it does not seem overwhelmingly dangerous, they are inclined simply to forget about it, instead of developing contingency plans in case it materializes. The group members know that no one among them is a superman, but they feel that somehow the group is a supergroup, capable of surmounting all risks that stand in the way of carrying out any desired course of action: 'Nothing can stop us!' Athletic teams and military combat units may often benefit from members' enthusiastic confidence in the power and luck of their group. But policy-making committees usually do not.

We would not expect sober government officials to experience such exuberant esprit de corps, but a subdued form of the same tendency may have been operating – inclining the President's advisers to become reluctant about examining the drawbacks of the invasion plan. In group meetings, this groupthink tendency can operate like a low-level noise that prevents warning signals from being heeded. Everyone becomes somewhat biased in the direction of selectively attending to the messages that feed into the members' shared feelings of confidence and optimism, disregarding those that do not.

When a cohesive group of executives is planning a campaign directed against a rival or enemy group, their discussions are likely to contain two themes, which embody the groupthink tendency to regard the group as invulnerable: (1) 'We are a strong group of good guys who will win in the end.' (2) 'Our opponents are stupid, weak, bad guys.' It is impressive to see how closely the six false assumptions fit these two themes. The notion running through the assumptions is the overoptimistic expectation that 'we can pull off this invasion, even though it is a long-short gamble.' The policy advisers were probably unaware of how much they were relying on shared rationalizations in order to appraise the highly risky venture as a safe one. Their overoptimistic outlook would have been rudely shaken if they had allowed their deliberations to focus on the potentially devastating consequences of the obvious drawbacks of the plan, such as the disparity in size between Castro's military forces of two hundred thousand and the small brigade of fourteen hundred exiles. In a sense, this difference made the odds against their long-short gamble 200,000 to 1,400 (over 140 to 1).

When discussing the misconceptions that led to the decision to approve the CIA's plan, Schlesinger emphasizes the gross underestimation of the enemy. Castro was regarded as a weak 'hysteric' leader whose army was ready to defect; he was considered so stupid that 'although warned by air strikes, he would do nothing to neutralize the Cuban underground.' This is a stunning example of the classical stereotype of the enemy as weak and ineffectual.

In a concurrence-seeking group, there is relatively little healthy skepticism of the glib ideological formulas on which rational policy-makers, like many other people who share their nationalistic goals, generally rely in order to maintain self-confidence and cognitive mastery over the complexities of international politics. One of the symptoms of groupthink is the members' persistence in conveying to each other the cliché and oversimplified images of political enemies embodied in long-standing ideological stereotypes. Throughout their deliberations they use the same old stereotypes, instead of developing differentiated concepts derived from an open-minded inquiry enabling them to discern which of their original ideological assumptions, if any, apply to the foreign policy issue at hand. Except in unusual circumstances of crisis, the members of a concurrence-seeking group tend to view any antagonistic out-group against whom they are plotting not only as immoral but also as weak and stupid. These wishful beliefs continue to dominate their thinking until an unequivocal defeat proves otherwise, where upon – like Kennedy and his advisers – they are shocked at the discrepancy between their stereotyped conceptions and actuality.

A subsidiary theme, which also involved a strong dose of wishful thinking, was contained in the Kennedy group's notion that 'we can get away with our clever cover story.' When the daily newspapers were already demonstrating that this certainly was not so, the undaunted members of the group evidently replaced the original assumption with the equally overoptimistic expectation that 'anyhow, the non-Communist nations of the world will side with us. After all, we **are** the good guys.'

Overoptimistic expectations about the power of their side and the weakness of the opponents probably enable members of a group to enjoy a sense of low vulnerability to the effects of any decision that entails risky action against an enemy. In order to maintain this complacent outlook, each member must think that everyone else in the group agrees that the risks can be safely ignored.

The illusion of unanimity When a group of people who respect each other's opinions arrive at a unanimous view, each member is likely to feel that the belief must be true. This reliance on consensual validation tends to replace individual critical thinking and reality-testing, unless there are clear-cut disagreements among the members. The members of a face-to-face group often become inclined, without quite realizing it, to prevent latent disagreements from surfacing when they are about to initiate a risky course of action. The group leader and the members support each other, playing up the areas of convergence in their thinking, at the expense of fully exploring divergences that might disrupt the apparent unity of the group. Better to share a pleasant, balmy group atmosphere than to be battered in a storm.

This brings us to the second outstanding symptom of groupthink manifested by the Kennedy team – a shared illusion of unanimity. In the formal sessions dealing with the Cuban invasion plan, the group's consensus that the basic features of the CIA plan should be adopted was relatively free of disagreement.

According to Sorensen, 'No strong voice of opposition was raised in any of the key meetings, and no realistic alternatives were presented.' According to Schlesinger, 'the massed and caparisoned authority of his senior officials in the realm of foreign policy and defense was unanimous for going ahead. . . . Had one senior advisor opposed the adventure, I believe that Kennedy would have canceled it. No one spoke against it.'

Perhaps the most crucial of Schlesinger's observations is, 'Our meetings took place in a **curious atmosphere of assumed consensus.**' His additional comments clearly show that the assumed consensus was an illusion that could be maintained only because the major participants did not reveal their own reasoning or discuss their idiosyncratic assumptions and vague reservations. President Kennedy thought that prime consideration was being given to his prohibition of direct military intervention by the United States. He assumed that the operation had been pared down to a kind of unobtrusive infiltration that, if reported in the newspapers, would be buried in the inside pages. Rusk was certainly not on the same wavelength as the President, for at one point he suggested that it might be better to have the invaders fan out from the United States naval base at Guantánamo, rather than land at the Bay of Pigs, so that they could readily retreat to the base if necessary. Implicit in his suggestion was a lack of concern about revealing United States military support as well as implicit distrust in the assumption made by the others about the ease of escaping from the Bay of Pigs. But discussion of Rusk's strange proposal was evidently dropped long before he was induced to reveal whatever vague misgivings he may have had about the Bay of Pigs plan. At meetings in the State Department, according to Roger Hilsman, who worked closely with him, 'Rusk asked penetrating questions that frequently caused us to reexamine our position.' But at the White House meetings Rusk said little except to offer gentle warnings about avoiding excesses.

As usually happens in cohesive groups, the members assumed that 'silence gives consent.' Kennedy and the others supposed that Rusk was in substantial agreement with what the CIA representatives were saying about the soundness of the invasion plan. But about one week before the invasion was scheduled, when Schlesinger told Rusk in private about his objections to the plan, Rusk, surprisingly, offered no arguments against Schlesinger's objections. He said that he had been wanting for some time to draw up a balance sheet of the pros and cons and that he was annoyed at the Joint Chiefs because 'they are perfectly willing to put the President's head on the block, but they recoil at doing anything which might risk Guantánamo.' At that late date, he evidently still preferred his suggestion to launch the invasion from the United States naval base in Cuba, even though doing so would violate President Kennedy's stricture against involving America's armed forces.

McNamara's assumptions about the invasion were quite different from both Rusk's and Kennedy's. McNamara thought that the main objective was to touch off a revolt of the Cuban people to overthrow Castro. The members of the group who knew something about Cuban politics and Castro's popular support must have had strong doubts about this assumption. Why did they fail to convey their misgivings at any of the meetings?

Suppression of personal doubts The sense of group unity concerning the advisability of going ahead with the CIA's invasion plan appears to have been based on superficial appearances of complete concurrence, achieved at the cost of self-censorship of misgivings by several of the members. From post-mortem discussions with participants, Sorensen concluded that among the men in the State Department, as well as those on the White House staff, 'doubts were entertained but never pressed, partly out of a fear of being labelled "soft" or undaring in the eyes of their colleagues.' Schlesinger was not at all hesitant about presenting his strong objections in a memorandum he gave to the President and the Secretary of State. But he became keenly aware of his tendency to suppress objections when he attended the White House meetings of the Kennedy team, with their atmosphere of assumed consensus:

> In the months after the Bay of Pigs I bitterly reproached myself for having kept so silent during those crucial discussions in the Cabinet Room, though my feelings of guilt were tempered by the knowledge that a course of objection would have accomplished little save to **gain me a name as a nuisance**. I can only explain my failure to do more than raise a few timid questions by reporting that one's impulse to blow the whistle on this nonsense was simply undone by the **circumstances of the discussion**.

Whether or not his retrospective explanation includes all his real reasons for having remained silent, Schlesinger appears to have been quite aware of the need to refrain from saying anything that would create a nuisance by breaking down the assumed consensus.

Participants in the White House meetings, like members of many other discussion groups, evidently felt reluctant to raise questions that might cast doubt on a plan that they thought was accepted by the consensus of the group, for fear of evoking disapproval from their associates. This type or fear is probably not the same as fear of losing one's effectiveness of damaging one's career. Many forthright men who are quite willing to speak their piece despite risks to their career become silent when faced with the possibility of losing the approval of fellow members of their primary work group. The discrepancy between Schlesinger's critical memoranda and his silent acquiescence during the meetings might be an example of this.

[· · · · ·]

Self-appointed mindguards Among the well-known phenomena of group dynamics is the alacrity with which members of a cohesive in-group suppress deviational points of view by putting social pressure on any member who begins to express a view that deviates from the dominant beliefs of the group, to make sure that he will not disrupt the consensus of the group as a whole. This pressure often takes the form of urging the dissident member to remain silent if he cannot match up his own beliefs with those of the rest of the group. At least one dramatic instance of this type of pressure occurred a few days after President Kennedy had said, 'we seem now destined to go ahead on a quasi-minimum basis.' This was still several days before the final decision was made.

At a large birthday party for his wife, Robert Kennedy, who had been constantly informed about the Cuban invasion plan, took Schlesinger aside and asked him why he was opposed. The President's brother listened coldly and then said, 'You may be right or you may be wrong, but the President has made his mind up. Don't push it any further. Now is the time for everyone to help him all they can.' Here is another symptom of groupthink, displayed by a highly intelligent man whose ethical code committed him to freedom of dissent. What he was saying, in effect, was, 'You may well be right about the dangerous risks, but I don't give a damn about that; all of us should help our leader right now by not sounding any discordant notes that would interfere with the harmonious support he should have.'

When Robert Kennedy told Schlesinger to lay off, he was functioning in a self-appointed role that I call being a 'mindguard.' Just as a bodyguard protects the President and other high officials from injurious physical assaults, a mindguard protects them from thoughts that might damage their confidence in the soundness of the policies to which they are committed or to which they are about to commit themselves.

[· · · · ·]

Docility fostered by suave leadership The group pressures that help to maintain a group's illusions are sometimes fostered by various leadership practices, some of which involve subtle ways of making it difficult for those who question the initial consensus to suggest alternatives and to raise critical issues. The group's agenda can readily be manipulated by a suave leader, often with the tacit approval of the members, so that there is simply no opportunity to discuss the drawbacks of a seemingly satisfactory plan of action. This is one of the conditions that fosters groupthink.

President Kennedy, as leader at the meetings in the White House, was probably more active than anyone else in raising skeptical questions; yet he seems to have encouraged the group's docility and uncritical acceptance of the defective arguments in favor of the CIA's plan. At each meeting, instead of opening up the agenda to permit a full airing of the opposing considerations, he allowed the CIA representatives to dominate the entire discussion. The President permitted them to refute immediately each tentative doubt that one of the others might express, instead of asking whether anyone else had the same doubt or wanted to pursue the implications of the new worrisome issue that had been raised.

Moreover, although the President went out of his way to bring to a crucial meeting an outsider who was an eloquent opponent of the invasion plan, his style of conducting the meeting presented no opportunity for discussion of the controversial issues that were raised. The visitor was Senator J. William Fulbright. The occasion was the climactic meeting of April 4, 1961, held at the State Department, at which the apparent consensus that had emerged in earlier meetings was seemingly confirmed by an open straw vote. The President invited Senator Fulbright after the Senator had made known his concern about newspaper stories forecasting a United States invasion of Cuba. At the meeting, Fulbright was given an opportunity to present his opposing views. In a 'sensible and strong' speech Fulbright correctly predicted many of the damaging effects the invasion would have on United States foreign relations. The President did not open the floor to discussion of the questions raised in Fulbright's rousing speech. Instead, he returned to the procedure he had initiated earlier in the meeting; he had asked each person around the table to state his final judgment and after Fulbright had taken his turn, he continued the straw vote around the table. McNamara said he approved the plan. Berle was also for it; his advice was to 'let her rip.' Mann, who had been on the fence, also spoke in favor of it.

Picking up a point mentioned by Berle, who had said he approved but did not insist on 'a major production,' President Kennedy changed the agenda by asking what could be done to make the infiltration more quiet. Following discussion of this question – quite remote from the fundamental moral and political issues raised by Senator Fulbright – the meeting ended. Schlesinger mentions that the meeting broke up before completion of the intended straw vote around the table. Thus, wittingly or unwittingly, the President conducted the meeting in such a way that not only was there no time to discuss the potential dangers to United States foreign relations raised by Senator Fulbright, but there was also no time to call upon Schlesinger, the one man present who the President knew strongly shared Senator Fulbright's misgivings.

Of course, one or more members of the group could have prevented this by-passing by suggesting that the group discuss Senator Fulbright's arguments and requesting that Schlesinger and the others who had not been called upon be given the opportunity to state their views. But no one made such a request.

The President's demand that each person, in turn, state his overall judgment, especially after having just heard an outsider oppose the group consensus, must have put the members on their mettle. These are exactly the conditions that most strongly foster docile conformity to a group's norms. After listening to an opinion leader (McNamara, for example) express his unequivocal acceptance, it becomes more difficult than ever for other members to state a different view. Open straw votes generally put pressure on each individual to agree with the appparent group consensus, as has been shown by well-known social psychological experiments.

[· · · · ·]

During the Bay of Pigs planning sessions, President Kennedy, probably unwittingly, allowed the one-sided CIA memoranda to monopolize the attention of the group by failing to circulate opposing statements that might have stimulated an intensive discussion of the drawbacks and might therefore have revealed the illusory nature of the group's consensus. Although the President read and privately discussed the strongly opposing memoranda prepared by Schlesinger and Senator Fulbright, he never distributed them to the policy-makers whose critical judgment he was seeking. Kennedy also knew that Joseph Newman, a foreign correspondent who had just visited Cuba, had written a series of incisive articles that disagreed with forecasts concerning the ease of generating a revolt against Castro. But, although he invited Newman to the White House for a chat, he did not distribute Newman's impressive writings to the advisory group.

The members themselves, however, were partially responsible for the President's biased way of handling the meetings. They need not have been so acquiescent about it. Had anyone suggested to the President that it might be a good idea for the group to gain more perspective by studying statements of opposing points of view, Kennedy probably would have welcomed the suggestion and taken steps to correct his own-sided way of running the meetings.

Conclusion

Although the available evidence consists of fragmentary and somewhat biased accounts of the deliberations of the White House group, it nevertheless reveals gross miscalculations and converges on the symptoms of groupthink. My tentative conclusion is that President Kennedy and the policy advisers who decided to accept the CIA's plan were victims of groupthink. If the facts I have culled from the accounts given by Schlesinger, Sorensen, and other observers are essentially accurate, the groupthink hypothesis makes more understandable the deficiencies in the government's decision-making that led to the enormous gap between conception and actuality.

The failure of Kennedy's inner circle to detect any of the false assumptions behind the Bay of Pigs invasion plan can be at least partially accounted for by the group's tendency to seek concurrence at the expense of seeking information, critical appraisal, and debate. The concurrence-seeking tendency was manifested by shared illusions and other symptoms, which helped the members to maintain a sense of group solidarity. Most crucial were the symptoms that contributed to complacent overconfidence in the face of vague uncertainties and explicit warnings that should have alerted the members to the risks of the clandestine military operation – an operation so ill conceived that among literate people all over the world the name of the invasion site has become the very symbol of perfect failure.

The groupthink syndrome

Symptoms of groupthink

The first step in developing a theory about the causes and consequences of groupthink is to anchor the concept of groupthink in observables by describing the symptoms to which it refers.

$$[\cdot \cdot \cdot \cdot \cdot]$$

The eight symptoms of groupthink include group products and processes that reinforce each other, as can be seen most clearly in the case study of the Bay of Pigs invasion plan. The symptoms can be divided into three main types, which are familiar features of many (although not all) cohesive groups observed in research on group dynamics.

Type I: Overestimations of the group – its power and morality

1. An illusion of invulnerability, shared by most or all the members, which creates excessive optimism and encourages taking extreme risks
2. An unquestioned belief in the group's inherent morality, inclining the members to ignore the ethical or moral consequences of their decisions

Type II: Closed-mindedness

3. Collective efforts to rationalize in order to discount warnings or other information that might lead the members to reconsider their assumptions before they recommit themselves to their past policy decisions
4. Stereotyped views of enemy leaders as too evil to warrant genuine attempts to negotiate, or as too weak and stupid to counter whatever risky attempts are made to defeat their purposes

Type III: Pressures toward uniformity

5. Self-censorship of deviations from the apparent group consensus, reflecting each member's inclination to minimize to himself the importance of his doubts and counterarguments

6. A shared illusion of unanimity concerning judgments conforming to the majority view (partly resulting from self-censorship of deviations, augmented by the false assumption that silence means consent)
7. Direct pressure on any member who expresses strong arguments against any of the group's stereotypes, illusions, or commitments, making clear that this type of dissent is contrary to what is expected of all loyal members
8. The emergence of self-appointed mindguards – members who protect the group from adverse information that might shatter their shared complacency about the effectiveness and morality of their decisions

Consequences

When a policy-making group displays most or all of the symptoms in each of the three categories, the members perform their collective tasks ineffectively and are likely to fail to attain their collective objectives as a result of concurrence-seeking. In rare instances, concurrence-seeking may have predominantly positive effects for their members and their enterprises. For example, it may make a crucial contribution to maintaining morale after a defeat and to muddling through a crisis when prospects for a successful outcome look bleak. But the positive effects are generally outweighed by the poor quality of the group's decision-making. My assumption is that the more frequently a group displays the symptoms, the worse will be the quality of its decisions, on the average. Even when some symptoms are absent, the others may be so pronounced that we can expect all the unfortunate consequences of groupthink.

To be more specific, whenever a policy-making group displays most of the symptoms of groupthink, we can expect to find that the group also displays symptoms of defective decision-making. Seven such symptoms [can be] listed on the basis of prior research on decision-making in government, industry, and other large organizations:

1. Incomplete survey of alternatives
2. Incomplete survey of objectives
3. Failure to examine risks of preferred choice
4. Failure to reappraise initially rejected alternatives
5. Poor information search
6. Selective bias in processing information at hand
7. Failure to work out contingency plans

How widespread is the groupthink syndrome?

At present we do not know what percentage of all major fiascoes are attributable to groupthink. Some decisions of poor quality that turn out to be fiascoes might be ascribed primarily to mistakes made by just one man, the chief executive. Others arise because of a faulty policy formulated by a group of executives whose decision-making procedures were impaired by errors having little or nothing to do with groupthink. For example, a non-cohesive committee may be made up of bickering factions so intent on fighting for political power within the government bureaucracy that the participants have little interest in examining the real issues posed by the foreign policy question they are debating; they may settle for a compromise that fails to take account of adverse effects on people outside their own political arena.

All that can be said from the historical case studies I have analyzed so far is that the groupthink syndrome sometimes plays a major role in producing large-scale fiascoes. In order to estimate how large the percentage might be for various types of decision-making groups, we need investigations of a variety of policy decisions made by groups of executives who have grossly miscalculated the unfavorable consequences of their chosen courses of action. Such investigations should also provide comparative results that are valuable for helping to determine the conditions that promote groupthink.

Sources

[The sources for most of the quotations used by Janis and the main bases for this account of the Bay of Pigs fiascoes are:

Schlesinger, Arthur M. (1965) *A Thousand Days*, Houghton Mifflin, Boston; Sorensen, T.C. (1966) *Kennedy*, Bantam, New York.

Schlesinger was a party to the decision-making process surrounding the Bay of Pigs, while Sorensen's book was based on extensive interviews with the president and others in the weeks following these events – Editors.]

The virtue of irrationality – decision making, action and commitment

NILS BRUNSSON

Making a decision is only a step towards action. A decision is not an end product. Practitioners get things done, act and induce others to act.

An action perspective makes it easier and important to observe that there exist both decisions without actions and actions without decisions. Some actions are not preceded by weighing of objectives, evaluating of alternatives or choosing; and decision processes and decisions do not always influence

Abridged extract reproduced with permission from Brunsson, N. (1972) The Irrationality of Action and Action Rationality: Decisions, Ideologies and Organizational Actions. *Journal of Management Studies*, **19**, no. 1, 24–44.

actions, particularly not when the actions precede the decisions. On the other hand, decision processes often comprise some of the processes associated with actions. Because managers and representatives in political bodies describe part of their work as decision making, decisions and decision making should remain important topics for study.

In fact, the very relationship between decision making and action helps explain why decisions deviate from normative rationality. Since decision processes aim at action, they should not be designed solely according to such decision-internal criteria as the norms of rationality; they should be adapted to external criteria of action. Rational decisions are not always good bases for appropriate and successful actions.

How can decisions lay foundations for actions? The next section attempts to answer this question.

Decisions as initiators of actions

Making decisions is just one way among several of initiating actions in organizations. However, it is a familiar one. Actions are often preceded by group activities which the participants describe as decision-making steps. Certain issues are posed in forms that allow them to be handled by decision processes: several alternative actions are proposed, their probable effects are forecasted, and finally actions are chosen. Sometimes the decision makers even formulate goals or other explicit criteria by which the alternatives can be evaluated. The final results are called decisions.

For decisions to initiate actions, they must incorporate cognitive, motivational and committal aspects. One cognitive aspect of a decision is expectation: the decision expresses the expectation that certain actions will take place. A decision also demonstrates motivation to take action, and it expresses the decision makers' commitments to specific actions. By making a decision, decision makers accept responsibility both for getting the actions carried out and for the appropriateness of the actions.

To go from decision to action is particularly complicated and difficult when there are several decision makers and several actors and when decision makers and actors are different persons. These conditions are typical of organizations. Thus, organizations should provide motivational and social links from decisions to actions. Strong motivations, sometimes even enthusiasm, are needed to overcome big intellectual or physical obstacles. Cooperating actors should be able to rely on certain kinds of behaviours and attitudes from their collaborators, so they should construct mutual commitments: the actors should signal to one another that they endorse proposed actions, for example, by presenting arguments in favour of them or by expressing confidence in success. Actors should also elicit commitments from those who will evaluate their actions afterwards, because committed evaluators are more likely to judge actions as successful (Brunsson, 1976).

Thinking, motivation and commitment are aspects of all actions. However, the importance of each aspect might differ in various situations, depending on such variables as the actors' time horizons, the degrees of change that the actions involve, and the power relationships within the organization. Cognitive activities probably become more important where the actors expect more information to be beneficial. Motivations would be more important where actors lack information needed for predicting the consequences of acting, where the negative consequences could be great, or where great efforts are essential; motivations would be less important where the actions are highly complex and the actors must collaborate extensively (Zander, 1971). Commitments would be more important where many people are involved in actions, agreements from many people are necessary, efforts must be tightly coordinated, or results depend upon the actions or evaluations of collaborators who are accessible through communication. Since motivations and commitments represent internal pressures for action, they are particularly influential where external pressures are weak. This is true of wait-and-see situations where people think that it may be possible to take no action: the actors can reject one proposed action without having to accept another at the same time.

The stronger the expectation, motivation and commitment expressed in a decision, the more power that decision exerts as a basis for action. Insofar as the constituents of decisions are determined by decision processes, the likelihoods of actions can be influenced by designing the decision processes. However, effective decision processes break nearly all the rules for rational decision making: few alternatives should be analyzed, only positive consequences of the chosen actions should be considered, and objectives should not be formulated in advance.

The following subsections explain how irrationalities can build good bases for organizational actions.

Searching for alternatives

According to the rational model, all possible alternatives should be evaluated. This is impossible, so the injunction is often reformulated as evaluating as many alternatives as possible.

In reality, it seems easier to find decision processes which consider few alternatives (typically two) than ones which consider many alternatives. It is even easy to find decision processes which consider only one alternative. This parsimony makes sense from an action point of view, because considering multiple alternatives evokes uncertainty, and uncertainty reduces motivation and commitment. If actors are uncertain whether a proposed action is good, they are less willing to undertake it and to commit themselves to making it succeed. For example, in order to facilitate product-development projects, uncertainty should not be analyzed but avoided (Brunsson, 1980). If people do not know which action will actually be carried out, they have to build up motivations for several alternatives at the same time, and this diffuses the motivations supporting any single alternative. For the same reasons, commitments may be dispersed or destroyed by the consideration of several alternatives. Therefore, very early in decision processes, if possible before the processes even start, decision makers should get rid of alternatives that have weak to moderate chances of being chosen.

On the other hand, alternatives with no chance to being chosen do not have these negative effects: they may even reinforce motivation and commitment. One strategy is to propose alternatives which are clearly unacceptable but which highlight by comparison the virtues of an acceptable alternative. This defines the situation as not being of the wait-and-see type: rejecting one alternative means accepting another. Another and more important effect is that commitments become doublesided: commitments arise not only through endorsements of acceptable alternatives but also through criticisms of unacceptable alternatives. Thus, considering two alternatives can lay a stronger foundation for action than considering only one alternative if one of the two alternatives is clearly unacceptable.

One example is the decision process following the merger of Sweden's three largest steel companies. The merger was supposed to make production more efficient by concentrating each kind of production in one steelworks. A six-month-long decision process considered several alternative ways of redistributing production. Besides the alternative that was actually chosen, however, only one alternative was investigated thoroughly. This was the alternative to make no change at all. Because this alternative would have made the merger meaningless, no one considered it a practical action.

Estimating consequences

Decision makers who want to make rational decisions are supposed to consider all relevant consequences that alternatives might have; positive and negative consequences should get equal attention. But such a procedure evokes much uncertainty, for inconsistent information produces bewilderment and doubt, and stimulates conflicts among decision makers (Hoffman, 1968). Also, it is difficult to weigh positive and negative consequences together (Slovic, 1966).

One way of avoiding uncertainty is to search for consequences in only one direction – to seek support for the initial opinion about an alternative. People tend to anchor their judgements in the first cues they perceive (Slovic, 1972; Tversky and Kahneman, 1974). Searching for positive consequences of an acceptable alternative has high priority, while negative consequences are suppressed. The purpose is not only to avoid uncertainty: active search for arguments in favour of an alternative also helps to create enthusiasm and to increase commitments. If negative consequences do pop up, adding more positive consequences can at least help to maintain commitment and motivation.

For example, in a company with high propensity to undertake innovative product-development projects, personnel spent most of their discussions collecting arguments in favour of specific projects. This helped them to build up enthusiasm for projects – an enthusiasm that they deemed necessary to overcome difficulties (Brunsson, 1976).

Evaluating alternatives

The rational model prescribes that alternatives and their consequences should be evaluated according to predetermined criteria, preferably in the form of objectives. Decision makers are told to start with objectives and then to find out what effects the alternatives would have on them. This is a dangerous strategy from the action point of view because there is a high risk that decision makers will formulate inconsistent objectives and will have difficulties assessing alternatives. Data are needed that are difficult or impossible to find, and different pieces of information may point in conflicting directions.

For producing action, a better strategy is to start from the consequences and to invent the objectives afterwards (Lindblom, 1959). Predicted consequences are judged to be good because they can be reformulated as desirable objectives. The relations between alternatives and objectives are not investigated in detail, only enough to demonstrate some positive links. The objectives are arguments, not criteria for choice; they are instruments for motivation and commitment, not for investigation. The argumentative role of objectives becomes evident in situations where objectives are abandoned after data indicate that they will not be promoted by preferred actions.

For instance, the calculations in the merged steel company actually demonstrated that the no-change alternative would be at least as profitable as the alternative that was chosen. The decision makers then shifted their criterion from profitability as defined in the calculations to criteria such as access to a harbour and the age of a steelworks – criteria which favoured the alternative to be chosen.

Choosing

Within the decision-making perspective, a decision is normally described as a choice which follows automatically from preceding analysis. But when decision making initiates action, a choice is not merely a statement of preference for one alternative but an expression of commitment to carrying out an action. A choice can be formulated in diverse ways which express different degrees of commitment and enthusiasm. Which people participate in choosing influences which people participate in acting.

A local government with an unstable majority postponed for eight years a decision about where to build new houses. Yet, at every time, there existed a majority favouring one location. Majority support was not thought to be a sufficient basis for the complicated and time-consuming planning work to follow (Brunsson, 1981; Jönsson, 1982).

Making rational use of irrationality

The purpose of action calls for irrationality. Some irrationalities are consistent with the prescriptions of Lindblom (1959) who argued that thorough rational analyses are irrelevant for the incremental steps in American national policy. But irrationality is even more valuable for actions involving radical changes, because motivation and commitment are crucial.

Much of the decision irrationality observed in decision processes can be explained as action rationality. The hypothesis that such may be the case is worth considering at least in situations where motivation and commitment are highly beneficial. For example, this kind of explanation can be applied to some of the strategic decisions described by Janis (1972). Much of the irrationality Janis observed in the decision of the Kennedy administration to invade Cuba can be explained by the fact that such risky and normally illegitimate actions needed extreme motivation and commitment to be adopted. Strong motivations and commitments seem actually to have arisen, and they led to very strong efforts to complete the action in spite of great difficulties and uncertainties.

According to Janis, better alternatives would have been found if the decision process had been more rational, giving room for more criticism, alternative perspectives and doubts. Perhaps so. But deciding more rationally in order to avoid big failures is difficult advice to follow. If the decisions should initiate actions, the irrationality is functional and should not be replaced by more rational decision procedures. Rational analyses are more appropriate where motivation and commitment offer weak benefits. This is true for actions which are less significant, less complicated and short-term. Lundberg (1961) observed that investment calculations are made for small, marginal investments but not for large, strategic ones. If one believes that rational decision processes lead to better choices, this observation should be disquieting. Moreover, important actions tend to be carried out with strong motivations and commitments, which make it difficult to stop or change directions if the actions prove to be mistakes.

There is also the opposite risk – that decision rationality impedes difficult but necessary actions. For actions involving major organizational changes, the magnitudes of the issues and the uncertainties involved may frighten people into making analyses as carefully as possible. At the same time, the uncertainty potentials and the involvements of many people heighten the risks that rational decision making will obstruct action.

One extreme and pathological case of decision making giving no basis for action is decision orientation. This occurs when people regard decision making as their only activities, not caring about the actions and not even presuming that there will be actions. In full accordance with the decision-making perspective, these people look upon decisions as end points. In one political organization, for instance, the politicians facilitated their decision making substantially by concentrating on making decisions and ignoring subsequent actions. Since the decisions were not to be carried out, the politicians did not have to worry about negative effects, and they could easily reach agreements. On the other hand, the lack of actions threatened the survival of the organization.

To sum up, rational decision-making procedures fulfill the function of choice – they lead to the selection of action alternatives. But organizations face two problems: to choose the right thing to do and to get it done. There are two kinds of rationality, corresponding to these two problems: decision rationality and action rationality. The one is not better than the other, but they serve different purposes and imply different norms. The two kinds of rationality are difficult to pursue simultaneously because rational decision-making procedures are irrational from an action perspective; they should be avoided if actions are to be facilitated.

References

Brunsson, N. (1976) *Propensity to Change*. Göteborg, Sweden: B.A.S.
—— (1980) 'The functions of project evaluation'. *R&D Management*, vol. 10, pp. 61–5.
—— (1981) *Politik och administration*. Stockholm: Liber.
Hoffman, P.J. (1968) 'Cue-consistency and configurality in human judgement'. In Kleinmetz, B. (ed.), *Formal Representation of Human Judgement*. New York: Wiley.
Janis, I.L. (1972) *Victims of Groupthink*. Boston, Mass.: Houghton Mifllin.
Jönsson, S.A. (1982) 'Cognitive turning in municipal problem solving'. *Journal of Management Studies*, vol. 19, pp. 63–73.
Lindblom, C.E. (1959) 'The science of "muddling through"'. *Public Administration Review*, vol. 19, pp. 79–88.
Lundberg, E. (1961) *Produktivitet och räntabilitet*, Stockholm: S.N.S.
Slovic, P. (1972) *From Shakespeare to Simon*. Portland: Oregon Research Institute.
Tversky, A. and Kahneman, D. (1974) 'Judgement under uncertainty: heuristics and biases'. *Science*, vol. 185, pp. 1124–31.
Zander, A. (1971) *Motives and Goals in Groups*. New York: Academic Press.

Motivation through job enrichment

FREDERICK HERZBERG

'Motivating' with KITA

In lectures to industry on the problem, I have found that the audiences are anxious for quick and practical answers, so I will begin with a straightforward, practical formula for moving people.

What is the simplest, surest, and most direct way of getting someone to do something? Every audience contains the 'direct action' manager who shouts, 'Kick him!' And this type of manager is right. The surest and least circumlocuted way of getting someone to do something is to kick him in the pants – give him what might be called the KITA.

There are various forms of KITA, and here are some of them:

Negative physical KITA. This is a literal application of the term and was frequently used in the past. It has, however, three major drawbacks: (1) it is inelegant; (2) it contradicts the precious image of benevolence that most organizations cherish; and (3) since it is a physical attack, it directly stimulates the autonomic nervous system, and this often results in negative feedback – the employee may just kick you in return. These factors give rise to certain taboos against negative physical KITA.

Negative psychological KITA. This has several advantages over negative physical KITA. First, the cruelty is not visible; the bleeding is internal and comes much later. Second, since it affects the higher cortical centers of the brain with its inhibitory powers, it reduces the possibility of physical backlash. Third, since the number of psychological pains that a person can feel is almost infinite, the direction and site possibilities of the KITA are increased many times. Fourth, the person administering the kick can manage to be above it all and let the system accomplish the dirty work. Fifth, those who practice it receive some ego satisfaction (one-upmanship), whereas they would find drawing blood abhorrent. Finally, if the employee does complain, he can always be accused of being paranoid, since there is no tangible evidence of an actual attack. Now, what does negative KITA accomplish? If I kick you in the rear (physically or psychologically), who is motivated? **I** am motivated; **you** move! Negative KITA does not lead to motivation, but to movement. So:

Positive KITA. Let us consider motivation. If I say to you, 'Do this for me or the company, and in return I will give you a reward, an incentive, more status, a promotion, all the quid pro quos that exist in the industrial organization,' am I motivating you? The overwhelming opinion I receive from management people is, 'Yes, this is motivation.'

I have a year-old Schnauzer. When it was a small puppy and I wanted it to move, I kicked it in the rear and it moved. Now that I have finished its obedience training, I hold up a dog biscuit when I want the Schnauzer to move. In this instance, who is motivated – I or the dog? The dog wants the biscuit, but it is I who want it to move. Again, I am the one who is motivated, and the dog is the one who moves. In this instance all I did was apply KITA frontally; I exerted a pull instead of a push. When industry wishes to use such positive KITAs, it has available an incredible number and variety of dog biscuits (jelly beans for humans) to wave in front of the employee to get him to jump.

Myths about motivation

Why is KITA not motivation? If I kick my dog (from the front or the back), he will move. And when I want him to move again, what must I do? I must kick him again. Similarly, I can charge a man's battery, and then recharge it, and recharge it again. But it is only when he has his own generator that we can talk about motivation. He then needs no outside stimulation. He **wants** to do it.

Hygiene vs. motivators

Let me rephrase the perennial question this way: How do you install a generator in an employee? A brief review of my motivation-hygiene theory of job attitudes is required before theoretical and practical suggestions can be offered. The theory was first drawn from an examination of events in the lives of engineers and accountants. At least 16 other investigations, using a wide variety of populations (including some in the Communist countries), have since been completed, making the original research one of the most replicated studies in the field of job attitudes.

The findings of these studies, along with corroboration from many other investigations using different procedures, suggest that the factors involved in producing job satisfaction (and motivation) are separate and distinct from the factors that lead to job dissatisfaction. Since separate factors need to be considered, depending on whether job satisfaction or job dissatisfaction is being examined, it follows that these two feelings are not opposites of each other. The opposite of job satisfaction is not job dissatisfaction but, rather, **no** job satisfaction; and, similarly, the opposite of job dissatisfaction is not job satisfaction, but **no** job dissatisfaction.

Stating the concept presents a problem in semantics, for we normally think of satisfaction and dissatisfaction as opposites – i.e., what is not satisfying must be dissatisfying, and vice versa. But when it comes to understanding the behavior of people in their jobs, more than a play on words is involved.

Two different needs to man are involved here. One set of needs can be thought of as stemming from his animal nature – the built-in drive to avoid pain from the environment, plus all the learned drives which become conditioned to the basic biological needs. For example, hunger, a basic biological drive, makes it necessary to earn money, and then money becomes a specific drive. The other set of needs relates to that unique human characteristic, the ability to achieve and, through achievement, to experience psychological growth. The stimuli for the growth needs are tasks that induce growth; in the industrial setting, they are the **job content**. Contrariwise, the stimuli inducing pain-avoidance behavior are found in the **job environment**.

The growth or **motivator** factors that are intrinsic to the job are: achievement, recognition for achievement, the work itself, responsibility, and growth or advancement. The dissatisfaction-avoidance or **hygiene** (KITA) factors that are extrinsic to the job include: company policy and administration, supervision, interpersonal relationships, working conditions, salary, status, and security.

A composite of the factors that are involved in causing job satisfaction and job dissatisfaction, drawn from samples of 1,685 employees, is shown in Fig. 3.9. The results indicate that motivators were the primary cause of satisfaction, and hygiene factors the primary cause of unhappiness on the job. The employees, studied in 12 different investigations, included lower-level supervisors, professional women, agricultural administrators, men about to retire from management positions, hospital maintenance personnel, manufacturing supervisors, nurses, food handlers, military officers, en-

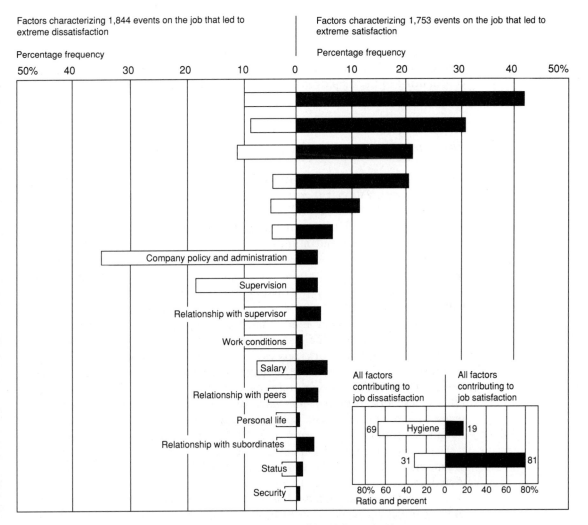

Figure 3.9 Factors affecting job attitudes, as reported in 12 investigations.

gineers, scientists, housekeepers, teachers, technicians, female assemblers, accountants, Finnish foremen, and Hungarian engineers.

They were asked what job events had occurred in their work that had led to extreme satisfaction or extreme dissatisfaction on their part. Their responses are broken down in the exhibit into percentages of total 'positive' job events and of total 'negative' job events. (The figures total more than 100% on both the 'hygiene' and 'motivators' sides because often at least two factors can be attributed to a single event; advancement, for instance, often accompanies assumption of responsibility.)

To illustrate, a typical response involving achievement that had a negative effect for the employee was, 'I was unhappy because I didn't do the job successfully.' A typical response in the small number of positive job events in the Company Policy and Administration grouping was, 'I was happy because the company reorganized the section so that I didn't report any longer to the guy I didn't get along with.'

As the lower right-hand part of the exhibit shows, of all the factors contributing to job satisfaction, 81% were motivators. And of all the factors contributing to the employees' dissatisfaction over their work, 69% involved hygiene elements.

Eternal triangle

There are three general philosophies of personnel management. The first is based on organizational theory, the second on industrial engineering, and the third on behavioral science.

The organizational theorist believes that human needs are either so irrational or so varied and adjustable to specific situations that the major function of personnel management is to be as pragmatic as the occasion demands. If jobs are organized in a proper manner, he reasons, the result will be the most efficient job structure, and the most favorable job attitudes will follow as a matter of course.

The industrial engineer holds that man is mechanistically oriented and economically motivated and his needs are best met by attuning the individual to the most efficient work process. The goal of personnel management therefore should be to concoct the most appropriate incentive system and to design the specific working conditions in a way that facilitates the most efficient use of the human machine. By structuring jobs in a manner that leads to the most efficient operation, the engineer believes that he can obtain the optimal organization of work and the proper work attitudes.

The behavioral scientist focuses on group sentiments, attitudes of individual employees, and the organization's social and psychological climate. According to his persuasion, he emphasizes one or more of the various hygiene and motivator needs. His approach to personnel management generally emphasizes some form of human relations education, in the hope of instilling healthy employee attitudes and an organizational climate which he

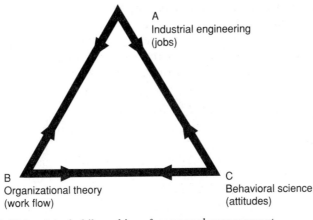

A
Industrial engineering
(jobs)

B
Organizational theory
(work flow)

C
Behavioral science
(attitudes)

Figure 3.10 'Triangle' of philosophies of personnel management.

considers to be felicitous to human values. He believes that proper attitudes will lead to efficient job and organizational structure.

There is always a lively debate as to the overall effectiveness of the approaches of the organizational theorist and the industrial engineer. Manifestly they have achieved much. But the nagging question for the behavioral scientist has been: What is the cost in human problems that eventually cause more expense to the organization – for instance, turnover, absenteeism, errors, violation of safety rules, strikes, restriction of output, higher wages, and greater fringe benefits? On the other hand, the behavioral scientist is hard put to document much manifest improvement in personnel management, using his approach.

The three philosophies can be depicted as a triangle, as is done in Fig. 3.10, with each persuasion claiming the apex angle. The motivation-hygiene theory claims the same angle as industrial engineering, but for opposite goals. Rather than rationalizing the work to increase efficiency, the theory suggests that work be enriched to bring about effective utilization of personnel. Such a systematic attempt to motivate employees by manipulating the motivator factors is just beginning.

The term **job enrichment** describes this embryonic movement. An older term, job enlargement, should be avoided because it is associated with past failures stemming from a misunderstanding of the problem. Job enrichment provides the opportunity for the employee's psychological growth, while job enlargement merely makes a job structurally bigger. Since scientific job enrichment is very new, this article only suggests the principles and practical steps that have recently emerged from several successful experiments in industry.

Job loading

In attempting to enrich an employee's job, management often succeeds in reducing the man's personal contribution, rather than giving him an opportunity for growth in his accustomed job. Such an endeavor, which I shall call horizontal job loading (as opposed to vertical loading, or providing motivator factors), has been the problem of earlier job enlargement programs. This activity merely enlarges the meaninglessness of the job. Some examples of this approach, and their effect, are:

- Challenging the employee by increasing the amount of production expected of him. If he tightens 10,000 bolts a day, see if he can tighten 20,000 bolts a day. The arithmetic involved shows that multiplying zero by zero still equals zero.
- Adding another meaningless task to the existing one, usually some routine clerical activity. The arithmetic here is adding zero to zero.
- Rotating the assignments of a number of jobs that need to be enriched. This means washing dishes for a while, then washing silverware. The arithmetic is substituting one zero for another zero.
- Removing the most difficult parts of the assignment in order to free the worker to accomplish more of the less challenging assignments. This traditional industrial engineering approach amounts to subtraction in the hope of accomplishing addition.

These are common forms of horizontal loading that frequently come up in preliminary brain-storming sessions on job enrichment. The principles of vertical loading have not all been worked out as yet, and they remain rather general, but I have furnished seven useful starting points for consideration in Table 3.3.

Table 3.3 Principles of vertical job loading

Principle	Motivators involved
A. Removing some controls while retaining accountability	Responsibility and personal achievement
B. Increasing the accountability of individuals for own work	Responsibility and recognition
C. Giving a person a complete natural unit of work (module, division, area, and so on)	Responsibility, achievement, and recognition
D. Granting additional authority to an employee in his activity; job freedom	Responsibility, achievement, and recognition
E. Making periodic reports directly available to the worker himself rather than to the supervisor	Internal recognition
F. Introducing new and more difficult tasks not previously handled	Growth and learning
G. Assigning individuals specific or specialized tasks, enabling them to become experts	Responsibility, growth, and advancement

A successful application

An example from a highly successful job enrichment experiment can illustrate the distinction between horizontal and vertical loading of a job. The subjects of this study were the stock-holder correspondents employed by a very large corporation. Seemingly, the task required of these carefully selected and highly trained correspondents was quite complex and challenging. But almost all indexes of performance and job attitudes were low, and exit interviewing confirmed that the challenge of the job existed merely as words.

A job enrichment project was initiated in the form of an experiment with one group, designated as an achieving unit, having its job enriched by the principles described in Table 3.3. A control group continued to do its job in the traditional way. (There were also two 'uncommitted' groups of correspondents formed to measure the so-called Hawthorne Effect – that is, to gauge whether productivity and attitudes toward the job changed artificially merely because employees sensed that the company was paying more attention to them in doing something different or novel. The results for these groups were substantially the same as for the control group, and for the sake of simplicity I do not deal with them in this summary.) No changes in hygiene were introduced for either group other than those that would have been made anyway, such as normal pay increases.

The changes for the achieving unit were introduced in the first two months, averaging one per week of the seven motivators listed in Table 3.3. At the end of six months the members of the achieving unit were found to be outperforming their counterparts in the control group, and in addition indicated a marked increase in their liking for their jobs. Other results showed that the achieving group had lower absenteeism and, subsequently, a much higher rate of promotion.

How was the job of these correspondents restructured? Table 3.4 lists the suggestions made that were deemed to be horizontal loading, and the actual vertical loading changes that were incorporated in the job of the achieving unit. The capital letters under 'Principle' after 'Vertical loading' refer to the corresponding letters in Table 3.3.

Steps to job enrichment

Now that the motivator idea has been described in practice, here are the steps that managers should take in instituting the principle with their employees:

1. Select those jobs in which (a) the investment in industrial engineering does not make changes too costly, (b) attitudes are poor, (c) hygiene is becoming very costly, and (d) motivation will make a difference in performance.
2. Approach these jobs with the conviction that they can be changed. Years of tradition have led managers to believe that the content of the jobs is sacrosanct and the only scope of action that they have is in ways of stimulating people.

Table 3.4 Enlargement vs. enrichment of correspondents' tasks in company experiment

Horizontal loading suggestions (rejected)	Vertical loading suggestions (adopted)	Principle
Firm quotas could be set for letters to be answered each day, using a rate which would be hard to reach.	Subject matter experts were appointed within each unit for other members of the unit to consult with before seeking supervisory help. (The supervisor had been answering all specialized and difficult questions.)	G
The women could type the letters themselves, as well as compose them, or take on any other clerical functions.	Correspondents signed their own names on letters. (The supervisor had been signing all letters.)	B
All difficult or complex inquiries could be channeled to a few women so that the remainder could achieve high rates of output. These jobs could be exchanged from time to time.	The work of the more experienced correspondents was proofread less frequently by supervisors and was done at the correspondents' desks, dropping verification from 100% to 10%. (Previously, all correspondents' letters had been checked by the supervisor.)	A
The women could be rotated through units handling different customers, and then sent back to their own units.	Production was discussed, but only in terms such as 'a full day's work is expected.' As time went on, this was no longer mentioned. (Before, the group had been constantly reminded of the number of letters that needed to be answered.)	D
	Outgoing mail went directly to the mailroom without going over supervisors' desks. (The letters had always been routed through the supervisors.)	A
	Correspondents were encouraged to answer letters in a more personalized way. (Reliance on the form-letter approach had been standard practice.)	C
	Each correspondent was held personally responsible for the quality and accuracy of letters. (This responsibility had been the province of the supervisor and the verifier.)	B,E

3. Brainstorm a list of changes that may enrich the jobs, without concern for their practicality.
4. Screen the list to eliminate suggestions that involve hygiene, rather than actual motivation.

5. Screen the list for generalities, such as 'give them more responsibility,' that are rarely followed in practice. This might seem obvious, but the motivator words have never left industry; the substance has just been rationalized and organized out. Words like 'responsibility,' 'growth,' 'achievement,' and 'challenge,' for example, have been elevated to the lyrics of the patriotic anthem for all organizations. It is the old problem typified by the pledge of allegiance to the flag being more important than contributions to the country – of following the form, rather than the substance.

6. Screen the list to eliminate any **horizontal** loading suggestions.

7. Avoid direct participation by the employees whose jobs are to be enriched. Ideas they have expressed previously certainly constitute a valuable source for recommended changes, but their direct involvement contaminates the process with human relations **hygiene** and, more specifically, gives them only a **sense** of making a contribution. The job is to be changed, and it is the content that will produce the motivation, not attitudes about being involved or the challenge inherent in setting up a job. That process will be over shortly, and it is what the employees will be doing from then on that will determine their motivation. A sense of participation will result only in short-term movement.

8. In the initial attempts at job enrichment, set up a controlled experiment. At least two equivalent groups should be chosen, one an experimental unit in which the motivators are systematically introduced over a period of time, and the other one a control group in which no changes are made. For both groups, hygiene should be allowed to follow its natural course for the duration of the experiment. Pre- and post-installation tests of performance and job attitudes are necessary to evaluate the effectiveness of the job enrichment program. The attitude test must be limited to motivator items in order to divorce the employee's view of the job he is given from all the surrounding hygiene feelings that he might have.

9. Be prepared for a drop in performance in the experimental group the first few weeks. The changeover to a new job may lead to a temporary reduction in efficiency.

10. Expect your first-line supervisors to experience some anxiety and hostility over the changes you are making. The anxiety comes from their fear that the changes will result in poorer performance for their unit. Hostility will arise when the employees start assuming what the supervisors regard as their own responsibility for performance. The supervisor without checking duties to perform may then be left with little to do.

After a successful experiment, however, the supervisor usually discovers the supervisory and managerial functions he has neglected, or which were never his because all his time was given over to checking the work of his subordinates. For example, in the R&D division of one large chemical company I know of, the supervisors of the laboratory assistants were theoretically responsible for their training and evaluation. These functions, however, had come to be performed in a routine, unsubstantial fashion. After the job enrichment program, during which the supervisors were not merely passive observers of the assistants' performance, the supervisors actually were devoting their time to reviewing performance and administering thorough training.

What has been called an employee-centered style of supervision will come about not through education of supervisors, but by changing the jobs that they do.

Concluding note

Job enrichment will not be a one-time proposition, but a continuous management function. The initial changes, however, should last for a very long period of time. There are a number of reasons for this:

- The changes should bring the job up to the level of challenge commensurate with the skill that was hired.
- Those who have still more ability eventually will be able to demonstrate it better and win promotion to higher-level jobs.
- The very nature of motivators, as opposed to hygiene factors, is that they have a much longer-term effect on employees' attitudes. Perhaps the job will have to be enriched again, but this will not occur as frequently as the need for hygiene.

Not all jobs can be enriched, nor do all jobs need to be enriched. If only a small percentage of the time and money that is now devoted to hygiene, however, were given to job enrichment efforts, the return in human satisfaction and economic gain would be one of the largest dividends that industry and society have ever reaped through their efforts at better personnel management.

The argument for job enrichment can be summed up quite simply: If you have someone on a job, use him. If you can't use him on the job, get rid of him, either via automation or by selecting someone with lesser ability. If you can't use him and you can't get rid of him, you will have a motivation problem.

The 'autonomous' work group

P. NEEDHAM

During the mid 1970s many manufacturing organisations were faced with seemingly intractable personnel problems which had their origin in social

Excerpt reproduced with permission from Needham, P. The Myth of the Self-Regulating Work Group. *Personnel Management*, pp. 29–31, August 1982.

and industrial conditions far removed from those of today. Many faced recruitment difficulties which were exacerbated by high labour turnover; industrial relations problems were accentuated by conditions of relatively full employment; and political developments suggested that the concept of industrial democracy was about to be moved from paper theory to industrial reality.

It was against this background that a number of assembly industries took a hard look at work structuring. Early experiments, such as those at Volvo and others on the continent, suggested that reorganisation of semi-skilled assembly work in such a way as to increase the scope of the job could improve job satisfaction for the operator. Success was claimed in some cases in reducing absenteeism, improving quality, reducing labour turnover and improving the overall industrial relations climate.

Considerable hopes were pinned on these reorganized methods, particularly by personnel and industrial relations specialists seeking long-term solutions to the traditional problems of running efficient assembly lines in post-war British industry. Work structuring seemed to get to the root of the problem in that, as research was increasingly demonstrating, most workers wanted more say in the day-to-day matters affecting their immediate working environment and were largely indifferent to the wider implications of industrial democracy. Moreover, enlarging semi-skilled jobs might bring other benefits. Greater self-regulation might enable factories to run with low levels of overhead, for instance, fewer line supervisors or quality control staff. The question was whether the assembly worker would respond positively to such unaccustomed freedom.

The case study given below describes an attempt in 1974 to reorganize assembly work in a medium-sized engineering company, and follows through its successes and failures up to the present time. It will be seen that work structuring in such an environment offered major benefits both to the company and to the individual operator but that, in order to sustain these, many traditional elements of control had to be restored. In the longer term, self-regulation, particularly when applied to work rate, quality and attendance, proved to be something of a myth.

The company concerned was part of a European multinational group, and was engaged in the design, manufacture and assembly of a range of domestic appliances. The management was progressive in its outlook, but operated in a fiercely competitive market, in which price and quality were of vital importance. In 1974 a decision was taken to manufacture a new range of appliances aimed at a growing UK and export market, which would provide the company with a much needed factory load.

Following lengthy discussions, a decision was made to assemble the new product using self-contained work groups rather than the assembly line techniques used for other products in the factory. This was done for a number of reasons:

- There would probably be a requirement for up to 60 'versions' of the basic design. The disruption to an assembly line of constant re-balancing would be considerable, whereas the work structuring concept implied great flexibility.

- There was traditionally a very low level of unemployment (less than one per cent up to 1980) in the district, and the industry with low profit margins had never been amongst the highest payers. The implication was that, whatever production system was adopted, it would have to be manned with assembly workers of varying ability and age range, and would have to be acceptable to women as well as men.
- The growth of industrial democracy suggested to management that 'line assembly' had a limited lifetime in the UK. It was also thought that production lines might be impossible to staff adequately on shifts because of absenteeism. If the product sold as well as expected, shift working would become essential.
- The market for these products was both cost and quality conscious. Therefore the system of production had to encourage responsibility for the quality of one's own work, and at the same time operate with the lowest possible overheads.
- Finally, the factory was proud of its record in industrial relations and promoting good conditions of employment. As an example of this, there had been no recourse to external disputes procedure with the main manual union (AUEW) in 20 years, with most issues being settled between stewards and superintendents. A strong 'consensus' style had built up over the years, and work structuring seemed consistent with this style.

The basis of the new assembly system was the 'module'. This term was adopted to describe a group of five (later six) assembly workers of compatible personalities and of similar age range and ability who agreed together on the rate of work and degree of responsibility they wished to 'contract' for. These factors in turn determined their piecework earnings. The payment system had two main components: a basic 40 hour dayrate and a payment by results bonus. The latter was based on two variables, whereby modules could opt for one of three levels of productivity and also for one of three levels of responsibility:

Basic, where each operator on the module performed a limited range of assembly tasks and passed the product on to another operator, who carried out the next stage of assembly. In essence the module operated as a mini assembly line.
Advanced, where each operator in the module assembled a complete product.
Exemplary, where, in addition to assembly through all the stages, the module achieved exemplary levels of attendance, quality and flexibility. This would include, for instance, absorbing waiting time and achieving low scrap levels.

Productivity was measured using advanced work-study techniques which related each stage of assembly to an effort rating, using appropriate allowances for relaxation, breakdowns and other contingencies. However, an important part of the arrangements from the operator's point of view was that, once the modules had completed their contracted number of machines, they could clean up their work area and spend the rest of the shift socialising. This system in time tended to encourage a high level of output in the early part of the shift in order to accumulate free time in the afternoon. The payment system at the outset was geared to encourage self-reliance – hence supervision was tacitly encouraged to 'make up' bonus earnings even where actual performance fell below contracted levels, rather than reduce pay to the level actually earned. This was because (at least in theory) the goodwill thus generated could be called upon when extra co-operation was called for – for instance if components were substandard and assembly more difficult.

Signs of success

For a period of almost five years the system worked very effectively under the influence of enlightened supervision and an ever-expanding market. From 1974 to 1979 output of the product quadrupled. Operators expressed satisfaction and the product was profitable. There were by this time more than 200 operators employed on modules. The modules had shown themselves to be extremely versatile. For instance, additional versions could be added to the product range with the minimum of disruption to production by the simple device of having one module specialize in that version. Labour flexibility represented little or no problem and the system was particularly useful when redeployment problems arose from other parts of the factory in that with such a large number of modules the range of employable people was very wide indeed. Any personnel officer familiar with the great difficulties encountered by many older employees in medium to heavy assembly jobs could recognize the major benefits of the module concept. Not surprisingly, operator satisfaction was very high and labour turnover was minimal.

At this stage any assessment of the reorganisation would have been likely to conclude that it had been a success. From a risky start the new product had established itself and was taking a high market share. Projections for future growth in output were made, and suggested that a factory extension would be needed to cope with demand. There was little doubt that the module system had played an important part in the success story. However, it was not an unqualified success.

Problems

First, absenteeism had been steadily growing from seven to eight per cent in the late '60s to 11–12 per cent by 1978, especially with the advent of full 'staff' conditions for all employees. Certified absences and night shift absence were the main problems, but an analysis in 1979 showed the average operator taking five weeks sickness absence per year, with no correlation with age or known serious illness. However, absenteeism was clearly a shop-floor problem – white collar staff seldom recorded absence levels higher than three per cent.

Although recruitment into modules was easier than on lines, it was also becoming difficult, and consequently standards had been somewhat lowered. In addition, a small machine shop elsewhere in the factory had been closed and the operators, mainly elderly or disabled, had been found jobs in assembly modules. Hence the proportion of modules opting for high productivity was decreasing, and the bonus 'slope' was simply not attractive enough.

Thirdly, work study rates were becoming slack, partly because of increasing operator expertise with what was now a well-established product and partly because of a shortage of experienced work study engineers to keep up to date on the effect of design changes on the rates. The rate of introduction of minor design changes, coupled with the large number of versions and of modules, imposed a great 'maintenance' burden on the work study department, which not surprisingly fell behind.

The result was that operators were finishing the contracted number early in the afternoon. This problem could not be tackled by opening up the earnings ceiling because of differential problems between top semi-skilled and bottom skilled rates, and also because of tight central management control over pay increases. Incomes policy exacerbated this situation and reduced further the incentive element of pay as a proportion of total earnings. In simple terms, it was just not worth the extra effort to produce more when an average card player could make more money using his spare time in the tea bars. Finally, the extent of supervision's willingness to 'make up' unearned bonus had become a serious problem, undermining an already unsatisfactory incentive slope.

At this time management began investigations into introducing an added value bonus scheme, such as had been introduced in other factories in the group. It offered a means of paying more, and could hence help recruitment and retention, whilst providing an incentive for accepting change – in particular to encourage the semi-skilled workforce to accept tighter rates of work. However, by the time the scheme was ready for introduction, the onset of the recession had considerably changed these problems – recruitment was no longer an issue, changes could be more easily introduced in working practices and manning levels, and moreover factory added value ratios had taken a severe knock with the loss of business which meant an added value bonus could only have been generated by using an artificially low baseline.

Some managers were by now becoming visibly disillusioned with the module system. Support departments such as quality assurance and materials management had always found the system irksome, since autonomous work groups tend to demand more attention from the services. This applies particularly to stock control, storage or work in progress, quality assurance, production engineering and financial control. Although direct supervision could be kept to a minimum, the modules consumed a lot of time and energy of support functions.

Traditional solutions

The upshot was that management began to examine some more traditional solutions. The external climate was gradually changing and a tough management stance was seen to be appropriate.

The productivity problem was partially tackled in late 1979, when a productivity clause was agreed as part of the annual wage negotiation. Under the terms of this agreement, the annual general increase was subject to a number of conditions including a complete re-timing of all assembly jobs. This entailed increases in output of between 10 and 60 per cent for the modules, depending on how much 'slack' was found in their rate. At the same time the piecework incentive was restored, with a 'dog leg' incentive slope which doubled the piecework earnings above a certain level of output. Also appeals for better attendance were issued, including a letter to each employee about the effect of absenteeism on the business.

The productivity deal was resisted strongly by the manual unions, who wished to trade increased pay for increased productivity on a one-for-one basis. However, they eventually agreed reluctantly to a 17 per cent pay increase, coupled with a tightening of rates by an average of 30 per cent.

By mid-1980, the situation seemed to have improved, with output increasing by 20 per cent over late 1979 with substantially the same workforce. The impact of the recession was probably somewhat delayed because the product had a seasonal aspect to sales, and high stocks in the early summer of 1980 did not cause undue concern. However, by July, stocks were equivalent to six months production and a series of steps had to be taken to reduce production and increase efficiency. The main measures adopted were as follows:

1

A redundancy exercise was carried out on a selective basis. First, the evening and night shift activities were reappraised. Night shift working was clearly one-third more expensive in basic wages alone because of the premium element. Coupled with this, however, were high absenteeism, high turnover and little commitment to the factory's overall objectives. The evening shift reappraisal proved more difficult because of a belief that part-time women, usually with children at school, might be persuaded into a seasonal pattern of work with a long summer lay-off. The beneficial effect of this on summer stocks might make this kind of work pattern attractive to the company even with 20 per cent shift premium. However, strong union pressure was exerted to protect full-time jobs rather than part-time.

Redundancy was carried out on day shift on a selective basis, and supervision and the union were consulted closely on questions of capability, flexibility and commitment. A points system was devised, and accordingly a considerable number of semi-skilled with well known problems of poor attendance, output and quality were selected. A conscious decision was made not to select serious ill-health cases for redundancy, since those were best tackled under sickness payment and if necessary early retirement provisions. However, two shop stewards who had led the battle against the productivity deal in 1979 were included in the list.

2

The absenteeism problem was solved by a combination of selective redundancy and blanket use of the disciplinary procedure. Employees with three spells or more of absence (irrespective of reason) were issued with a first formal warning, on the basis that attempts to resolve the problems by traditional methods had brought no improvement, and that by now the survival of the business was at stake. Interestingly, one of the company's main competitors announced a complete suspension of their sick pay scheme at the same time. Accordingly, almost 25 per cent of the total semi-skilled workforce were seen by the personnel department and issued with a first formal warning, irrespective of reasons for the various absences. An undertaking was given by the company that before any individual progressed to a final warning, a thorough investigation of the background circumstances would be conducted.

However, in the following six months no-one needed to be seen again about absence, and the level reduced to under three per cent – less than a third of the comparable 1979 figure.

3

Re-rating of jobs by work study engineers was continued and ran into increasing shop floor resistance. Two national level conferences were held before some of these new rates were agreed, and shop stewards began to demand more say in the rating of jobs.

However, there was no appetite on the shop floor for serious resistance to those various measures. Communication exercises were conducted in which supervision explained the need for improvement in efficiency as part of the requirement for survival. Instinctively, the shop floor accepted that the old state of affairs could not continue but it was clear that these measures had opened up shop floor/staff divisions which had previously not been so acutely felt.

In retrospect, management concluded that if autonomous work groups were to remain a serious alternative to traditional assembly lines, a very disciplined approach was going to be needed. In particular some of the more traditional management controls and functions would have to be retained to ensure that the benefits deriving from greater job satisfaction and greater flexibility were not obtained at the expense of efficiency and operating costs. In increasingly difficult trading conditions, there is clearly no room for any slackness in approach to costs: moves towards more socially advanced conditions need to be carefully monitored so that additional costs are not incurred.

Autonomous groups working is still a serious alternative to repetitive line assembly in a society which continues to dislike the dehumanising influence of many traditional assembly methods. But in the struggle to retain market share such concepts will need to be stripped of woolly idealism if they are to prove effective. In particular, the idea still embraced by many personnel managers that job redesign leads to greater self-regulation looks increasingly dubious.

Early forms of worker resistance – swing riots

E.J. HOBSBAWM and G. RUDÉ

A remarkable feature of the labourers' movement of 1830, distinguishing it from many others of its kind, was its multiformity: arson, threatening letters, 'inflammatory' handbills and posters, 'robbery', wages meetings, assaults on overseers, parsons and landlords, and the destruction of different types of machinery all played their part. There were only three cases of rioting over enclosure, two of them in Oxfordshire; and food riots, still prevalent in the East Anglian riots of 1816, were now almost entirely confined to Cornwall, a last bastion of this traditional form of the small consumers' protest.

Yet behind these multiform activities, the basic aims of the labourers were singularly consistent: to attain a minimum living wage and to end rural unemployment. To attain these objects, they resorted to means that varied with the occasion and the opportunities at hand. They might take the elementary course of meeting to determine the amount that should be asked for, drafting a 'paper' or 'document' for presentation to their employers and, should resistance be encountered, accompanying their demands by 'illegal assemblies' and threats of violence: such cases were particularly frequent in the Kentish Weald, Berkshire, Hampshire, Essex, Suffolk, and both parts of Sussex. Yet, even here, there was considerable variety in both the procedures adopted and the rates demanded. Wages meetings were generally, in their inception at least, on a village basis; but they might easily spread to embrace groups of neighbouring villages, as in the Maidstone area and in the Kent and Sussex Weald; they might invade the select vestry of the parish or local market town; or the labourers might assemble in larger meetings like those convened at Rushmere Heath, near Ipswich, or at Mile End, near Colchester, on 5 and 6 December.

Abridged excerpts reproduced with permission from Hobsbawm, E.J. and Rudé, G. *Captain Swing*, pp. 163–6, 178–9, 187 and 224–5; published by Lawrence and Wishart Ltd, London, 1969.

Again, the rates demanded varied from one county to another. In Kent and Sussex, where wages were relatively high, the wage demanded for an able-bodied married man was 2s 6d a day in summer and 2s 3d in winter. These rates were occasionally repeated elsewhere, as at Kintbury in Berkshire and at Stotfold in Bedfordshire.

Other forms of pressure to increase wages included attacks on overseers, justices and parsons, and far less frequently on farmers: these account for a large proportion of the cases appearing in the indictments as 'riots'. Of a different order altogether were the levies of money, beer and food on householders and passers-by. These played a large part in some counties, but not in others; and were most prevalent in Berkshire, Wiltshire and Hampshire. The first example of this type of rioting appears to have been at East Sutton, near Maidstone, at the end of October, when the Radical shoemaker John Adams, persuaded Sir John Filmer to hand over two sovereigns, as his men 'had come from afar and wanted refreshment'. From this comparatively modest beginning such levies became a regular feature of the riots as they spread westwards. To some extent, too, they changed their purpose.

This type of 'robbery' (as it is generally termed in the indictments) assumed considerable proportions, particularly in Hampshire, where more rioters were indicted on this charge than on any other. But, even in these southern and midlands counties, it was not so much this form of disturbance, impressive as it was, as machine-breaking that set its stamp on the whole labourers' movement. In fact, the distinctive hall-mark of 'Swing' – even more than arson or the threatening letter that gave the riots their name – was the breaking of agricultural machinery. It was by no means universal: there were no threshing machines broken in Bedfordshire, Lincoln or Surrey and only one machine was broken in Cambridgeshire, in Suffolk and in the Sussex Weald; but, taking the riots as a whole, it was the most constant and the most frequent of the rioters' activities. Between 28 August 1830, when the first threshing machine was broken in East Kent, and 3 September 1832, when a final, solitary machine was destroyed in a Cambridgeshire village, we have counted a total of 387 threshing machines – and 26 other agricultural machines – in twenty-two counties. The purpose, here too, was to force up wages and 'make more work': for the introduction of threshing machines in the Canterbury area in the summer of 1830 was seen by the Kentish labourers as the greatest single threat to their means of existence. As the riots spread west and into the midlands counties, other farming implements, such as cast iron ploughs, harvesters, chaff-cutters, haymakers and seed and winnowing machines, were added to the labourers' targets: we have noted such cases in Hampshire, Wiltshire, Berkshire, Buckingham, Gloucester and Norfolk. And from the barns where the machines were housed it was natural that the rioters' attention should occasionally be diverted to the foundries and workshops where they were forged or manufactured. This accounts for the major part of the 'industrial' machine-breaking that occurred in foundries and factories at Andover, Fordingbridge, Hungerford and

Wantage. In addition, paper-machines were destroyed at High Wycombe, Colthrop, Taverham and Lyng, and other machines were destroyed by sawyers, needle-makers and weavers at Redditch, Loughborough and Norwich. Yet fears expressed that the labourers' initiative would release a general outbreak of industrial machine-breaking were never realized, and as far as the labourers were concerned, it was the threshing machine, far more than any other, that was the symbol of injustice and the prime target of their fury.

Yet to many contemporary observers the most notable and memorable of 'Swing' activities were the dispatch of threatening letters and incendiary attacks on farms, stacks and barns. There were good reasons for this: it was by such means that the movement began in the summer of 1830 around Sevenoaks and Orpington; they were widely reported, far more so than the destruction of machines; and, being carried on at dead of night and under conditions that made it easy to escape detection, they led to the wildest rumours and were followed by comparatively few prosecutions. Among such rumours was the constantly repeated tale that 'gentlemen' or 'strangers' were travelling round the countryside in 'green gigs', making mysterious inquiries about wage-rates and threshing machines, distributing money and firing stacks with incendiary bullets, rockets, fire balls or other devilish devices.

[T]he village [was] the centre and starting-point of all 'Swing's' multiform activities. It was here that a nucleus of militants initiated action and built up support, by persuasion or intimidation, before putting their demands before the local parson or farmer. It was from here, too, that the local movement radiated outwards and swept up other villages as it gained impetus and momentum. The typical agent of propagation was the itinerant band, which marched from farm to farm, swelling its numbers by 'pressing' the labourers working in the fields or in their cottages at night. There was always a certain ceremonial attending such operations. The leader might wear a white hat or ride on a white horse; flags were carried, and horns were blown to arouse the villagers and warn them of the rioters' approach. In the earlier (and later) days, when the militants were more inclined to fear detection, raiding parties might blacken their faces and do their work at night; but as the movement developed, riots took place in open day, and were public performances and at times assumed a festive air. There were frequent reports of the gaiety and good humour with which the labourers set about their work; and, in Dorset, Mary Frampton, the sister of a local justice, described the rioters at Winfrith 'as being in general very fine-looking young men, and particularly well dressed as if they had put on their best clo' for the occasion'.

The atmosphere was, however, not always so light-hearted, and there are equally frequent reports of the violent, even ferocious, language used by rioting groups. Terms such as 'blood for supper' or 'blood for breakfast', or the more traditional threat of 'bread or blood', were voiced on numerous occasions.

In fact, no single life was lost in the whole course of the riots among farmers, landlords, overseers, parsons or the guardians of law and order – not even among the 'specials' for whom the labourers felt a particularly strong revulsion. Farmers were rarely molested, but there were occasional beatings-up of 'specials', overseers and parsons. In tithe-and-wages riots in particular, parsons were frequently 'mobbed'; and other labourers refusing the 'press-gang's' summons might be thrown in the pond, carried away by force, or otherwise manhandled.

[T]his was essentially a labourers' movement with essentially economic ends. This was the view of the more responsible of the government's agents in the countries, who were not greatly impressed by the stories of 'strangers in gigs' and 'itinerant' Radicals or incendiaries, and said as much. From East Kent Sir Edward Knatchbull wrote that he saw 'no political association and no extending of insubordination outside the labourers' ranks'. In East Sussex George Maule, legal adviser to the Home Office, could detect 'no bad feeling among the peasantry against the Government'. From Norfolk, Colonel Brotherton wrote that he could not 'possibly conceive anything so inconceivable as a distinct corps of incendiaries gliding thru the country unperceived'. In Wiltshire, a senior magistrate rejected all exaggerated reports 'attributing the calamity to political incendiaries'; and Brotherton concluded that 'the insurrectionary movement seems to be directed by no plan or system, but merely actuated by the spontaneous feeling of the peasants, and quite at random.' By and large, their verdict appears to be a just one.

In all, 1,976 prisoners were tried by 90 courts sitting in 34 counties. We may briefly tabulate the sum total of their sentences as follows:

Sentenced to death:	252 (of these 233 commuted, mainly to transportation, some to prison).
Executed:	19
Transported:	505 (of these only 481 sailed).
Prison:	644
Fined:	7
Whipped	1
Acquitted or bound over:	800

Taken as a whole, were these sentences peculiarly harsh? In terms of death sentences and executions, they followed the usual pattern of the times: there were nineteen executions, but all but three of them for arson. Yet in terms of men transported, they were quite remarkably severe. No less than 481 persons were wrested from their families, and shipped 12,000 miles away with virtually no hope of ever returning to their homes. In the south of England, there were whole communities that, for a generation, were stricken by the blow. From no other protest movement of the kind – from neither Luddites nor Chartists, nor trade unionists – was such a bitter price exacted.

Industrial sabotage

L. TAYLOR and P. WALTON

They had to throw away half a mile of Blackpool rock last year, for, instead of the customary motif running through its length, it carried the terse injunction 'Fuck Off'. A worker dismissed by a sweet factory had effectively demonstrated his annoyance by sabotaging the product of his labour. In the Christmas rush in a Knightsbridge store, the machine which shuttled change backwards and forwards suddenly ground to a halt. A frustrated salesman had demobilized it by ramming a cream bun down its gullet. In our re-searches we have been told by Woolworth's sales girls how they clank half a dozen buttons on the till simultaneously to win a few minutes' rest from 'ringing up'. Railwaymen have described how they block lines with trucks to delay shunting operations for a few hours. Materials are hidden in factories, conveyor belts jammed with sticks, cogs stopped with wire and ropes, lorries 'accidentally' backed into ditches. Electricians labour to put in weak fuses, textile workers 'knife' through carpets and farmworkers co-operate to choke agricultural machinery with tree branches.

Our data include examples of acts which only temporarily disconcert the management, and of those which have shut an entire factory. Sometimes the behaviour involves only one person, but often the active or passive coopera-tion of hundreds is observable. It may occur just once or twice in the history of the industry or be an almost daily experience in the workers' life. To do justice to such a range of activity we use a broad definition of industrial sabotage – that rule-breaking which takes the form of conscious action or inaction directed towards the mutilation or destruction of the work environ-ment (this includes the machinery of production and the commodity itself).

The covert and ambiguous nature of much industrial sabotage sounds like a good reason for steering clear of the topic. However, the following reasons suggest that the subject may have some general sociological as distinct from psychological significance.

(i)   Industrial sabotage may be an important index of underlying industrial conflict.
(ii) Industrial sabotage may have behavioural and motivational links with other deviant behaviour which occurs outside the workplace.
(iii) The study of industrial sabotage illuminates the problem of 'irrational' behaviour.

Obviously searching for meanings is a sensible activity only if we assume that the behaviour we examine is meaningful to the actor. If it is true that industrial sabotage is often 'irrational', 'gratuitous', 'mindless', then it would

Abridged excerpts reproduced from Taylor, L. and Walton, P. Industrial Sabotage: Motives and Meanings, in Cohen, S. (ed.) *Images of Deviance*, pp. 219–23, 225–6 and 242; published by Penguin, Harmondsworth, 1971.

save time and effort to refer it straightaway to the psychoanalyst for interpretation in terms of unconscious desires and hidden motives. But we must be careful about imputing irrationality simply on the basis of superficial impressions; behaviour which may be generally referred to as 'meaningless' may not appear so to the actor, or indeed to the members of his sub-culture.

When we come to look at all the accounts we have of the meaning of sabotage, derived from the several sources we described earlier, we find three main types emerging.

Our three types show individuals attempting to destroy or mutilate objects in the work environment in order (i) to reduce tension and frustration, or (ii) to facilitate the work process, or (iii) to assert some form of direct control.

[· · · · ·]

Unplanned smashing and spontaneous destruction are the signs of a powerless individual or group – our experience suggests that they principally occur in industries which are in an almost 'pre-trade-union' state, where there is a lack of any general shared consciousness amongst the workers such as might be found in industries with a history of collective industrial action.

Utilitarian sabotage is to be expected principally in industries where the worker has to 'take on the machine' in order to push up his earnings – his working against the clock encourages such secondary adjustments. An unintended consequence of time and motion studies and improved technology in the factory may be the development by workers of more sophisticated ways of 'beating the clock'. Where sabotage is encountered, we expect to find a history of militant activity, a generalized recognition of the target for the attack and a readiness to sacrifice short-term gains for long-term objectives in a situation in which the opportunities for official protest are circumscribed.

The power of collective action

R. HYMAN

Organized and unorganized conflict

The distinction between organized and unorganized conflict is of great analytical importance (though occasionally difficult to draw in practice). While both types of activity represent workers' response to a work situation

Abridged excerpt reproduced with permission from Hyman, R. *Strikes*, pp. 56–9; published by Macmillan Ltd, London, 4th edn, 1989. Copyright © Richard Hyman 1972, 1977, 1984, 1989.

which causes dissatisfaction or deprivation, the nature and implications of this response differ markedly. Put simply, in unorganized conflict workers typically respond to the oppressive situation in the only way open to them **as individuals**: by withdrawal from the source of discontent, or, in the case of certain forms of individual sabotage or indiscipline, by reacting against the immediate manifestation of oppression. Such reaction rarely derives from any calculative strategy; indeed, unorganized expressions of conflict 'are often not regarded as conflict by the persons in the situation' (Scott *et al.*, 1963: 40).

Organized conflict, on the other hand, is far more likely to form part of a conscious strategy to change the situation which is identified as the source of discontent.

Forms of conflict as alternatives

Evidence from a number of studies suggests that in any industrial situation in which workers experience sufficiently acute deprivations, unrest will be expressed in some form. The circumstances of the case will however influence what form this expression of conflict takes. Thus in any situation, the different varieties of industrial conflict may represent alternatives.

For discontent to be expressed in a strike, a minimum of worker solidarity and organization is presupposed almost by definition.

> The very action of striking is a collective act and implies a certain amount of understanding and belief in the efficaciousness of mass action. While it is true that strikes are occasionally spontaneous outbursts due to accidental circumstances or long periods of repression, one may generalize to the extent of saying that workers with no feeling of solidarity or common interest would be unlikely to undertake a strike.
>
> (*Griffin, 1939: 98*)

While car workers are sufficiently cohesive to display their unrest in strike action, 'with young unskilled women in the clothing industry, say, it may appear in a high rate of labour turnover' (Knowles, 1952: 210). (This does not mean, incidentally, that women are never prominent in industrial disputes; the London match girls' strike of 1888 is one of the most famous episodes of British labour history, and many other examples of female militancy are cited by Knowles. Indeed, women clothing workers took part in one of the most prominent stoppages of 1970. But women tend to be employed in industries and occupations where collective organization is least strong, and they strike far less frequently than men.)

There is statistical evidence that different types of conflict function as alternatives. Knowles concluded that 'figures covering the end-period of the Second World War suggest that strikes and absenteeism in coal-mining are to some extent "interchangeable"' (1952: 225). Subsequently a more detailed study in the same industry has offered corroboration (Scott *et al.*, 1963). Miners in higher-skilled occupations, who form more cohesive work groups and possess greater bargaining strength, are most likely **both** to pursue grievances through the formal negotiating procedure **and** to engage in strikes, go-slows, and overtime bans. Lower-skilled groups, who figure least prominently in such collective activities, have the highest level of involvement in the measurable forms of unorganized conflict. Very similar findings emerge from a study in American manufacturing industry: 'apathetic' work groups which lack sufficient cohesion to engage in collective conflict 'were not trouble-free, but only superficially so. . . . There was evidence of worker discontent, but often it was not found in terms of specific demands or grievances' (Sayles, 1958: 8).

One implication of such findings is that attempts to suppress specific manifestations of conflict, **without removing the underlying causes of unrest**, may merely divert the conflict into other forms. There is the case of the major motor company which, two decades ago, dismissed a number of leading shop stewards as 'trouble-makers'. The resulting demoralization at shop-floor level led to a temporary fall in strike figures; but absenteeism, accidents, and turnover all rose sharply (Turner *et al.*, 1967: 190–1). (It may be significant that labour turnover in the strike-prone car industry appears much lower than in manufacturing industry generally.) In coal-mining, the period of contraction since the mid-1950s has been associated both with a decline in strike action and with a rise in absenteeism (Handy, 1968). While these examples show the expression of conflict changing from organized to unorganized form, the reverse may also occur. It one Midland factory, after severe local unemployment had reduced the normally high rate of turnover, an unprecedented series of strikes took place (Hyman, 1970). It is plausible to assume that disgruntled employees who would normally have found more congenial jobs elsewhere were instead induced to take collective action to improve conditions.

Just as the expression of unrest may change between organized and unorganized form, so situations will influence what type of organized conflict is more regularly used. Flanders has noted 'the increasing use of "cut price" industrial action such as overtime bans, working to rule or going slow' (1970: 112); this may be seen as reflecting an economic situation in which workers have been stimulated to growing self-assertiveness, but because of mortgage and HP commitments are perhaps less willing than previously to lose earnings through strike action. (This point should not be overstressed: on occasion workers **are** ready to make major sacrifices in a dispute, and in any case few strikers initially anticipate a protracted struggle. Today, moreover, the presence in many households of more than one wage-earner ensures some income even during a strike.) If social and economic conditions can influence the choice of 'cut-price sanctions', so, more dramatically, can managerial policy. When firms in the American rubber industry (with union collaboration) introduced severe disciplinary penalties for unofficial strikers, workers turned from stoppages to go-slows, with considerable success: 'management has found slow-downs more difficult to combat . . . Moreover, they do not carry the opprobrium of walkouts in the eyes of the public'

(Kuhn, 1961: 176–7). Other American employers have had the same experience: a typical comment is 'Give me a good clean wildcat any day' (Slichter *et al.*, 1960: 671). The predominant view of those British managers who have had experience of both is also that other sanctions are more effective than strikes. It may be predicted that if anti-strike legislation in Britain does reduce the number of stoppages, this is likely to accelerate the growth of alternative forms of collective action. Those responsible for the Industrial Relations Act paid little heed to this possibility; presumably they were unwilling to admit that the very structure of work in industry generates conflict, and that the strike is only its most manifest form of expression.

References

Flanders, A. (1970) *Management and Unions*, London: Faber and Faber.
Griffin, J.I. (1939) *Strikes: A Study in Quantitative Economics*, New York: Columbia University Press.
Handy, L.J. (1968) 'Absenteeism and Attendance in the British Coal-Mining Industry'. *British Journal of Industrial Relations*, 6, pp. 37–50.
Hyman, R. (1970) 'Economic Motivation and Labour Stability'. *British Journal of Industrial Relations*, 9, pp. 159–78.
Knowles, K.G.J.C. (1952) *Strikes: a Study in Industrial Conflict*. Oxford: Blackwell.
Sayles, L.R. (1958) *The Behaviour of Industrial Work Groups*, New York: Wiley.
Scott, W.H., Mumford, E., McGivering, I.G., and Kirkby, J.M. (1963) *Coal and Conflict*, Liverpool: Liverpool University Press.
Slichter, S.H., Healy, J.J., and Livernash, E.R. (1960) *The Impact of Collective Bargaining on Management*, Washington: Brookings.
Turner, H.A., Clark, G., and Roberts, G. (1967) *Labour Relations in the Motor Industry*, London: Allen and Unwin.

Further Reading

Rose, N. (1989) *Governing The Soul: The shaping of the private self*, Routledge, Chapters 6–9. (See also further reading for Chapters 2 and 5.)

Rose, M. (1975) *Industrial Behaviour*, Penguin, 2nd edn, 1988. (Extremely good on Taylor and Mayo, Parts I and III respectively, and very good generally.)

Eldridge, J.E.T. (1975) *Sociology and Industrial Life*, Nelson. (Particularly pp. 45–64 on resistance and the 'Effort Bargain'.)

Issues for discussion

1. To what extent are 'classical' approaches to managing organisations still relevant?
   Readings: Thompson, Weber, Taylor, Coch and French, Fiedler, Herzberg and Needham (all Chapter 3)
2. To what extent are 'classical' and 'human relations' approaches to managing organisations compatible?
   Readings: Taylor, Mayo, Fiedler, Coch and French, Herzberg and Needham (all Chapter 3)
3. Can and should decision making in organisations be rational?
   Readings: Kumar (Chapter 1 – both)
   Merton (Chapter 2)
   Weber, Janis and Brunsson (all Chapter 3)
4. Compare and contrast different forms of worker resistance.
   Readings: Roethlisberger and Dickson, Hobsbawm and Rudé, Taylor and Walton, and Hyman (all Chapter 3)
5. To what extent do 'classical' and 'human relations' approaches to management represent different responses to worker resistance?
   Readings: all in Chapter 3

PART TWO

CRITICAL ISSUES

This final part of the book deals with three areas of current concern in the study of organisations and behaviour. They are:

1. flexibility;
2. culture and quality; and
3. alienation and stress.

Any number of areas might have been selected. The readings chosen are the focus of recent intellectual and managerial interest, and provide illustrations of the central themes of the book: the development of organisation and identity as historical processes.

4

Flexibility

The idea that organisational structures, and workers within them, should be able to respond quickly and flexibly to changing market and consumer demands is not new. We find Marx in the nineteenth century, for example, introducing the notion of an industrial reserve army (see Friedman in Chapter 1) to explain the means by which workers who are usually considered surplus to requirements are called upon in times of boom and rejected when the economy turns downward into recession. But what forms does flexibility commonly take and who does it most affect?

In the first reading Burns and Stalker contrast two types of managerial system: mechanistic and organic. The mechanistic structure is closely associated with bureaucracy (see Weber in Chapter 3) and operates efficiently in stable environmental conditions. The organic structure on the other hand is, they argue, better suited to unstable or dynamic environments and enables the pooling of the creative talent of organisation members to deal with particular tasks or projects breaking down the rigid hierarchies of bureaucracy.

Burns and Stalker make clear the need for a 'common culture' of shared values and beliefs to underpin these organic relationships, and enable members to work towards collectively agreed objectives.

Flexibility is also the central theme of the next reading from Atkinson and the organising principle of his core-periphery model. Atkinson argues that the central features of organisation structure and working life have undergone recent changes. As managers 'slim down' their workforce into a 'lean' core of employees, they increasingly make use of peripheral workers who float in contractual orbit around the organisation's centre. With 'plug-in' and 'plug-out' jobs, called upon as and when needed as sub-contractors or agency staff, workers in the periphery suffer 'numerical flexibility' and insecurity at the mercy of the dominant firms and the vagaries of market demand. Core workers, on the other hand, are said to enjoy stable career patterns in return for 'functional flexibility', the willingness to adapt to new demands and learn new skills.

The reading from Pollert, however, calls Atkinson's model into doubt and brands it 'a model in search of reality' – the triumph of

hope over wisdom and scholarly insight. More than this, Pollert
questions its status as a management strategy, pointing out that
long-term labour market and employment trends play a significant
part in organisational change.

Interestingly, some ten years before Atkinson published his research Barron and Norris had identified a dual labour market
stratified along gender lines. Here, men were in the primary labour
market and enjoyed enhanced employment conditions to women,
who were, by and large, in the insecure, unstable, secondary labour
market. In any event, as they make clear, the dual labour market is
not a new phenomenon. It had been characteristic of colonial and
neo-colonial societies, and had been identified along ethnic lines
in America before their research began. They are aware of the
difficulties of drawing boundaries around the two types of labour
market, but make an interesting case for segregation along gender
lines.

The flexibility debate has also featured quite strongly in the
British press, the source of the final reading in this chapter. Hirst
and Zeitlin's article appeared in the *Guardian*'s 'Debate' columns
and summarises the implications of the flexibility literature for
Britain's economic performance. Incorporating the notion of 'flexible
specialisation' which encompasses multi-skilling and the custom-
isation of goods, they argue for a revitalisation of British industry,
suggesting that 'our ideas of flexibility have made us less, not more,
competitive'.

Mechanistic and organic systems of management

TOM BURNS and G.M. STALKER

Simon (1958) suggests that, by common knowledge, a large number of the decisions we ordinarily make, in business and elsewhere, fall within the limits of a 'programme': 'Under certain circumstances when an individual or an organization is confronted with a situation requiring decision, the decision process goes off quickly and smoothly – almost as though no decision were being made at all, but the matter had been decided previously.' By contrast, 'non-programmed' decisions involve 'much stirring about, deliberation, discussion, often vacillation'. The distinction is said to resemble that drawn by other, psychologist, students of decision-making between 'habitual behaviour' and 'genuine decisions' or between 'routine' and 'critical' decisions.

Our own studies suggest that there are industrial concerns for which non-programmed decision-making is a normal function; indeed, that this kind of activity takes up most management time, and is its most important function. Such firms, in so far as they are successful, have either spontaneously or deliberately worked out a kind of management system which will facilitate non-programmed decision-making. In exploiting human resources in this new direction, such concerns have to rely on the development of a 'common culture', of a dependably constant system of shared beliefs about the common interests of the working community and about the standards and criteria used in it to judge achievement, individual contributions, expertise, and other matters by which a person or a combination of people are evaluated. A system of shared beliefs of this kind is expressed and visible in a code of conduct, a way of dealing with other people. This code of conduct is, in fact, the first sign to the outsider of the presence of a management system appropriate to changing conditions.

Mechanistic and organic systems

We are now at the point at which we may set down the outline of the two management systems which represent for us the two polar extremities of the forms which such systems can take when they are adapted to a specific rate of technical and commercial change. The case we have tried to establish from the literature, as from our research experience, is that the different forms assumed by a working organization do exist objectively and are not merely interpretations offered by observers of different schools.

Abridged excerpts reproduced from Burns, T. and Stalker, G.M. *The Management of Innovation*, pp. 103–5, 114 and 118–25; published by Tavistock (Routledge), London, 1961.

Both types represent a 'rational' form of organization, in that they may both, in our experience, be explicitly and deliberately created and maintained to exploit the human resources of a concern in the most efficient manner feasible in the circumstances of the concern. Not surprisingly, however, each exhibits characteristics which have been hitherto associated with different kinds of interpretation. For it is our contention that empirical findings have usually been classified according to sociological ideology rather than according to the functional specificity of the working organization to its task and the conditions confronting it.

We have tried to argue that these are two formally contrasted forms of management system. These we shall call the mechanistic and organic forms.

A **mechanistic** management system is appropriate to stable conditions. It is characterized by:

(a) the specialized differentiation of functional tasks into which the problems and tasks facing the concern as a whole are broken down;

(b) the abstract nature of each individual task, which is pursued with techniques and purposes more or less distinct from those of the concern as a whole; i.e., the functionaries tend to pursue the technical improvement of means, rather than the accomplishment of the ends of the concern;

(c) the reconciliation, for each level in the hierarchy, of these distinct performances by the immediate superiors, who are also, in turn, responsible for seeing that each is relevant in his own special part of the main task.

(d) the precise definition of rights and obligations and technical methods attached to each functional role;

(e) the translation of rights and obligations and methods into the responsibilities of a functional position;

(f) hierarchic structure of control, authority and communication;

(g) a reinforcement of the hierarchic structure by the location of knowledge of actualities exclusively at the top of the hierarchy, where the final reconciliation of distinct tasks and assessment of relevance is made;

(h) a tendency for interaction between members of the concern to be vertical, i.e., between superior and subordinate;

(i) a tendency for operations and working behaviour to be governed by the instructions and decisions issued by superiors;

(j) insistence on loyalty to the concern and obedience to superiors as a condition of membership;

(k) a greater importance and prestige attaching to internal (local) than to general (cosmopolitan) knowledge, experience, and skill.

The **organic** form is appropriate to changing conditions, which give rise constantly to fresh problems and unforeseen requirements for action which cannot be broken down or distributed automatically arising from the functional roles defined within a hierarchic structure. It is characterized by:

(a) the contributive nature of special knowledge and experience to the common task of the concern;

(b) the 'realistic' nature of the individual task, which is seen as set by the total situation of the concern;

(c) the adjustment and continual re-definition of individual tasks through interaction with others;

(d) the shedding of 'responsibility' as a limited field of rights, obligations and methods. (Problems may not be posted upwards, downwards or sideways as being someone's else's responsibility);

(e) the spread of commitment to the concern beyond any technical definition;

(f) a network structure of control, authority, and communication. The sanctions which apply to the individual's conduct in his working role derive more from presumed community of interest with the rest of the working organization in the survival and growth of the firm, and less from a contractual relationship between himself and a non-personal corporation, represented for him by an immediate superior;

(g) omniscience no longer imputed to the head of the concern; knowledge about the technical or commercial nature of the here and now task may be located anywhere in the network; this location becoming the *ad hoc* centre of control authority and communication;

(h) a lateral rather than a vertical direction of communication through the organization, communication between people of different rank, also, resembling consultation rather than command;

(i) a content of communication which consists of information and advice rather than instructions and decisions;

(j) commitment to the concern's tasks and to the 'technological ethos' of material progress and expansion is more highly valued than loyalty and obedience;

(k) importance and prestige attach to affiliations and expertise valid in the industrial and technical and commercial milieux external to the firm.

One important corollary to be attached to this account is that while organic systems are not hierarchic in the same sense as are mechanistic, they remain stratified. Positions are differentiated according to seniority – i.e. greater expertise. The lead in joint decisions is frequently taken by seniors, but it is an essential presumption of the organic system that the lead, i.e. 'authority', is taken by whoever shows himself most informed and capable, i.e. the 'best authority'. The location of authority is settled by consensus.

A second observation is that the area of commitment to the concern – the extent to which the individual yields himself as a resource to be used by the working organization – is far more extensive in organic than in mechanistic systems. Commitment, in fact, is expected to approach that of the professional scientist to his work, and frequently does. One further consequence of this is that it becomes far less feasible to distinguish 'informal' from 'formal' organization.

Thirdly, the emptying out of significance from the hierarchic command system, by which co-operation is ensured and which serves to monitor the working organization under a mechanistic system, is countered by the development of shared beliefs about the values and goals of the concern. The growth and accretion of institutionalized values, beliefs, and conduct, in the form of commitments, ideology, and manners, around an image of the concern in its industrial and commercial setting make good the loss of formal structure.

Finally, the two forms of system represent a polarity, not a dichotomy; there are, as we have tried to show, intermediate stages between the extremities empirically known to us. Also, the relation of one form to the other is elastic, so that a concern oscillating between relative stability and relative change may also oscillate between the two forms. A concern may (and frequently does) operate with a management system which includes both types.

The organic form, by departing from the familiar clarity and fixity of the hierarchic structure, is often experienced by the individual manager as an uneasy, embarrassed, or chronically anxious quest for knowledge about what he should be doing, or what is expected of him, and similar apprehensiveness about what others are doing. Indeed, as we shall see later, this kind of response is necessary if the organic form of organization is to work effectively. Understandably, such anxiety finds expression in resentment when the apparent confusion besetting him is not explained. In these situations, all managers some of the time, and many managers all the time, yearn for more definition and structure.

On the other hand, some managers recognize a rationale of nondefinition, a reasoned basis for the practice of those successful firms in which designation of status, function, and line of responsibility and authority has been vague or even avoided.

[· · · · ·]

The distinctive feature of the organic system is the pervasiveness of the working organization as an institution. In concrete terms, this makes itself felt in a preparedness to combine with others in serving the general aims of the concern. Proportionately to the rate and extent of change, the less can the omniscience appropriate to command organizations be ascribed to the head of the organization; for executives, and even operatives, in a changing firm it is always theirs to reason why. Furthermore, the less definition can be given to status, roles, and modes of communication, the more do the activities of each member of the organization become determined by the real tasks of the firm as he sees them than by instruction and routine. The individual's job ceases to be self-contained; the only way in which 'his' job can be done is by his participating continually with others in the solution of problems which are real to the firm, and put in a language of requirements and activities meaningful to them all. Such methods of working put much heavier demands on the individual.

We have endeavoured to stress the appropriateness of each system to its own specific set of conditions. Equally, we desire to avoid the suggestion that either system is superior under all circumstances to the other. In particular, nothing in our experience justifies the assumption that mechanistic systems should be superseded by organic in conditions of stability. The beginning of administrative wisdom is the awareness that there is no one optimum type of management system.

Reference

Simon, H.A. (1958) 'The Role of Expectations in an Adaptive or Behaviouristic Model', in Bowman (ed.), *Expectations, Uncertainty and Business Behaviour*, Social Science Research Council, New York.

The dual labour market

R.D. BARRON and G.M. NORRIS

In the last few years studies of the labour market in the developed capitalist societies have begun to recognize the importance of the stratification of the labour market into a primary sector – containing relatively well-rewarded and stable jobs; and a secondary sector – containing lower paid and insecure occupations. The investigation of the causes of poverty in the advanced societies, particularly in deprived urban areas, has increasingly directed the attention of economists and sociologists towards the reality of significant barriers to upward mobility for the less skilled in the labour market and away from the 'human capital' emphasis on individual deficiencies as prime or sole causes of economic deprivation. In colonial and neo-colonial economies dualism is an obvious feature of the labour market, since modern, highly capitalized industries co-exist with a primitive, labour-intensive economy, and industrial workers in the primary sector are clearly separated from traditional rural and craft workers. Dualism in Western labour markets is less obvious, however, except in those areas where salient social divisions have highlighted the distinction between the two sectors as well as reinforcing their intensity. Thus it was the reality of the work experience of black people in the United States which awakened academic interest in labour market dualism in that country.

A dual labour market is one in which:

1. There is a more or less pronounced division into higher paying and lower paying sectors;
2. Mobility across the boundary of these sectors is restricted;

Abridged excerpts reproduced from Barron, R.D. and Norris, G.M. Sexual Divisions and the Dual Labour Market, in Barker, D.L. and Allen, S. *Dependence and Exploitation in Work and Marriage*, pp. 47, 49–50 and 64; published by Longman, London, 1976.

3. Higher paying jobs are tied into promotional or career ladders, while lower paid jobs offer few opportunities for vertical movement;
4. Higher paying jobs are relatively stable, while lower paid jobs are unstable.

This model also emphasizes the extent to which pay inequalities between the primary and secondary sectors are reinforced by other factors; primary sector jobs, it suggests, will also provide good fringe benefits, better working conditions, and so on. Some writers would probably stress the particular form which the division between primary and secondary sectors takes – for example, racial lines of cleavage may be an obvious institutional barrier between the two sectors; or the secondary economy may characteristically contain certain sorts of industry. But these versions of the dual labour market model are merely special instances of the general model outlined in the above four propositions.

In our view, not shared by some authors, dualism in a labour market can cut through firms, industries, and industrial sectors. Although some firms or industries may be mainly primary employers, it is possible for a single employer or industry to contain both primary and secondary labour markets provided that the four conditions are met. Furthermore, dualism is essentially a matter of degree. Some labour markets are more dualistic than others, but probably most labour markets are neither wholly dualistic nor entirely unsegmented. To establish the extent of dualism in a national labour market would be a formidable methodological task, probably requiring a cluster analysis technique to establish inter-correlations between pay, conditions and promotion prospects of jobs and mobility behaviour of job holders.

Such an exercise, which is beyond the scope of this paper, has yet to be undertaken.

[None the less, it] seems to us that women are the main secondary workforce in Britain, and that the fact that the primary-secondary division coincides with sexual divisions in the labour market has obscured the existence of dualism in the British labour market. Many researchers have ignored the dualistic aspects of the market because they have been concentrating upon the jobs held by men, and have therefore noticed inequalities rather than major structural barriers. This is not to say that there are not secondary 'dualisms' or divisions **within** particular occupational labour markets, but the existence of these should not be allowed to blind us to the larger divisions between men and women at work and between primary and secondary jobs.

The flexible firm

J. ATKINSON

'British firms don't have manpower strategies; they just have manpower tactics writ large.' This comment, made by a senior personnel director in response to questions about new employment strategies, seems to sum up both the weaknesses and the strengths of British manpower management. On the one hand, it implies that manpower policies are often the unplanned outcome of business initiatives which have been taken without serious consideration of their manpower implications. But, on the other hand, it also implies that such policies are subordinate to business needs and do not have any independent rationale. It also suggests that responses to changing economic circumstances are likely to be empirical and pragmatic. A research programme conducted at the Institute of Manpower Studies (IMS) over the last year has been considering where such empiricism and pragmatism is taking manpower policy.

Although it is possible to identify some sectors of the economy (and some firms) whose experience has been different, several important common themes can be found underpinning the employment plans of most UK companies. Among the most important are:

Market stagnation: The combination of world recession, of the UK's unusually deep and prolonged share of that recession, and of a widespread inability to compete effectively in world markets, has led to a managerial imperative with the permanent reduction of unit labour costs.

Job loss: Virtually all UK firms have undergone an enforced and dramatic reduction in employment levels, which have often been as expensive in cash terms as they have been painful for employee relations.

Uncertainty: Despite Treasury optimism about a national growth rate of three per cent, many firms appear privately more cautious about the pace of an upswing and, more importantly, are not relying on growth being sustained. As a result, such firms are anxious not to overcommit themselves in terms of employment or investment.

Technological change: The increasing pace, and decreasing cost, of technological change means that the firm (and its employees in particular) needs to be capable of responding quickly to substantial changes in either product lines or production methods (and probably both).

Working time: As reductions in basic hours have continued, so employers have increasingly been forced to reconsider the most effective deployment of worked time. This has led to a widespread view among employers that any further reductions of working time can only be sustained through restructuring worked time, often in quite unconventional ways.

Abridged excerpt reproduced with permission from Atkinson, J. Manpower Strategies for Flexible Organisations. *Personnel Management*, August 1984, 28–31.

As a result, firms have found themselves under pressure to find more flexible ways of manning which take account of these new market realities. They have put a premium on achieving a workforce which can respond quickly, easily and cheaply to unforeseen changes, which may need to contract as smoothly as it expands, in which worked time precisely matches job requirements, and in which unit labour costs can be held down. At the same time, employers have recognized that the current state of the labour market, with high unemployment, few shortages of labour, and a weakened trade union movement, will help them secure these aims. So, there are both strong pressures to achieve a more flexible workforce and greater opportunities to do so now than in the past.

What is flexibility?

Our research suggests that firms are really looking for three kinds of flexibility – functional, numerical and financial.

Functional flexibility is sought so that employees can be redeployed quickly and smoothly between activities and tasks. This might mean the deployment of multiskilled craftsmen moving between mechanical, electrical and pneumatic jobs; it might mean moving workers between indirect and direct production jobs; or it might mean a complete change of career from, say, draughtsman to technical sales. As products and production methods change, functional flexibility implies that the same labour force changes with them, in both the short and medium term.

Numerical flexibility is sought so that headcount can be quickly and easily increased or decreased in line with even short term changes in the level of demand for labour. It might mean that hire and fire policies can be more easily implemented, or that hiring gives way to a looser contractual relationship between manager and worker. The end result would be that at any time the number employed/working exactly matched the number needed.

Financial flexibility is sought for two reasons; first, so that pay and other employment costs reflect the state of supply and demand in the external labour market. Of course, there is little novel in the suggestion that employers wish to hire labour as cheaply as possible. The significance lies more in relativities and differentials between groups of workers than in an across-the-board push to reduce wages, and the implications include a continued shift to plant level bargaining and widening differentials between skilled and unskilled worker. Secondly, and probably of greater importance in the long term, pay flexibility means a shift to new pay and remuneration systems that facilitate either numerical or functional flexibility, such as assessment-based pay systems in place of rate-for-the-job systems.

There is little that is new in any of these management aspirations, but what is new is the growing trend for firms explicitly to seek all three forms of flexibility. We have seen attempts to build each of them into the basic approach to manning, rather than treating flexibility as an additional extra to be secured through a productivity deal. The relative priority accorded to each form of flexibility by a particular organisation will determine how closely it comes to resemble the 'contractual', the 'professional' or the 'federal' models described in Professor Handy's article. So widespread have aspirations for greater flexibility become that many employers now expect to introduce changes which will restructure the work experience of some, or perhaps all, of their labour force.

For these employers, a change in the organisation of work is seen as the best way of achieving greater flexibility from the workforce. As a result a new employment model is beginning to emerge which makes it much easier to secure all three kinds of flexibility.

The new model involves the break up of the orthodox hierarchical structure of the firm in such a way that radically different employment policies can be pursued for different groups of worker. The new divisions are much less likely to be based on blue or white collar distinctions, but rather on the separation of jobs which are specific to a particular firm from those involving only general skills. The firm-specific skills might range from production manager to maintenance occupations, and the non-specific from systems analyst to driver. Both can be found at all levels in a company.

The result is shown in the diagram (Fig. 4.1) which represents the organisational structure which many UK firms are trying to introduce. The new structure involves the break-up of the labour force into increasingly peripheral, and therefore numerically flexible groups of workers, clustered about a numerically stable core group which will conduct the organisation's key, firm-specific activities. At the core, the emphasis is on functional flexibility; shifting to the periphery, numerical flexibility becomes more important. As the market grows, the periphery expands to take up slack; as growth slows, the periphery contracts. At the core, only tasks and responsibilities change; the workers here are insulated from medium term fluctuations of the market, whereas those in the periphery are more exposed to them.

Workers in the core group are full-time permanent career employees: say, managers, designers, technical sales staff, quality control staff, technicians and craftsmen. Their employment security is won at the cost of accepting functional flexibility both in the short term (involving cross-trade working, reduced demarcation, and multi-discipline project teams) as well as in the longer term (changing career and retraining). Terms and conditions of employment are designed to promote functional flexibility. This often involves single status conditions, and the displacement of 'rate-for-the-job' by pay systems which reward the acquisition and deployment of new skills, and which are at least partly based on performance assessment. But the central characteristic of this group is that their skills cannot readily be bought-in. The firm is therefore seeking to separate them from a wider labour market.

'[First] peripheral group' workers are also full-time employees, but enjoy a lower level of job security and have less access to career opportunities. In effect they are offered a job, not a career. For example, they might have

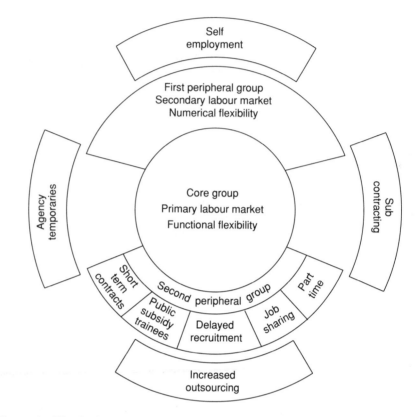

Figure 4.1 The flexible firm.

clerical, supervisory, component assembly and testing occupations. The key point is that their jobs are 'plug in' ones, and not firm-specific. As a result, the firm looks to the external labour market to fill these jobs, and seeks to achieve numerical and financial flexibility through a more direct and immediate link to the external labour market than is sought for the core group. Functional flexibility is not sought and, because these jobs tend to be less skilled, little training or retraining is needed. A lack of career prospects, systematization of job content around a narrow range of tasks, and a recruitment strategy directed particularly at women, all tend to encourage a relatively high level of labour turnover, which itself facilitates easy and rapid numerical adjustment to product market uncertainty.

If the firm needs to supplement the numerical flexibility of the first peripheral group with some functional flexibility, then a second peripheral group can be distinguished. They are on contracts of employment designed to combine the two. Part-time working is probably the best example of this – the jobs having all the characteristics of those in the first peripheral group, with their deployment often structured to match changing business needs – twilight shifts, overlaid shifts or peak manning etc. Jobsharing, short-term contracts, public subsidy trainees and recruitment through temporary contracts all perform a similar function – maximizing flexibility while minimizing the organization's commitment to the worker's job security and career development.

Where jobs are not at all firm-specific, because they are very specialized (e.g. systems analysis) or very mundane (e.g. office cleaning), firms are increasingly likely to resource them outside, through the use of sub-contracting, self-employed jobbers, temporary help agencies and the like. This not only permits great numerical flexibility (the firm deciding precisely how much of a particular service it may need at any time), but it also encourages greater functional flexibility than direct employment (as a result of a greater commitment of the self-employed to getting the job done, the greater specialisation of sub-contractors, or the relative powerlessness of the worker in this context, according to your taste). Privatization in public sector agencies is perhaps the most well-known aspect of this trend to the use of outsourcing. The most radical breaks with past practices are perhaps represented by 'networking' and 'teleworking' but both are only part of a much broader externalization of functions across the broad areas of the UK labour market.

Implications for employees

The implication of these changes for employees is that an individual's pay, security and career opportunities will increasingly be secured at the expense of the employment conditions of others, often women, more of whom will find themselves permanently relegated in dead-end, insecure and low paid jobs. Within the core group employees will increasingly enjoy security of employment provided they are both capable of and willing to retrain. Outside it, employment security is reduced, and retraining costs are unlikely to be borne by employers. Hence secondary workers are likely to become more job specific at a time when technology is substantially changing the content of many such jobs. In the external group, some workers, notably the self-employed sub-contractors, may find themselves without job or employment security, and with the entire responsibility for providing business support and training for themselves.

In the core group promotion prospects are generally favourable, although career development will increasingly involve mastering new skills. Career movement for secondary workers will involve changing employers and will therefore be restricted. Within firms new training structures for sustaining a supply of key employees in the core group may need to be developed, as internal career paths which existed in a unitary internal labour market will no longer be available. For secondary employees (particularly in the second peripheral group), conditions of employment will deteriorate substantially: payments for non-worked time (holidays, sickness and pension) are likely to be most badly affected. Among primary workers, conditions are likely to improve, with the twin aim of creating a homogeneous group of employees and encouraging retention. For all groups the relationship between pay and time worked is likely to change. For core workers, pay will often be increasingly determined by individual performance, rather than through collective agreement. For the peripheral groups pay is likely to vary more explicitly with hours worked, as employers try to match their labour inputs more precisely to their needs over time. For the externals, pay is likely to be influenced by performance, but in this case, more akin to a 'fee-for-work-done' rather than hours attended. An across-the-board approach to rates for any job is therefore likely to become more difficult to sustain.

To put it simply, two sorts of change in work organization seem to be under way. First, the gap between the conditions of employment of these different groups of worker is widening. At the core, job security, single status conditions and performance-related pay systems contrast with the relatively poor conditions, insecurity and pay levels driven down by competition in the labour market, which are found among most peripheral and external groups. Second the numerical balance between these groups appears to be changing, with some managers anxious to push as many jobs as possible into peripheral or external categories.

The obvious implication is that a single approach to manpower management is unlikely to be appropriate to both groups. Nor can it be assumed that conventional forms of management can simply be grafted into any of the emerging groups. Very few of the firms involved with this work had introduced new management structures, but there was a widespread recognition that changes in emphasis were needed.

Table 4.1 shows how those changes might be structured. For simplicity it concentrates on the opposing ends of the organized spectrum – the core group and externals. The approach to the two peripheral groups is likely to involve elements of both. It can be seen that the focus of the managerial system is quite different for each group; for the core group the focus is the employee, for the externals the focus is the job. Similarly, the principal form of management control is facilitating the effective deployment of core group workers, as opposed to monitoring delivery of the job against specification for the externals. This might well involve a participative approach to core group management, compared with a more directive approach to externals.

Table 4.1 Managing the flexible firm

	Core group	External
Focus for management	Employee	Job
Instrument of control	Effecting deployment	Delivery against specification
Management style	Participative	Directive
Remuneration system	Wage for time worked	Fee for work done
Motivation/Incentive system	Performance appraisal	Delivery on schedule
Supply	Recruitment and training	Competitive tender severance

The table also shows that these divergent approaches to management need to be supported by different rationales for personnel policy. The basis of employment shifts from a salary based on time worked to a fee for work done (among external groups). Incentive payments vary from performance-related at the core to time-related among externals (e.g. bonus for early delivery, penalty payment for late delivery). Labour supply at the core is assured through the recruitment of potential and the provision of extensive training and retraining facilities; among externals it may be assured through competitive tender, or through the establishment of ex-employees on a new contractual basis.

The management of unorthodox work systems is clearly an issue requiring a good deal more research than we have been able to devote to it. One thing is clear however, the relegation of some parts of a firm's activities to a peripheral or external status will not eliminate managerial shortcomings; for example, the solution to a problem of low productivity among maintenance engineers is unlikely to be so simple as to push regular maintenance work out to contract, making it 'Somebody else's problem'. Reorganization for flexibility does not remove the need for effective management, but it can reproduce that need on a more favourable terrain.

Reference

Handy, C. (1984) 'The Organisation Revolution and How to Harness It', *Personnel Managment*, July.

The flexible firm: a model in search of reality

A. POLLERT

The model of the 'flexible firm' has achieved wide currency and acclaim. The model postulates two kinds of worker flexibility. Functional flexibility embraces the crossing of occupational boundaries, multi-skilling, and a willingness to adjust to production demands. It is provided by a 'core' of stable, skilled employees who enjoy relatively secure employment. Numerical flexibility, including part-time and temporary work and sub-contracting, enables a firm to adjust labour force levels rapidly. Such flexibility is provided by a 'periphery' of workers who are easily disposable and who face considerable insecurity.

Abridged excerpt reproduced from Pollert, A. The 'Flexible Firm': A Model In Search Of Reality (or A Policy In Search Of A Practice)? *Warwick Papers in Industrial Relations*, December 1987, no. 19, pp. i–iii (summary).

The empirical evidence

Contrary to the model's assertions, a managerial concern with labour flexibility is not new. It was a central element in the productivity bargaining of the 1960s and 1970s, while the segmentation of the labour market was extensively analysed by dual labour market theories. What is new is the model's translation of segmentation as a process into a deliberate managerial strategy for large firms. The evidence does not support this. An analysis of data on developments in temporary and part-time work, self-employment, sub-contracting, outworking, freelancing, and homeworking shows that these cannot be explained by a deliberate strategy to create an employment periphery. The public sector is an exception, but this fact raises further questions about the model, which gives no attention to this sector. Much of the expansion of insecure and irregular work can be explained by sectoral shifts in the structure of employment, by cost-cutting measures, and by rationalization; other changes reflect a host of managerial practices and not simply a strategy of flexibility. There is also little evidence of widespread developments towards functional flexibility or employment security of a 'core'.

Conceptual problems

Definitions of core and periphery are shifting and unsatisfactory. The identification of the core can easily become circular: core workers have secure employment, and the fact of such employment is used as evidence for the presence of a core. The fact that a group of workers enjoys relatively secure employment does not mean that it is treated as part of the core of the business. And some groups performing 'core' functions, such as women shop workers or young workers in the fast food industry, have neither secure employment nor privileged pay. The groups which are seen as crucial can, moreover, shift; and key skills can be bought in and not be provided by the 'core' (systems analysis being an obvious example).

The 'flexible firm' model also suffers by its uneasy alliance of description, prescription, and prediction. A radical and deliberate shift towards a strategy of flexibility is both asserted and denied. And the discussion is not related to earlier developments in the real world or to existing theories. An unrealistic picture of a radical break from the past is created, and this is projected into the future as an inevitable trend.

Policy and practice

The model claims to offer a practical policy for firms. Yet it breaks down in several ways. It is vague as to the precise kinds of flexibility which a firm might pursue. It neglects possible counter-productive effects of flexibility. And in emphasising numerical flexibility it diverts attention from the evidence which shows that Britain lags other countries in training and development: the model does not see a systematic lack of training as a problem which management needs to do something about.

The model concentrates on labour flexibility as a panacea. The probability that changes in labour arrangements are the result of far wider concerns with production organization, marketing, and industrial relations is not considered.

Origin and context of the model

If the flexible firm model is so flawed, how has it sustained such success? It has come to prominence because of a general concern with 'Japanisation' and because it offers an easily understandable picture of complex developments. The concepts of core and periphery seemed to give some logic and direction to firms' labour practices.

The emergence of the model needs to be seen in the context of developments in its home, the Institute for Manpower Studies. The Institute developed its studies of manpower planning and analysis during years of economic growth, and it has adapted to the new climate of recession and contraction by producing new approaches to labour market issues. Its traditional role of mediating between private firms and the government has also changed in the light of new public policies on employment and the labour market as well as new managerial philosophies.

Conclusions

Although superficially persuasive, the model rests on an uncertain basis of confused assumptions and unsatisfactory evidence. The assertion of a new polarization between core and periphery is misleading. It should be abandoned in favour of a more historically and theoretically informed analysis.

Knowing the buzz word is not enough

PAUL HIRST and JONATHAN ZEITLIN

Flexibility has been a key buzz word for British management in the 1980s. It is a symbol of the resolve to overcome past problems and to match our competitors.

In practice it has boiled down to two objectives: creating a more flexible and responsive labour force freed from rigid union job demarcations and conditions of employment; and creating the flexible firm, which avoids being trapped in one line of business, and which differentiates by expansion and acquisitions.

The rhetoric is one thing, the reality is another. British-style flexibility has failed to change deep-seated national patterns in both manufacturing organization and company management. A revolution has taken place in manufacturing organization since the mid-1970s in Germany, Italy, Japan and certain regions of the US. It has created a new paradigm of industrial efficiency – 'flexible specialization' – and with it new forms of competitive advantage in manufacturing.

Flexible specialization is bad news for Britain, because its key features are the most difficult to import. They stem from different social institutions and different attitudes. They do not consist in readily transferable management practices or technologies that can be bought off-the-shelf.

Flexible specialization is the production of a wide and changing range of semi-customised goods using general purpose, flexible machinery and broadly-skilled, adaptable workers who are given high levels of responsibility. It contrasts with the mass production of standardized goods using highly dedicated machinery and low-skilled labour assigned to fragmented tasks with low levels of discretion.

Flexible specialization developed in the 1970s. The ability to produce a range of products enabled manufacturers to exploit changing patterns of demand by expanding the output of the most successful lines. It also enabled them to exploit new markets by changing their product range without massive re-tooling and is used by multinationals and small business alike.

However, it has two characteristic forms of organization.

Firstly, the industrial district, a region with a population of predominantly small and medium-sized firms. Examples of such regions are Baden-Württemberg in Germany, and Emilia-Romagna in Italy. Emilia-Romagna, with its capital city Bologna, is one of the fastest growing districts in Europe, where nearly every firm has less than 100 employees.

The basic feature of industrial districts is that they have developed institutions that enable their member firms both to compete and to co-operate with one another.

Co-operation enables them to attain equivalents to economies of scale through sharing collective services. Such services provide key inputs such as suitably trained labour, low-cost finance, common R&D and marketing facilities. Such co-operation also provides resources that cannot be bought on the market, like trust between firms, and between management and workers.

The second organizational form may seem surprising, but it relates to multinationals. The flexibly specialized big firm is generally firmly located in one large industrial area.

What makes it different is that the demands of a shifting mix of products force the firm to keep its internal structures and external contacts with other firms open to re-combination. Such a firm will allow its subsidiaries relatively high autonomy, it will create new groups for projects, depending on the specialization of its subsidiaries, and it will link outward in suitable partnerships in developing new projects.

Such a firm mirrors in its internal structure the flexibility and capacity to recombine for new tasks and new conditions offered by the industrial district.

This is quite different from the strategy of top management in British conglomerates, which tend to behave like a portfolio manager by spreading risk and buying into profitable areas.

Big British firms seek security through diversity, and buy into different industries; but they also seek the highest possible domestic share in key sectors, buying up the competition whenever they can. The British answer to competition is concentration, not productive flexibility and emphatically not co-operation.

If this analysis is right, them Britain faces a series of big problems. Our ideas of flexibility have made us less, not more, competitive. Our 'flexible' workers are the worst-trained in the advanced world, and our training practices are inadequate to sustain our relatively low-skilled and hierarchically directed workforce.

Our managerial structures are too rigid to allow subsidiary firms the autonomy they need to innovate, to invest and to develop horizontal links with other firms. Our regional economies have become so weakly differentiated, that we now have few candidates for development into successful industrial districts.

Our governmental system is very centralized and our small business sector is starved of low-cost finance. We have moved so far in the direction of a wholly competitive and market-based economy that it is difficult even to imagine the patterns of sharing work and co-operation one finds among firms in Italy and Japan.

Yet this is the direction in which we must move. To do so will involve a massive loosening of the rigidities in our overcentralized and highly concentrated governmental and economic system.

Revitalising British industry's competitiveness goes beyond economics and challenges the very roots of how we organize ourselves as a society and a polity.

Further reading

Rose, M. (1975) *Industrial Behaviour*, Penguin, 2nd edn, 1988. (Particularly Chapter 36, 'The Artisans are Coming Back'.)

Haralambos, M. (1980) *Sociology: Themes and Perspectives*, Unwin Hyman, 3rd edn. (Particularly pp. 345–51 for a succinct and excellent overview of the flexibility debate.)

Atkinson, J. and Gregory, D. (1986) 'A Flexible Future: Britain's Dual Labour Force', *Marxism Today*, April 1986. (Compare this with the reading from Atkinson in this book which was taken from *Personnel Management* which is a good example of how academics write for different audiences. While the *Personnel Management* article is aimed at managers, the *Marxism Today* article is addressed to Trade Unionists to 'find a creative response to the employers' drive for flexibility'.)

Issues for discussion

1. 'There is no new thing under the sun' Ecclesiastes 1: 9. Discuss with reference to the concept of flexibility in organisations.
   Readings: all in Chapter 4
2. Compare and contrast different ways of achieving flexibility in organisations.
   Readings: all in Chapter 4
3. 'Flexibility is good for everyone.' Discuss.
   Readings: all in Chapter 4

5

Culture and quality

The idea that values, beliefs and affiliations are important elements in ensuring social cohesion has roots in the work of Durkheim and Mayo as we saw in Chapters 1 and 3. It has resurfaced more recently in the search for corporate success and 'excellence' (cf. Peters and Waterman 1982). What is particularly interesting about this literature is the corporate concern to reconstruct or recast identity in the corporate image or, at the very least, to clone 'organisation man' (see Whyte and Kanter in Chapter 2). The reading from Pascale and Athos illustrates this trend. In discussing the case of Delta Airlines, for example, they quote the company psychologist who screens applicants for the job of stewardess in order to 'determine their sense of cooperativeness or sense of teamwork [at Delta] you don't just join a company, you join an objective'.

This use of corporate culture as a control device (used increasingly in association with psychological assessments, cf. Hollway 1984) comes out clearly in the reading from Ray, who points to its Durkheimian legacy. Ray sees this as the most recent in a series of control devices which developed through bureaucratic and humanistic phases to the present concern with culture – though not everyone would agree with the implication that humanist approaches replaced bureaucratic ones in practice.

Further evidence of the tendency to manipulate culture can be seen in two recent developments: Quality Circles and Total Quality Management.

Very popular particularly in the 1980s in the West following on the so-called Japanese economic 'miracle', Quality Circles were enthusiastically experimented with and often dropped as a result of managerial distrust (and worker suspicion). The reading from Bradley and Hill defines Quality Circles and the first reading from Hill shows how, in Britain, they are unlikely ultimately to be successful. Two further readings from Hill recount the recent implementation of Total Quality Management. An important point made by Hill is that while Quality Circles were managerially inspired attempts to effect cultural change from below, Total Quality Management is 'driven from the top' and more likely to succeed as a result.

The reading from Höpfl *et al.* draws together this chapter on culture and quality, reviewing briefly the literature and reporting the experience of managerial attempts to change culture and introduce Total Quality Management. Höpfl is writing for *Personnel Review*, a journal aimed at personnel or human resource managers, yet her conclusions are interestingly radical. Such programmes, she argues, are likely to evoke quite contradictory feelings with employees vacillating from 'excessive commitment' to 'excessive resentment' in a confused and painful questioning of their very identity.

In this sense the visionary missions of corporate culture enthusiasts may prove to be little more than flawed Messianic quests to re-enchant the barren rational landscape of a capitalism in trouble. More than this, it seems that they may contain within them the potential for a radically different interpretation of the world from the one being touted and carry the very seeds of their own destruction (Binns 1993). If forms of participative co-operation, an integral part of the heady apparatus of cultural invocation, are introduced into organisations which have been set up in a capitalist environment – geared to profit over human need – the contradictions may just become all too transparent to those involved.

References

Binns, D. (1993) 'Total Quality Management, Organisation Theory and the New Right: A Contribution to the Critique of Bureaucratic Totalitarianism', *UEL Occasional Papers on Business, Economy Business and Society*, Paper no. 11.

Hollway, W. (1984) 'Fitting work: psychological assessment in organisations', in Henriques J. *et al.*, *Changing the Subject*, Methuen, pp. 26–59.

Peters, T.J. and Waterman, R.M. Jun. (1984) *In Search of Excellence*, Harper & Row.

Corporate cultures

RICHARD PASCALE and ANTHONY ATHOS

In management, as in music, there is a base clef as well as a treble. The treble generally carries the melody in music, and melody's equivalent in management is the manager's style. A manager's style – the way he focuses his attention and interacts with people – sets the 'tune' for his subordinates and communicates at the **operational** level what his expectations are and how he wants business conducted. Beneath these messages is a deeper rhythm that communicates more fundamentally. The bass in music – whether hard rock or a classical symphony – often contains much of what moves the listener. So, too, the 'bass' of management conveys meanings at a deeper level and communicates what management **really** cares about. These messages can influence an organization profoundly. In Japanese organizations, a great deal of managerial attention is devoted to ensuring the continuity and consistency of these 'bass clef' messages.

[W]e have variously referred to these 'bass' clef messages as an organization's 'significant meanings,' 'shared values,' and 'spiritual fabric.' For clarity, we will adopt one all inclusive term to describe these characterizations: **superordinate goals** – the goals above all others. They are the seventh element in our framework. Superordinate goals provide the glue that holds the other six – strategy, structure, systems, style, staff, and skills – together. When all are fitted together, organizations tend to become more internally unified and self-sustaining over time.

Superordinate goals play a pragmatic role by influencing implementation at the operational level. Because an executive cannot be everywhere at once, many decisions are made without his knowledge. What superordinate goals do, in effect, is provide employees with a 'compass' and point their footsteps in the right direction. For example, at IBM that translates into never sacrificing customer service; at Matsushita it means never cheating a customer by knowingly producing or selling defective merchandise. These values permit the CEOs[1] to influence the actions of their employees, to help the employees make correct independent decisions. These value systems act as 'tie breakers' in close cases, those in which decisions otherwise might be made the wrong way.

Year after year, decade after decade, Delta Air Lines has been the most consistent money-maker in the airline industry. Undoubtedly, its route structure, concentrated in the fast-growing South, has contributed to its success. But route structure alone cannot explain Delta's performance – for

Abridged excerpt from Pascale, R.T. and Athos, A.G. *The Art of Japanese Management*, pp. 177–99; published by Penguin Books Ltd, Harmondsworth, 1981. Reprinted by permission of the Peters Fraser & Dunlop Group Ltd.

[1] CEO: Chief Executive Officer [Editors].

neither United Airlines (with its dominant position in America's busiest air terminal, Chicago) nor American Airlines (with the lion's share of the market in fast-growing Dallas/Fort Worth) has been able to match Delta's performance over the long term.

Delta considers its key to success in the highly competitive and largely undifferentiated airline industry to be **service**. (As we saw, for a time Carlson succeeded in inculcating this idea at United, where it worked equally well.) Delta considers service to be the direct result of a motivated and friendly work force. Delta's approach, which includes virtually open-door access for all of its 36,500 employees, has enabled the airline to maintain its esprit de corps and remain non-union in an industry plagued by labor-management strife. Delta's management **style** and strongly reinforced **super-ordinate goals** are largely responsible for this achievement (Guyon, 1980, p. 13).

At the heart of Delta's philosophy is 'the Delta family feeling.' More than a slogan, it is what makes Delta different. This 'family' emphasis was introduced and nurtured by the airline's founder and has been carefully institutionalized. 'It's just a feeling of caring within the company,' says Delta's current chairman, W. Thomas Beebe.

It's difficult to find workers with serious complaints at Delta. The firm promotes from within, pays better than most airlines and rarely lays off workers. These policies are what makes the 'family feeling' real. When other airlines were slashing employment during the 1973 oil embargo, Mr. Beebe told senior management: 'Now the time has come for the stockholders to pay a little penalty for keeping the team together.' Notice how the superordinate goal of preserving the 'family feeling' took precedence over near-term profits and return on investment.

Like Matsushita, Delta pays attention to the socialization of new employees. It makes sure employees embrace the 'family' concept by emphasizing it in training programs and at meetings. It also carefully screens job applicants. Stewardess candidates, for example, are culled from thousands of applicants, interviewed twice and then sent to Delta's psychologist, Dr. Sidney Janus. 'I try to determine their sense of cooperativeness or sense of teamwork,' he says. At Delta, 'you don't just join a company, you join an objective.'

The Delta example sheds light on several features of effective superordinate goals. First, they need to tie into higher-order human values. Second, they need to be consistent with the other six S's, especially the firm's **style** and **staffing** and **systems** practices. Third, management needs to be meticulous in respecting these values (even if it means sacrificing short-term profits) or they will be seen as empty slogans.

Kinds of superordinate goals

Effective superordinate goals should be (1) significant, (2) durable, and (3) achievable. Most tend to fall into one or more of the following categories:

1. **The company as an entity**
   Here the whole organization is reinforced as an entity one lives within and should identify with and belong to, and which is deserving of admiration and approval from employees and society (e.g., Delta's belief in the 'family feeling').
2. **The company's external markets**
   Here the emphasis is on the value of the company's products or services to humanity, and on those factors important in maintaining this value – that is, quality, delivery, service, and customers' needs (e.g., Matsushita's belief in advancing the standard of living in Japan by distributing reliable and affordable electrical products).
3. **The company's internal operations**
   Here attention is focused on such things as efficiency, cost, productivity, inventiveness, problem solving, and customer attention (e.g., Delta's emphasis on 'service' and Matsushita's dedication to first-class production engineering).
4. **The company's employees**
   Here attention is paid to the needs of groups of people in reference to their productive function, and to individual employees as valued human beings in a larger context – that is, human resource systems, growth and development, opportunity and rewards, individual attention and exceptions (e.g., Matsushita's commitment to developing employees not only for the firm's benefit but to contribute to each employee's personal growth over a lifetime).
5. **The company's relation to society and the state**
   Here the values, expectations, and legal requirements of the surrounding larger community are explicitly honored, such as beliefs in competition, meritocracy, the necessity of obeying the law, or being sensitive to other nations' customs (e.g., Matsushita sees itself as a major contributor in restoring Japanese status and prestige).
6. **The company's relation to culture (including religion)**
   Here the underlying beliefs about 'the good' in the culture are honored – beliefs in our own case largely derived from Judeo-Christian tradition, and including such things as honesty, and fairness, e.g. (the strong influence of religion in shaping the Matsushita philosophy – which reinforces many Confucian and Buddhist values including harmony, solidarity, discipline and dedication).

IBM, then and now

IBM has for many years been one of our most successful and effective US corporations. It is known for its remarkable development of strategy, structure, systems, style, skill, and staff, and the fit among them, **and** for its equally advanced development of superordinate goals.

In a 1940 *Fortune* article describing the company and its president (Thomas John Watson), the author's imagery is initially surprising. For example, he describes the young Mr. Watson as having the appearance and behavior of a 'somewhat puzzled divinity student' who 'began to confect the aphoristic rules of thumb that have since guided his life and policies. "Ever onward," he told himself. "Aim high and think in big figures; serve and sell; he who stops being better stops being good.". . . Mr. Watson caused the word THINK to be hung all over the factory and offices. . . . Generally it is framed, sometimes graven on pediments in imperishable granite or marble, again embossed in brass, yet again lettered in gold on a purple banner, but always and everywhere it is there. . . . Whether you particularly agree with [what Mr. Watson is saying] you listen. . . . Mr. Watson's monumental simplicity compels you to do so. . . . Let him discourse on the manifest destiny of I.B.M., and you are ready to join the company for life. Let him retail plain homilies on the value of Vision, and a complex and terrifying world becomes transparent and simple. Let him expound the necessity for giving religion the preference over everything else, and you **could not help falling to your knees**. . . . Everybody in the organization is expected to find the ubiquitous THINK sign a constant source of inspiration, as the weary travelers of old found new strength in the wayside crucifixes' (Burck, 1940).

That the author found such images useful to **his** purpose does not necessarily mean, of course, that such images captured an important truth about the company. They could have been useful mostly in capturing the writer's **reaction** to IBM and Mr. Watson. But three senior executives quoted in the article add weight to the 'religious' impression. One said: 'Mr. Watson has spread his benign influence over the earth, and everywhere it has touched, people have gained, mentally and morally, materially and spiritually.' Another remarked: 'I think that we do not always count our blessings. Every so often we should all of us stop and think of the many things that have been done for each member of this organization.' A third echoes a similar theme: 'Mr. Watson gave me something I lacked – the vision and the foresight to carry on in this business, which from that day forward I have never had any thought of leaving.'

There is an implied reference to cultural values of gratitude, faith, and commitment. There is repeated reference to the beneficial impact of Mr. Watson on **individuals**. The tone is evangelical. In the 1930s, society's acceptance of various absolutes was not yet much undermined by existential beliefs and moral relativism, and there was still widespread acceptance of the use in business of explicit, usually Christian, religious metaphors.

[· · · · ·]

In the years since 1940, IBM's expression of its beliefs, and its ways of honoring them, has become what seems fair to call 'more sophisticated.' The approach is much more analogous to the best functioning of some of our established formal religions. There is less obvious conformity required, more subtlety in technique, more complexity acknowledged in goals, and thus more skill required to behave 'well.' Yet the more recent statements of

IBM's superordinate goals, the basic beliefs reinforced within the present firm, can be seen as having evolved from the first Mr. Watson's original efforts. And that IBM has been at it so long gives the present beliefs the enormous advantage of a successful and shared history. A recent statement of IBM's basic beliefs is as follows:

Basic beliefs

A sense of accomplishment and pride in our work often go hand in hand with a basic understanding of what we're all about, both as individuals and as a company. IBM is fortunate to have a timeless statement of its purpose – in its basic beliefs.

The underlying meaning of these beliefs was best expressed by Tom Watson, Jr., in his McKinsey Foundation Lectures at Columbia University in New York in 1962, when he said:

I firmly believe that any organization, in order to survive and achieve success, must have a sound set of beliefs on which it premises all its policies and actions.

Next, I believe that the most important factor in corporate success is faithful adherence to those beliefs.

And finally, I believe that if an organization is to meet the challenges of a changing world, it must be prepared to change everything about itself except those beliefs as it moves through corporate life.

In other words, the basic philosophy, spirit, and drive of an organization have far more to do with its relative achievements than do technological or economic resources, organizational structure, innovation, and timing. All these things weigh heavily in success. But they are, I think, transcended by how strongly the people in the organization believe in its basic precepts and how faithfully they carry them out.

What is this set of beliefs Watson was talking about? There are three:

Respect for the individual. Respect for the dignity and the rights of each person in the organization.

Customer service. To give the best customer service of any company in the world.

Excellence. The conviction that an organization should pursue all tasks with the objective of accomplishing them in a superior way.

In addition to these basic beliefs, there is a set of fundamental principles which guide IBM management in the conduct of the business. They are:

- To give intelligent, responsible, and capable direction to the business.
- To serve our customers as efficiently and as effectively as we can.
- To advance our technology, improve our products and develop new ones.
- To enlarge the capabilities of our people through job development and give them the opportunity to find satisfaction in their tasks.

- To provide equal opportunity to all our people.
- To recognize our obligation to stockholders by providing adequate return on their investment.
- To do our part in furthering the well-being of those communities in which our facilities are located.
- To accept our responsibilities as a corporate citizen of the US and in all the countries in which we operate throughout the world.

[· · · · ·]

It will be clear immediately that, over time, the tradeoffs and balance will require a lot of managerial skill applied constantly in order to confirm these principles and their modes of application in the minds of thousands of people. If one assumes, as we do, that IBM really works at living up to its basic beliefs and principles, and if one assumes, as we do, that such effort has a powerful effect on the company's success, then it becomes possible to set aside the skepticism often reserved for high-minded pronouncements of top executives. If it is **not** just fluff, then it is a powerful and positive force indeed.

[· · · · ·]

Western history and superordinate goals

By an accident of history, we in the West have evolved a culture that separates man's spiritual life from his institutional life. This turn of events has had a far-reaching impact on modern Western organizations. Our companies freely lay claim to mind and muscle, but they are culturally discouraged from intruding upon our personal lives and deeper beliefs.

In the West, many managers feel both the employee and the organization are culturally conditioned to an arm's-length relationship. This causes the firm to let the employee fend for himself in adversity and draw upon the problematic spiritual resources available to him from friends, family, and religious affiliations.

What is needed in the West is a nondeified, nonreligious 'spiritualism' that enables a firm's superordinate goals to respond truly to the inner meanings that many people seek in their work – or, alternatively, seek in their lives and could find at work if only that were more culturally acceptable.

Western institutions are, in fact, backing into this role. Two forces are at work: employees seeking more meaning from their jobs and demanding more concern from the corporation, and legislative pressures enforcing a broad range of personal services, including employee rights to counseling. In response to these forces, most major firms now describe these activities as 'Human Resource Management' instead of 'Personnel' – it is to be hoped, the first step in adopting a larger perspective. Most larger firms also provide assistance to employees dealing with chronic personal problems, such as divorce, alcoholism, and stress. And, as noted earlier, some of our most outstanding companies have long acknowledged a larger role in the lives of their employees and foster greater interdependence among them. All are remarkably 'Japanese' when we look at them closely. Their success may have important implications for Western organizations of the future.

References

Burck, G. (1940) 'International Business Machines', *Fortune*, January, pp. 36–40.
Guyon, J. (1980) 'Family Feeling at Delta Creates Loyal Workers, Enmity of Unions', *Wall Street Journal*, Monday, July 17, p. 13.

Corporate culture as a control device

CAROL AXTELL RAY

Organizational or corporate culture, and the focus in this paper is upon private US corporations, provides an extremely interesting and current example of the management process and how it changes. Just one of the debates which has emerged around the topic of organization culture is whether culture is something an organization has, or whether culture is something an organization is (Smircich, 1983, p. 347). Put differently, is culture a variable or a metaphor? In this paper, culture is treated as a variable, a potential control variable.

First, a brief definition of corporate culture is necessary, as well as a description of its functions. In organizations, culture may be defined as an amalgam of beliefs, ideologies, language, ritual and myth (Pettigrew, 1979). Put more succinctly, 'It's the way we do things around here' (Deal and Kennedy, 1982). This does not, however, mean formal ways of doing things. Indeed, the crucial feature which distinguishes the use of culture from other forms of management is that culture is conveyed to its participants through the expression of sentiments, beliefs, and attitudes (Pfeffer, 1981). Thus it appeals to the emotional, non-rational, affective elements within employees. Corporate culture, then, is different from the usual methods of operation within US firms, those of quantitative analysis, planning, formal rules and sanctions, the numerative rationalist approach which dominates business schools (Deal and Kennedy, 1982).

As far as top management is concerned, what is important is the articulation and channelling of the culture in directions which supply employees with guidelines and which promote a system of strongly-held, shared values. Recognition that the effects of a company's culture may be positive or

Abridged excerpt reproduced with permission from Ray, C.A. (1986) Corporate culture: The last frontier of control? *Journal of Management Studies*, **23**, 287–97.

negative for the purpose of corporate leaders (Martin and Siehl, 1983), or that the culture of upper management is not necessarily a unitary one shared by all organizational participants (Thompson and Wildavsky, 1986), means that conscious attempts must be made to dispense the culture in ways that are perceived as helpful in achieving the goals of corporate leaders. Put another way, the effects of culture should not be left to chance. Proper implementation, then, leads to internalization of desired values and norms. This internalization, whether or not conveyed through a formal indoctrination process, makes constant surveillance of workers unnecessary (Pfeffer, 1981). Everyone 'way down the line' knows the handful of guiding values (Peters and Waterman, 1982).

Each accentuated component of a corporation's culture, proponents believe, has an important purpose and, in one way or another, encourages employees to accept, even embrace, the goals and values of the leaders of the enterprise and, at the same time, promotes a sense of belongingness in all participants.

As is always the case, managers must implement this strategy of control. The proponents of the use of corporate culture (Deal and Kennedy, 1982; Peters and Waterman, 1982) draw heavily on the work of Barnard: 'The inculcation of belief in the real existence of a common purpose is an essential executive function . . . [the manager] is primarily an expert in the promotion and protection of values' (1938, pp. 28, 87, 88). Deal and Kennedy state the case even more strongly. It is the explicit challenge to management to make '. . . thousands and thousands of people . . . have a strongly ingrained sense of the company's values' (1982). If management meets this challenge, employees identify more completely with the firm and see their own interests as congruent with it (Athos and Pascale, 1981). The manager becomes an evangelist, a shaman, a statesperson. Properly implemented, the use of culture as a managerial strategy is seen to be potentially very effective in promoting loyalty, enthusiasm, diligence and even devotion to the enterprise.

Durkheim and corporate culture

Why might employees embrace corporate culture? In the USA, advocates of its use are ready with an answer. Ties to community and church have weakened and people's affiliatory needs are not being met. More, these losses of ties have led to a concomitant loss of meaning in individuals' lives. Since meaning is something that everyone desperately needs, individuals will sacrifice a great deal to institutions which supply it (Ouchi and Johnson, 1978; Athos and Pascale, 1981). Aside from the obvious parallels between the above and Durkheim's concepts regarding the positive uses of the division of labour, there is a more subtle and interesting application of his work.

Indeed it is in the various writings of Durkheim that a conceptual framework for discussions of corporate culture may be found. The theme which appears repeatedly in Durkheim's work is that of morality. For him, moral behaviour implies conformity to norms, a sense of 'ought'. It also implies structures or limits within which individuals know what they can legitimately expect to achieve. Finally, morality is, above all, social in nature. By this Durkheim meant that morality begins with disinterest in self and attachment to something larger than self; it is a solidary attachment to a group and suggests sacrifice to it (1933, p. 398).

Initially Durkheim believed that the division of labour would become the chief source of social solidarity and thus the foundation of moral order. Yet he later discarded this notion not only because he viewed exchange relations as temporary, but also because the utilitarian nature of the workplace may be classified as falling into his realm of the profane. The realm of the profane, for Durkheim, consists of the concrete, the rational, the material; it elicits neither sentiment nor emotion. Sources of morality were to be found in Durkheim's realm of the sacred (1965, p. 243). He noted that the sacred realm is actually a function which promotes and maintains cohesion among members of society. So when Durkheim speaks of religion, its sacred aspects are not that the bonds between individuals and their gods are strengthened but that the bonds between the individuals and the community are strengthened (1965, p. 258). The religious impulse had, however, faded. Where, then, would be the locus of morality? Durkheim finally settles upon society itself. Society is appropriate because it is exterior and superior to its members, it brings out the best in all individuals. Recognition of society's attributes and beneficence elicits sentiment and emotion which are also sustained through the use of much ritual, ceremony and heavy symbolism which revivify previous historical moments of collective ferment and effervescence (1965, pp. 240, 252, 263).

While the protagonists of corporate culture in the USA do not seem familiar with the work of Durkheim, they have stumbled upon his central ideas. Rather than society as the sacred realm, the enterprise becomes sacred. Employees at all levels in the firm become quasi-parishioners. Indeed, the corporation is spoken of as a potential source of non-deified, non-religious spirituality (Athos and Pascale, 1981). Thus, in cases where a company's culture acts as a strong integrating variable, we may in fact speak of encumbents as organizational 'members', members who we may be tempted to go so far as to say possess a 'corporate consciousness' (Clegg and Dunkerley, 1980, p. 122). The rites, rituals, ceremonies and symbolism contribute to the elicitation of sentiment and emotion and, in Durkheimian terms, keep the eyes of all participants fixed on the same goal and concurring in the same faith (1973, pp. 48, 161, 92). Advocates of corporate culture even recognize the dualism of human nature about which Durkheim wrote (1973, p. 158). Employees want, on the one hand, to be unique and 'stand out' yet, on the other, desire cession to the whole. This seeming paradox is resolved by strong-culture companies, US style, stressing the importance of each individual; everyone has a chance to be a 'winner' (Peters and Waterman, 1982). In this way, both the collectivist and individualistic aspects of people might be reconciled. For Durkheim, the struggle within individuals between devotion to self and devotion to society is natural, yet society emerges victorious for it penetrates consciousness and fashions it (1973, p. 163). Among the corporate culture advocates, however, one should substitute the word 'company' for the word 'society'.

In this regard, corporate culture as a method of control strongly resembles what Etzioni (1961) called 'moral involvement' by participants in organizations (Hofstede, 1980, p. 48). This, according to Etzioni, is typically found in religious orders, totalitarian parties, voluntary associations and sometimes in certain professional institutions such as hospitals and universities. Note that for-profit organizations are not present on Etzioni's list. What the above organizations' members share is a sense of mission, typically a profound belief in improving the human condition in one way or another.

The crisis of bureaucratic control

We are now in a position to discuss how it is that the manipulation of a corporation's culture has come to the fore as the latest and possibly most powerful form of control.

In Edwards' discussion of the transformation of the workplace in the USA (1979), he describes the emergence of **bureaucratic control**. Rather than domination being exercised by individual bosses or by the pace of machinery, domination is embedded in the social and organizational structure of the firm (1979, p. 131).

Edwards argues that bureaucratic control shapes people into more firm-orientated individuals. This is due, in part, to the fact that the criteria for evaluating employees concentrate more on behavioural attributes or personal traits than upon skill. He portrays wage-earners as owing their demeanour and affection to the firm (1979, p. 148). Yet, while bureaucratic control may prompt individuals to act **as if** the company is their source of meaning and commitment that is an entirely different matter from seriously believing it. In other words, control remains externalised rather than becoming internalised (Lebas and Weigenstein, 1986). Following Durkheim, the individualistic nature of this kind of control precludes the solidarity and bonding which a 'moral' organization could generate. Workers may well become career- or security-orientated but the material, concrete nature of such an orientation leaves the system of bureaucratic control in the realm of the profane.

The limits of humanistic control

Bureaucratic control, then, could no longer stand alone. Various strands of human relations styles of management moved into the foreground of many companies' *répertoire* of control techniques. Mayo (1933; 1945) is clearly responsible for the two major contributions to human relations techniques of management. While Mayo drew on the work of Durkheim he was, it seems, only familiar with Durkheim's piece on suicide. Mayo had noticed with some alarm that society was not fulfilling its integrative function. Rather than, however, turning his attention to the possibility of integrating individuals into the firm as a whole, Mayo concentrated his analysis upon the effects of the environment of the individual on the individual in the small group (Clegg and Dunkerley, 1980). This particular focus of Mayo, and his assertion that management must encourage the developing and sustaining of the small work group or team and, more, allow employees to have a say in the organization of their productive activity (1945, pp. 70, 73) has, without doubt, influenced such managerial techniques as 'participative decision making' and 'team building labs'.

The second strand of human relations was developed from Mayo's observations that managers need to be careful listeners, they need to be 'fair' and they must be trained in logical understanding (1933, pp. 110, 183, 185). This generated the counselling ideology in management as opposed to the old authoritarian methods. Mayo was, after all, responding to the dehumanizing effects of Taylorism, and also to deskilling and increased task fragmentation. He viewed workers as not simply 'economic' individuals but as inherently sociable and cooperative. Later, industrial psychologists would use Mayo's works as a basis for 'job enrichment', 'job enlargement', and 'job rotation' plans. All these developments attempted to offset the future-orientated, individualistic, competitive features of bureaucratic control by trying to shape wage-earners into present-orientated, cooperative people who will devote themselves to the task at hand, the here-and-now, and the immediate work group whose cooperation is necessary if the goals of management are not to be defeated (Mayo, 1945, p. 111).

In the US, human relations styles of management were not implemented to any large extent until the termination of World War II. The widespread labour unrest which followed coincided with the dissemination of the work of Kurt Lewin and his students, followers and associates, especially Douglas McGregor. Unlike Mayo and his associates, the Lewinians were not subject to the critical barrages launched by social scientists, and within a few years, human relations was in place as management theory and practice in progressive US firms.

Continuing with a Durkheimian analysis, the reason that humanistic control fails as any sort of ultimate method of control is because, again, it does not possess the capabilities to generate sentiment or emotion. While it may encourage employees to interact in more cooperative ways within the small work group, there is still no method by which individuals may span or broach the vertical divisions in the corporation in order to have a direct, unmediated connection with the goals and values of dominant *élites*. There is nothing within humanistic control which promotes senses of the broader collectivity. In the last analysis, human relations, as Mills acerbically put it, attempts to conquer work alienation within the bounds of work alienation (1951).

Corporate culture as the ultimate control?

While it is certainly not a new wish among corporate leaders, or leaders of any kind, that lower level participants should devote themselves to the organization, what is new is the recognition that the generation and elicitation of employees' devotion to the enterprise cannot be accomplished by simply 'fixing' the rewards system, the task, the employees, or the managers. The latest strategy of control implies that the top management team aims to have individuals possess direct ties to the values and goals of the dominant *élites* in order to activate the emotion and sentiment which might lead to devotion, loyalty and commitment to the company. In this sense, the use of corporate culture is analogous to Rousseau's notion of the individual citizen's relationship to the General Will. When viewed this way, we find that man is free inside the society (the corporation) but the legislator (the chief executive) is to lead him to the knowledge of the General Will (corporate policy) which will serve the entire collectivity (Shorris, 1981).

To recapitulate, the three methods of control that are being discussed look like this:

Bureaucratic Control
manipulation of rewards → loyalty → increased productivity

Humanistic Control
'satisfying' task or work group life → loyalty → increased productivity

Culture Control
manipulation of culture including myth, ritual → love of firm and its goals → increased productivity

Note that the three types contain different underlying assumptions about human nature. Bureaucratic control views people as rational, economic, competitive, future-orientated individuals. Humanistic control views people as sociable, desiring satisfying work, present-orientated and cooperative. Control by corporate culture views people as emotional, symbol-loving, and needing to belong to a superior entity or collectivity.

It is only this last form of control which has the potential to qualify the firm as lying in Durkheim's realm of the sacred. This method of control, then, seems to contain possibilities of being extremely powerful in ensnaring workers in a hegemonic system.

At this time there is no persuasive evidence, however, that the manipulation of US corporations' cultures really functions as a form of control. It is even less certain that its use as a management strategy is generalizable to other societies any more than other management techniques which have been espoused in the United States. And if it is learned that employees have embraced the culture of the firm, this does not necessarily preclude worker resistance. Resting within the concept of corporate culture is the notion of shared values and a heightened sense of collectivity; it implies commitment to the firm rather than to career or lesiure activities. But control by corporate culture has within it the essential contradiction that while individuals may become more enthusiastic, productive and committed to the corporation, they will, at the same time, be labouring in collective ways and sharing collective values. In the dominant belief system of US top management, any source of homogenization of employees is potentially threatening. The homogenization of emotion and sentiment may cut through divisions among workers and lead to intensified interaction and frequency of discourse. Increased employee demands and activism are among the possible consequences.

References

Athos, A.G. and Pascale, R. (1981) *The Art of Japanese Management*, New York: Warner Books.

Barnard, C. (1938) *The Functions of the Executive*, Cambridge: Harvard University Press.

Clegg, S. and Dunkerley, D. (1980) *Organization, Class and Control*. London: Routledge and Kegan Paul.

Deal, T.E. and Kennedy, A.A. (1982) *Corporate Cultures*. Reading, Mass.: Addison-Wesley.

Durkheim, E. (1933). *The Division of Labor in Society*. New York: Free Press.

— (1965) *The Elementary Forms of the Religious Life*. New York: Free Press.

— (1973) *On Morality and Society*: Selected Writings (Bellah, R. (ed.)). Chicago: University of Chicago Press.

Edwards, R. (1979) *Contested Terrain: The Transformation of the Workplace in the Twentieth Century*. New York: Basic Books.

Etzioni, A. (1961) *A Comparative Analysis of Complex Organizations*. New York: Free Press.

Hofstede, G. (1980) 'Motivation, leadership, and organization: do American theories apply abroad?' *Organizational Dynamics*, vol. 9, no. 1, pp. 42–63.

— (1984) 'Cultural dimensions in management and planning'. *Asia Pacific Journal of Management*, vol. 1, no. 2, pp. 81–99.

Lebas, M. and Weigenstein, J. (1986) 'Management control: The Roles of Rules, Markets and Culture', *Journal of Management Studies*, vol. 23, no. 3, May, pp. 259–272.

Martin, J.A. and Siehl, C. (1983) 'Organizational culture and counterculture: an uneasy symbiosis'. *Organizational Dynamics*, vol. 12, no. 2, pp. 52–64.

Mayo, E. (1933) *The Human Problems of an Industrial Civilization*. New York: Macmillan Company.

— (1945) *The Social Problems of an Industrial Civilization*. Cambridge, Mass.: Harvard University Press.

Mills, C.W. (1951) *White Collar*. New York: Oxford University Press.

Ouchi, W.G. and Johnson, J.B. (1978) 'Types of organizational control and their relationship to emotional well-being'. *Administrative Science Quarterly*, vol. 23, no. 2, pp. 293–317.

Peters, T.J. and Waterman, Jr. R.H. (1982) *In Search of Excellence*. New York: Harper and Row.

Pettigrew, A. (1979) 'On studying organizational cultures'. *Administrative Science Quarterly*, vol. 24, no. 2, pp. 570–81.

Pfeffer, J. (1981) 'Management as symbolic action: the creation and maintenance of organizational paradigms'. In Cummings, L.L. and Staw, B. (eds), *Research in Organizational Behavior*, vol. 3. Greenwich, Conn.: JAI Press.

Shorris, E. (1981) *The Oppressed Middle: Politics of Middle Management, Scenes from Corporate Life*. New York: Anchor Press/Doubleday.

Smirich, L. (1983) 'Concepts of culture and organizational analysis'. *Administrative Science Quarterly*, vol. 28, no. 3, pp. 339–58.

Thompson, M. and Wildavsky, A. (1986) 'A Cultural Theory of Information Bias in Organizations', *Journal of Management Studies*, vol. 23, no. 3, May, pp. 273–86.

What quality circles are

KEITH BRADLEY and STEPHEN HILL

Western management literature is now repleat with analyses of Japanese managerial practice and what can be learned from this (Pascale and Athos, 1981; Ouchi, 1981), the movement to meet the perceived Japanese challenge by emulation of Japanese methods being encapsulated neatly in the Ford Motor Company's epithet 'after Japan'. An aspect of the Japanese model that receives attention is *ringi seido* or bottom-up management, which is operationalized through the use of quality circles. Quality circles involve small groups of between 5 and 10 employees who work together and volunteer to meet regularly to solve job-related problems. Usually meetings take place during company time, but the frequency varies; some are weekly while others are monthly. Normally though not always led by supervisors, circles aim to improve quality, reduce production costs, raise productivity and improve safety.

Specific characteristics distinguish quality circles from other managerial techniques such as project groups, joint problem solving and job laboratories. Firstly, quality circles have a permanent existence and meet regularly, and are not *ad hoc* creations to solve specific problems. Secondly, participants decide their own agenda of problems and priorities. Finally, all circle members are trained to use specialized tools of quality management which include elementary statistics.

Three important assumptions underlie quality circles: one, all employees, and not just managers or technical experts, are capable of improving quality and efficiency; two, among employees there exists a reservoir of relevant knowledge about work processes, which, under conventional work practices, is difficult to tap; three, quality is an integral part of the entire production process. It is not an adjunct but the responsibility of every employee.

The intellectual pedigree of the Japanese quality circle concept is a synthesis of several discrete stands. During the 1950s, Deming's (1970) thesis

Abridged excerpt reproduced from Bradley, K. and Hill, S. (1983) After Japan: The Quality Circle Transplant and Productive Efficiency. *British Journal of Industrial Relations*, **21**, 291–311.

that statistical analysis would reveal causes and solutions to problems, and that quality should be inbuilt rather than inspected for, received detailed examination by Japanese industrialists. Equal attention was paid to Juran (1967 and 1976), who argued that the quality assurance function should be decentralized throughout an organization rather than remain a specialized function. The final strand was the American behavioural science research on motivation and job satisfaction with which the Japanese were familiar, which suggested that productive efficiency and worker morale, defined as job satisfaction and involvement in company objectives, improved as a result of increased employee participation in job-related decisions.

The quality circle movement has become a world-wide phenomenon: in Japan in 1978, an estimated 4 million employees were in circles, 12.5 per cent of the working population (Cole, 1979a); in 1981, there were reported to be 750 US corporations and governmental agencies (Burck, 1981) and over 100 British companies with circles (Lorenz, 1981); circles are also found in Brazil, Canada, France, Korea and Sweden (Intersocial, 1980; Labour Trends, 1981). The evidence on their economic effects is not comprehensive, and failure to increase profitability of operations may well be less likely to be reported than success, nevertheless there are reliable reports from a number of firms of considerable cost savings and efficiency gains resulting from the introduction of quality circles, often as a result of many small improvements that cumulatively add up.

References

Burck, C.J. (1981) 'Working Smarter', *Fortune*, June 15, July 27, August 24.
Cole, R.E. (1979) *Work, Mobility and Participation*, Berkeley, California: University of California Press.
Deming, W. (1970) *Statistical Control of Quality in Japan*, Union of Japanese Scientists and Engineers, Tokyo.
Intersocial (1980) *Intersocial*, no. 58.
Juran, J.N. (1967) 'The QC circle phenomenon', *Industrial Quality Control*, no. 23.
— (1976) *Quality Control Handbook*, McGraw Hill, New York.
Labor Trends (1981) 'Brazil-Japan Encounter', *Labor Trends*, vol. 11, November 25.
Lorenz, C. (1981) 'Learning from the Japanese – Quality Circles', *Financial Times*, January 26, 27, 28, 30, February 2, 3, 4, 6.
Ouchi, W.G. (1981) *Theory Z*. Reading, Mass.: Addison-Wesley.
Pascale, R.T. and Athos, A.G. (1981) *The Art of Japanese Management*. Simon Schuster, New York.

Quality circles in Britain

STEPHEN HILL

Quality circles

The quality circle evidence can be summarized briefly as it is reported in more detail elsewhere (Bradley and Hill 1983; 1987; Hill 1991). At their peak in the mid-1980s, quality circles were to be found in at least 400 British companies, making this numerically the largest innovation in participative quality management. Yet by the end of the decade the boom was over and most companies had wound up their programmes. In the firms under investigation, employers had opted for circles in order to improve the quality of operations and to change human relations and company culture. All had also made other changes in their style of communications and their employment practices to the same end, the most substantial of which was the introduction of single status employment in about forty per cent of cases. In the event, while circles promoted minor operational improvements, they did little to change human relations and company culture. In few cases did more than ten per cent of the eligible employees choose to join and most people displayed indifference verging on hostility to circles. The idea of greater participation in decisions was popular, but circles were not seen as an appropriate vehicle.

Despite the importance senior managers had attached to quality improvement and quality circles, the recalcitrance of junior and middle managers was the major single cause of their collapse. This was partly a result of organizational design and the failure to integrate improvement into the existing structure. Circles create organizational dualism by setting up a structure parallel to the normal chain of command. Managers claimed this was not in their own best interests. They were responsible for circles but had no authority over them: they could not determine who joined nor what was discussed, since membership was voluntary and circles chose their own agenda. Moreover, they thought that the contribution low level employees could make to improvement was slight. The presence of the parallel circle hierarchy of facilitators and senior managers drawn from elsewhere in the firm meant a manager was exposed to outside scrutiny. Circles had elaborate and inflexible formal procedures which were time consuming and cumbersome. Resistance was also partly due to managerial culture, since few middle managers were committed to the principle of participative management with regard to their own subordinates. However, they were attracted by the idea of having more participation in the decisions taken above them in the hierarchy and resented that they were expected to extend participation downwards when they themselves did not have the same rights upwards.

Abridged excerpt reproduced with permission from Hill, S. (1991) How Do You Manage A Flexible Firm? The Total Quality Model. *Work, Employment and Society*, **5**, 397–415.

These findings indicate that circles on their own, outside a context of total quality management, are unlikely to work. They highlight the need to consider the managerial response to quality improvement, the difficulty top management may face in winning the cooperation of lower levels, the relative lack of participation of these levels in the decisions that affect them, and the issue of appropriate organization. They also demonstrate the reluctance of labour to become involved in quality improvement on a voluntary basis when the mechanism of involvement is the quality circle.

References

Bradley, K. and Hill, S. (1983) 'After Japan: the quality circle transplant and productive efficiency', *British Journal of Industrial Relations*, vol. 21, pp. 291–311.
Hill, S. (1991) 'Why Quality Circles Failed but Total Quality Might Succeed', *British Journal of Industrial Relations*, vol. 29, no. 4, pp. 541–568.

The nature of total quality management (TQM)

STEPHEN HILL

Quality management is only one of the changes occurring as companies learn how to become more flexible, and it is as much a methodology as a distinct set of practices. The issues it addresses, however, are crucial. TQM is the exemplar of how companies organize themselves for success in modern product markets.

The principles of quality management

Japanese-style modern quality management grew out of the postwar application of statistical process control (SPC) to manufacturing processes, in order to replace inspection for defects after the event by the prevention of errors, and quality management has retained this 'hard' face: any process should be analysed systematically by means of appropriate and rigorous techniques. The 'soft' face is the emphasis given to mobilizing everyone around the goal of continuous quality improvement, training them in the techniques of improvement and enlisting their active commitment by means of participation and new employment relations. There are a number of quality management gurus, but certain common principles can be identified (Hill 1992; Oakland 1989).

1. **Quality is defined as conformance to the requirements of the customer.**
   'Fitness for use' is the exact definition. This includes 'quality of design';

Abridged excerpt reproduced with permission from Hill, S. (1991) How Do You Manage A Flexible Firm? The Total Quality Model. *Work, Employment and Society*, 5, 397–415.

that is, the design of goods and services is to a specification that meets the needs of the customer and not the producer. 'Quality of conformance' comes second, and covers the more common notion of quality as being conformance to a specification; that is, a product does what it is designed to do and is free of defects. If a product does not incorporate quality of design, it is irrelevant whether it is produced in a quality manner. Quality therefore comprises both effectiveness and efficiency. To put this another way: first you need to know that you are doing the right thing, then you make sure that you are doing it right.

2. **There are internal as well as external customers.** The internal customer is the next process. An organizational unit receives inputs from the previous process and transforms these to produce outputs for the next (if they do not produce directly for the external customer). As a 'customer', a unit should expect conformance to its own requirements, while as a supplier it has an obligation to conform to the requirements of others.

3. **Appropriate performance measures are used routinely to assess quality of design and conformance and initiate corrective action when performance is below standard.** The use of these (e.g. market research, competitive benchmarking of products and processes against other firms, SPC and the cost of quality) leads companies to collect different types of information and to diffuse it more widely.

4. **New organizational arrangements are required.** Top level oversight of the improvement process is necessary. This is normally achieved by a steering committee of senior managers drawn from a range of functions that reports directly to the chief executive. It allocates responsibility for the attainment of corporate quality policies, determines the procedures to be employed and monitors outcomes. Subsidiary units, such as divisions and individual establishments, set up similar committees reporting to their local senior management. Arrangements are also required for organized communication between departments and across functions, because quality management involves a greater flow of information outside the normal vertical lines of communication. There is an assumption that large-scale organization promotes compartmentalism and inward-looking attitudes within sub-units. While the internal customer principle should open up communication and improve coordination, in practice organizations also need more formal arrangements to ensure interdepartmental and crossfunctional collaboration and new agencies that cut across internal boundaries such as special project teams. Teamwork and small group activities for improvement are also promoted throughout the organization, wherever naturally occurring groups are to be found within the existing structure. Groups are expected to identify and solve quality problems that lie within their own areas of responsibility and competence.

5. **Wider participation in decision-making is essential.** Various assumptions inform this position. The first is that everyone in an organization has relevant knowledge and experience to contribute to the improvement of efficiency and effectiveness. Second, traditional managerial practices and

organizational arrangements do not harness this potential to contribute in a satisfactory manner. Third, given the right setting most people welcome the opportunity to contribute to improvement. Fourth, people are more likely to become committed to quality improvement on a daily basis if they are involved in making the relevant decisions.

6. **An appropriate culture is required if everyone in the organization is to endorse the objectives and routinely follow the procedures of quality management.** This is a culture of high-trust social relationships and respect for individuals, a shared sense of membership of the firm, and a belief that continuous improvement is for the common good. Substantial changes in prevailing employment practices regarding low level employees may be needed to make this possible.

7. **The quality of the final product or service results from every single activity in an organization.** Therefore each individual must maintain and improve the quality of what he or she does and cooperate with others to enhance their collective activities. However, some employees are more important than others: as managers have the major responsibility for quality improvement and managerially controlled systems are the prime sources of quality failures, the preceding principles apply *a fortiori* to managers.

Quality management theory does not prescribe any single best practice and firms are encouraged to tailor the application of the principles to their individual circumstances. The exception is the Quality Circle, which the Japanese regard as an essential part of TQM on the shop floor and for which there is a precisely specified structure and set of procedures (Lillrank and Kano, 1989).

References

Hill, S. (1992) 'People and quality', in Bradley, K. (ed.) *People and Performance*, Aldershot: Gower.

Lillrank, P. and Kano, N. (1989) *Continuous Improvement: Quality Control Circles in Japanese Industry*, Ann Arbor, Mi.: University of Michigan.

Oakland, J. (1989) *Total Quality Management*, Oxford: Heinemann.

Why total quality management might succeed

STEPHEN HILL

Four companies with TQM were investigated in two phases of research. These included the European subsidiary of a US office automation company and the British company in the same industry that was used for the employee

Abridged excerpt reproduced with permission from Hill, S. (1991) Why Quality Circles Failed But Total Quality Management Might Succeed. *British Journal of Industrial Relations*, **29**, 541–68.

survey cited above, from the first phase. In 1988, the US company was in the fifth year of TQM and had extended this to all employees including those on the shop-floor two years earlier. Most of the research was carried out in the manufacturing division employing 5000 staff, slightly less than half of these being located in Britain. The British company was in the second year of the programme at the conclusion of the QC study in 1988 and shortly afterwards extended TQM throughout the company. Follow-up visits in 1989 and 1990 tracked the programme through to its fourth year. In late 1989 and early 1990, two additional companies were investigated as part of the research for the separate project on technological innovation. One was the British subsidiary of a US manufacturer of components for the automotive industry with 5500 UK staff. This started on TQM in 1985 and extended it to the shop-floor in 1988. The other was a British manufacturer of precision engineering components with 1200 UK staff. TQM was a year old and confined to management, and the company was unsure when it would extend the scheme. Case-study methods were used in all four companies, involving interviews and discussions among all levels of management and with union representatives and other employees, and inspection of the companies' own documentation.

Discussion

Two of the companies had been working along TQM lines for more than four years and a third for more than three; thus, it is reasonable to assume that the halo effect that accompanies major organizational innovations, when managers tend to be bullish and to talk up the latest activity, would no longer have been a major distorting factor at the time these investigations were conducted.

Most of the blame for the failure of quality circles to realize the business improvement and cultural change objectives of senior managers should be assigned to middle managers, and the response of the middle levels of the organization must be related, in turn, to the failure of senior managers to establish appropriate organizational designs. TQM avoids the problem of parallel and dualistic structures by integrating quality management into existing hierarchies. The point at which each reporting line converged in these companies was the top establishment manager. This was also where overall responsibility for quality management resided. Every company also modified its operating systems and procedures to include quality manage-ment as part of the normal method of managing and as a component of every managerial job. Quality control professionals had a facilitating role, training and advising people in other functional areas, but no direct re-sponsibility for quality improvement. Improvement was therefore part of a unified structure that prevented organizational dualism.

An appropriate design is more than just the right structures, systems and procedures, however, and the companies still found they had to contend with backsliding and less than full commitment among certain middle and

senior managers. In particular, a number of people failed to develop participative teamworking among subordinates and to pursue improvement using
the tools of quality management systematically. Both the office automation
companies had started with the assumption that TQM should be taken up
voluntarily and that managers would willingly adopt the required attitudes
and behaviour, provided the people at the top created the appropriate
organizational arrangements and climate, but they introduced significant
changes in the fourth years of their programmes when they decided to use
their normal methods of rewarding desired behaviours and punishing deviations in order to make TQM stick. In the US company, the widely publicized
dismissal of a top corporate manager who resisted the prescribed techniques
was seen by managers in Britain as an important symbolic act that would
encourage the others to conform. These developments extended the assimilation of improvement into the everyday fabric of these organizations. The
automotive company remained less concerned than the others to monitor
the process and was more interested in quality improvement results, but
managers were quite clear that delivering improvements would be rewarded
in terms of their careers. In sum, managers came to understand over time,
as the result of their experience of using quality management procedures
and the actions of their bosses, that TQM directly affected their own interests: it helped them to manage more effectively, it increased their own
participation, and it carried both positive and negative sanctions. One may
conclude with the simple proposition that top management will increase the
likelihood of a successful outcome to planned organizational change, in this
case the cultural shift required by quality management, when it finds ways to
align this with the self-interest of individual managers.

  While there is firm evidence of the tangible business benefits of TQM and
clear indications that cultural change within management was under way, it
is not possible to be so definite about cultural change among shop-floor and
office employees. Anthropologists and ethnographers define culture as
comprising standardized and patterned behaviours as well as mental constructs such as values, beliefs, attitudes and assumptions (Singer, 1968),
although organizational theorists have placed greater emphasis on the latter
than the former. Taking the attitudinal element, there is some indication
that people identify with elements of the TQM culture, but the quality of
this evidence is unclear. However, as previous research has shown that rank-
and-file employees in Britain value the more 'egalitarian' style of managing
and the opportunities that Japanese management systems provide for high-
quality work and rekindling the work ethic (White and Trevor, 1983), a
positive evaluation of TQM by people in the present study would not be
unexpected. Wilkinson *et al.* (1991) also report favourable employee responses to TQM in two companies that have recently implemented quality
management. The behavioural evidence is firmer, and by their actions many
employees show that quality management has been internalized and is
becoming a normal way of working. The effects of the other changes that
preceded the formal adoption of TQM, such as the upwards harmonization

of terms and conditions of employment and new production concepts, should not be regarded as confusing the issue, because such developments are treated within TQM theory as components of quality management. Thus there is some support for a second proposition, that people at the bottom of company hierarchies are receptive to TQM culture; although to establish whether this holds good, and how widely and under what conditions, requires further research on attitudes and perceptions.

These firms have maintained participation at the base of their organizations beyond the point in the cycle of control and legitimation where one might have expected it to be dropped; nor is it a sham. My own observations of work tasks and improvement teams in action, together with the perceptions of workers, stewards and supervisors, indicate that rank-and-file employees have become more involved in issues that were previously the prerogative of management. The examples of a quality improvement team taking charge of a plant relocation and of work-group autonomy are the most dramatic illustrations, but the routine use of improvement teams and the enlargement of jobs confirms the picture. This is not to be starry-eyed about the nature of participation at this level. In the main, it has been confined to issues related to work tasks and work organization at the point of production. The area of autonomous decision-making varies from case to case and has been most extensive where group working concepts are implemented. Where solutions to problems involve financial expenditure or have repercussions elsewhere in the organization, it is common for labour to propose while management makes the decision. Nevertheless, rank-and-file employees do have more say than before, so TQM meets at least part of their aspirations for more participation.

Finally, there are sound theoretical reasons for believing that top management now has a real interest in making participation work at all levels. These relate to other changes in organizations over the last few years and give enhanced participation a basis in the material conditions of production rather than just as an ideological prop of management. Quality circles were introduced within conventional organizational structures that combined bureaucratic and Taylorist principles. Despite their demise as the result of the failure of companies to find appropriate mechanisms of integration, some of them showed briefly that participation could deliver efficiency gains, even in conventional firms, by accessing the local knowledge of those doing a particular job. The TQM firms, however, were trying to change on a broad front and were using quality management as a method of tying together the components of change and as a model of the desired end state. In common with many American and British organizations, they had delayered and destaffed their lower and middle management in order to reduce costs, while at the same time looking for a more rapid and effective response to the contemporary product market requirements of variety, change and quality. Delayering management promotes some decentralization of decision-making and an enlargement of jobs that affects roles at and near the bottom of companies. Rapid response puts a new premium on internal flexibility and better horizontal co-ordination, which gives an additional impetus to wider roles at each hierarchical level as people collaborate across the organization rather than push issues upwards, shifting from mechanistic towards more organic ways of working. TQM provides a workable method of handling such changes, and it must be viewed as an influential and effective paradigm for flexible organizations (Hill, 1991).

It is therefore obvious that the strategy of changing organizations from below by means of quality circles was bound to fail. The belief that change would convect upwards ignored the realities of organizational power and inertia and underestimated the difficulty of transforming companies in a 'quality' direction. The unwillingness of top managers to deal with the issue of organizational design by creating appropriate systems and structures and attaching positive and negative sanctions – in other words, their refusal to manage change – reduced what little chance quality circles may have had. Even TQM, which is massively resourced, driven from the top and works with the grain of management, is liable to falter without the additional reinforcement of organizational controls. The difference now is that the people who rule corporations appear far more determined to succeed with this latest development than they ever were in the past.

References

Hill, S. (1991) 'How do you manage a flexible firm? The total quality model'. *Work, Employment and Society*, vol. 5, pp. 397–415.

White, M. and Trevor, M. (1983) *Under Japanese Management*. London: Heinemann Educational.

Wilkinson, A., Allen, P., and Snape, E. (1991) 'TQM and the management of labour'. *Employee Relations*, vol. 13, pp. 24–31.

Excessive commitment and excessive resentment: issues of identity

H. HÖPFL *et al.*

The last ten years have seen a proliferation of literature on the subject of organizational culture. Much of the writing within the management perspective has regarded organizational culture as a variable to be manipulated and managed to strategic ends. Corporate culture change has been viewed as a means of improving corporate performance by securing greater employee commitment and identification with corporate values. According to Willmott,

Abridged excerpts reproduced with permission from Höpfl, H. *et al.* (1992) Values and Valuations: The Conflicts between Culture Change and Job Cuts. *Personnel Review*, 21, 24–5 and 30–6. © MCB University Press.

theorists have either regarded culture as a critical variable to be manipulated to improve performance or as a 'root metaphor' to describe and explain social phenomena in organizations and there has been a consequent absence of critical analysis in the literature. Schein's cultural model is a case in point. This has been particularly influential in offering both a definition of culture and suggestions for a diagnostic approach to the study of organizational culture. Schein defines culture as the 'basic assumptions and beliefs that are shared by members of an organization', a definition which in various formulations appears in innumerable accounts and studies of organizational culture. Bate argues that a 'key feature of culture is that it is shared – it refers to ideas, meanings and values people hold in common'. Sathe contends that,

> People feel a sense of commitment to an organization's objectives when they identify with those objectives and experience some emotional attachment to them. The shared beliefs and values that compose culture help generate such identification and attachment.

The notion of shared beliefs and values is regarded as unproblematic. This [article] addresses the simplification at the heart of assumptions of shared meaning and of the managerial prerogative to undertake 'the management of meaning'. Consequently, whether regarded as a root metaphor, a functional variable or as an instrument of increased management control, the study of culture and corporate values requires further empirical examination.

Linstead and Grafton Small argue that corporate culture 'is the term used for a culture devised by management and transmitted, marketed, sold or imposed on the rest of the organisation', that it has an internal and external image and that it 'includes actions and belief – the rites, rituals, stories, values which are offered to organisational members as part of the seductive process of achieving membership and gaining commitment'. This definition of corporate culture provides a valuable starting point because it is rooted in managerial assumptions regarding entitlement to manipulate the social aspects of work or as Willmot puts it, 'by enabling employees to derive a sense of meaning and purpose from using their discretion to put corporate values into practice . . . non-rational aspects of organisation . . . can be colonised by management'. In these views of corporate culture, commitment to the organization is increased as the individual's sense of identity is brought into line with the values of the corporate culture. Whether from a theoretical standpoint or as the basis of managerial action, what needs to be challenged is the 'naive preoccupation with shared values as a route to organisational success'.

Undoubtedly, organizational cultures will affect individuals and their construction of reality but propositions regarding the power of organizations to manage the construction of meaning require more careful analysis.

Changing culture: The BT experience

During 1984, the Telecommunications Act not only provided for the privatisation of British Telecom, but ended its exclusive privilege of providing telecommunications systems within the UK. This was a fundamental change in the way in which the business, then under the Chairmanship of Sir George Jefferson, operated. The business had to become responsive to market forces, as it was now answerable to the market analysts and shareholders.

This resulted in an organizational change to make 27 District General Managers responsible for their own budgets and performance. The districts were semi-autonomous profit centres, an effort to move away from civil service bureaucracy. However, experience showed that there were some fundamental problems with this approach.

In 1989 a project examined British Telecom's ability to meet customer needs, and found:

- A company organized around geography – not customers
- Up to six layers of general managers
- Up to 12 layers of management
- A lack of focus – no one person in charge; different priorities in different districts.

From these findings, a plan was formulated to focus the organization on the customer's needs. Called Project Sovereign, it was launched in April 1990, and meant a major change in structure which the Chairman said would provide a framework for a complete culture change.

The structure of the organization was changed to widen spans of control, and reduce the layers of management to no more than six, which meant that 6,000 management jobs disappeared. The planned reduction in numbers was limited to managerial grades, although as recruitment was frozen, staff numbers throughout the business fell through natural wastage.

The Management Early Release Scheme (MERS) was voluntary, although targeted either at managers in their 40s or over, or those whose jobs disappeared under the new organization. Generally, managers who requested release were allowed to go, and those who wanted to stay were allowed to do so. However, of those targeted, few stayed. Many managers within BT are on personal contracts which run for a year, and it was realized that these contracts could be terminated at their end, resulting in redundancy without the favourable terms and conditions that MERS offered.

Project Sovereign announced the top layers of management in the new organization first. These managers were then able to select their own teams, and were given a great deal of autonomy to do so. Once chosen, this next tier of management was announced, and the process repeated. This was in itself a huge change from the way BT operated prior to privatization, when job vacancies were filled by those 'in line', and managers usually had no choice over their staff.

This process created a great deal of uncertainty among the lower levels of management, many of whom were left uninformed, and consequently insecure, for a long time. It undoubtedly created opportunities and promotions for some, but many were either left with no job or were placed in a post with which they were unfamiliar – which they did not want.

Certainly, six months into Sovereign, morale was low throughout the organization. At the Chairman's Conference in November 1990, Iain Vallance acknowledged that it was 'hard going', and that BT staff were concerned that 'people values' had been abandoned. He stated that the way to deal with the problems would be by returning to the basics of Total Quality. Since 1986, BT has been committed to Total Quality Management (TQM) as the way of achieving its 'Vision' of being the world's top tele-communications agency.

Vallance simplified BT's values into five easily remembered one-liners:

- We put our customers first
- We are professional
- We respect each other
- We work as one team
- We are committed to continous improvement.

These were the espoused values of the new culture that the chairman wanted to create.

On 1 April 1991, the new organization came into being; at the same time the new corporate identity was launched. The name was changed to BT and a new logo was introduced, representing two human figures, one listening, one speaking, brought together by BT's technology and understanding of customers needs.

Now, nearly two years after Sovereign was first announced, BT is reaching a period of stability. Change has not stopped, but the pace has slowed a little. Morale has improved from a year and a half ago, especially among the managers, and is noticeably better among more senior managers than the first line managers. There are several reasons for this.

Managers understand that 'putting the customer first' is the path for BT, like many other businesses, to follow. As a large organization, it has too many overheads to be able to compete solely on price – the service element is crucial. It was generally accepted, even by those who have left the company, that BT was too 'top heavy', over-managed, and that 'releasing' so many managers was necessary for survival. They are also aware that those managers who did leave were treated well. The terms and conditions of MERS were extremely favourable, people were given assistance from outplacement agencies, and most could choose their leaving date.

There is performance-related pay for all managerial grades, and there are substantial bonuses for achievement against objectives. Much bureaucracy has been removed, and managers now have more discretion over their areas of responsibility. Greater management autonomy over team selection has made team members feel more valued. Total Quality Management has initiated an improved communications programme with mandatory monthly team meetings and one to one meetings with the next level of management.

So morale has improved. The question of whether or not culture change has been achieved needs to be addressed.

There are some external signs that BT is becoming more customer-oriented. Language provides one example. Within BT the term 'subs' was used for subscribers, a term now rarely heard. Customers are now referred to as 'customers'. The value of putting customers first is repeated and talked about, but not questioned. For many it is not a deep-seated belief.

Another change is in the way in which BT undertakes selection. Formerly, managers were promoted from within. Career progression was slow, but fairly predictable. BT now recruits a proportion of its managers externally. The chairman, when talking of systems and processes in his November 1990 speech cautioned 'wherever we can, we should look externally and avoid the BT habit of entirely reinventing the wheel'. This is generally felt to be a desirable change within the company.

The influx of 'new blood' has had the effect of 'rounding out' teams and committees. Styles of working in the organization tended to be bureaucratic, and the new staff have had the effect of bringing the full set of characteristics needed to make effective teams. They have also had a positive effect on morale to some extent by introducing a 'good' external perspective of the organization. This has lead to some healthy debate. They also praise the staff canteens, pay, social and welfare facilities, which within the organization are often taken for granted.

The 'down' side of this policy is that there are now managers who have made a career move to BT to gain experience, who expect to move on after a few years. This means losing the type of long-term commitment at senior level, which people who have worked their way up through the company can give. Corporate values are in this sense societal values. They are reflected in the language, in working arrangements and styles, but they are contextual rather than an intrinsic part of culture. To this extent values are arguably contingent on the business environment, liable to change over time.

Many BT staff no longer have the belief that they are 'stamped BT to the core', as one manager put it. This is perhaps an indication of a 'healthier' relationship between the employee and the organization.

In BT, all the major changes in the organization have been directed at the management. Starting in 1986 TQM was directed mainly at managers. Senior managers attended a one week workshop, and all managers had a three-way workshop. Clerical and engineering people had at most a half day appreciation.

Other programmes for managers are the leadership programme, manager as leader and coach, and customer calling programme. Managers were the group affected by the Sovereign changes the most, with the work of clerical and engineering grades mainly unchanged, although often with a different management hierarchy.

In November 1991, a programme called Involving Everyone was launched, and will be extended to all BT's staff within 12 months. One thousand people a day will attend one of the 30 or so Event Centres around the country: a complex logistics exercise. The programme starts at the Event Centre, with exercises that communicate BT's mission and vision, the importance of Total Quality and teamwork. However, much of the work is designed to continue through the medium of team meetings – already in place. The emphasis is on teamwork, the recognition of internal as well as external customers, and the drive for continual improvement. It is hoped that this will provide the mechanism to get Total Quality into the 'bloodstream' of the company.

The programme relies on the managers to lead their people through, and potentially it will have a greater effect on the culture of BT than any initiative so far. Again, quoting from the chairman's 1990 speech '. . . we should (not) underestimate the hunger to be involved which exists out there . . . the potential strength of involving every single one of our employees'.

Most efforts of culture change have been directed only at part of BT – the part that senior managers perceived need it most, that is, the management of the organization.

Commitment and self-perception

The level of intervention on which corporate culture operates is inadequate to sustain radical change in the individual. On the contrary, it tends to offer meanings and reality definitions which have only situational validity. On this level, the notion of shared corporate values accords with other performance motivated techniques, behaviours and practices. The assumption that culture can be manipulated is a theoretical simplification which requires closer scrutiny. In any interaction there is always more difference than similarity in the perception and interpretation of events. Given this and the implicit contradiction in the notion of management development it is arguable that culture change programmes have promoted debate, scepticism, evaluation of corporate meaning versus personal meanings, challenged espoused values and had the effect of raising issues which had previously been taken for granted. Against the promotion of corporate values and ideals individuals have been able to explore antithetical views of work and role and personal meanings, to examine the relationship between their work behaviour and their subjective experiences. Such processes are inevitably painful and employees may vacillate between excessive commitment, where the company appears to offer the only source of meaning, to excessive resentment, where the company is perceived to be the source of all disjunct experience. Yet these experiences are common everyday experiences which are not specific to the world of work but part of the human condition. The real seduction which corporate bodies hold is an implicit notion of their own immortality of a metaphysical and transcendent reality which exists and endures beyond the membership of the individuals of which they are, at any one time, made up. Corporate survival and meanings, therefore, become confused with individual meanings and the awareness of mortality. Frenetic activity postpones the moment of realization in which individual meaning is confronted. Culture change programmes and, indeed, change programmes in general, initiate the radical reflections by which issues of identity are confronted.

Finally, the question of how individuals react to redundancy in organizations which have undergone major culture change provides some interesting insights. It appears from the work that has been going on [in BT] that employees who are leaving the companies do not feel that the companies have reneged on a 'values contract'. They do not relate their experiences to a fundamental hypocrisy in espoused values. Many have a powerfully realistic perception of the culture change, its purposes and outcomes, as being performance aspects of the business. Obviously, personal experience is likely to be different. Those leaving the organization may experience bitterness and, initially, a sense of betrayal, may lose a sense of their own worth and the integrating meaning structures which are associated with work and identity. Away from the purposive and directional activities of the organization they are re-confronted by their own mortality. In short, culture change progarammes have opened up the distinction between management development as a motivational technique and management development as development of the person and, in doing so, have put on the corporate agenda experiential discontinuities between appearance and subjective experience; between apparently shared meanings and 'espoused' values and personal meanings, individual values. The debate has now been taking place for a number of years and demonstrates widely different perceptions of companies, their objectives and values. It has fostered a more balanced style of management, a more realistic attitude to commitment, a more critical perspective, a healthier appreciation of the individual's psychological contract of work and a greater awareness of the performance aspects of work. All in all, this presents interesting challenges for management development in the 1990s.

References

Ackroyd, S. and Crowdy, P. (1989) 'Can Culture Be Managed? Working with "Raw" Material: The Case of the English Slaughtermen', *Personnel Review*, vol. 19, no. 5, pp. 3–13.

Anthony, P.D. (1989) 'The Paradox of the Management of Culture or "He Who Leads Is Lost" ', *Personnel Review*, vol. 19, no. 4, pp. 3–8.

Bate, P. (1984) 'The Impact of Organizational Culture on Approaches to Organizational Problem Solving', *Organization Studies*, vol. 5, no. 1, pp. 43–66.

Derr, C.B. and Laurent, A. (1989) 'The Internal and External Career: A Theoretical and Cross-cultural Perspective', in Arthur, M.B., Hall, D.T., and Lawrence, B.S. (eds), *Handbook of Career Theory*, Cambridge University Press, Cambridge.

Höpfl, H.J. (1991) 'The "Corpse" in the Deconstruction of Culture: Some Observations on Dissonant Experience and Its Treatment in Organisational Life', paper presented to the SCOS Conference, Copenhagen, June.

Kirkbride, P.S. (1987) 'Personnel Management and Organisational Culture: A Case of Deviant Innovation?', *Personnel Review*, vol. 16, no. 1, pp. 3–9.

Lawrence, G. (1985) 'Management Development – Some Ideals, Images and Realities', in Colman, A.D. and Geller, M.H. (eds), *Group Relations Reader 2*, A.K. Rice Institute, Washington, DC.

Linstead, S.L. and Grafton Small, R.G. (1991) 'On Reading Organizational Culture', *Organization Studies*, vol. 13, no. 3.

Pascale, R. (1985) 'The Paradox of "Corporate Culture": Reconciling Ourselves to Socialization', *California Management Review*, vol. XXVII, no. 2, pp. 26–41.

Sathe, V. (1983) 'Implications of Corporate Culture: A Manager's Guide to Action', *Organizational Dynamics*, Autumn.

Schein, E.H. (1984) 'Coming to a New Awareness of Organizational Culture', *Sloan Management Review*, Winter.

— (1985) *Organizational Culture and Leadership: A Dynamic View*, Jossey-Bass, San Francisco, CA.

Sievers, B. (1986) 'Beyond the Surrogate of Motivation', *Organization Studies*, vol. 7, no. 4, pp. 335–51.

— (1990) 'The Diabolization of Death: Some Thoughts on the Obsolescence of Mortality in Organization Theory and Practice', in Hassard, J. and Pym, D. (eds), *The Theory and Philosophy of Organizations, Critical Issues and Perspectives*, Routledge, London.

— (1990) 'Zombies or People – What Is the Product of Work? Some Considerations about the Relation between Human and Non-human Systems in Regard to the Sociotechnical-Systems Paradigm', in Turner, B. (ed.), *Organizational Symbolism*, Walter de Gruyter, Berlin.

Smircich, L. and Morgan, G. (1982) 'Leadership: The Management of Meaning', *Journal of Applied Behavioral Science*, vol. 18, no. 3, pp. 257–73.

Smith, P.B. and Peterson, M.F. (1988) *Leadership, Organizations and Culture*, Sage, London.

Willmott, H. (1991) 'Strength Is Ignorance: Slavery Is Freedom: Managing Culture in Modern Organizations', paper presented at the SCOS Conference, Copenhagen, June.

Further reading

Rose, N. (1989) *Governing the Soul: The shaping of the private self*, Routledge, Chapter 10. (see also further reading for Chapters 2 and 3.)

Binns, D. (1993) *Total Quality Management, Organisation Theory and the New Right: A Contribution to the critique of Bureaucratic Totalitarianism*, University of East London Occasional Papers on Business, Economy and Society, Paper No. 11.

Issues for discussion

1. How successful are strategies involving a) corporate culture and b) Total Quality Management likely to prove as a control device?
   Readings: all in Chapter 5
2. Examine connections between organisational culture and quality.
   Readings: all in Chapter 5
3. Examine the implications for organisational identities of a) corporate culture and b) Total Quality Management.
   Readings: Whyte (Chapter 2)
              Kanter (Chapter 2)
              all readings Chapter 5, particularly Höpfl

6

Alienation and stress

It has become commonplace in the literature on organisations and behaviour at work to see alienation as one of the major consequences of the adoption of classical management theories and techniques. The implications of this are drawn out by Braverman in the first reading in this chapter, the attrition of craft knowledge and autonomy leading to dehumanisation and degradation – to alienation.

For Marx alienation was firmly rooted in the economic system of industrial capitalism which prevented workers from realising their true identities as creative beings. The loss of self, of identity and of freedom, is documented in the reading from Marx and expanded in the reading by Fromm.

Alienation can be termed an 'essentially contested' concept in that it has often been used by a number of different social scientists to help explain aspects of the human condition. In the reading which follows Fromm, Wright Mills explores aspects of alienation, and the threats it poses to reason and freedom.

In pointing to alienation as one of the consequences of historically specific social relationships, social scientists have helped to distinguish between private troubles and public issues, a guiding principle in the work of Wright Mills. If you are the only unemployed person among a working population of many millions he argues, then you will experience the trouble privately, alone, whereas if you are part of an army of unemployed workers the issue becomes public and solutions of a social structural kind explored.

So too with stress, a topic currently enjoying something approaching vogue status among psychologists as a private trouble to be assessed and addressed individually through such interventionary practices as one-to-one counselling. But what if stress, like unemployment, were to be recognised as a public issue, connected closely to social structural relationships?

The reading from Selye introduces stress in medical terms, recounting what he calls the general adaptation syndrome. This is followed by a reading from Eyer and Sterling which focuses on causes and consequences for people at work whose identities come under strain through stress-related pressures. Eyer and Sterling use data from America to locate stress in a specific historical context as the product of the vagaries and relentless pressures of capitalism. The bodily insults deriving from the internal and external dictates of production are documented all too painfully in this reading, which outlines the harrowing consequences of such contemporary work features as unemployment and flexibility in the competitive drive for profit.

Corporate reaction to the outward manifestations of stress in the workplace has been slow but steady as businesses wake up to the spiralling costs of health-care insurance and litigation. The reading from Cooper provides some illuminating case material from American courts to show how the recent interest in corporate health derives more from enlightened self-interest than any clear sense of altruism.

The final reading from Clark pulls this chapter together, linking private troubles to public issues and calling for a sociological analysis of stress rooted in the historical structures of patriarchy, alienation and anomie. The reading demonstrates how identities – in this case gender – interact with other elements of the social structure to produce differing experiences of stress. Patriarchy, in essence the control and domination of women by men, is highlighted as a feature of relationships at work interacting with other aspects of work relations to produce heightened effects of stress for women.

On this count the very structure of social relationships and organised life itself create, mould, influence and adversely affect vulnerable if tenacious identities. This indicates all the more need for investigation of historically constituted forms of organisation and identity, through analysis of social structure. This is a fitting end to the chapter and the book as a whole.

The degradation of work

H. BRAVERMAN

The separation of mental work from manual work reduces, at any given level of production, the need for workers engaged directly in production, since it divests them of time-consuming mental functions and assigns these functions elsewhere. This is true regardless of any increase in productivity resulting from the separation. Should productivity increase as well, the need for manual workers to produce a given output is further reduced.

A necessary consequence of the separation of conception and execution is that the labor process is now divided between separate sites and separate bodies of workers. In one location, the physical processes of production are executed. In another are concentrated the design, planning, calculation, and record-keeping. The preconception of the process before it is set in motion, the visualization of each worker's activities before they have actually begun, the definition of each function along with the manner of its performance and the time it will consume, the control and checking of the ongoing process once it is under way, and the assessment of results upon completion of each stage of the process – all of these aspects of production have been removed from the shop floor to the management office. The physical processes of production are now carried out more or less blindly, not only by the workers who perform them, but often by lower ranks of supervisory employees as well. The production units operate like a hand, watched, corrected, and controlled by a distant brain.

The concept of control adopted by modern management requires that every activity in production has its several parallel activities in the management center: each must be devised, precalculated, tested, laid out, assigned and ordered, checked and inspected, and recorded throughout its duration and upon completion. The result is that the process of production is replicated in paper form before, as, and after it takes place in physical form. Just as labor in human beings requires that the labor process take place in the brain of the worker as well as in the worker's physical activity, so now the image of the process, removed from production to a separate location and a separate group, controls the process itself. The novelty of this development during the past century lies not in the separate existence of hand and brain, conception and execution, but the rigor with which they are divided from one another, and then increasingly subdivided, so that conception is concentrated, insofar as possible, in ever more limited groups within management or closely associated with it. Thus, in the setting of antagonistic social relations, of alienated labor, hand and brain become not just separated, but divided and hostile, and the human unity of hand and brain turns into its opposite, something less than human.

This paper replica of production, the shadow form which corresponds to the physical, calls into existence a variety of new occupations, the hallmark of which is that they are found not in the flow of things but in the flow of paper. Production has now been split in two and depends upon the activities of both groups. Inasmuch as the mode of production has been driven by capitalism to this divided condition, it has separated the two aspects of labor; **but both remain necessary to production, and in this the labor process retains its unity**.

The separation of hand and brain is the most decisive single step in the division of labor taken by the capitalist mode of production. It is inherent in that mode of production from its beginnings, and it develops, under capitalist management, throughout the history of capitalism, but it is only during the past century that the scale of production, the resources made available to the modern corporation by the rapid accumulation of capital, and the conceptual apparatus and trained personnel have become available to institutionalize this separation in a systematic and formal fashion.

The destruction of craftsmanship during the period of the rise of scientific management did not go unnoticed by workers. Indeed, as a rule workers are far more conscious of such a loss while it is being effected than after it has taken place and the new conditions of production have become generalized. Taylorism raised a storm of opposition among the trade unions during the early part of this century; what is most noteworthy about this early opposition is that it was concentrated not upon the trappings of the Taylor system, such as the stopwatch and motion study, but upon its essential effort to strip the workers of craft knowledge and autonomous control and confront them with a fully thought-out labor process in which they function as cogs and levers. In an editorial which appeared in the *International Molders Journal*, we read:

> The one great asset of the wage worker has been his craftsmanship. We think of craftsmanship ordinarily as the ability to manipulate skillfully the tools and materials of a craft or trade. But true craftsmanship is much more than this. The really essential element in it is not manual skill and dexterity but something stored up in the mind of the worker. This something is partly the intimate knowledge of the character and uses of the tools, materials and processes of the craft which tradition and experience have given the worker. But beyond this and above this, it is the knowledge which enables him to understand and overcome the constantly arising difficulties that grow out of variations not only in the tools and materials, but in the conditions under which the work must be done.

The editorial goes on to point to the separation of 'craft knowledge' from 'craft skill' in 'an ever-widening area and with an ever-increasing acceleration," and describes as the most dangerous form of this separation the gathering up of all this scattered craft knowledge, systematizing it and concentrating it in the hands of the employer and then doling it out again only in the form of minute instructions, giving to each worker only the knowledge needed for the performance of a particular relatively minute task. This process, it is evident, separates skill and knowledge even in their narrow relationship. When it is completed, the worker is no longer a craftsman in any sense, but is an animated tool of the management.

A half-century of commentary on scientific management has not succeeded in producing a better formulation of the matter.

Reference

Hoxie, R.F. (1918) *Scientific Management and Labour*, New York and London.

Alienated labour

K. MARX

The worker becomes poorer the more wealth he produces, the more his production increases in power and extent. The worker becomes an ever cheaper commodity the more commodities he produces. The **devaluation** of the human world grows in direct proportion to the **increase in value** of the world of things. Labour not only produces commodities; it also produces itself and the workers as a **commodity** and it does so in the same proportion in which it produces commodities in general.

This fact simply means that the object that labour produces, its product, stands opposed to it as **something alien**, as a **power independent** of the producer. The product of labour is labour embodied and made material in an object, it is the **objectification** of labour. The realization of labour is its objectification. In the sphere of political economy this realization of labour appears as a **loss of reality** for the worker, objectification as **loss of and bondage to the object**, and appropriation as **estrangement**, as **alienation**.

So much does the realization of labour appear as loss of reality that the worker loses his reality to the point of dying of starvation. So much does objectification appear as loss of the object that the worker is robbed of the objects he needs most not only for life but also for work. Work itself becomes an object which he can only obtain through an enormous effort and with spasmodic interruptions. So much does the appropriation of the object

Abridged excerpts reproduced with permission from Marx, K. *Economic and Philosophic Manuscripts*, pp. 323–4 and 326–32; published by Lawrence and Wishart, London, 1975.

appear as estrangement that the more objects the worker produces the fewer can he possess and the more he falls under the domination of his product, of capital.

All these consequences are contained in this characteristic, that the worker is related to the **product of his labour** as to an **alien** object. For it is clear that, according to this premise, the more the worker exerts himself in his work, the more powerful the alien, objective world becomes which he brings into being over against himself, the poorer he and his inner world become, and the less they belong to him. It is the same in religion. The more man puts into God, the less he retains within himself. The worker places his life in the object; but now it no longer belongs to him, but to the object. The greater his activity, therefore, the fewer objects the worker possesses. What the product of his labour is, he is not. Therefore, the greater this product, the less is he himself. The externalization [*Entäusserung*] of the worker in his product means not only that his labour becomes an object, an **external** existence, but that it exists **outside him**, independently of him and alien to him, and begins to confront him as an autonomous power; that the life which he has bestowed on the object confronts him as hostile and alien.

Up to now we have considered the estrangement, the alienation of the worker only from one aspect; i.e. his **relationship to the products of his labour**. But estrangement manifests itself not only in the result, but also in the **act of production**, within the **activity of production** itself.

The estrangement of the object of labour merely summarizes the estrangement, the alienation in the activity of labour itself.

What constitutes the alienation of labour?

Firstly, the fact that labour is **external** to the worker, i.e. does not belong to his essential being; that he therefore does not confirm himself in his work, but denies himself, feels miserable and not happy, does not develop free mental and physical energy, but mortifies his flesh and ruins his mind. Hence the worker feels himself only when he is not working; when he is working he does not feel himself. He is at home when he is not working, and not at home when he is working. His labour is therefore not voluntary but forced, it is **forced labour**. It is therefore not the satisfaction of a need but a mere **means** to satisfy needs outside itself. Its alien character is clearly demonstrated by the fact that as soon as no physical or other compulsion exists it is shunned like the plague. External labour, labour in which man alienates himself, is a labour of self-sacrifice, of mortification. Finally, the external character of labour for the worker is demonstrated by the fact that it belongs not to him but to another, and that in it he belongs not to himself but to another. Just as in religion the spontaneous activity of the human imagination, the human brain and the human heart detaches itself from the individual and reappears as the alien activity of a god or of a devil, so the activity of the worker is not his own spontaneous activity. It belongs to another, it is a loss of his self.

The result is that man (the worker) feels that he is acting freely only in his animal functions – eating, drinking and procreating, or at most in his dwelling and adornment – while in his human functions he is nothing more than an animal.

It is true that eating, drinking and procreating, etc., are also genuine human functions. However, when abstracted from other aspects of human activity and turned into final and exclusive ends, they are animal.

We have considered the act of estrangement of practical human activity, of labour, from two aspects: (1) the relationship of the worker to the **product of labour** as an alien object that has power over him. This relationship is at the same time the relationship to the sensuous external world, to natural objects, as an alien world confronting him in hostile opposition. (2) The relationship of labour to the **act of production** within **labour**. This relationship is the relationship of the worker to his own activity as something which is alien and does not belong to him, activity as passivity, power as impotence, procreation as emasculation, the worker's **own** physical and mental energy, his personal life – for what is life but activity? – as an activity directed against himself, which is independent of him and does not belong to him. **Self estrangement**, as compared with the estrangement of the **object** mentioned above.

We now have to derive a third feature of **estranged labour** from the two we have already looked at.

Man is a species-being, not only because he practically and theoretically makes the species – both his own and those of other things – his object, but also – and this is simply another way of saying the same thing – because he looks upon himself as the present, living species, because he looks upon himself as a **universal** and therefore free being.

Species-life, both for man and for animals, consists physically in the fact that man, like animals, lives from inorganic nature; and because man is more universal than animals, so too is the area of inorganic nature from which he lives more universal. Just as plants, animals, stones, air, light, etc., theoretically form a part of human consciousness, partly as objects of science and partly as objects of art – his spiritual inorganic nature, his spiritual means of life, which he must first prepare before he can enjoy and digest them – so too in practice they form a part of human life and human activity.

Estranged labour not only (1) estranges nature from man and (2) estranges man from himself, from his own active function, from his vital activity; because of this it also estranges man from his **species**. It turns his **species-life** into a means for his individual life. Firstly it estranges species-life and individual life, and secondly it turns the latter, in its abstract form, into the purpose of the former, also in its abstract and estranged form.

For in the first place labour, **life activity**, **productive life** itself appears to man only as a **means** for the satisfaction of a need, the need to preserve physical existence. But productive life is species-life. It is life-producing life. The whole character of a species, its species-character, resides in the nature of its life activity, and free conscious activity constitutes the species-character of man. Life itself appears only as a **means of life**.

The animal is immediately one with its life activity. It is not distinct from that activity; it is that activity. Man makes his life activity itself an object of his will and consciousness. He has conscious life activity. It is not a determination with which he directly merges. Conscious life activity directly distinguishes man from animal life activity. Only because of that is he a species-being. Or rather, he is a conscious being, i.e. his own life is an object for him, only because he is a species-being. Only because of that is his activity free activity. Estranged labour reverses the relationship so that man, just because he is a conscious being, makes his life activity, his **being**, a mere means for his **existence**.

The practical creation of an **objective world**, the **fashioning** of inorganic nature, is proof that man is a conscious species-being, i.e. a being which treats the species as its own essential being or itself as a species-being. It is true that animals also produce. They build nests and dwellings, like the bee, the beaver, the ant, etc. But they produce only their own immediate needs or those of their young; they produce one-sidedly, while man produces universally; they produce only when immediate physical need compels them to do so, while man produces even when he is free from physical need and truly produces only in freedom from such need; they produce only themselves, while man reproduces the whole of nature; their products belong immediately to their physical bodies, while man freely confronts his own product.

Consciousness, which man has from his species, is transformed through estrangement so that species-life becomes a means for him.

(3) Estranged labour therefore turns **man's species-being** – both nature and his intellectual species-powers – into a being **alien** to him and a **means** or his **individual existence**. It estranges man from his own body, from nature as it exists outside him, from his spiritual essence, his **human** essence.

(4) An immediate consequence of man's estrangement from the product of his labour, his life activity, his species-being, is the **estrangement of man from man**. When man confronts himself, he also confronts **other** men. What is true of man's relationship to his labour, to the product of his labour and to himself, is also true of his relationship to other men, and to the labour and the object of the labour of other men.

In general, the proposition that man is estranged from his species-being means that each man is estranged from the others and that all are estranged from man's essence.

Man's estrangement, like all relationships of man to himself, is realized and expressed only in man's relationship to other men.

In the relationship of estranged labour each man therefore regards the other in accordance with the standard and the situation in which he as a worker finds himself.

The **alien** being to whom labour and the product of labour belong, in whose service labour is performed and for whose enjoyment the product of labour is created, can be none other than **man** himself.

If the product of labour does not belong to the worker, and if it confronts him as an alien power, this is only possible because it belongs to **a man other** than the worker. If his activity is a torment for him, it must provide **pleasure** and enjoyment for someone else. Not the gods, not nature, but only man himself can be this alien power over men.

Consider the above proposition that the relationship of man to himself becomes **objective** and **real** for him only through his relationship to other men. If therefore he regards the product of his labour, his objectified labour, as an **alien, hostile** and powerful object which is independent of him, then his relationship to that object is such that another man – alien, hostile, powerful and independent of him – is its master. If he relates to his own activity as unfree activity, then he relates to it as activity in the service, under the rule, coercion and yoke of another man.

Thus through **estranged, alienated labour** the worker creates the relationship of another man, who is alien to labour and stands outside it, to that labour. The relation of the worker to labour creates the relation of the capitalist – or whatever other word one chooses for the master of labour – to that labour. **Private property** is therefore the product, result and necessary consequence of **alienated labour**, of the external relation of the worker to nature and to himself.

Private property thus derives from an analysis of the concept of **alienated labour**, i.e. **alienated man**, estranged labour, estranged life, **estranged man**.

An enforced **rise in wages** (disregarding all other difficulties, including the fact that such an anomalous situation could only be prolonged by force) would therefore be nothing more than better **pay for slaves** and would not mean an increase in human significance or dignity for either the worker or the labour.

Alienation

E. FROMM

By alienation is meant a mode of experience in which the person experiences himself as an alien. He has become, one might say, estranged from himself. He does not experience himself as the center of his world, as the creator of his own acts – but his acts and their consequences have become his masters, whom he obeys, or whom he may even worship. The alienated person is out of touch with himself as he is out of touch with any other person. He, like the others, are experienced as things are experienced; with the senses and with common sense, but at the same time without being related to oneself and to the world outside productively.

The older meaning in which 'alienation' was used was to denote an

Abridged excerpts reproduced from Fromm, E. *The Sane Society*, pp. 120–1 and 177–84; published by Routledge & Kegan Paul, London, 1963.

insane person; *aliéné* in French, *alienado* in Spanish are older words for the psychotic, the thoroughly and absolutely alienated person. ('Alienist,' in English, is still used for the doctor who cares for the insane.)

In the last century the word 'alienation' was used by Hegel and Marx, referring not to a state of insanity, but to a less drastic form of self-estrangement, which permits the person to act reasonably in practical matters, yet which constitutes one of the most severe socially patterned defects. In Marx's system alienation is called that condition of man where his 'own act becomes to him an alien power, standing over and against him, instead of being ruled by him.'[1]

What becomes the meaning of **work** in an alienated society?

We have already made some brief comments about this question in the general discussion of alienation. But since this problem is of utmost importance, not only for the understanding of present-day society, but also for any attempt to create a saner society, I want to deal with the nature of work separately and more extensively in the following pages.

Unless man exploits others, he has to work in order to live. However primitive and simple his method of work may be, by the very fact of production, he has risen above the animal kingdom; rightly has he been defined as 'the animal that produces.' But work is not only an inescapable necessity for man. Work is also his liberator from nature, his creator as a social and independent being. **In the process of work, that is, the molding and changing of nature outside of himself, man molds and changes himself.** He emerges from nature by mastering her; he develops his powers of co-operation, of reason, his sense of beauty. He separates himself from nature, from the original unity with her, but at the same time unites himself with her again as her master and builder. The more his work develops, the more his individuality develops. In molding nature and re-creating her, he learns to make use of his powers, increasing his skill and creativeness. Whether we think of the beautiful paintings in the caves of Southern France, the ornaments on weapons among primitive people, the statues and temples of Greece, the cathedrals of the Middle Ages, the chairs and table made by skilled craftsmen, or cultivation of flowers, trees or corn by peasants – all are expressions of the creative transformation of nature by man's reason and skill.

In Western history, craftsmanship, especially as it developed in the thirteenth and fourteenth centuries, constitutes one of the peaks in the evolution of creative work. Work was not only a useful activity, but one which carried with it a profound satisfaction. The main features of craftsmanship have been very lucidly expressed by C.W. Mills. 'There is no ulterior motive in work other than the product being made and the processes of its creation. The details of daily work are meaningful because they are not detached in the worker's mind from the product of the work. The worker is free to

---

[1] K. Marx, *Capital*. cf. also Marx-Engels, *Die Deutsche Ideologie* (1845/6), in K. Marx, *Der Historische Materialismus, Die Frübschriften*, S. Landshut and D.P. Mayer, Leipzig, 1932, II, p. 25.

control his own working action. The craftsman is thus able to learn from his work; and to use and develop his capacities and skills in its prosecution. There is no split of work and play, or work and culture. The craftsman's way of livelihood determines and infuses his entire mode of living.'[2]

With the collapse of the medieval structure, and the beginning of the modern mode of production, the meaning and function of work changed fundamentally, especially in the Protestant countries. Man, being afraid of his newly won freedom, was obsessed by the need to subdue his doubts and fears by developing a feverish activity. The outcome of this activity, success or failure, decided his salvation, indicating whether he was among the saved or the lost souls. **Work, instead of being an activity satisfying in itself and pleasureable, became a duty and an obsession.** The more it was possible to gain riches by work, the more it became a pure means to the aim of wealth and success. Work became, in Max Weber's terms, the chief factor in a system of 'inner-worldly asceticism,' an answer to man's sense of aloneness and isolation.

However, work in this sense existed only for the upper and middle classes, those who could amass some capital and employ the work of others. For the vast majority of those who had only their physical energy to sell, work became nothing but forced labor. The worker in the eighteenth or nineteenth century who had to work sixteen hours if he did not want to starve was not doing it because he served the Lord in this way, nor because his success would show that he was among the 'chosen' ones, but because he was forced to sell his energy to those who had the means of exploiting it. The first centuries of the modern era find the meaning of work divided into that of **duty** among the middle class, and that of **forced labor** among those without property.

The religious attitude toward work as a duty, which was still so prevalent in the nineteenth century, has been changing considerably in the last decades. Modern man does not know what to do with himself, how to spend his lifetime meaningfully, and he is driven to work in order to avoid an unbearable boredom. But work has ceased to be a moral and religious obligation in the sense of the middle-class attitude of the eighteenth and nineteenth centuries. Something new has emerged. Ever-increasing production, the drive to make bigger and better things, have become aims in themselves, new ideals. Work has become alienated from the working person.

What happens to the industrial worker? He spends his best energy for seven or eight hours a day in producing 'something.' He needs his work in order to make a living, but his role is essentially a passive one. He fulfills a small isolated function in a complicated and highly organized process of production, and is never confronted with 'his' product as a whole, at least not as a producer, but only as a consumer, provided he has the money to buy 'his' product in a store. He is concerned neither with the whole product in its physical aspects nor with its wider economic and social aspects. He is

[2] C.W. Mills, *White Collar*, Oxford University Press, New York, 1951, p. 220.

put in a certain place, has to carry out a certain task, but does not participate in the organization or management of the work. He is not interested, nor does he know why one produces this, instead of another commodity – what relation it has to the needs of society as a whole. The shoes, the cars, the electric bulbs, are produced by 'the enterprise,' using the machines. He is a part of the machine, rather than its master as an active agent. The machine, instead of being in his service to do work for him which once had to be performed by sheer physical energy, has become his master. Instead of the machine being the substitute for human energy, man has become a substitute for the machine. **His work can be defined as the performance of acts which cannot yet be performed by machines.**

Work is a means of getting money, not in itself a meaningful human activity. P. Drucker, observing workers in the automobile industry, expresses this idea very succinctly: 'For the great majority of automobile workers, the only meaning of the job is in the pay check, not in anything connected with the work or the product. Work appears as something unnatural, a disagreeable, meaningless and stultifying condition of getting the pay check, devoid of dignity as well as of importance. No wonder that this puts a premium on slovenly work, on slowdowns, and on other tricks to get the same pay check with less work. No wonder that this results in an unhappy and discontented worker – because a pay check is not enough to base one's self-respect on.'[3]

This relationship of the worker to his work is an outcome of the whole social organization of which he is a part. Being 'employed,'[4] he is not an active agent, has no responsibility except the proper performance of the isolated piece of work he is doing, and has little interest except the one of bringing home enough money to support himself and his family. Nothing more is expected of him, or wanted from him. He is part of the equipment hired by capital, and his role and function are determined by this quality of being a piece of equipment. In recent decades, increasing attention has been paid to the psychology of the worker, and to his attitude toward his work, to the 'human problem of industry'; but this very formulation is indicative of the underlying attitude; there is a human being spending most of his lifetime at work, and what should be discussed is the **'industrial problem of human beings,'** rather than **'the human problem of industry.'**

Most investigations in the field of industrial psychology are concerned with the question of how the productivity of the individual worker can be increased, and how he can be made to work with less friction; psychology has lent its services to 'human engineering,' an attempt to treat the worker and employee like a machine which runs better when it is well oiled. While Taylor was primarily concerned with a better organization of the technical use of the worker's physical powers, most industrial psychologists are mainly concerned with the manipulation of the worker's psyche. The underlying

---

[3] cf. Peter F. Drucker, *Concept of the Corporation*, The John Day Company, New York, 1946, p. 179.
[4] The English 'employed' like the German *angestellt* are terms which refer to things rather than to human beings.

idea can be formulated like this: if he works better when he is happy, then let us make him happy, secure, satisfied, or anything else, provided it raises his output and diminishes friction. In the name of 'human relations,' the worker is treated with all devices which suit a completely alienated person; even happiness and human values are recommended in the interest of better relations with the public. Thus, for instance, according to *Time* magazine, one of the best-known American psychiatrists said to a group of fifteen hundred Supermarket executives: 'It's going to be an increased satisfaction to our customers if we are happy . . . It is going to pay off in cold dollars and cents to management, if we could put some of these general principles of values, human relationships, really into practice.' One speaks of 'human relations' and one means the most in-human relations, those between alienated automatons; one speaks of happiness and means the perfect routinization which has driven out the last doubt and all spontaneity.

The alienated and profoundly unsatisfactory character of work results in two reactions: one, the ideal of complete **laziness**; the other a deep-seated, though often unconscious **hostility** toward work and everything and everybody connected with it.

It is not difficult to recognize the widespread longing for the state of complete laziness and passivity. Our advertising appeals to it even more than to sex. There are, of course, many useful and labor saving gadgets. But this usefulness often serves only as a rationalization for the appeal to complete passivity and receptivity. A package of breakfast cereal is being advertised as **'new – easier to eat.'** An electric toaster is advertised with these words: ' . . . the most distinctly different toaster in the world! Everything is done **for** you with this new toaster. You need not even bother to lower the bread. Power-action, though a unique electric motor, **gently takes the bread right out of your fingers!'** How many courses in languages, or other subjects are announced with the slogan 'effortless learning, no more of the old drudgery.' Everybody knows the picture of the elderly couple in the advertisement of a life-insurance company, who have retired at the age of sixty, and spend their life in the complete bliss of having nothing to do except just travel.

Radio and television exhibit another element of this yearning for laziness: the idea of 'push-button power'; by pushing a button, or turning a knob on my machine, I have the power to produce music, speeches, ball games, and on the television set, to command events of the world to appear before my eyes. The pleasure of driving cars certainly rests partly upon this same satisfaction of the wish for push-button power. By the effortless pushing of a button, a powerful machine is set in motion; little skill and effort is needed to make the driver feel that he is the ruler of space.

But there is far more serious and deep-seated reaction to the meaninglessness and boredom of work. It is a hostility toward work which is much less conscious than our craving for laziness and inactivity. Many a businessman feels himself the prisoner of his business and the commodities he sells; he has a feeling of fraudulency about his product and a secret contempt for it.

He hates his customers, who force him to put up a show in order to sell. He hates his competitors because they are a threat; his employees as well as his superiors, because he is in a constant competitive fight with them. Most important of all, he hates himself, because he sees his life passing by, without making any sense beyond the momentary intoxication of success. Of course, this hate and contempt for others and for oneself, and for the very things one produces, is mainly unconscious, and only occasionally comes up to awareness in a fleeting thought, which is sufficiently disturbing to be set aside as quickly as possible.

The cheerful robot

C. WRIGHT MILLS

On reason and freedom

[W]e must now raise the question in an ultimate form: among contemporary men will there come to prevail, or even to flourish, what may be called The Cheerful Robot?

We know of course that man can be turned into a robot, by chemical and psychiatric means, by steady coercion and by controlled environment; but also by random pressures and unplanned sequences of circumstances. But can he be made to want to become a cheerful and willing robot? Can he be happy in this condition, and what are the qualities and the meanings of such happiness? It will no longer do merely to assume, as a metaphysic of human nature, that down deep in man-as-man there is an urge for freedom and a will to reason. Now we must ask: What in man's nature, what in the human condition today, what in each of the varieties of social structure makes for the ascendancy of the cheerful robot? And what stands against it?

The advent of the alienated man and all the themes which lie behind his advent now affect the whole of our serious intellectual life and cause our immediate intellectual malaise. It is a major theme of the human condition in the contemporary epoch and of all studies worthy of the name. I know of no idea, no theme, no problem, that is so deep in the classic tradition – and so much involved in the possible default of contemporary social science.

It is what Karl Marx so brilliantly discerned in his earlier essays on 'alienation'; it is the chief concern of Georg Simmel in his justly famous essay on 'The Metropolis'; Graham Wallas was aware of it in his work on *The Great Society*. It lies behind Fromm's conception of the 'automaton'. The fear that such a type of man will become ascendant underlies many of

Abridged excerpt reproduced from Wright Mills, C. *The Sociological Imagination*, pp. 189–91 and 193–5; published by Penguin, Harmondsworth, 1970. Copyright © Oxford University Press.

the more recent uses of such classic sociological conceptions as 'status and contract', 'community and society'. It is the hard meaning of notions [like] Riesman's 'other-directed' and Whyte's 'social ethic'. And of course, most popularly, the triumph – if it may be called that – of such a man is the key meaning of George Orwell's *1984*.

On the positive side – a rather wistful side nowadays – the larger meanings of Freud's 'id', Marx's 'Freiheit', George Mead's 'I', Karen Horney's 'spontaneity', lie in the use of such conceptions against the triumph of the alienated man. They are trying to find some centre in man-as-man which would enable them to believe that in the end he cannot be made into, that he cannot finally become, such an alien creature – alien to nature, to society, to self. The cry for 'community' is an attempt, a mistaken one I believe, to assert the conditions that would eliminate the probability of such a man, and it is because many humanist thinkers have come to believe that many psychiatrists by their practice produce such alienated and self-rationalized men that they reject these adaptive endeavours. Back of all this – and much more of traditional and current worrying and thinking among serious and sensible students of man – there lies the simple and decisive fact that the alienated man is the antithesis of the Western image of the free man. The society in which this man, this cheerful robot, flourishes is the antithesis of the free society – or in the literal and plain meaning of the word, of a democratic society. The advent of this man points to freedom as trouble, as issue, and – let us hope – as problem for social scientists. Put as a trouble of the individual – of the terms and values of which he is uneasily unaware – it is the trouble called 'alienation'. As an issue for publics – to the terms and values of which they are mainly indifferent – it is no less than the issue of democratic society, as fact and as aspiration.

Freedom is not merely the chance to do as one pleases; neither is it merely the opportunity to choose between set alternatives. Freedom is, first of all, the chance to formulate the available choices, to argue over them – and then, the opportunity to choose. That is why freedom cannot exist without an enlarged role of human reason in human affairs. Within an individual's biography and within a society's history, the social task of reason is to formulate choices, to enlarge the scope of human decisions in the making of history. The future of human affairs is not merely some set of variables to be predicted. The future is what is to be decided – within the limits, to be sure, of historical possibility. But this possibility is not fixed; in our time the limits seem very broad indeed.

Stress; the general adaptation syndrome and dissonances of adaptation

HANS M.D. SELYE

Stress – an introduction

Since the first description of the 'alarm reaction,' a decade ago, many publications have dealt with this phenomenon and with the 'general adaptation syndrome,' of which it forms a part.

Interest in the general adaptation syndrome has recently received a further impetus as a result of investigations suggesting that some of the most important diseases of human pathology (such as hypertension) may represent by-products of the endocrine reactions, which are at play in the general adaptation syndromey, [I]t is essential to give a clear definition of the subject and the terminology to be used.

The general adaptation syndrome is the sum of all non-specific, systemic reactions of the body which ensue upon long continued exposure to stress. [W]e were struck by the fact that certain manifestations are always the same, irrespective of the specific nature of the eliciting damaging agent. It is the sum of these non-specific adaptive reactions that is referred to as the 'general adaptation syndrome.' It has been found, furthermore, that if an organism is continuously exposed to a certain type of stress, the resulting general adaptation syndrome evolves in three distinct stages, namely, those of the 'alarm reaction,' the 'stage of resistance' and the 'stage of exhaustion.' Perhaps because historically the alarm reaction was the first to be described, or because of its striking name, it received the greatest attention in the literature. Indeed, some workers fail to distinguish clearly between the alarm reaction and the general adaptation syndrome as a whole. It is especially important, therefore, to emphasise that the former is merely the first stage of the latter.

The alarm reaction is the sum of all non-specific systemic phenomena elicited by sudden exposure to stimuli to which the organism is quantitatively or qualitatively not adapted.

Hence, the alarm reaction may in turn be subdivided into two more or less distinct phases: the phase of **shock** and the phase of **counter-shock**. If exposure to damage is not very sudden or if the damaging agent to which the organism is exposed is relatively mild, counter-shock phenomena may become evident without any preceding phase of actual 'shock'.

It seems appropriate, therefore, to say that shock is a condition of suddenly developing, intense, systemic (general) damage. This definition, though perhaps not very instructive, is necessarily correct, since it is merely a brief

Abridged excerpt reproduced from Selye, H.M.D. (1946) The General Adaptation Syndrome and Dissonances of Adaptation. *The Journal of Clinical Endocrinology*, **6**, 118–35.

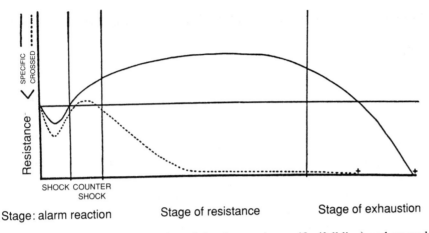

Figure 6.1 Schematic representation of the changes in specific (full line) and crossed (dotted line) resistance during the three stages of the general adaptation syndrome.

outline of the essential phenomena which induced physicians to coin the term 'shock.' This latter term always implies a suddenly developing condition, so that damage caused by chronic ailments cannot be thus described. It also implies that the damage is systemic (or general).

The **stage of resistance** represents the sum of all non-specific systemic reactions elicited by prolonged exposure to stimuli to which the organism has acquired adaptation as a result of continuous exposure. It is characterized by an increased resistance to the particular agent to which the body is exposed and a decreased resistance to other types of stress. Thus the impression is gained that, during the stage of resistance, adaptation to one agent is acquired 'at the expense of' resistance to other agents.

Finally, **the stage of exhaustion** represents the sum of all non-specific systemic reactions which ultimately develop as the result of very prolonged exposure to stimuli to which adaptation had been developed, but could no longer be maintained.

[I]t was found that even a perfectly adapted organism cannot indefinitely maintain itself in the stage of resistance. If exposure to abnormal conditions continues adaptation wears out, the lesions characteristic of the alarm reaction (involution of lymphatic structures, adrenal enlargement, gastrointestinal ulcers) reappear and the **stage of exhaustion** develops during which further resistance becomes impossible.

Apparently, even a fully inured organism cannot indefinitely maintain its adaptation when continuously exposed to a great amount of stress. It is this observation which led to the concept of 'adaptation energy.' Apparently, under the influence of continuous adaptive work, the adaptability or 'adaptation energy' of the organism is eventually exhausted. The time at which this breakdown of adaptation occurs, is referred to as the 'stage of exhaustion.'

Stress related mortality and social organization

JOSEPH EYER and PETER STERLING

Abstract: Modern capitalist social organization, through intensified, conflicted work and the destruction of cooperative, supportive forms of social community, causes a large excess mortality among adults in developed countries. This excess mortality is most strikingly evident in the comparison of vital rates for advanced capitalist societies whith those of undisrupted hunter-gatherers.

In the twentieth century United States, this excess mortality has varied markedly with the social fate of successive generations entering the labor market. The excess was high for the large cohort entering the labor market before the depression, low for the small cohort entering in the 1930s and with the boom, 1940–55; and now high once again for the baby boom children, entering the labor market since about 1960. Though death rates for heart disease and other stress-related diseases are now declining as the small cohort moves into older middle age, death rates are rising for the baby boom children at ages 15–30. If past experience with the first large cohort of the twentieth century is a valid guide, this new large cohort of baby boom children will suffer a large increase in death rates for cirrhosis of the liver, cancer, and heart disease, as it moves into maximal risk ages by the 1990s.

Contemporary medicine transforms a largescale social problem into a problem in the motivation of individuals, for which marketable commodities, including therapy programs, surgery, and drugs are seen as the typical solutions. Therefore it mystifies and defuses potential autonomous awareness and organization looking to a different kind of society. The reintegration of cooperative community, with its consequences in the reduction of work intensity and the dealienation of labor, is however associated with a marked reduction of stress. The cooperative assertion of mass-scale cooperative community may therefore prove to be the most effective therapy for the diseases of modern capitalism.

Stress-related mortality and social organization

Since the late 1950's there have been dramatic increases in the death rates for adults of certain ages, particularly males. At ages 20–24, death rates have risen 21% for white males and 26% for blacks, 1961–68, and 7% and 30%, respectively at ages 35–39. The problem is not really new, for despite the continuous expansion of medical care and its recent availability to the

Abridged excerpt reproduced with permission from Eyer, J. and Sterling, P. (1977) Stress-related Mortality and Social Organization. *Review of Radical Political Economy*, **9**, 1–44. [The original article contains a wealth of statistical data and references to which the enthusiastic reader is referred. It has been omitted from this reading because of lack of space. – Editors].

urban poor there has been little improvement in male life expectancy at older ages since the 19th century.

On the other hand, the high, and in some cases, rising death rates for ages beyond adolescence are less directly related to the defects in our system of medical care than they are to the organization of our whole society. [W]e argue that extremely important contributions to adult death rates are made by the chronic stresses that result from the kinds of human relations that are fundamental to social organization under capitalism. We start by summarising what is meant by stress and review some of the mechanisms by which it can lead to pathology. Next, we describe some of the relations between stress and social organization. Finally, we examine the causes of death for various age groups and the historical variations of age-specific death rates, indicating how these point strongly to the role of stress in the deaths of adults under capitalism.

A general conclusion is that a large component of adult physical pathology and death must be considered neither acts of God nor of our genes, but a measure of the misery caused by our present social and economic organization.

Somatic effects of stress

Stress arises in situations in which an individual is called upon to respond with some sort of coping behavior but in which he is either unable to respond or uncertain that he will be able to. These conditions lead to psychological and physiological arousal. Arousal consists of a series of internal changes that prepare the body for 'fight or flight' – or for dealing attentively and forcefully with the stimulus in some other way. Among the acute changes (over seconds, minutes) are: a rise in heart rate and blood pressure; changes in the distribution of blood, e.g., more to brain and muscle, less to skin and stomach; a release into the blood of energy-producing compounds such as glucose and fatty acids. Some changes, for example, a rise in metabolic rate, occur more slowly and last for hours, days, or weeks during which time there is a gradual restoration of the body to the pre-stress condition.

Both the acute and restorative changes are initiated and coordinated by the brain through its control of the autonomic and endocrine systems.

It is fair to say that not a single cell in the body is unaffected by these alterations of nervous and endocrine activity.

The sources of stress may be either physical or psychological. Selye, for example, was able to produce in rats a characteristic stress syndrome (enlarged adrenal, reduced thymus, and stomach ulcers, etc.) by exposing them to a variety of noxious physical or emotional stimuli. Although there has been much emphasis in stress research on physical stress, it is now recognized that it is the emotional response to the physical change which causes the stress syndrome physiologically. Furthermore in humans signals for arousal can be so thoroughly internalized that the full response can occur spontaneously or in response to objectively innocuous external stimuli.

There is evidence that the atherosclerotic process itself is stimulated by stress. Frequent and violent changes in blood pressure, resulting from acute activation of the sympathetic nervous system, leads to vascular damage through stretching and tearing of blood vessel walls. Chronic high blood pressure leads to fibrous deposition at points of mechanical stress in blood vessels. Although the mechanisms for chronic elevation of blood pressure are not understood in detail, there is evidence that 'essential hypertension' is stress-related.

In urban societies average blood pressure is much higher than in agricultural societies. Furthermore, in urban societies blood pressure generally increases with age once adulthood is reached. In agricultural and pastoral societies this increase is less marked and is entirely absent in some of those societies that are least affected by modern development. Among the highest average blood pressures and the greatest incidence of essential hypertension in the world are found among blacks in the United States, particularly in the rural South. This cannot be attributed in any simple way to a genetic predisposition because the tribal stocks from which United States blacks are descended are not hypertensive. Neither can nutrition be a large factor in the population effect because there is no strong correlation between diet (salt consumption, for example) and average blood pressure levels.

Finally, it has been found that when diet, blood pressure, smoking and exercise are controlled for, a certain behavioral style is associated with a 2–6 times increased risk of coronary heart disease. Some of the characteristics of the 'coronary prone behavior pattern' are 'extremes of competitiveness, striving for achievement, aggressiveness (sometimes stringently repressed), haste, impatience, restlessness, hyperalertness, explosiveness of speech, tenseness of facial musculature, and feelings of being under the pressure of time and under the challenge of responsibility'. These characteristics, of course, are signs of chronic arousal, so that all of the mechanisms mentioned above are working full-time. Furthermore, the 'coronary prone behavior pattern' is often associated with many of the other characteristics that were controlled for in these studies, i.e., with consumption of cigarettes, little time for exercise and so on. It is important in this connection that women with coronary prone behavior patterns have a death rate close to that of coronary prone men despite the well-known large sex differential in coronary heart disease.

Ulcers are another pathology in which chronic stress has a clear causal relation.

All of these changes are controlled by the autonomic nervous system. In fact, one last resort 'treatment' for an ulcer is sever its supply from the vagus nerve, the link between stress and acid secretion.

Chronic, heavy demand on the insulin secreting cells of the pancreas may exhaust the cells and promote the development of diabetes, an important cause of rising death rates at ages 25 and up.

In animals the body's immune system is powerfully suppressed by corticosteroids secreted during stress. Such an effect in humans would lead to increased susceptibility to infectious diseases, such as pneumonia and influenza which are still important causes of death. Through the same mechanism, stress may also have a role in cancer. Although the process by which normal cells become malignant is poorly understood, it is known that the body's immune system is essential in the defense against such cells. Partial suppression of the immune system during stress, e.g. by elevated cortisol, may be partly responsible for the rising death rates from cancer.

Sources of stress and their relation to death rates

When people are asked in surveys to rank stressful events, the top of the list is generally occupied by family break-up, death of relatives, job insecurity and job changes, and migration. All of these stresses that people feel to be major are associated with increased mortality.

Divorce

[T]he death rates for divorced men are two to four times higher than for married men. These differences are true for almost all causes of death, for example, coronary heart disease and cancer as much as suicide. There is a similar difference in age-specific death rates between married and divorced women, but the difference is somewhat smaller. This suggests that the protective effect of marriage against stress is smaller for women than for men.

[W]idowers also have increased mortality. In a study where surviving spouses were matched with controls for age and sex, surviving spouses showed a ten-fold excess deaths over the controls. As in the case of divorce, men had twice the increase in mortality risk from bereavement as women.

Migration

Death rates for migrants also tend to be higher than for those who remain in stable communities.

Unemployment

The most dramatic indicator of the relation between job insecurity and stress is the suicide rate. For men of all labor market ages there is a peak in suicide for each peak in unemployment. The fluctuations of suicide rate for women during this century are not nearly as large as those for men, presumably because women have not been as 'exposed' to unemployment.

Death rates from ulcers also show clear fluctuations with the business cycle. Among working-age males, for each unemployment peak there is an ulcer death rate peak. On one interpretation, it is possible to relate each peak in ulcer deaths to a prior unemployment peak, with a lag of between 1 and 3 years. Alternatively, one might emphasize the stresses which rise with the boom of the business cycle, such as overwork. Ulcer death rate peaks, which generally occur during the boom, would then be produced without a lag.

Finally the distribution of life stresses is also related to income. Unemployment, job turnover, migration, divorce and separation are all highest for the poor. These are the concrete social stresses that probably account for the largest part of the differential in death rates by income.

The evidence presented thus far suggests: (1) physiological mechanisms exist through which stress can produce pathology; (2) there are strong correlations between age-specific death rates and events that people report as stressful; (3) the death rates from chronic disease that have risen in the United States during the twentieth century are not merely the result of reducing deaths from infectious disease; they probably reflect increased social stress. We may now ask how these stressful events are related to social structure, how there came to be so much stress.

Cultural variation in stress

Ninety percent of the humans that have ever lived have been hunter-gatherers, 6% have been agricultural (10,000 years), and only 4% have been industrial (a few hundred years). Although the life of primitive man has been viewed, since Hobbes, as 'nasty, brutish, and short', quite a different picture emerges from current anthropological research.

[S]tress indices are very low for these populations.

It is evident that the sources of stress important in modern societies hardly exist among hunter-gatherers.

Blood pressures are not only low, but show little change with age.

With agriculture the work week did not increase very much. It is estimated that 'slash and burn' agriculture requires about 10–30 hours per week and that plow agriculture, such as was prevalent in Europe during the Middle Ages, requires 30–35 hours per week. This figure is similar for nonagricultural occupations in the Middle Ages. It has been estimated, for example, that the average work week of miners in the 15th century was 35 hours. Much time remained for leisure and ritual activities. There were prohibitions against working at night and during religious holidays, which in 16th century Bavaria occupied 99–190 days of the years. The situation was dramatically reversed with the development of capitalism. Thus, the number of weeks per year that British workers had to work for subsistence increased five-fold in a little over two centuries: 10 weeks in 1495, 20 weeks in 1564, 48 weeks in 1684, 52 weeks in 1726.

The division of labor was small by today's standards and little technical change occurred in the course of a single generation. As a consequence, youth followed their parent's occupations and were incorporated into the economy without strain. Furthermore, because the pace of work and technological change was slow, older people could continue to be wise and useful. Unemployment and job insecurity were still meaningless concepts.

This is not to paint a universal agricultural idyll. For example, the estimated work week under irrigation agriculture is 50–70 hours, and this form was frequently associated with intense class exploitation, e.g., in China, Egypt and in the Incan civilization.

Sources of stress under capitalism

The social relations that bound people together in agricultural societies were shattered by the development of commodity production under competitive capitalism. The competition demands continuous improvements in efficiency and productivity. These are achieved with a 'flexible' labor force, a fast pace, and relentless technological change.

The labor force: external controls

The 'flexible' labor force required under capitalism is one that is treated, not according to rules fixed by tradition, but one that can be manipulated as required by the opportunities for investment and profit. There are a number of features to this flexibility, each of which contributes to social stress.

Perhaps the most stressful period is during the creation of the labor force. The removal of the family and kin system from its central position of control over production is the first step in capitalist development. This has been accomplished in all cases by taking advantage of every natural, legal and economic opportunity to force people off the land and into the cities, and by taking the craft tools out of the hands of the craftsman and the regulation of production from the craft guild. The result is a 'free' labor force, which has no way to live but to sell its labor power. This process occurred in Europe during the 17–19th centuries and was the source of labor not only for European, but also for American industrialization. The process has been repeated in the United States during this century, in the dust bowl during the 1930's, in the rural South since the 1940's, in Puerto Rico, etc. The laborers arrive in the city streamlined, stripped of all ties but those of the nuclear family, ready to work anywhere at any job, for any wage.

Mobility and turnover are hallmarks of the 'flexible' work-force.

Another aspect of 'flexibility' is the infinite division of labor required for efficient capitalist production. Workers must submit to this division though it robs most work of any intrinsic pleasure. The rapid pace of this type of production is itself a chronic stress and, further, robs workers of the pleasure of socializing that to some extent would mitigate the dullness of the labor. Shaped by these requirements most work has become so unpleasant in quality, in pace, or both that workers 'burn out' quickly.

Given the pace of technological change, the accumulated experience of age is not only valueless, it is laughable. The accumulated social experience is also useless because of the demoralization of older people and their physical separation from the youth.

Unemployment is a phenomenon of modern society. Wherever economists study 'under-developed' peoples, they must study unemployment, not as an overt phenomenon of joblessness and lack of income, leading to individual destitution – but as 'hidden unemployment'. The kin and friendship relations of peasant societies support people who are not working to the limits of their capacity. Individual productivity thus becomes the criterion for creating an 'unemployment' statistic for these societies. Clearly this is nothing like unemployment as we know it, especially in the area of stressful social impact.

Given the negative characteristics of modern work detailed above, unemployment and the threat of it play an important role in manipulating the labor force to maintain flexibility and efficiency. The highly stressful effects of joblessness or job insecurity are prime motivators, ranking beside the wage in workers' awareness. Thus unemployment is not simply an unfortunate by-product of more efficient, flexible, progressive economic organization, it is essential to its functioning as a social system.

Another feature of capitalist organization that disrupts community and the possibilities for its formation are the economic cycles: the 3–4 year business cycle and the large (15–30 year) swings. Associated with each of these cycles, there is invariably a rise of most of the stressful events we have listed: job insecurity and turnover, migration (in search of work), family breakup, and slowing of the rate of new family formation.

Internal control of the work force

The molding of the work force is complete when the longings and fantasies that remain after the suppression of affiliative and sensual impulses are used to stimulate consumption. This helps the economy and helps maintain the level of striving. In fact, work, striving, and competition, that were in earlier societies means to get something, have been in our culture so internalized that they are ends in themselves. The goods, power, security, etc. that accumulate in the struggle are rarely satisfying. It is no wonder that professors do not relax on achieving tenure or that the highest Federal officials cannot keep their hands from the till.

The chronic, competitive striving, the central adaptation for success under capitalism, is synonymous with chronic stress since it requires and generates constant physiological arousal. This primary adaptation is seen in extreme form in the coronary-prone behavior pattern described earlier. There are, of course, those who fail to adapt or for whom the cost of adaptation is very high. The cost takes myriad forms: alcoholism (8 million Americans), withdrawal into chronic illness such as ulcer, mental 'illness', and suicide.

In summary, we argue that the economic and cultural forces in capitalist society create chronic stress by (1) disrupting attempts to reestablish communal ties, (2) molding competitive, striving people who find it difficult to build these ties even when external forces of disruption are removed. In the next section we describe the changes in mortality patterns that accompany capitalist development and that provide quantitative evidence for the relation between stress-mortality and capitalism.

Rise of stress-related mortality with industrialization

The relation between stress and mortality can be seen clearly be examining the mortality patterns in countries that shift from a predominately traditional, agricultural to a predominately industrial, capitalist social organization. Two features are the same wherever comparative statistics are available. First, there is a rise in those causes of death that show the greatest modern urban-rural differential: suicide, homicide, ulcer, coronary heart disease, ect.

[S]uicide increased in Sweden by almost a factor of 10 between 1785–1965. The increase was dramatic for the rural as well as the urban areas. This is not surprising since, as already noted, the transition to urban life depends upon severe economic and social disruption in the countryside.

The second constant feature in the mortality patterns during the rural-urban transition is the sharp rise in the death rates of young adults. Before industrialization, mortality is high in infancy, low in childhood, and shows a continuous, but gradual, rise after adolescence.

The pattern of an elevated death rate for 15–30 year olds and its later spread to older ages appears in all regions where capitalist development occurs.

The historical trend of the male-female differential in age-specific death rates indicates that the socially disruptive effects of industrialization have been especially serious for men. In the United States, for instance, the sex differential in life expectancy has widened since 1900 from 2 years to 7.

The differential in the total death rate has widened with development because women have benefited more from public health and medical measures reducing infectious disease, while suffering less rise of coronary heart disease, hypertension, ulcers, suicide, cirrhosis and other stress-related causes. These data clearly imply that there has been a disproportionately large rise of social stress, for men, in modern development.

Rise in stress for youth: 1957–1970s

Parallelling the rise in mortality there have been increases in other stress indicators at these ages: a rise in mental hospital admissions and residency rates, rise in illegitimacy, venereal disease, and a fall in the rate of marriage accompanied by increased marital breakup. While alcohol consumption has risen among all age groups, there is some evidence that it has risen faster for young people recently. The birth rate has fallen to a level below the previous historical low in the Depression of the 1930s; and the suicide rate for 15–24 year olds is now at a new historical high.

After 1955 the new, large cohort began to enter the labor market, and the competitive situation for young people intensified. Even though the proportions of young people going to high school and college expanded markedly through this period, and after 1964, the draft absorbed temporarily up to 80% of the increase in new labor market entrants, the unemployment rate of young people not in school or the army doubled from the fifties to the sixties. This increase was matched by the beginning of the rise of suicide and other causes of death during a period in which the unemployment and suicide rates for the older, small cohort were steady or falling.

The behavior of the unemployment rate alone cannot account for the **accelerating** rise of stress pathology for young people in the 1960s and early 1970s. In the next section we examine other social changes which have added successively to the stress experienced by the large cohort, and help to account for this accelerating rise of stress death rates.

Additional sources of social stress

Accompanying the intensified competition within the young, large cohort have been a series of shifts in the structure of the labor market which cause increased stress. Since the second world war, the distribution of newly available jobs has progressively shifted toward those requiring greater education – toward white collar and service jobs and away from manual labor. The black and poor white migrants from the family farm, who were easily absorbed into the urban labor market, 1940–55, have been increasingly unemployable in the economy of the sixties and seventies. The migration has not abated, however, since welfare payments have enormously expanded in the Northern and Western cities. The net impact of these changes has been to create a demoralized population, living in run-down ghettos on very little money, but not starving to death. This transition has been accompanied by a massive breakdown of marriage among the recent migrants and a disruption of previously stable ethnic neighborhoods.

Within the young, large, cohort, the rich have gotten richer and the poor poorer.

Young people have responded vigorously to these changes by attempting to create new forms of community. These attempts were at the heart of the civil rights movement, the peace movement, the creation of the youth counterculture, the expansion of premarital sexual relations, and the movement toward communal and cooperative forms of living. The defeat of these movements by mass shootings, government-directed counter-insurgency disruption, and divisive cooptation, as well as the disappearance of a mass base with the end of the draft, has undoubtedly added another substantial component to the rise of stress for young people in the early 1970s.

Health prospects for the baby boom children

[W]e can see that the baby boom cohort is not the first in capitalist social history to suffer a dramatic rise of stress pathology. The groups entering the labor market between 1880 and 1925 experienced a larger upswing of pathology, starting from lower levels. Of the many factors contributing to this rise of stress at the turn of the century, the alienation and intensification of work was perhaps the most important. The specific pattern of diseases expressing stress was also influenced by the switch from alcohol to tobacco as the major drug of alienated work in the population.

Members of the baby boom cohort are now dying of behavioral causes which reflect acute stress: suicide, homicide, accidents, drug deaths. The suicide rate for this group has surpassed previous historical peaks and is still rising. The ulcer death rate has turned upward, in contrast to the rapidly falling rates at older ages. If past experience with the first highly-stressed cohort of the twentieth century is a valid guide, the baby boom children will suffer a large increase in death rates for cirrhosis of the liver, cancer, and heart disease as they move into maximal risk ages for these diseases by the 1990s.

The impact of depression and recovery

Superimposed on the effects of the various cohorts is the impact of movement toward economic depression since 1968.

[T]he death rate as a whole rises during business booms and declines during depressions. The most rapid and sustained death rate declines in the whole series – 1872–78, 1881–86, 1892–97, 1908–15, 1919–21, 1929–33, 1936–38, 1942–49, and 1968–75 – all occurred when unemployment was rising.

This seemingly paradoxical relationship reflects the fact that heart disease, stroke, cancer, cirrhosis, diabetes, accidents, influenza–pneumonia, and many smaller causes of death such as ulcers rise during the boom with the lengthening of hours of work, the increase of migration, and its attendant community disintegration. Only suicide and homicide, among death rates, rise and fall with unemployment and its family consequences during depressions. Clearly the social sources of stress which rise during boom outweigh the effects of economic depression on the death rate as a whole.

[Any] recent health gains are clearly the product of the labor market strength of a majority of workers – the small cohort. This same labor market strength, by limiting hours of work and the intensity of work, while ensuring higher wages, has retarded the advance of the productivity of labor and squeezed capitalists' profits. The strength of the small cohort workers has thus been a fundamental factor in bringing on the depression of the mid-1970s, which in turn has further beneficial impacts on health by reducing the hours of work and community disruption still more.

Traditionally, capitalism has resolved this kind of problem by the introduction of new technology designed to undermine the control over life and work exerted by worker groups in strong positions. Such transformation of the workplace requires an expansion of investable surplus. Since the late 1960s, the ruling class has sought to gain this new capital by cutbacks in the use of surplus for social welfare, education and health care services won by the political struggles of the small cohort. In addition, an economic strategy of raising unemployment rates to moderately high levels – enough to break the small cohort's strength, but not enough to stimulate mass disaffection and independent initiative – has been consistently pursued. These policies have not yet resulted in a fundamental redistribution of social surplus in favor of capital.

If the baby boom children continue to bear the brunt of redistributive measures, the prospective increase in death rates for this group as it moves into maximal risk ages for heart disease, cancer, and cirrhosis will be that much larger.

How has medicine responded to these problems?

So far, only superficial technical solutions have been offered. For example, a major response to the drug problem has been the introduction of methadone and a push to develop an arsenal of narcotics antagonists. In fact, the major response to psychological disorder has been for the last 20 years pharmacological: for depression, 'antidepressants': for anxiety, 'anti-anxiety' agents; for hyperactive children, stimulants, etc.

Ironically, many treatments for a variety of stress-related illnesses act not by removing the causes of the illness but by destroying the capacity of the organ to respond to the cause, often by removing the organ or by severing its connection with the brain. Thus 'ultimate cures' for ulcer are vagotomy or removal of the duodenum; a response to hypertension may be blockage of the sympathetic nervous system: a response to severe mental disturbance may be psychosurgery. Medicine is increasingly forced to intervene with heroic measures whose side effects are often only slightly less unpleasant than the original disease.

The irony of treating stress pathology by destroying the capacity of the organs to respond to the stress or removing them, is lost on much of the medical profession, which sees only its duty to the individual.

There are at least four problems with this sort of medicine. One is that it is not 'cost effective'. Technical solutions to rising death rates from stress pathology are far more expensive than the public health measures that reduced the death rate in the past. Coronary by-pass operations and blood dialysis are two well-known examples. Stress pathologies are the source of an increasing proportion of the deaths and will require an increasing share of the social product for their treatment.

A second problem is that high technology curative medicine will probably be ineffective in dealing with these problems.

Though the per capita consumption of anti-anxiety agents has risen sharply in the last decades, stress death rates have risen at an accelerating pace. Though major tranquilisers are credited with emptying out the mental hospitals, they have not prevented a sharp upswing in admissions and residency rates for youth from the large cohort. The highest death rates are now found in the large metropolises, which also have the highest number of doctors per capita, hospital beds per capita and medical expenditures per capita. The 'great medical centers' are often located right in the midst of the areas of highest chronic pathology – the slums. Rural areas with low doctors per capita and low medical expenditures have the lowest death rates. To add yet another paradox, as a result of Medicare and Medicaid, the poor now have more doctor visits per capita than the rich, and have equal access, at least on paper, to the high-quality high technology private facilities. However, the death rate differential between these two groups has probably increased since the mid-sixties. These data strikingly indicate the irrelevance of high cost curative medicine to overall health in society.

A third problem is the the technical approach contributes additionally and powerfully to the breakdown of community responsible for the diseases in the first place. Death is no longer treated as part of the human life cycle. Life and death are no longer related to bonds between human beings but to treatment by technicians. The growth of this trend increases one's fear, passivity, and sense of helplessness – factors which have been directly implicated in the impact of stress on increased sickness. Doctors increasingly lose their capacity to reduce stress, and in the process, lose their roles as healers.

Finally, it seems just plain inappropriate to view these diseases as mere technical defects in the body's machinery rather than as dramatic evidence of the fear and pain pervading people's lives. Even if technical advances can be developed cheaply, they are not an appropriate response. For example, there are claims that cingulotomy (a psychosurgical operation) is 'effective' in treating alcoholism in the sense that destruction of the cingulum may relieve feelings that lead to drinking. The cost of a cingulotomy is low, roughly that of an abortion. What sort of society, however, deals with the problems of 9 million people by destroying their capacity to **feel** tension and anxiety? It seems equally inappropriate to view atherosclerosis and lung cancer primarily as technical challenges.

New directions

The most human solution, and in the long run the only real one, is to halt the social disruption and recreate relaxed community. Work should no longer be a high pressure activity kept going by the threat of a variety of social punishments. People should not be socialized to put themselves under chronic stress in order to produce. The ideals of competitive material achievement must be replaced by ideals of cooperative mutual development of social relationships. The barriers separating work from home and children should be broken down, and both men and women should be free to develop themselves and create in a relaxed atmosphere. Material aspirations should be stabilized, and industry automated and put on a maintenance basis. Capital accumulation should give way to living.

That this prescription is not just a list of leftist slogans, the applicability of which to modern life is dubious, is demonstrated by the social attempts to deal with stress pathology that have already been made. Behavior modification techniques, for instance, have been used to help people reduce blood pressure, stop smoking, or lose weight. That these methods are successful shows that sociopsychological factors are important in these diseases, in contrast to irreversible, possibly genetic, physiological alterations. However, outside the reinforcement situation, they start smoking again, and blood pressure increases, since the rewards and punishments of the surrounding society have not been changed.

Various techniques of relaxation have been widely propagated – self-hypnosis, progressive relaxation, Yoga, Transcendental Meditation. As with behavior modification, these methods have large impacts on physiological stress indicators during relaxation sessions. People who become consistent practitioners of these methods show a decided reduction of chronic stress indicators. The problem is that the great majority of people who try these techniques cannot become consistent practitioners due to the pressure of their own socialization and their immediate environment.

People have tried to create new forms of intimate community – encounter groups, sensitivity training, organizational development – but the impact at best has been limited. People are opening up to new possibilities but their social relationships are not transformed. Intimate group meetings have been used to deal specifically with stress-related problems, as in the cases of Alcoholics Anonymous, Synanon, or Weight Watchers. These groups have only limited success also, which may be due to a number of things. Many of these groups share the practice of mutual denunciation and negative reinforcement to get people to shape up to the Protestant Ethic and perform. [T]his simply is a repeating phase in the total problem for an alcoholic or addict, a step in the circle of the game, not a move outside it. Others, like Weight Watchers, do not use such methods, but also fail to alter the relevant social relations which are the source of stress; they only create a community supportive of a very particular change. All of these groups work, not with the natural network of people involved with a person suffering from stress pathology, but with relative strangers.

The impact of altering the whole environment of social reinforcers is dramatically illustrated in the experiments with a token economy in mental hospitals. Mental hospitals usually reinforce pathological behavior. The token economy is an attempt to reinforce 'normal' behavior. By this method, chronic back ward schizophrenics are transformed from helpless asocial beings into people who can feed, clothe and take care of themselves, engage in work and play, and go through halfway houses back into the world of society as it is. Of course, many of them return to the hospital, since the reinforcers **in society**, particularly in their intimate networks, have not changed. Their 'sickness' is necessary to the relationships they have with people on the outside.

Another limit to these methods will come when an attempt is made to find this open space for large numbers of people. While it may be possible to transform a depressed, demoralized migrant agricultural laborer into a college graduate with high income prospects, it is clearly impossible to do this for all, or even the majority, of lower class people. In a pyramid of social power which always has the same dimensions the rise of one individual is matched by the relative fall of another. The difficulties of 'preventive psychiatry' in the 1960s surround this very problem.

We have already pointed out how essential social disruption is to the process of 'free' labor migration following in the path of capital's pursuit of higher profit rates. Since constantly rising productivity requires such disruption, stopping the disruption and rebuilding community will greatly limit productivity advance. Similarly, mass relaxation by the **majority** of men who share the coronary prone behavior pattern would undermine productivity, the profits of capitalist firms, and thence the growth process itself. As cross-cultural studies have demonstrated, no achievement syndrome, no rapid growth. Thus the real problem clearly emerges: to initiate a successful community forming process which abolishes social hierarchy in the whole society and stops the capital accumulation process, with its attendant disruption and family structures aimed at socialization for high-pressure productivity.

In the historical statistics of developed countries, the effective kind of community forming process occurs also during mass strikes and popular uprisings, which are accompanied by sharp declines in the suicide rate. The rate rises back to, or above, previous levels as these movements are defeated as well. The defeat of these movements is also associated, of course, with a great increase of official homicide, and in some cases which required prolonged military seige to overcome the insurgents, the diseases associated with starvation and the breakdown of public health systems.

These data make it crystal clear that although this method of community formation is very effective in reducing stress, it too has limits imposed directly by the power of the ruling class in this society. While it solves the problems unresolved by therapy of small groups or by mass formation of pseudocommunity as in Suburbia, it is impossible so long as the ruling class retains its military power and cultural hegemony. Successful revolutions, however, overcome both of these problems, through fraternization with the military forces, and through an Enlightenment, begun many years previous, which creates a new worldview, causes a loss of confidence in the ruling ethic among the rulers themselves, and facilitates political division among the rulers at the point of revolutionary crisis, so that the ruling hegemony is then at best contradictory and usually nonexistent.

Since the genuine community forming processes that occur in mass uprisings may be the most effective therapy for chronic stress pathology, we believe that medical science should devote primary energies toward investigating this effect and furthering its practical application. In this paper we have made some contributions toward one aspect of this task, the formation of a new worldview.

Looking back over the facts we have discussed, it is easy to understand why Virchow, reflecting on the revolutions of 1848 in Europe, said: 'Medicine is nothing but a social science. Politics is nothing but medicine on a large scale.'

Stress and industry: altruism or big business?

CARY L. COOPER

The road to health in American firms

Health promotion in American industry is big business now.

Are American employers, after all these years, becoming more compassionate, altruistic, concerned about their employees, instead of being obsessed with their profit margins?

The answer is 'You must be kidding!' American industry is facing an enormous and ever spiralling bill for employee health care costs. Individual insurance costs rose by 50 per cent over the past two decades, but the employers' contribution rose by over 140 per cent. It has also been estimated that over $700 million a year is spent by American employers to replace the 200,000 men aged 45 to 65 who die or are incapacitated by coronary artery disease alone. Top management at Xerox estimate that the cost of losing just one executive to heart disease or other stress-related illnesses costs the organization $600,000.

[W]orkplace stress is indeed creating an enormous cost to industry – through increased sick leave, absenteeism, labour turnover, ill health, lost production and lower morale. There is another source of growing costs, too. More and more employees, in American companies at least, are litigating against their employers, through the worker compensation regulations and laws, in respect of job-related stress. For example, in California, the stress-related compensation claims for psychiatric injury now total over 3,000 a year, since the California Supreme Court upheld its first stress-disability case in the early 1970s.

J.M. Ivancevich and his colleagues at the University of Houston cite three important precedents.

In 1955, in Bailey v. American General, a Texas court provided the first test case in the United States. Bailey was an iron worker on a scaffolding who saw a colleague plunge to his death, while escaping death himself. He went back to work, but gradually he began to have frequent black-outs, and became paralysed. He also had a number of behaviour problems, such as sleeping difficulties and extreme sensitivity to pain. The court ruled in Bailey's favour.

A more dramatic case occurred in 1960. The Michigan Supreme Court, in the case of Carter v. General Motors, ruled that an assembly worker's

Abridged excerpt reproduced from Cooper, L. (1985) The Road to Health in American Firms. *New Society*, 6 September, 335–6.

psychological breakdown might have been due not only to the difficulty of keeping up with the machine-paced work, but also to repeated criticisms from his supervisor. One must remember that worker compensation in the United States is meant to provide employees with compensation 'for all work-related injuries.' In Carter v. General Motors, this was broadly interpreted. The significance of the case was that it deviated from previous rulings that only a 'discreet, identifiable accident' could be compensated for. Carter was subjected to stress over a long period, which culminated in his breakdown. It was in this case that the term, 'cumulative trauma,' was first established.

The final case was Alcorn v Arbo Engineering in 1970. Alcorn was a lorry driver who was in disagreement with management over his union activities. As a result of abusive behaviour by managers, Alcorn claimed that he suffered physical and emotional distress, which led to insomnia, nausea and other symptoms. He won his claim. As Ivancevich concludes: 'In effect, [the case] argued that the supervisor's words, style and actions constituted a 'sudden emotional event' sufficient to establish a valid claim for compensation.'

This may help to explain the burgeoning stress management programmes and health promotion activities which are taking place in American industry. If the employer is at least seen to be doing something about workplace stress, then he may have an easier ride in the courts.

So it is fair enough to be cynical about why many US companies are involved in health promotion. All the same there are now some dramatic effects in reducing the medical costs to industry.

By far the most comprehensive and best researched of these programmes was undertaken by Control Data Corporation, one of the largest American computer companies. Like many major US firms, it is now 'self-insured' – covering its employees direct – and therefore has control of its own health care costs. Its programme is called STAYWELL. It is provided for the 22,000 Control Data employees and their spouses in 14 American cities as a 'free corporate benefit.' It has five components: stopping smoking, weight control, cardio-vascular fitness, stress management and improved diet (particularly, cutting down on cholesterol, salt and sugar).

But what is the outcome? The evidence is startling.

Most revealing of all, those employees who entered the cardio-vascular fitness programme, and reduced their hypertension levels, had less than half the health care costs of those who did not.

The motives of corporate America may not be altruistic. But their employees stand a good chance of living longer and healthier than their counterparts in Britain.

References

Cooper, C.L. (1983) *Stress Research: issues for the eighties*, Wiley.
Ivancevich, J.M., Matteson, M.T., and Richards, E.P. (1985) 'Who's liable for stress on the job?' *Harvard Business Review*, March–April.

Patriarchy, alienation and anomie: new directions for stress research

HEATHER CLARK

Stressors

[R]esearch into stress [at work] has been mainly on 'stressors', and there are many, but the perception of these and their effects is, on the whole, gender-blind. References are made to individuals and for 'individual' read men and where, increasingly, women are acknowledged they are immediately subsumed into the more traditional linear approach and meticulously researched.

If we look at a discussion of organisational structure [for example] we find it analysed (Burke op cit: 83) in terms of work overload, role conflict, supervisor relations but with the unquestioned assumption that the organisational structure itself is neutral. 'It is a taken-for-granted non-problematic feature of social organisation' (Hearn *et al.*, 1989: 14–15). Both 'organisation' and 'the organisation' are the result of knowledge, practices and processes built up over time and which are then reflected in a powerful discourse based on ideas of rationality, efficiency, productivity and control – quite what these mean, and for whom is questionable given the activities on the part of some organisations in the 1980's and 1990's – Union Carbide in Bhopal, Barlow-Clowes, Hanson – ICI, BCCI worldwide. Research will then be couched in empirical and pragmatic terms and the deeper level of analysis of the concepts not undertaken; this deeper level is assumed to contain the irrational, the ideological and the chaotic, i.e. not scientific, which in turn is seen as part of woman's nature and is excluded. What one then also excludes is the possibility of understanding a large part of the experience which one is purporting to explain in the first place.

It is not total exclusion, there is some research by social psychologists that endeavours to cover the environment of work and marital and family effects and shows that women in,

> 'junior, middle and senior management are experiencing a greater number of high stress factors and manifestations than their male counterparts . . .
> . . . The other disturbing findings which emerge from this study centre on the overwhelming evidence that the majority of the additional pressures at work experienced by female managers are stress factors beyond their control and based largely on prejudice and discrimination from both corporate policy and other people at work.'
>
> (*Davidson and Cooper, 1983: 189*)

Abridged excerpt from Clark, H. (1991) Women, Work and Stress: New Directions. *University of East London Occupational Papers on Business, Economy and Society*, no. 3, 8–24.

They note that management (especially higher level management) remains a male-dominated preserve (Davidson and Cooper ibid: Lewis and Cooper, 1988).

These studies do suggest ways of eliminating stress but it is more narrowly aimed at management training, or advocating that legislative and policy makers 'do' something, or, at counselling the individual to relax. The analysis goes no further into the prejudice and discrimination discussed above.

Yet this is the area that needs analysis but cannot be so analysed with the range of concepts and methods in use at present. Prejudice and discrimination are very deep seated and will take more than exhortations to politicians, lawyers and managers to 'do' something, although if and when the economic costs of not 'doing' become relevant, there may then be direct intervention by management to introduce counselling. (Cooper, 1985).

The Equal Pay Act and Equal Opportunity legislation have been in existence for 20 years now (1970, 1975 & 1986). The Acts clearly outlaw discrimination in employment on grounds of sex but if one looks at the E.O.C's research 'Barriers to Fair Selection' in 1988 (a multi-sector study of recruitment pratices) what do we find? It is shot through with stereotypical ideas about women by male managers whether the positions are for un-skilled, skilled or managerial posts. (Collinson: 1988).

There is some research which looks at structural problems but we need to go beyond the narrow confines of particular disciplines to find it (Eyer and Sterling, 1977). Brown & Harris' research into 'vulnerability' and the provoking agents of depression considered the 'possibility of a more direct involvement of the social environment in disorder' (Brown and Harris, 1978: 5). Irrespective of the physical, biological or psychiatric basis, they were concerned, 'with how she perceives and reacts emotionally to [these] changes [but argued] no one has found it easy to translate [this] into effective research'. (op cit. 5)

However, Brown & Harris are taken to task over the statistical elements of their 'vulnerability' model (Lyon, 1986) which Brown (1986) dismisses arguing that –

> It is impossible at the moment to conceive of a way of arriving at true
> ratio scales to measure phenomena such as degree of stress . . . we have
> no way of establishing a basic quantum of stress as we have of weight'
> (1986: 603).

It seems there is a justification for looking further for ways of defining, understanding and acting to remove stress. We can, with McKenna & Ellis in their counterpoint to Davidson and Cooper,

> 'consider that practitioners in organisational design should be provided
> with academic advice from a thorough, selective and well grounded
> analysis of the focal topic' (1981),

which in its turn requires that practitioners in organisational design, as well as others, be first made aware of just what that particular element of stress consists (Gutek, 1989; Collinson and Collinson, 1989).

Well, what is this stress? How does it come about?

'To use an analogy from physics, stress arises because of the impact of an environmental force on a physical object; the object undergoes strain and this reaction may result in temporary distortion but equally it could lead to permanent distortion. In human terms any situation that is seen as burdensome, **threatening**, **ambiguous**, or boring is likely to produce stress'. (my emphasis)

(McKenna, 1987: 382)

'Stress arises in situations in which an individual is called upon to respond with some sort of coping behaviour but in which he (sic) is either **unable to respond** or **uncertain** that he (sic) will be able to '
(my emphasis)

(Eyer and Sterling, 1977: 2)

These two definitions, one from a psychologist the other from a biologist and consultant physician point the way for further research.

New directions I

Many of the research methods considered so far have produced limited research, the results of which are gender-blind in the main and considered valid only when the research is statistically precise. My argument is that life is not statistically precise and that a more sociological understanding of women's position would make clear the extra level of permanent ambiguity and ambivalence she lives under which has been defined as a component of stress.

It is not suggested for one moment that other [forms of] stress do not exist. Women and men will continue to show signs of stress at work and their personality, their physical and mental abilities, together with the effects of their circumstances and those of the work place will interact with the expectations, or lack of them, present in their work. The existing frameworks however have not specified where to look for the answers to this gendered element although raised secondarily by some (Davidson and Cooper; Brown and Harris) and alluded to by others. It is not being argued here that all psychologists are the same, or that they assume or accept the conventional paradigm referred to earlier as the norm, but that stress is being only selectively researched and the structurally induced level not addressed. Stress appears to be increasing in the changing and more flexible conditions of work. Certainly more is being written about it. 'Estimates vary on the cost of stress related illness to industry but figures in excess of 40 million lost working days' are given. (Lucas as quoted in Thompson and McHugh, 1990: 324). It is still treated as a 'private' trouble for individuals rather than the 'public' issue it has become (Mills, 15: op cit.). One woman cannot change the structure as she might be able to her job (Hugill, 1991) although this is doubtful too, 'being travellers in a country whose language we don't know' (Coward, 1991).

The psychological structural bridge between the person and the social structure is also now better documented and understood (Elias, 1991; Hollway, 1982, 1991) if not yet widely used at the empirical level. Human beings are both the independent person with personality and identity, together with their collective history and social arrangements – their 'social habitus' – a concept that makes it possible to see women (and men) as an accumulation of, and sharing with others, all that her particular society and sex has lived through. This, together with her own personal characteristics, 'creating a more or less individual style . . . what might be called an unmistakable individual handwriting that grows out of the social script' (Elias, 182–3). Similar ideas conceiving the 'I' and the collective 'we' as one, are to be found in the researches of Bourdieu in his work on the linguistic habitus (Thompson, 1984: 53). It appears at the same time in the more radical/ feminist analysis as 'man-made' language (Spender, 1982: 12) and more abstractly theoretical again in Giddens' concept of structuration (Thompson, 150). Hollway too, in following Foucault's analysis of knowledge as power creating discourses and constructing subjects, questions the 'production' of psychology and its partiality. It has produced, 'knowledge which attributes responsibility for stress to the individual rather than the organisation' (Hollway, op cit.: 179). Further evidence of the effect of the social and economic environment on the body and mind with the resultant stress and ill-health can be found in Doyal (1981: 93). Analysing the structural effects on stress for women appears to have possibilities.

There is no intention to be directive or overly precise about the possible uses of the concepts alienation and anomie. They are two among many sociological concepts that take as their starting point the analysis of structures and both are likely to be able to 'converse' with the stressful effects of those structures. Both are problematic in use and remain essentially contested concepts because of their moral underpinnings.

I shall use as a basis John Horton's 'Dehumanisation of Anomie & Alienation' (1964) in which he argues that, 'contemporary definitions have confused, obscured and changed the classical meaning'. For example, research such as Blauner's (1964) which related alienation of the workers to the objective nature of the work process and their subjective feeling states. His research findings do not carry the same powerful implications of Marx's own use of the concept. 'Alienation for Marx and anomie for Dukheim were metaphors for a radical attack on the dominant institutions and values of industrial society. They attacked similar behaviour, but from opposing perspectives.' Problems of power and change for Marx were problems about the maintenance of order for Dukheim. 'Anomie concentrates on culture or culture transmitted in social organisation; alienation on the hierarchy of control in the organisation itself.' There is a strong ethical stance and concern over the, 'social process, values and assumptions about the relation between man (*sic*) and society', '. . . neither Durkheim nor Marx was interested in abstract historical and psychological definitions', but in modern definitions it is, 'precisely the original, radical, historical and sociological content which has been removed or altered'.

Much of the evidence in the psychological, managerial and other texts shows this to have increasingly taken place to the degree that it is now de-radicalised and 'ideologically' neutral with its models, paradigms and generalities purporting to be objective whilst offering a reading that removes the contradictions of gender (and much else besides) and is thus denuded. They are a-historical abstractions in which assumptions and values are hidden and not only not questioned but researched and structured in such a way that it is inconceivable that there would (or could) be any questions to be asked.

There are problems in operationalising the concept of alienation but Horton argues that alienation is a problem of 'legitimacy of social control; it is a problem of power defined as domination'. This is precisely what women are finding at work as they begin to enter the higher levels of some organisations. They are voicing their unhappiness at the personal level in many other ways (Networking in the 300 group being one example) whilst the statistics of the continuing imbalance between women and men at the higher levels in organisations are very public knowledge. The apprehension of these experiential states i.e. domination, lack of control, does give rise to

"THE JOB WILL INVOLVE YOU DOING THE WORK, AND ME TAKING THE CREDIT ......"

Mary Holland

Spellbound Books, Moss St., Dublin 1.

Figure 6.2 'The job will involve you doing the work, and me taking the credit . . .'

alienatory stress. How do women identify with the end result of their labours when it is managed, owned and controlled by men? The cartoon here is but one example of alienation; the underlying stress level is as yet undiscussed – not withstanding the Equal Opportunities legislation of 20 years and the latest research by the E.O.C. (1991) into the NHS. Women were 70% of the total workforce but the health authorities had done very little towards making women 'equal'. Where there was a written policy 75% did not monitor it and 84% had not appointed anyone whose chief responsibility it would be (Brindle, 1991). Women are also alienated from themselves, whilst not always recognising it. They are treated as a commodity, and are part of the reserve army of labour to be called into action as and when required. This is part of the 'double exploitation' of women, their 'sole responsibility' for the domestic sphere is still not considered to be really important; if it were, it would appear on the agendas of all types of political and economic organisation.

There are clear differences between the concepts of exploitation and oppression – the one concerning wage-labour, the other patriarchy. Yet there is clear overlap between women's private and public lives, even if it appears in different guises.

Women occupy many different structural work locations, for example manager (which will be discussed in the next section), factory worker and homeworker. Consider examples of these two latter 'ghettoised' situations (a) the factory in which a majority of workers are women making clothes. A 'domestic' enclave is thus produced, with the only men employed as the managers. Poor wages and conditions are the norm, the camaraderie of the women covering up the exploitation and lack of control by the women (Westwood, 1984) and (b) the well documented and traditional part-time and homeworking areas of the economy and the increased 'flexibility' being introduced in them (Huws, 1984; Atkinson, 1984). There are different levels and degrees of alienation and stress enamating from them. Consciousness of ambiguity and ambivalence will affect 'token' women in positions of authority differently from these women in the factory or at home, working at low skill levels and/or in isolation. The stress for the homeworker may well be visible in depression and other signs of ill-health because the effect of traditional values of women's inferiority are more keenly felt in isolation even when not consciously articulated. Whereas there is a 'buffer' zone of camaraderie between the felt sense of alienation and the dominant values for the factory women so that the more extreme effects are deflected (Parkin, 1972).

Evidence so far shows that the concept of alienation is likely to be difficult to translate into an operational definition given the different notions as to what exactly the word means. What was it that Humpty Dumpty said? – 'when I use a word, it means just what I choose it to mean – neither more nor less' (Carroll, 1962). What does remain in the classical definition is the idea, and effect, of being a subordinate group under the permanent domination of a 'superordinate' group and that there will be various ways in which that effect will manifest itself, stress being one of them. Yet this insight is not incorporated into factually neutral research which is 'safer' politically and certainly more likely to get funding and be published (Hanmer and Leonard, 1984).

The academic specialisation of labour which, by necessity, restricts both methods and knowledge, fails to build a coherent 'picture' overall thus pieces of the jigsaw are missing and remain so. For example, Eyer & Sterling suggested in 1977 that capitalist social organisation was showing an increase in stress-related mortality and argued that a 'reintegration of cooperative community . . . reduction of work intensity and the dealienation of labour is associated with a marked reduction of stress'. Brown & Harris too showed that poor women with isolated life-styles in their research were vulnerable to depression. Davidson & Cooper came near to discussing women's stress in structural terms when they isolated prejudice and discrimination as being something over which women have no control.

These insights are undeveloped and are likely to remain so until such time as structural concepts are used in which to embed them. One such concept is alienation. In its Marxist sense, in the context of wage labour, it would be an interesting way of analysing stress. This would help focus on the similarities of stress experienced by women and men. In its classical sense the concept of alienation promises insights into stress felt by women, as women, as a subordinate group.

New directions II

Anomie appears to offer an even more fruitful area for further research. John Horton again, 'Anomie refers to the problems of social control in a social system', where the 'values are conflicting or absent, or the individuals not socialised to the cultural directives'. Where this is the case individuals are suffering from normlessness. I will argue that this is precisely what many women suffer from whilst at work.

Anomie then is the state of being outside the main culture, women are and suffer direct stress from being so.

The culture that exists in organisations does not reflect women, it is traditionally male-oriented in every way (Hearn, op cit.; Cooper, op cit.). The male role models incorporate generalised expectations of men, about men and for men; women are not in this scheme and although they are now moving into higher managerial posts, they are still seen as 'outsiders' (Savage, op cit.) with no social support (Huber op cit.). They have no control over male attitudes towards them (Cooper and Davidson op cit.). 'I don't want a bright woman on my board' (Holberton and Cookson, 1991). The administration, the hierarchy and the competitive nature of the organisation is shown to be stressful for women to operate in successfully (Hearn et al. op cit.). An example of this is a company electrician in Patricia Lunneburg's research commenting on her male colleagues, 'They're all keyed to competition, [and] those competitive work attitudes and ethics lower the quality of their work' (1990). The women in this study had consciously developed coping behaviours to enhance their means of control.

These contradictory situations for women will always be the 'norm'. They may not always exhibit extreme distress because they have learned the ability to both 'accommodate' and 'resist' which all women do more or less consciously. Accommodation and resistance are those coping strategies against ideologically contradictory and mutually exclusive sex-role appropriate behaviours:

(a) 'nurturance of men and children in a domestic situation, submissiveness and non-competition with men outside the domestic situation'

and

(b) 'the achieving of self-esteem and success in the non-domestic competitive world of work'.

(Anyon, 1983: 19)

Nevertheless, this juggling of the conflicting messages in a man's world does not eliminate the stress. The capitalist culture of work does not represent or reflect women's experience or existence. However adept at 'conjuring' she becomes, the underlying level of anomie is always present. The attitudes, values and behaviour at work are male and even where there are many women working together, the overall patriarchal expectations of them, and organisation for them, will still prevail.

In the last few years there has been an interesting development in managerial research which exemplifies the rigidity of work-place culture. The 'fashionable' notion of the 'excellent' company (Peters and Waterman, 1982) with its exhortation for a strong corporate culture and missionary zeal among employees to imbibe and uphold company values is an appealing one at present.

The idea is not new. We find it in the work of Mayo and his advocacy of the need for a 'human relations' approach which, in turn, was influenced by the earlier ideas of Durkheim on the effect of the division of labour and its resultant 'little sense of belonging to a community' (Rose, 1978: 14; Hill, 1981: 90).

Ray argues that because, 'ties to community and church have weakened and peoples' affiliatory needs are not being met . . . this had led to a concomitant loss of meaning in individual's lives'. The original moral commitment to the community appears to have been translated by management into a commitment to, and control by, the enterprise (Carol Axtell Ray, 1986). If this happens there is likely to be an even narrower interpretation of the male oriented culture and the stress factor for women will be greater. They are unlikely to share in this particularly heightened sense of 'collectivity' of totalitarian sameness. The over-riding commitment to a collective pursuit of competitive edge for short term gain is exemplified in 'Hanson and I.C.I' (Adcroft et al., 1991). Financial engineering of this kind may be a good example of narrow missionary purposes but its appeal is clearly limited. And, what happens to Equal Opportunities?

Concluding remarks

The New Directions suggested here are by no means certain to 'succeed' used alone. They offer the possibility of a wider perspective within which other research into stress would then carry more meaning.

I have, I hope, given some idea of where the classical concepts have relevance. Alienation is more problematic than Anomie, which does appear quite clearly to offer scope. Power to control their own existence is not yet in women's hands and the increasing number of them in professional occupations has not yet reduced the general sexual stereotyping that exists in the culture of organisations giving rise to ambiguity for the women. A radical stance will encompass those critical questions about the group under analysis; 'people who ask questions of this order may be said to share a common perspective . . . the commonality rests in the questions asked and certainly not in the answers given' (Eldridge, 1971: 139). We would want to know the source of the alienation and anomie that women suffer and why it happens. What – and where – is the evidence that will help to shed light on this?

Those researchers into women's stress, in any discipline, who are interested in the same questions will use structural concepts in which to embed them. It is the questions that matter – the research, however difficult, will produce results of interest and of understanding with the possibility of change instead of statistically correct sterility. The stress is real, patriarchy and capitalism and the structures they embody are real. Let us then take some new directions!

> 'Why strive for knowledge of reality if this knowledge cannot serve us in life?'
>
> (*Emile Durkheim,*
> *The Rules of Sociological*
> *Method, 1964: 48*)

References

Adcroft, A., Cutler, T. Haslam, C., Williams, J., and Williams, K. (1991) *Hanson and ICI: The Consequences of Financial Engineering, PEL Occasional Paper on Business Economy and Society*.

Anyon, J. (1983) In Walker, S. and Barton, L. (eds), '*Intersections of Gender & Class: Accommodation and Resistance by Working Class & Affluent Females to Contradictory Sex-Role Ideologies' Gender, Class & Education*, Falmer Press.

Atkinson, J. (1984) 'Manpower Strategies for Flexible Organisations', *Personnel Management*, August, pp. 28–31.

Blauner, R. (1964) *Alienation & Freedom*, Univ. of Chicago Press.

Brindle, D. (1991) *'NHS Accused of widely practised discrimination'* in the Guardian, 2nd August.

Briner, R. and Hockey, R.J. (1988) 'Operator Stress & Computer-based Work', in Cooper, C.L. and Payne, R. (eds), *Causes, Coping & Consequences of Stress at Work*, Wiley.

Brown, G.W. (1986) 'Statistical Interaction and the Role of Social Factors in the Aetiology of Clinical Depression', in *Sociology*, vol. 20, no. 4, pp. 601–6, BSA.

— and Harris, T. (1978) *Social Origins of Depression*, Tavistock.

Burke, R.J. (1988) 'Sources of Managerial & Professional Stress' in Cooper, C.L. and Payne, R. (ed.), *Causes, Coping & Consequences of Stress at Work*, Wiley.

Carroll, L. (1962) *Alice's Adventures in Wonderland & Through The Looking, Glass*, Puffin.

Collinson, D.L. (1988) *Barriers to Fair Selection—a multi-sector study of recruitment practices*, Equal Opps. Commission Research Series, HMSO.

— and Collinson, M. (1989) 'Sexuality in the Workplace: The Domination of Men's Sexuality' in Hearn, J., Sheppard, D, Tancred-Sheriff and Burrell G. (eds), *The Sexuality of Organisation*, Sage.

Cooper, C. (1985) 'The Road to Health in American Firms' *New Society*, 6th Sept.

— Cooper, R.D., and Eaker, L.H. (1988) *Living with Stress*, Penguin.

Coward, R. (1991) 'The Best Man for the Job', the *Guardian*, 18.7.91.

Davison, M. and Cooper, C. (1981) 'Occupational Stress in Female Managers—A Review of the Literature' in *Journal of Enterprise Management*, vol. 3, no. 2, pp. 115–138.

— (1983) *Stress & the Woman Manager*, Robertson (Oxford).

Doyal, L. and Pennel, I. (1979) *The Political Economy of Health*, Pluto Press.

Durkheim, E. (1938) *The Rules of Sociological Method*, Free Press, New York, 1964.

Eldridge, J.E.T. (1971) *Sociology & Industrial Life*, Nelson.

Elias, N. (1991) *The Society of Individuals*, Blackwell.

Eyer, J. and Sterling, P. (1977) 'Stress Related Mortality & Social Organisation', *Review of Radical Political Economy*, vol. 9, no. 1, pp. 1.44.

Fletcher, B.C. (1988) 'The Epidemiology of Occupational Stress' in Cooper, C.L. and Payne, R. (eds), *Causes, Coping & Consequences of Stress at Work*, Wiley.

Foucault, M. (1981) *The History of Sexuality*, vol. I, Penguin.

— (1979) *Discipline & Punish*, Peregrine.

Giddens, A. (1991) *Modernity and Self-Identity*, Polity.

Gutek, B. (1989) 'Sexuality in the Workplace: Key issues in Social Research and Organisational Practice,' in Hearn, J., Sheppard, D., Tancred-Sheriff and Burrell (eds), *The Sexuality of Organisation*, Sage.

Hanmer, J. and Leonard, D. (1984) 'Negotiating the problem: the DHSS & research on violence in marriage' in Bell, C. and Roberts, H. (eds), *Social Researching, Politics, Problems, Practice*, RKP.

Hearn, J., Sheppard, D., Tancred-Sheriff and Burrell G. (eds) (1989) *The Sexuality of Organisation*, Sage.

Hill, S. (1981) *Competition & Control at Work*, Gower.

Holberton, S. and Cookson, C. (1991) 'Women breach boardroom bar', *Financial Times* 11.2.91.

Hollway, W.A. (1982) Identity & Gender Differences in Adult Social Relations, unpub. *Phd. Birkbeck* College, Univ. of London.

Hollway, W. (1991) *Work Psychology & Organisational Behaviour*, Sage.

Horton, J. (1964) 'The Dehumanisation of Anomie & Alienation', *British Journal of Sociology* vol. 15.

Huber, J. (1974) 'Ambiguities in Identity Transformation From Sugar & Spice to Professor', *Notre Dame Journal of Education* vol. 2, no. 4, Winter.

Hugill, B. (1991) 'Women set for victory on lecture posts "bias"' *Observer* 14.7.91.

Huws, U. (1984) *The New Homeworkers*, Low Pay Unit, Pamphlet No. 28.

Lewis, S.N.C. and Cooper, C.L. (1988) 'Stress in Dual-Earner Families' in Gutek, B., Stromberg, A. and Larwood, L. (eds), *Women & Work: An Annual Review*, vol, 3, Sage (USA).

McKenna, E.F. (1987) *Psychology in Business*, Lawrence Erlbaum Associates Ltd.

McKenna, E. and Ellis, T. (1981) 'Counterpoint to Davidson & Cooper' in *Journal of Enterprise Management*, vol. 3, no. 2, pp. 139–142.

Mills, C. Wright (1970) *The Sociological Imagination*, Pelican (orig. Oxford Univ. Press 1959 N. York).

Parkin, F. (1972) *Class Inequality & Political Order*, Paladin.

Peters, T.J. and Waterman, R.H. Jr. (1982) *In Search of Excellence*, Harper & Row, New York.

Ray, C.A. (1986) 'Corporate Culture: The last Frontier of Control?' *Journal of Management Studies* 23.3 May 1986.

Rose, M. (1978) *Industrial Behaviour*, Penguin.

Savage, W. (1986) *A Savage Enquiry—who controls childbirth*, Virago.

Schutz, A, (1970) 'Concept and Theory Foundation in the Social Sciences' in Emmet, D. and MacIntye, A. (eds), *Sociological Theory and Philosophical Analysis*, Macmillan.

Spender, D. (1982) *Invisible Women—The Schooling Scandal*, Writers & Readers.

Suswin, M. (1986) 'It's not what they say it's the way that they say it' the *Guardian* 6/10/86.

Thompson, J.B. (1984) *Studies in the Theory of Ideology*, Polity.

Thompson, P. and McHugh, D. (1990) *Work Organisations*, Macmillan.

Westwood, S. (1984) *All Day and Every Day*, Pluto.

Further reading

Bell, D. (1962) *The End of Ideology: on the Exhaustion of Political Ideas in the Fifties*, Free Press, New York, pp. 358–67 (on alienation).

Eldridge, J.E.T. (1971) *Sociology and Industrial Life*, Nelson, Part 3 (on alienation).

Clark, H. (1991) *Women, Work and Stress: New Directions*, University of East London Occasional Papers on Business, Economy and Society, Paper No. 3.

Davidson, M.J. and Cooper, C.L. (1992) *Shattering the Glass Ceiling: The Woman Manager*, Paul Chapman Publishing.

Spencer, A. and Podmore, D. (eds) (1987) *In a Man's World: Essays on Women in Male-Dominated Professions*, Tavistock.

Issues for discussion

1. Examine the relationship between alienation and stress.
   Readings: all in Chapter 6
2. To what extent are alienation and stress inevitable in contemporary organisational life?
   Readings: Friedman (Chapter 1)
           Bell (Chapter 1)
           Thompson (Chapter 3)
           and all in Chapter 6
3. Examine the consequences for organisational identities of a) alienation and b) stress.
   Readings: all in Chapter 6.

Author index

Subject index